THE VALM

Bibek Debroy is a renowned economist, scholar and translator. He has worked in universities, research institutes, industry and for the government. He has widely published books, papers and articles on economics. As a translator, he is best known for his magnificent rendition of the Mahabharata in ten volumes, and additionally the *Harivamsha*, published to wide acclaim by Penguin Classics. He is also the author of *Sarama and Her Children*, which splices his interest in Hinduism with his love for dogs.

PRAISE FOR *THE MAHABHARATA*

'The modernization of language is visible, it's easier on the mind, through expressions that are somewhat familiar. The detailing of the story is intact, the varying tempo maintained, with no deviations from the original. The short introduction reflects a brilliant mind. For those who passionately love the Mahabharata and want to explore it to its depths, Debroy's translation offers great promise . . .'—*Hindustan Times*

'[Debroy] has really carved out a niche for himself in crafting and presenting a translation of the Mahabharata . . . The book takes us on a great journey with admirable ease'—*Indian Express*

'The first thing that appeals to one is the simplicity with which Debroy has been able to express himself and infuse the right kind of meanings . . . Considering that Sanskrit is not the simplest of languages to translate a text from, Debroy exhibits his deep understanding and appreciation of the medium'—*The Hindu*

'Debroy's lucid and nuanced retelling of the original makes the masterpiece even more enjoyably accessible'—*Open*

'The quality of translation is excellent. The lucid language makes it a pleasure to read the various stories, digressions and parables'—*Tribune*

'Extremely well-organized, and has a substantial and helpful Introduction, plot summaries and notes. The volume is a beautiful example of a well thought-out layout which makes for much easier reading'—*Book Review*

'The dispassionate vision [Debroy] brings to this endeavour will surely earn him merit in the three worlds'—*Mail Today*

'Debroy's is not the only English translation available in the market, but where he scores and others fail is that his is the closest rendering of the original text in modern English without unduly complicating the readers' understanding of the epic'—*Business Standard*

'The brilliance of Ved Vyasa comes through, ably translated by Bibek Debroy'—*Hindustan Times*

# THE VALMIKI RAMAYANA 1

## Translated by Bibek Debroy

**PENGUIN BOOKS**

An imprint of Penguin Random House

PENGUIN BOOKS

USA | Canada | UK | Ireland | Australia
New Zealand | India | South Africa | China

Penguin Books is part of the Penguin Random House group of companies
whose addresses can be found at global.penguinrandomhouse.com

Published by Penguin Random House India Pvt. Ltd
7th Floor, Infinity Tower C, DLF Cyber City,
Gurgaon 122 002, Haryana, India

First published in Penguin Books by Penguin Random House India 2017

10 9 8 7 6

ISBN 9780143428046

Typeset in Sabon by Manipal Digital Systems, Manipal
Printed at Replika Press Pvt. Ltd, India

www.penguin.co.in

MIX
Paper from
responsible sources
FSC® C016779

*For Professor Shailendra Raj Mehta*

# Contents

# Acknowledgements

This journey, with Penguin, started more than a decade ago. It is a journey of translating Sanskrit texts into English, in unabridged form. It commenced with the Bhagavad Gita in 2006, followed by the Mahabharata (2010 to 2014) and the Harivamsha (2016). It continues with the Valmiki Ramayana and will be followed by the Puranas. To the best of my knowledge, the great translator, Manmatha Nath Dutt (1855–1912), is the only other person who has accomplished the 'double' of unabridged translations of both the Valmiki Ramayana and the Mahabharata in English. In this journey with Penguin, special thanks to Meru Gokhale, Ambar Sahil Chatterjee and Paloma Dutta. All three have made this journey easier to traverse.

My wife, Suparna Banerjee (Debroy), has not only been *patni*, she has been *grihini* and *sahadharmini* too. Had she not provided an enabling and conducive environment, juggling professional commitments and carving out the time required for translating would have been impossible. यः तया सह स स्वर्गो निरयो यस्त्वया विना (2.27.16).

This translation is based on the Critical Edition brought out (between 1951 and 1975) by the Oriental Institute, now part of Maharaja Sayajirao University, Baroda. When I started work on translating the Mahabharata in 2009, there was a thought, however hazy, of attempting the Valmiki Ramayana too. Therefore, one had to acquire the seven published volumes of the Critical Edition. Those who have tried this acquisition will testify this is no mean task. Multiple channels and multiple efforts failed. The Oriental Institute is not known for its marketing and distribution successes.

The context changed in 2015, because I joined the government. By then, I had still not been able to get copies of the Critical Edition. What with joining the government, which made finding time difficult, and an inability to get the text, I remarked to my wife that destiny willed otherwise. A few months later, on a flight, I found myself seated next to Shailendra Mehta, economist, scholar, friend, and currently president, director and distinguished professor at MICA, Ahmedabad. 'What next, after the Mahabharata?' asked Shailendra and I described my frustration. A few weeks down the line, Shailendra Mehta walked into my office, lugging a trolley bag, with all seven volumes in them. 'All yours,' he said. What destiny willed was clear enough. The dedication of this three volume set to Shailendra is a paltry attempt to say thank you.

'What next, after the Valmiki Ramayana?' Life moves on to the Puranas, beginning with the Bhagavata Purana. At one point, the Mahabharata translation seemed like a mammoth task, stretching to infinity. With the major Puranas collectively amounting to four times the size of the Mahabharata, they are more monumental than the mammoth. But as always, if it so wills, destiny finds a way.

# Introduction

The Ramayana and the Mahabharata are known as *itihasa*s. The word itihasa means 'it was indeed like that'. Therefore, the word is best rendered as legend or history, and not as myth. This does not mean everything occurred exactly as described. In a process of telling and retelling and oral transmission, embellishments are inevitable. However, the use of the word itihasa suggests a core element of truth. There were two great dynasties—*surya vamsha* and *chandra vamsha*.[1] The first proper king of the surya vamsha was Ikshvaku and the Ramayana is a chronicle of the solar dynasty, or at least a part of its history. Similarly, the first king of the chandra vamsha was Ila and the Mahabharata is a chronicle of the lunar dynasty. The Puranas also describe the histories of the solar and lunar dynasties. Though there are some inconsistencies across genealogies given in different Puranas, the surya vamsha timeline has three broad segments: (1) from Ikshvaku to Rama; (2) from Kusha to Brihadbala; and (3) from Brihadbala to Sumitra. In that stretch from Ikshvaku to Rama, there were famous kings like Bharata (not to be confused with Rama's brother), Kakutstha, Prithu, Yuvanashva, Mandhata, Trishanku, Harishchandra, Sagara, Dilipa, Bhagiratha, Ambarisha, Raghu, Aja and Dasharatha. These ancestors explain why Rama is referred to as Kakutstha, Raghava or Dasharathi.

Rama had two sons—Lava and Kusha. Ikshvaku and his descendants ruled over the kingdom of Kosala, part of today's Uttar Pradesh. The Kosala kingdom lasted for a long time, with

[1] The solar and the lunar dynasty, respectively.

the capital sometimes in Ayodhya and sometimes in Shravasti. When Rama ruled, the capital was in Ayodhya. After Rama, Lava ruled over south Kosala and Kusha ruled over north Kosala. Lava's capital was in Shravasti, while Kusha's capital was in Kushavati. We don't know what happened to Lava thereafter, though he is believed to have established Lavapuri, today's Lahore. The second segment of the surya vamsha timeline, from Kusha to Brihadbala, doesn't have any famous kings. Brihadbala was the last Kosala king. In the Kurukshetra War, he fought on the side of the Kouravas and was killed by Abhimanyu. The third segment of the surya vamsha timeline, from Brihadbala to Sumitra, seems contrived and concocted. Sumitra is described as the last king of the Ikshvaku lineage, defeated by Mahapadma Nanda in 362 BCE. Sumitra wasn't killed. He fled to Rohtas, in today's Bihar.

The Ramayana isn't about these subsequent segments of the timeline. Though there are references to other kings from that Ikshvaku to Rama stretch, it isn't about all of that segment either. Its focus is on Rama. It is difficult to date the poet Kalidasa. It could be anytime from the first century CE to the fifth century CE. Kalidasa wrote a *mahakavya*[2] known as *Raghuvamsha*. As the name of this mahakavya suggests, it is about Raghu's lineage, from Dilipa to Agnivarna, and includes Rama. But it isn't exclusively about Rama. Ramayana is almost exclusively about Rama. That's the reason it is known as रामायण = राम + अयण. अयन means travel or progress. Thus, Ramayana means Rama's progress. There is a minor catch though. अयन means travel or progress and अयण is a meaningless word. The word used in Ramayana is अयण, not अयन. This transformation occurs because of a rule of Sanskrit grammar known as internal *sandhi*. That is the reason रामायन becomes रामायण.

Who is Rama? The word राम means someone who is lovely, charming and delightful. There are Jain and Buddhist versions (*Dasharatha Jataka*) of the Rama account and they differ in significant details from the Ramayana story. For instance, in Jain accounts, Ravana is killed by Lakshmana. In *Dasharatha Jataka*,

[2] Epic.

Sita is Rama's sister. In Ramayana and Purana accounts, Rama is Vishnu's seventh *avatara*.[3] Usually, ten avataras are named for Vishnu, though sometimes, a larger number is also given. When the figure is ten, the avataras are *matsya*,[4] *kurma*,[5] *varaha*,[6] *narasimha*,[7] *vamana*,[8] Parashurama, Rama, Krishna, Buddha and Kalki (Kalki is yet to come). In the cycle of creation and destruction, *yugas*[9] follow each other and one progressively goes down *krita yuga* (alternatively *satya yuga*), *treta yuga*, *dvapara yuga* and *kali yuga*, before the cycle starts again. In the list of ten avataras, matysa, kurma, varaha and narasimha are from the present krita yuga; Vamana, Parashurama and Rama are from the present treta yuga; Krishna is from dvapara yuga; and Buddha and Kalki are from kali yuga. Rama was towards the end of treta yuga. (In the 'Uttara Kanda', dvapara yuga has started.) Just as Krishna's departure marked the transition from dvapara yuga to kali yuga, Rama's departure marked the transition from treta yuga to dvapara yuga.

When did these events occur? It is impossible to answer this question satisfactorily, despite continuous efforts being made to find an answer. At one level, it is an irrelevant question too. There is a difference between an incident happening and it being recorded. In that day and age, recording meant composition and oral transmission, with embellishments added. There was noise associated with transmission and distribution. It is impossible to unbundle the various layers in the text, composed at different points in time. Valmiki is described as Rama's contemporary, just as Vedavyasa was a contemporary of the Kouravas and the Pandavas. But that doesn't mean today's Valmiki Ramayana text is exactly what Valmiki composed, or that today's Mahabharata text

---

[3] Incarnation, or descent.
[4] Fish.
[5] Turtle.
[6] Boar.
[7] Half-man, half-lion.
[8] Dwarf.
[9] Eras.

is exactly what Krishna Dvaipayana Vedavyasa composed. Therein lies the problem with several approaches to dating.

The first and favoured method of dating is undoubtedly the astronomical one, based on positions of *nakshatra*s and *graha*s,[10] or using information about events like eclipses. However, because layers of the text were composed at different points in time, compounded by precession of the equinoxes, this leads to widely divergent dates for an event like Rama's birth, ranging from 7323 BCE to 1331 BCE. Second, one can work with genealogies, notwithstanding problems of inconsistencies across them. One will then obtain a range of something like 2350 BCE to 1500 BCE. Third, one can work with linguistics and the evolution of language, comparing that of the Ramayana to other texts. Fourth, one can work with the archaeological evidence, such as the pottery discovered in sites known to be associated with the Ramayana. Even then, there will be a wide range of dates, from something like 2600 BCE to 1100 BCE. Fifth, one can consider geography, geology, changes in the course of rivers. Finally, there are traditional views about the length of a *manvantara*[11] or yuga. Given the present state of knowledge, it is impossible to impart precision to any dating of the incidents in the Ramayana. Scholars have grappled with the problem in the past and will continue to do so in the future. This may be an important question. But from the point of view of the present translation, it is an irrelevant one.

The present translation is about the Ramayana text. But what is the Ramayana text? After a famous essay written by A.K. Ramanujan in 1987 (published in 1991), people often mention 300 Ramayanas. It is impossible to fix the number, 300 or otherwise, since it is not possible to count satisfactorily—or even define—what is a new rendering of the Ramayana story, as opposed to a simple retelling, with or without reinterpretation. Contemporary versions, not always in written form, are continuously being rendered. There are versions of the Ramayana story in East Asia (China, Japan),

---

[10] Constellations/stars and planets.
[11] Lifespan of a Manu.

South-East Asia (many countries like Thailand, Indonesia and Malaysia), South Asia (Nepal, Sri Lanka) and West Asia (Iran). As mentioned earlier, there are Buddhist and Jain versions. Every state and every language in India seems to have some version of the Rama story. Our impressions about the Rama story are often based on such regional versions, such as, the sixteenth-century *Ramcharitmanas* by Goswami Tulsidas. (Many of these were written between the twelfth and seventeenth centuries CE.) Those depictions can, and will, vary with what is in this translation. This translation is about the Sanskrit Ramayana. But even there, more than one text of the Sanskrit Ramayana exists—Valmiki Ramayana, Yoga Vasishtha Ramayana, Ananda Ramayana and Adbhuta Ramayana. In addition, there are versions of the Ramayana story in the Mahabharata and in the Puranas. With the exception of the Ramayana story in the Mahabharata, the Valmiki Ramayana is clearly the oldest among these. This is a translation of the Valmiki Ramayana and yes, there are differences between depictions in the Valmiki Ramayana and other Sanskrit renderings of the Rama story.

If one cannot date the incidents of the Ramayana, can one at least conclusively date when the Valmiki Ramayana was written? Because of the many layers and subsequent interpolations, there is no satisfactory resolution to this problem either. The Valmiki Ramayana has around 24,000 *shloka*s, a shloka being a verse. The Mahabharata is believed to have 100,000 shlokas, so the Valmiki Ramayana is about one-fourth the size of the Mahabharata. These 24,000 shlokas are distributed across seven *kanda*s—'Bala Kanda' (Book about Youth), 'Ayodhya Kanda' (Book about Ayodhya), 'Aranya Kanda' (Book of the Forest), Kishkindha Kanda (Book about Kishkindha), 'Sundara Kanda' (Book of Beauty), 'Yuddha Kanda' (Book about the War) and 'Uttara Kanda' (Book about the Sequel). Kanda refers to a major section or segment and is sometimes translated into English as Canto. 'Canto' sounds archaic, 'Book' is so much better. This does not mean the kanda-wise classification always existed. For all one knows, initially, there were simply chapters. In this text itself, there is a reference to the Valmiki Ramayana possessing 500 *sarga*s. The

word sarga also means Book, but given the number 500, is more
like a chapter. (For the record, the text has more than 600 chapters.)
Most scholars agree 'Uttara Kanda' was written much later. If one
reads the 'Uttara Kanda', that belief is instantly endorsed. The 'Uttara
Kanda' doesn't belong. This isn't only because of the content, which
is invariably mentioned. It is also because of the texture of the text,
the quality of the poetry. It is vastly inferior. To a lesser extent, one
can also advance similar arguments for the 'Bala Kanda'. Therefore,
the earlier portions were probably composed around 500 BCE. The
later sections, like the 'Uttara Kanda', and parts of the 'Bala Kanda',
were probably composed around 500 CE. It isn't the case that all later
sections are in 'Uttara Kanda'.

There is a mix of earlier and later sections across all kandas.
The word kanda also means trunk or branch of a tree. The
Mahabharata is also classified into such major sections or Books.
However, in the Mahabharata, these major sections are known as
parvas. The word parva also means branch. However, parva suggests
a smaller branch, one that is more flexible. Kanda suggests one that
is more solid, less flexible. There may have been slight variations
in shlokas across different versions of the Sanskrit Mahabharata,
but fundamentally the Sanskrit Mahabharata is a single text. The
original text expanded, like a holdall, to include everything. Those
different versions have been 'unified' in a Critical Edition published
by the Bhandarkar Oriental Research Institute, Poona (Pune). In the
case of the Valmiki Ramayana, with its kanda-kind of classification,
the evolution seems to have been different. If someone was unhappy
with what Valmiki had depicted, he simply composed another
Ramayana. In Sanskrit, mention has already been made of the Yoga
Vasishtha Ramayana, Ananda Ramayana and Adbhuta Ramayana.
This continued to happen with vernacular versions.

This translation is of the Valmiki Ramayana. It is necessary to
stress this point. Both the Ramayana and the Mahabharata are so
popular that one is familiar with people, stories and incidents. That
doesn't necessarily mean those people, stories and incidents occur in
the Valmiki Ramayana in the way we are familiar with them. Just
as the Bhandarkar Oriental Research Institute produced a Critical

Edition of the Mahabharata, between 1951 and 1975, the Oriental
Institute, Baroda, produced a Critical Edition of the Valmiki
Ramayana. This translation is based on that Critical Edition,
published sequentially between 1958 and 1975. Producing a Critical
Edition meant sifting through a large number of manuscripts of
the Valmiki Ramayana. The editors had around 2000 manuscripts
to work with. Not all of these were equally reliable. Therefore, in
practice, they worked with fifty to hundred manuscripts, the specific
number depending on the kanda in question. It is not that there were
significant differences across the manuscripts and broadly, there
was a Southern Recension (version) and a Northern one, the latter
sub-divided into a North-Western and a North-Eastern one. The
earliest of these written manuscripts dates to the eleventh century
CE. In passing, the language may have been Sanskrit, but the script
wasn't always Devanagari. There were scripts like Sharada, Mewari,
Maithili, Bengali, Telugu, Kannada, Nandinagari, Grantha and
Malayalam. Since this translation is based on the Baroda Critical
Edition, it is necessary to make another obvious point. Even within
the Sanskrit Valmiki Ramayana, not everything we are familiar with
is included in the Critical text. For instance, the configuration of
nakshatras and planets at the time of Rama's birth is not part of the
Critical text. Nor is the bulk of one of the most beautiful sections
of the Valmiki Ramayana, Mandodari's lamentation. Those are
shlokas that have been excised. That's also the case with a shloka
that's often quoted as an illustration of Lakshmana's conduct. नाहं
जानामि केयूरं नाहं जानामि कुण्डलं । नूपुरं तु अभिजानामि नित्यं पादाभिवन्दनात्॥ This
is a statement by Lakshmana to the effect that he cannot recognize
the ornament on Sita's head or her earrings. Since he has always
served at her feet, he can only recognize her anklets. This too has
been excised. There are instances where such excision has led to a
break in continuity and inconsistency and we have pointed them
out in the footnotes.

There are two numbers associated with every chapter. The
first number refers to the kanda, while the second number, within
brackets, refers to the number of the chapter (sarga) within that
kanda. Thus, Chapter 1(33) will mean the thirty-third chapter in

'Bala Kanda'. The table below shows the number of chapters and shlokas we have in the Critical Edition. The Critical text has 606 chapters, 106 more than the 500 sargas mentioned in the text itself. And there are 18,670 shlokas. If one considers chapters and shlokas from non-Critical versions, irrespective of which version it is, there are almost 650 chapters and just over 24,000 shlokas. Compared to such non-Critical versions, very few chapters have been excised from 'Bala', 'Ayodhya', 'Aranya', 'Kishkindha' or 'Sundara' kandas. The excision is primarily from 'Yuddha' and 'Uttara' kandas. The excision of shlokas is uniformly spread throughout the kandas, though most excision, relatively speaking, is from the 'Ayodhya', 'Yuddha' and 'Uttara' kandas.

| Name of kanda | Number of chapters | Number of shlokas |
|---|---|---|
| Bala Kanda | 76 | 1941 |
| Ayodhya Kanda | 111 | 3160 |
| Aranya Kanda | 71 | 2060 |
| Kishkindha Kanda | 66 | 1898 |
| Sundara Kanda | 66 | 2487 |
| Yuddha Kanda | 116 | 4435 |
| Uttara Kanda | 100 | 2689 |
| Total | 606 | 18,670 |

Valmiki is the first poet, *adi kavi*. By the time of classical Sanskrit literature, some prerequisites were defined for a work to attain the status of mahakavya. Kalidasa, Bharavi, Magha, Shri Harsha and Bhatti composed such works. Though these notions and definitions came later, the Valmiki Ramayana displays every characteristic of a mahakavya and is longer than any of these subsequent works. The story of how it came about is known to most people who are familiar with the Ramayana. The sage Valmiki had gone, with his disciple Bharadvaja, to bathe in the waters of the River Tamasa. There was a couple of *krouncha*[12] birds there, in the act of making

---

[12] Curlew.

love. Along came a hunter[13] and killed the male bird. As the female bird grieved, Valmiki was driven by compassion and the first shloka emerged from his lips. Since it was composed in an act of sorrow—*shoka*—this kind of composition came to be known as shloka. So the Ramayana tells us. Incidentally, this first shloka doesn't occur in the first chapter. It isn't the first shloka of the Valmiki Ramayana. The incident and the shloka occur in the second chapter. More specifically, it is the fourteenth shloka in the second chapter and is as follows. मा निषाद प्रतिष्ठां त्वमगमः शाश्वतीः समाः। यत्क्रौंचमिथुनादेकमवधीः कামमोहितम् ॥ 'O nishada! This couple of curlews was in the throes of passion and you killed one of them. Therefore, you will possess ill repute for an eternal number of years.'

Till a certain period of history, all Sanskrit works were in poetry or verse, not in prose. The Vedangas are limbs or auxiliaries and the six Vedangas are *shiksha*,[14] *chhanda*,[15] *vyakarana*,[16] *nirukta*,[17] *jyotisha*[18] and *kalpa*.[19] These are needed to understand not just the Vedas, but also Sanskrit works. Chhanda is one of these. Chhanda can be translated as metre and means something that is pleasing and delightful. Chhanda *shastra* is the study of metres or prosody. Sanskrit poetry wasn't about what we tend to identify as poetry today, the act of rhyming. Chhanda begins with the concept of *akshara*, akin to, but not exactly identical with, the English concept of syllable, that is, part of a word with a single vowel sound. Other than possessing a single vowel sound, an akshara must not begin with a vowel. Aksharas can be *hrasva* or *laghu*—light or L—and *guru*—heavy or G. Simply stated, with a short vowel, the akshara is L and with a long vowel, the akshara is G. There are some additional conditions, but we needn't get into those. Every verse consists of four *pada*s, the word pada meaning one quarter. Depending on how

---

[13] *Nishada.*
[14] Articulation and pronunciation.
[15] Prosody.
[16] Grammar.
[17] Etymology.
[18] Astronomy.
[19] Rituals.

many aksharas there are in a pada and the distribution of those aksharas into L and G, there were a variety of metres. Depending on the subject and the mood, the poet consciously chose a metre. Analysing in this way, there were more than 1300 different metres. One of the most popular was *anushtubh*. This figures prominently in the Valmiki Ramayana, the Mahabharata and the Puranas. The anushtubh structure meant eight aksharas in each pada, with a total of thirty-two aksharas. In addition, for anushtubh, in every pada, the fifth akshara would have to be L and the sixth akshara would have to be G. In classical Sanskrit literature, conditions were also applied to the seventh akshara, but such refinements came later. For that first verse, the decomposition runs as follows: (1) L L L G L G L G; (2) L G L G L G L G; (3) L L G G L G G L; (4) G G L L L G G L. (1) *ma ni sha da pra tish tham*; (2) *tva ma ga mah shash vati sa mah*; (3) *yat kroun cha mi thu na de ka*; (4) *ma va dhi ka ma mo hi tam*. It is not that Valmiki only used anushtubh. There are actually sixteen different metres in the Valmiki Ramayana.

It is impossible to capture the beauty of chhanda in an English translation. One can attempt to do a translation in verse, but it will fail to convey the beauty. If the original text is poetry, one starts with an initial question. Should one attempt a translation in verse or in prose? This translation is based on the premise that the translation should be as close as possible to the original Sanskrit text. One should not take liberties with the text. This translation is therefore almost a word-to-word rendering. If one sits down with the original Sanskrit, there will be almost a perfect match. In the process, deliberately so, the English is not as smooth as it might have been, had one taken more liberties, and this is a conscious decision. Had one attempted a translation in verse, one would perforce have had to take more liberties. Hence, the choice of prose is also a deliberate decision. As composers, there is quite a contrast between Valmiki and Vedavyasa. Vedavyasa focuses on people and incidents. Rarely does the Mahabharata attempt to describe nature, even if those sections are on geography. In contrast, Valmiki's descriptions of nature are lyrical and superlative, similar to Kalidasa. A translation can never hope to transmit that flavour. There is no substitute to reading the original Sanskrit, more so for the Valmiki Ramayana than for the Mahabharata.

Which occurred earlier, the incidents of the Ramayana or the Mahabharata? Which was composed earlier, the Ramayana or the Mahabharata? The Ramayana incidents occurred in treta yuga, the Mahabharata incidents in dvapara yuga. Rama was an earlier avatara, Krishna a later one. Hence, the obvious deduction is that the Ramayana incidents predated those of the Mahabharata—an inference also bolstered by the genealogy and astrological arguments mentioned earlier. However, and not just for the sake of being perverse, consider the following. Geographically, the incidents of the Mahabharata mostly occur along an east–west axis, along either side of what used to be called Uttarapath, the northern road, more familiar as Grand Trunk Road or National Highway (NH) 1 and 2. The incidents of the Ramayana often occur along a north–south axis, along what used to be called Dakshinapath, the southern road. Sanjeev Sanyal[20] has made the point that while Uttarapath remained stable over time, the Dakshinapath during Rama's time was different from the subsequent Dakshinapath, with the latter more like today's NH 44. To return to the point, the geographical terrain of the Mahabharata was restricted to the northern parts of the country, with the south rarely mentioned. The Aryan invasion theory has been discredited because of a multitude of reasons, but myths and perceptions that have lasted for decades are difficult to dispel. However, regardless of the Aryan invasion theory, the Ramayana reveals a familiarity with the geography of the southern parts of the country that the Mahabharata does not. The fighting in the Mahabharata, in the Kurukshetra War, is cruder and less refined. In the Ramayana, bears and apes may have fought using trees and boulders, but humans did not. A human did not tear apart another human's chest and drink blood. The urbanization depicted in the Ramayana is rarely found in the Mahabharata. We have cited these counter-arguments to make a simple point. Which incident

[20] *Land of the Seven Rivers: A Brief History of India's Geography*, Sanjeev Sanyal, Penguin, 2012.

occurred earlier and which text was composed earlier are distinct questions. They should not be confused. Even if the Ramayana incidents occurred before the incidents of the Mahabharata, that doesn't automatically mean the Ramayana was composed before the Mahabharata. The Rama story occurs in the Mahabharata, known as the 'Ramopakhyana' section. There is no such reference to the Mahabharata incidents in the Ramayana. This is the main reason for arguing that the Ramayana was composed before the Mahabharata.

The relationship between the 'Ramopakhyana' and the Valmiki Ramayana is also of scholarly interest. Which was earlier? Did one borrow from the other, or did both have a common origin? That need not concern us. What should be stressed is the obvious—the Valmiki Ramayana wasn't composed at a single point in time and there is a difference between the original composition and the present text, as given to us say in the Critical Edition. If bears and apes fought with the help of trees and boulders, and Angada suddenly kills someone with a weapon, that part is probably a later composition, with the composer having deviated from the original template. If a verse is in anushtubh, but deviates from the L–G pattern, this may have been a conscious decision, but in all probability, reflects the inferior skills of a subsequent poet. If we take the Critical text as it stands, while there are no direct references to the incidents of the Mahabharata, there are plenty of indirect allusions. There are shlokas reminiscent of the Bhagavatgita. When Bharata comes to Rama to inform him about Dasharatha's death, Rama asks him about the welfare of the kingdom, reminiscent of similar questions asked by Narada to Yudhishthira. In the Valmiki Ramayana, there are references to kings of the lunar dynasty (Yayati) and incidents (Ilvala and Vatapi) that are only described in the Mahabharata. The evidence may be circumstantial and speculative, but it is the following. It is as if the later composers knew about the Mahabharata incidents and the text, but consciously avoided any direct references.

Why is another translation of the Valmiki Ramayana needed? Surely, there are plenty floating around. That's not quite true. Indeed, there are several translations of the Valmiki Ramayana, including some recent ones, but they are abridged. In any act of abridgement, some sections are omitted or summarized. Abridged translations, no matter how good they are, are not quite a substitute for unabridged translations, which bring in the nuances too. To the best of my knowledge, the list of unabridged translations of the Valmiki Ramayana is the following: (1) Ralph T.H. Griffith;[21] (2) Manmatha Nath Dutt;[22] (3) Hari Prasad Shastri;[23] (4) Desiraju Hanumanta Rao and K.M.K. Murthy;[24] and (5) Robert P. Goldman.[25] Given the timelines, the Goldman translation is the only one based on the Critical Edition. Having translated the Mahabharata,[26] it was natural to translate the Valmiki Ramayana. The intention was to do a translation that was popular in style. That meant a conscious decision to avoid the use of diacritical marks, as would have been the case had one used IAST (International Alphabet of Sanskrit Transliteration). If diacritical marks are not going to be used, there may be problems rendering names, proper and geographic. We have sought to make the English renderings as phonetic as is possible. Thus, we use 'Goutama' to refer to the sage of that name—although others have often referred to him elsewhere as 'Gautama'. We have chosen Goutama on the logic that if Gomati is not Gamati, why should Goutama be rendered as Gautama? There remains the question of what one does with vowel sounds. How does one differentiate the short sound from the long? Should Rama be written as Raama and Sita as Seeta? That seemed to be too artificial and contrary to popular usage. On rare occasions, this does

---

[21] *The Ramayana of Valmiki, translated into English verse*, Ralph T.H. Griffith, E.Z. Lazarus and Company, London, 1895.

[22] *Valmiki Ramayana*, Manmatha Nath Dutt, R.K. Bhatia, Calcutta, 1891–92. Manmatha Nath Dutt (Shastri) was one of India's greatest translators (in English). He also translated the Mahabharata and several Puranas.

[23] *The Ramayana of Valmiki*, Hari Prasad Shastri, Shanti Sadan, London, 1952.

[24] This is net based, on the site http://www.valmikiramayan.net/ and leaves out 'Uttara Kanda'.

[25] *The Ramayana of Valmiki: An Epic of Ancient India*, Robert P. Goldman, Princeton University Press, 1984 to 2016.

[26] *The Mahabharata*, Bibek Debroy, Penguin (India), 10 volumes, 2010–2014, boxed set 2015.

cause a problem, with a danger of confusion between the ape Taara and his daughter Taaraa, Vali's wife. Such occasions are however rare and we have explained them. However, there are also instances where we have deviated from popular usage. Hanumat is a case in point, where Hanuman seemed to be too contrary to grammatical principles. There are some words that defy translation, *dharma* is an example. Hence, we have not even tried to translate such words. The Goldman translation is academic in style. This translation's style is more popular. Therefore, there is no attempt to overburden the reader with extensive notes. However, a straight translation may not be self-explanatory. Hence, we have put in footnotes, just enough to explain, without stretching the translation.

As with the Mahabharata, the Valmiki Ramayana is a text about dharma. Dharma means several different things—the dharma of the four *varna*s and the four *ashrama*s, the classes and stages of life; the governance template of *raja dharma*, the duty of kings; principles of good conduct, *sadachara*; and the pursuit of objectives of human existence, *purushartha*—dharma, *artha* and *kama*. As with the Mahabharata, the Valmiki Ramayana is a *smriti* text. It has a human origin and composer, it is not a *shruti* text. Smriti texts are society and context specific. We should not try to judge and evaluate individuals and actions on the basis of today's value judgements. In addition, if the span of composition was one thousand years, from 500 BCE to 500 CE, those value judgements also change. The later composers and interpreters may have had problems with what the earlier composers authored. A case in point is when Sita is being abducted by Ravana. At a certain point in time, men and women universally wore an upper garment and a lower one. When she is being abducted through the sky, Sita casts aside and throws down not just her ornaments, but her upper garment too. As this translation will illustrate, this caused problems for subsequent composers and interpreters.

To return to the notion of dharma—transcending all those collective templates of dharma—there is one that is individual in nature. Regardless of those collective templates, an individual has to decide what the right course of action is and there is no universal answer as to what is right and what is wrong. There are always contrary pulls of dharma, with two notions of dharma pulling in different directions. It is not immediately obvious which is superior. Given the trade-offs, an individual makes a choice and suffers the consequences. Why is there an impression that these individual conflicts of dharma are more manifest in the Mahabharata than in the Ramayana?

The answer probably lies in the nature of these two texts. What is the difference between a novel and a long story, even when both have multiple protagonists? The difference between a novel and a long story is probably not one of length. A novel seeks to present the views of all protagonists. Thus, the Mahabharata is a bit like a novel, in so far as that trait is concerned. A long story does not seek to look at incidents and actions from the point of view of every protagonist. It is concerned with the perspective of one primary character, to the exclusion of others.

If this distinction is accepted, the Valmiki Ramayana has the characteristics of a long story. It is Ramayana. Therefore, it is primarily from Rama's point of view. We aren't told what Bharata or Lakshmana thought, or for that matter, Urmila, Mandavi or Shrutakirti. There is little that is from Sita's point of view too. That leads to the impression that the Mahabharata contains more about individual conflicts of dharma. For the Valmiki Ramayana, from Rama's point of view, the conflicts of dharma aren't innumerable. On that exile to the forest, why did he take Sita and Lakshmana along with him? Was Shurpanakha's disfigurement warranted? Why did he unfairly kill Vali? Why did he make Sita go through tests of purity, not once, but twice? Why did he unfairly kill Shambuka? Why did he banish Lakshmana? At one level, one can argue these are decisions by a personified divinity and therefore, mere humans cannot comprehend and judge the motives. At another level, the unhappiness with Rama's decisions led to the composition of alternative versions of the Ramayana. Note that Sita's questions about dharma remained unanswered. If you are going to the forest as an ascetic, why have you got weapons with you? If the *rakshasa*s[27]

---

[27] Demons.

are causing injuries to hermits, punishing the rakshasas is Bharata's job, now that he is the king. Why are you dabbling in this? Note also Rama's justification at the time of Sita's first test. It wasn't about what others would think, that justification came later. The initial harsh words reflected his own questions about Sita's purity. Thus, Rama's conflicts over dharma also exist. It is just that in the Valmiki Ramayana, it is about one individual alone.

In conclusion, this translation is an attempt to get readers interested in reading the unabridged Valmiki Ramayana. Having read abridged versions, and there is no competition with those, to appreciate the nuances better, one should read the unabridged. And, to appreciate the beauty of the poetry, one should then be motivated to read the text in Sanskrit. A translation is only a bridge and an unsatisfactory one at that.

# CHAPTER ONE

# *Bala Kanda*

1

# Chapter 1(1)

Narada[1] was a bull among sages, devoted to austerities and self-studying. He was an ascetic and supreme among those who were eloquent. Valmiki asked him, 'Right now, who in this world is valorous and possesses all the qualities? Who knows about *dharma*[2] and about what has been done? Who is truthful in his words and firm in his vows? Who also possesses good conduct and is engaged in the welfare of all creatures? Who is also learned and capable? Who alone is the handsome one? Who has control over his own self and has conquered anger? Who is radiant and devoid of jealousy? When his anger is aroused in a battle, whom are even the gods scared of? I wish to hear about all this. My curiosity is great. O great sage! You are the person who is capable of knowing about this kind of man. Narada knew about the three worlds.[3] On hearing these words, he was delighted.

[1] Narada was a son born to Brahma through Brahma's mental powers.

[2] We will not translate the word dharma, because there is no satisfactory word that captures all of its nuances —duty, good behaviour, morality, ethics, governance (for kings) and the metaphysical or the spiritual. The nuance depends on the context.

[3] Heaven, earth and the nether regions. Alternatively, heaven, earth and the region between heaven and earth.

He invited Valmiki to listen and said, 'O sage! The many qualities you have recounted are extremely rare. Using my intelligence, I will tell you about such a man. I have heard about him.[4] He was born in the lineage of Ikshvaku[5] and he is known to people as Rama. He is self-controlled in his soul and immensely valorous. He is radiant, possesses fortitude and is capable of controlling.[6] He is intelligent and follows good policy. He is eloquent and handsome. He is a destroyer of enemies. He possesses broad shoulders and mighty arms. His neck is like a conch shell and his cheekbones stand out. His chest is broad and his bow is huge. He is a subjugator of enemies and his collarbones are hidden. His arms stretch down to his knees and he possesses an excellent head and a beautiful forehead. His tread is superb. He is medium in size and his limbs are well proportioned. He is pleasant in complexion and powerful. His chest is muscled and his eyes are large. He is prosperous and possesses all the auspicious qualities. He knows about dharma. He is firm in adhering to the truth and is devoted to the welfare of the subjects. He is famous and full of learning. He is pure, controlled and has restrained himself. He is a protector of the world of the living and is also a protector of dharma. He knows the truth about the Vedas and Vedangas and is skilled in *dhanurveda*.[7] He knows the truth about all the sacred texts. He is resplendent and has knowledge of the *smriti* texts.[8] He is virtuous and is loved by all the people. He can discriminate and is not distressed in his soul. Just as all rivers head towards the ocean, all virtuous people approach him. He is noble[9] and impartial towards everyone. He alone is the

---

[4] From Brahma. Narada recounts the core story of the Ramayana, in brief.

[5] The first king of the solar (*surya*) dynasty.

[6] This second reference to control is with reference to the senses and vices.

[7] The Vedas are Rig Veda, Sama Veda, Yajur Veda and Atharva Veda. The six Vedangas are *shiksha* (articulation and pronunciation), *chhanda* (prosody), *vyakarana* (grammar), *nirukta* (etymology), *jyotisha* (astronomy) and *kalpa* (rituals). Dhanurveda is the science of war or fighting.

[8] This can also be translated as possessing an excellent memory. However, the sacred texts are of two types—shruti and smriti. The texts mentioned earlier, as ones that Rama knows, are shruti texts. Therefore, it seems natural to interpret this as smriti texts.

[9] The word used is *arya*.

handsome one. The one who extends Kousalya's[10] lineage thus possesses all the qualities. In his gravity, he is like the ocean. In his patience, he is like the Himalayas. He is like Vishnu in valour.[11] He is as handsome as the moon. In his rage, he is like the fire of destruction.[12] In generosity, he is like the lord of riches.[13] Yet again, he is like Dharma[14] in truthfulness. Rama possesses such qualities and truth is his valour. He is the eldest and possesses the best of qualities. He is Dasharatha's beloved son. In his affection, the lord of the earth wished to instate him as the heir apparent.[15] His wife, Kaikeyee, saw that arrangements were being made for the consecration.[16] The queen asked for the boons that she had been granted earlier—that Rama be exiled and Bharata be anointed. The king was bound by the sanctity of his words and by the noose of dharma. Dasharatha banished his beloved son, Rama. To follow the instruction in his father's words and to do what would bring pleasure to Kaikeyee, the brave one honoured the pledge and left for the forest. When he left, his beloved brother, Lakshmana, the extender of Sumitra's joy and full of affection and humility, followed him. Rama's wife, Sita, is supreme among women and possesses all the auspicious qualities. She also followed him, like Rohini follows the moon.[17] For some distance, the citizens and his father, Dasharatha, also followed him and then took leave of his son in Shringaverapura, on the banks of the Ganga.[18] They went from one forest to another forest and crossed rivers that were full of large

[10] Rama's mother.

[11] This sentence is used to argue that the idea of Rama as Vishnu's incarnation is a later one.

[12] The fire that comes at the time of the destruction of a *yuga* (era).

[13] Kubera.

[14] The god of dharma.

[15] Dasharatha wanted to make Rama the crown prince.

[16] Dasharatha had three wives—Kousalya, Kaikeyee and Sumitra. Dasharatha had granted two boons to Kaikeyee earlier, boons she was going to redeem when the time was right. Bharata was Kaikeyee's son. Lakshmana and Shatrughna were Sumitra's sons.

[17] The twenty-seven *nakshatras* are married to the moon god, though the moon god loves Rohini (Aldebaran) more. The nakshatras are not quite stars, they can also be constellations.

[18] Shringaverapura is in Uttar Pradesh, near Allahabad.

quantities of water. Finally, they arrived in Chitrakuta, under Bharadvaja's control.[19] In that beautiful forest, the three of them constructed a beautiful abode and dwelt there happily, like the gods and the *gandharva*s.[20] When Rama left for Chitrakuta, lamenting with sorrow on account of his son, King Dasharatha went to heaven. When he died, the *brahmana*s, with Vasishtha at the forefront, wished to instate Bharata as the king, but the immensely strong one did not desire the kingdom. The brave one went to the forest and falling at Rama's feet, sought his favours.[21] Bharata's elder brother repeatedly asked Bharata to return and for the sake of the kingdom, gave him his sandals. With his desire unsatisfied, he touched Rama's feet. Wishing to wait for Rama's return, he began to rule the kingdom from Nandigrama.[22] Rama discerned that he might return there again and so might citizens and other people. Single-minded, he entered Dandaka.[23] He slew the *rakshasa*[24] Viradha and saw Sharabhanga.[25] He met Suteekshna, Agastya and his brother.[26] Following Agastya's words, he received Indra's bow and arrow, a sword and two inexhaustible quivers and was extremely pleased.[27] Rama dwelt in that forest. With the other forest dwellers, all the sages approached him, so that the *asura*s and rakshasas could be slain. While he dwelt there, a rakshasa lady named Shurpanakha, who resided in Janasthana and could assume any form at will, was disfigured.[28] Goaded by Shurpanakha's words, all the rakshasas

[19] It is difficult to pin down Chitrakuta now—it could have been in Uttar Pradesh, Madhya Pradesh or Chhattisgarh. Bharadvaja was a sage.

[20] Semi-divine species, companions of Kubera, celestial musicians.

[21] Bharata wanted Rama to return and become king, but Rama refused. Thereupon, Bharata returned with Rama's sandals, which would be placed on the throne.

[22] A village near Ayodhya.

[23] Rama was single-minded that his exile should not be disturbed. Etymologically, the forest of Dandaka, or Dandakaranya, has a sense of punishment, that is, it is a place to which one was exiled or banished. Today, Dandakaranya straddles several central Indian states.

[24] Demon.

[25] A sage. Suteekshna is another sage.

[26] Agastya's brother.

[27] He obtained these weapons from Agastya, Indra having given them to Agastya.

[28] Lakshmana severed her nose and ears. Janasthana is a place in Dandakaranya. The place where Shurpanakha's nose (and ears) were severed is identified as Nashika.

attacked—Khara, Trishira and the rakshasa Dushana. In the ensuing battle, Rama slew them and their followers. He killed fourteen thousand rakshasas. On hearing that his kinsmen had been killed, Ravana became senseless with rage. He summoned and sought the help of the rakshasa named Maricha. Maricha tried to restrain Ravana several times. "O Ravana! You will not be pardoned if you oppose someone as powerful as him." Ravana, goaded by destiny, did not pay any heed to these words. With Maricha, he went to his[29] hermitage. The two princes were drawn far away by the one versed in *maya*.[30] Having slain the vulture Jatayu, he[31] abducted Rama's wife. On hearing about the vulture being killed and on hearing about Maithilee, Raghava was tormented by sorrow.[32] He lamented, his senses distracted. In that state of grief, he cremated the vulture, Jatayu. While he was searching for Sita in the forest, he saw a rakshasa. His name was Kabandha. He was malformed and terrible to see. The mighty-armed one killed him. While he[33] ascended upwards towards heaven, he told him about Shabaree, who was a follower of dharma. "O Raghava! This ascetic lady is full of dharma. Go to her." The immensely energetic one, the slayer of enemies, went to Shabaree. Shabaree worshipped Dasharatha's son in the proper way. On the shores of the Pampa, he met the ape, Hanumat.[34] On Hanumat's words, he met Sugriva. The immensely strong Rama told Sugriva everything that had happened. In affection and full of grief, the king of the apes told Rama everything about the enmity.[35] The ape also told him about Vali's strength. Rama promised that he would kill Vali. However, Sugriva always suspected the extent of

[29] Rama's.

[30] Maya is the power of illusion. Maricha used these powers to adopt the form of a deer and draw Rama and Lakshmana away.

[31] Ravana.

[32] Maithilee is Sita, daughter of the king of Mithila, Janaka. The kingdom was Videha, the capital was Mithila. Sita is thus also known as Vaidehi. Raghu was one of Rama's ancestors. Hence, Rama is referred to as Raghava.

[33] Kabandha.

[34] Hanumat is Hanuman, Hanumat being the correct way of translating the name. The lake Pampa is near Hampi, in Karnataka.

[35] The enmity between Vali and Sugriva.

Raghava's valour. Dundubhi's gigantic skeleton was there.[36] To establish credibility, Raghava used the big toe on his foot to fling this ten *yojana*s away.[37] Yet again, with one single and large arrow, he pierced seven *sala* trees.[38] To generate confidence, he also dispatched a mountain to the nether regions. After this, the giant ape was assured and delighted in his mind. He went with Rama to Kishkindha[39] and to the mouth of the cave. Sugriva, supreme among apes and golden brown in complexion, started to roar there. On hearing this loud roar, the lord of the apes[40] emerged. Following Sugriva's words, he killed Vali in the encounter. Raghava returned the kingdom to Sugriva and instated him there. The bull among apes summoned all the apes. To search for Janaka's daughter, he sent them in all the directions. The strong Hanumat heard the words of the vulture, Sampati.[41] He leapt over the salty ocean that extended for one hundred yojanas. He reached the city of Lanka, ruled by Ravana. He saw Sita meditating in the forest of Ashoka. To establish Vaidehi's confidence, he gave her the sign[42] he had been given. He comforted her and broke down the gate. He killed five foremost commanders and seven sons of ministers. Having crushed the brave Aksha, he allowed himself to be captured. Because of a boon received from the grandfather,[43] he knew that he was capable of freeing himself from any weapon. However, the brave one wished to tolerate the rakshasas and those who had captured him. With the exception of Maithilee Sita, he burnt down the city of Lanka. To bring pleasure to Rama and to give him the news, the giant ape then returned. Having reached, he circumambulated the great-souled Rama. The one whose soul is immeasurable reported the truth about how he had seen Sita. With Sugriva, he[44] went to the shores

[36] A gigantic demon in the form of a buffalo, killed by Vali.
[37] A yojana is a measure of distance, between 8 and 9 miles.
[38] A large tree, *Shorea robusta*.
[39] The kingdom of the apes.
[40] Vali.
[41] Jatayu's elder brother.
[42] Rama's ring.
[43] Brahma.
[44] Rama.

of the great ocean. He agitated the ocean with arrows that were like the rays of the sun. The ocean, the lord of the rivers, showed himself. On the words of the ocean, he[45] asked Nala to construct a bridge. Using this, he went to the city of Lanka and killed Ravana in a battle. He instated Vibhishana, Indra among rakshasas, in the kingdom of Lanka. Because of the great-souled Raghava's deeds, the mobile and immobile objects in the three worlds and the gods and the sages were satisfied. Supremely content, all the gods worshipped him. Having accomplished his task, Rama was delighted and devoid of anxiety. Having obtained a boon from the gods, he revived all the slain apes. Ascending Pushpaka,[46] he left for Nandigrama. In Nandigrama, with his brothers, the unblemished one removed his matted hair. Rama got Sita back and also got back his kingdom. The people are joyous and delighted. Those who are scrupulous in following dharma are nurtured. There is recovery from disease. There are no famines and everything is devoid of fear. No man has to witness the death of his son. Women are not ignoble and never become widows. They are devoted to their husbands. There is no fear from the wind. Creatures never get submerged in water. There is no fear from fire. It is exactly as it was in *krita yuga*.[47] He performs one hundred horse sacrifices and gives away a lot of gold. Following the appropriate ordinances, he gives away crores of cattle to the learned. Raghava will establish one hundred royal lineages that possess all the qualities. In this world, he will engage the four *varna*s[48] in their own respective tasks. Rama will thus honour the kingdom for eleven thousand years and then go to Brahma's world.

'This is a sacred account and destroys all sins. It is auspicious and in conformity with the Vedas. If a person reads about this

---

[45] Rama.

[46] A celestial vehicle, *vimana*. This belonged originally to Kubera, but was seized by Ravana.

[47] There are four yugas—*satya* (krita), *treta*, *dvapara* and *kali*. Everything worsens as one moves from krita yuga to kali yuga. Though the incidents of the Ramayana occur in treta yuga, it seems as if it is krita yuga.

[48] Brahmanas, *kshatriyas*, *vaishyas* and *shudras*.

conduct, he is cleansed of all sins. A man who reads the account of the Ramayana has a long life, with his sons, grandsons and followers. After death, he obtains greatness in heaven. A brahmana who reads this becomes eloquent in speech, a kshatriya obtains lordship over land, a merchant[49] obtains the fruits of trading and a shudra person obtains greatness.'

# Chapter 1(2)

Hearing Narada's words, who was accomplished in speech, the great sage,[50] with dharma in his soul, worshipped him, accompanied by his disciple. Having been worshipped in the proper way, the celestial sage, Narada, took his leave and departed through the sky[51] to the world of the gods. After some time had passed,[52] the sage went to the banks of the Tamasa, not very far from the Jahnavee.[53] The great sage reached the banks of the Tamasa. With his disciple standing next to him, he saw that this *tirtha* was free from all mud.[54] He said, 'O Bharadvaja![55] Look. This tirtha is free from all mud. It is beautiful and the waters are pleasing, like the mind of a virtuous man. O son![56] Place the water pot here and give my garment made of bark. I will immerse myself in this supreme tirtha of Tamasa.' Bharadvaja was thus addressed by the great-souled Valmiki. Controlled and attentive towards his preceptor, he gave the sage the garment made of bark. The one who had controlled

[49] That is, a vaishya.

[50] Valmiki.

[51] Alternatively, left for heaven.

[52] The text uses the word *muhurta*. It is a measure of time. More specifically, it is a span of forty-eight minutes.

[53] Jahnavee is the Ganga and Tamasa is a tributary that flows through Madhya Pradesh and Uttar Pradesh. Valmiki's hermitage was on the banks of the Tamasa.

[54] A tirtha is a sacred place of pilgrimage with water where one can have a bath.

[55] Valmiki's disciple.

[56] The word used is *tata*. Though it means son, it is affectionately used for anyone who is younger or junior.

his senses received the garment made of bark from his disciple. He
advanced, glancing in every direction at the great forest.

Near the spot, the illustrious one saw a couple of curlews[57]
wandering around, attached to each other. The sound they made
was beautiful. There was a *nishada*[58] who bore evil intent towards
those who resided there. While he looked on,[59] he killed the male
one from that couple. Limbs covered with blood, it trembled on
the ground. On seeing it slain, the wife lamented in piteous tones.
The sage had dharma in his soul. He saw that the bird had been
brought down by the hunter and was moved by compassion. Full
of compassion and on seeing the female curlew that was weeping,
the brahmana recognized this as *adharma*. He spoke these words.
'O nishada! This couple of curlews was in the throes of passion and
you killed one of them. Therefore, you will possess ill repute for an
eternal number of years.'[60] Having said this, a thought arose in his
heart. 'Overcome by sorrow on account of the bird, what is this that
I have uttered?' The intelligent and immensely wise one reflected on
this. Having made up his mind, the bull among sages spoke these
words to his disciple. 'While I was overcome by grief, these words
emerged. They have rhythm and metre and are arranged in *pada*s
with an equal number of *akshara*s. This and nothing else will be
a shloka.'[61] The sage spoke these supreme words to his disciple
and he accepted them cheerfully. The preceptor was also content.
Following the prescribed rites, the sage performed his ablutions in
that tirtha. He returned, thinking about the purport of what had
transpired. Bharadvaja, the humble and learned disciple, followed
his preceptor at the rear, having filled the water pot.

[57] The *krouncha* bird.
[58] The nishadas were hunters who dwelt in mountains and forests.
[59] Valmiki looked on.
[60] This celebrated verse (shloka) is regarded as the beginning of Sanskrit poetry.
[61] There is an implied pun on the etymology of the word shloka, from *shoka* (sorrow).
Sanskrit poetry has different kinds of metres. This particular one is known as *anushtubh*.
An akshara is not quite a syllable, but syllable is a good enough approximation. Pada
means a quarter and an anushtubh shloka possesses four padas, with eight syllables in each
pada. That celebrated verse has these attributes.

The one who knew about dharma entered the hermitage with his disciple. Seating himself, he conversed about other things, but continued to meditate on what had happened. The lord Brahma, the creator of the worlds, himself arrived there. The immensely energetic one, with four faces, arrived there to see the bull among sages. Seeing him, the self-controlled Valmiki was at a loss for words. Supremely astounded, he quickly arose and joined his hands in salutation. He worshipped the god and honoured him with *padya*, *arghya* and a seat.[62] Having prostrated himself in the proper way, he asked him about his welfare. Worshipped in this wonderful way, the illustrious one seated himself. He instructed the great sage, Valmiki, to also be seated. In the presence of the grandfather of the worlds himself, Valmiki sat down, his mind still meditating on what had happened. 'His intelligence clouded by a sense of enmity, that evil-souled one[63] created a hardship. Without any valid reason, he killed a curlew that sang in such beautiful tones.' He was again overcome by sorrow on account of the curlew. Full of sorrow, in his mind, he again chanted the shloka. Brahma smiled at the bull among sages and said, 'You have composed a structured shloka. There is no need to think about this. O brahmana! The metre and the speech arose from me. O supreme among sages! This was so that you could recount Rama's conduct in its entirety. In this world, the intelligent Rama possesses all the qualities and has dharma in his soul. He possesses fortitude and you have heard about his conduct from Narada, everything that the intelligent Rama did, openly and in secret, with Sumitra's son, and all that concerns the rakshasas. You know about Vaidehi's conduct, whether it has been revealed or is a secret. All that is unknown will also become known to you. In the *kavya*[64] you compose, not a single word will be false and there will be nothing that will not happen. In structured and beautiful shlokas, compose the auspicious account of Rama's conduct. As long as there are mountains and as long as there are rivers on this

---

[62] These are objects always offered to a guest—padya (water to wash the feet), achamaniya (water to wash the mouth/face), arghya (a gift) and asana (a seat).

[63] The hunter.

[64] A long poem.

earth, till such a time, this Ramayana account will circulate in the worlds.[65] As long as Rama's account, composed by you, circulates, till that time, you will reside in the upper regions, the nether regions and even in my world.' Having spoken these words, the illustrious Brahma vanished. With his disciple, the sage, Valmiki, was struck by great wonder. All the disciples again chanted the shloka.

Cheerful and extremely surprised, they chanted it repeatedly. It was chanted by the great sage in four padas, with an equal number of aksharas in each. Because of repeated recitation and because it emerged from sorrow, it came to be known as a shloka.[66] Thus, intelligence came to Valmiki and thinking about it in his mind, he composed the entire Ramayana kavya. He decided that this is what he should do. In beautiful padas, the broad-minded and illustrious one composed the account of the illustrious Rama's conduct, with an equal number of aksharas in hundreds of shlokas. The generous and intelligent sage composed a kavya that brought him fame.

## Chapter 1(3)

Having heard everything about the intelligent one's[67] conduct, which was in conformity with dharma, the one with dharma in his soul again sought out all that was known about this. Following dharma, the sage touched water,[68] joined his hands in salutation and stood on a mat of *darbha*[69] grass, facing the east. He sought out a chart for progress.[70] The birth of the extremely brave Rama, who showed his favours towards everyone, was loved by the worlds, his perseverance, amiability and devotion to the truth; the many

[65] Literally, *Ramayana* means Rama's progress (*ayana*).

[66] There is the implication that something becomes a shloka when it is recited by others, not just the composer.

[67] Rama's. Having heard from Narada.

[68] Water is touched before an auspicious act.

[69] Sacred grass. It is not clear whether he stood, or seated himself.

[70] What follows is a description of what is in the Ramayana. The sentence is incomplete (without a subject and a verb), not unusual in Sanskrit.

other wonderful deeds with Vishvamitra as an aide, the shattering of the bow and the marriage with Janakee; the dispute between Rama and Rama[71] and the qualities of Dasharatha's son, Rama's consecration and Kaikeyee's evil intentions; the obstacle created for the consecration and Rama's exile, the miserable lamentations of the king[72] and his departure for the world hereafter; the sorrow of the ordinary subjects and the separation from the ordinary subjects, the conversation with the king of the nishadas[73] and the charioteer's return; the crossing of the Ganga and the meeting with Bharadvaja, having obtained Bharadvaja's permission, their sight of Chitrakuta; the construction of an abode and Bharata's arrival there to seek Rama's favours, the performance of the water rites for the father; the consecration of the sandals and the residence in Nandigrama, the departure for Dandakaranya and the meeting with Suteekshna; Anasuya's problem and the granting of an ointment for the body, the conversation with Shurpanakha and her disfigurement; the slaying of Khara and Trishira and Ravana's rise,[74] the slaying of Maricha and Vaidehi's abduction; Raghava's lamentations and the slaying of the king of the vultures, the sighting of Kabandha and the sighting of Pampa; the sighting of Shabaree and the sighting of Hanumat, the lamentations of the great-souled Raghava in Pampa; the departure for Rishyamuka and the meeting with Sugriva, the generation of friendship between the two and the conflict between Bali and Sugriva; the crushing of Bali and the bestowal on Sugriva,[75] Tara's lamentations and the agreement to reside there until the monsoon nights were over; the rage of the Raghava lion[76] and the gathering of the army, the departure in various directions and a description of the earth; the gift of the ring and the sighting of the bear's den, their fasting to death[77] and their sighting of Sampati;

[71] Parashurama.
[72] Dasharatha.
[73] Guha.
[74] A consequent rise in Ravana's wrath.
[75] The kingship of the apes.
[76] At Sugriva's delay.
[77] Because the apes had not been able to find Sita.

the ascent of the mountain and the leap across the ocean, the
solitary entry into Lanka in the night[78] and thinking about what
should be done; the visit to the liquor room and an examination
of the fortifications, the visit to Ashoka forest and the sighting of
Sita; the giving of the sign[79] and Sita's address, the censure of the
rakshasa ladies and Trijata's nightmare; Sita's gift of the jewel and
the destruction of the trees, the driving away of the rakshasa ladies
and the slaying of the guards; the capture of the son of Vayu,[80] his
roaring and the burning down of Lanka, the seizure of the honey
on the leap back; the presentation of the jewel and the assurance
of Raghava, the meeting with the ocean and Nala's construction
of the bridge; the crossing of the ocean and the siege of Lanka in
the night, the meeting with Vibhishana and the recounting of the
method of killing;[81] the slaying of Kumbhakarna and the crushing
of Meghanada, Ravana's destruction and the regain of Sita in that
city of enemies; the instatement of Vibhishana and the sighting
of Pushpaka, the departure for Ayodhya and the meeting with
Bharata; and the disbandment of all the soldiers and arrangements
for Rama's crowning, the delight brought to his own kingdom and
Vaidehi's exile. In this kavya, the illustrious *rishi* Valmiki described
everything that happened as long as Rama was on earth and all that
would occur in the future, thereafter.[82]

# Chapter 1(4)

When Rama obtained his kingdom, the illustrious rishi Valmiki,
in control of his soul, composed the entire account of his
conduct, in wonderful padas. The immensely wise one recounted
what had happened and what would transpire in the future,

---

[78] By Hanumat.
[79] The ring.
[80] The wind god; Hanumat was Vayu's son.
[81] Vibhishana explained how Ravana could be killed.
[82] After Rama had left earth.

thereafter. Having composed it, the lord thought about who would recount the tale. While the great sage was thinking about this in his mind, in the garb of sages, Kusha and Lava came and touched his feet. The illustrious princes, Kusha and Lava, knew about dharma. He saw that the two brothers, residents of the hermitage, possessed melodious voices. He saw that these two intelligent ones were accomplished in the Vedas. Since this only served to extend the Vedas, the lord gave this to them, the entire Ramayana kavya and Sita's greatness of character. The sage who was devoted in his vows told them about Poulastya's[83] death. This is to be read and sung in pleasant tones, categorized into three scales and seven notes.[84] It possesses rhythm that can be adjusted to the tunes of stringed instruments. This kavya is sung in *hasya, shringara, karunya, roudra, veera, bhayanaka, beebhatsa* and other *rasa*s.[85] They[86] possessed the knowledge of the gandharvas[87] and were accomplished in pausing and pitching their voices. Those two brothers had melodious voices and looked like gandharvas. They possessed beauty and the auspicious signs. They were sweet in speech. Having emerged from Rama's body, they were like two mirror images of him. The kavya was a supreme account and devoted to dharma, those two princes learnt it in its entirety, reciting it in the proper way, without any blemishes. Those two great-souled and immensely fortunate ones were seen to possess all the qualities and knew about the truth. Controlled, and as instructed, they sang this in assemblies of sages, brahmanas and the virtuous. On one occasion, they were seated in a gathering of sages, cleansed in their souls. They sung the kavya in their presence. On hearing this, all the sages had tears in their eyes.

---

[83] Ravana's.

[84] *Svara* (note) can be in seven tones—*shadja, rishabha, gandhara, madhyama, panchama, dhaivat* and *nishada*, commonly known as sa-re-ga-ma-pa-dha-ni. The three scales are *udatta* (high), *anudatta* (low) and *svarita* (accented).

[85] There are nine rasas (emotions) in aesthetics—shringara (romance), hasya (comedy), karunya (compassion), roudra (ferocity), beebhatsa (disgusting), bhayanaka (horrible), veera (heroic), *adbhuta* (wonderful) and *shanta* (peaceful). However, other rasas are also sometimes mentioned.

[86] Kusha and Lava.

[87] Singing, dancing and music.

They were filled with great wonder and uttered words of praise. All the sages, devoted to dharma, were delighted. They praised the singing of Kusha and Lava, who deserved to be praised. 'Wonderful! This song, in particular the shlokas, are melodious. Although all this happened a long time ago, it is as if we have witnessed it now. Those two immersed themselves in it and sung it in accordance with the sentiments. Accomplished in a wealth of svaras, they sang together, melodiously and with affection.' The great sages, who could pride themselves on their austerities, praised those two in this way. They sang in beautiful tones, full of deep meaning and affection. Delighted, a sage who was there gave them a water pot. Delighted, another extremely illustrious sage gave them garments of bark. The account composed by the sage,[88] arranged in successive sections, was extraordinary and would be a foundation for poets who would come in the future.

Those two singers were praised everywhere. On one occasion, while they were thus singing on the royal road, Bharata's elder brother[89] saw them. Rama, the slayer of enemies, honoured the two brothers, Kusha and Lava, who deserved to be praised, and brought them to his own abode. The lord, the scorcher of enemies, seated himself on a golden and divine throne. His advisers and brothers were seated around him. Rama saw those two handsome ones, with *veenas*,[90] and spoke to Lakshmana, Shatrughna and Bharata. 'They are as radiant as the gods. Let this account be heard from them. It is structured into wonderful and meaningful padas. Let it be properly sung by these two, who possess melodious voices. These two sages, Kusha and Lava, bear all the marks of kings, but are great ascetics. Listen to the great account they speak about. It brings prosperity even to me.' Those two were accomplished in the different techniques and modes of singing. Urged by Rama, they sang. And in that assembly, Rama was also gradually immersed in their narration.

[88] Valmiki.
[89] Rama.
[90] Stringed musical instrument.

# Chapter 1(5)

Beginning with Prajapati,[91] several victorious and unrivalled kings have ruled over this entire earth. There was one named Sagara, who dug up the ocean.[92] When he advanced, his sixty thousand sons surrounded him. This was the lineage of the Ikshvakus, one of great-souled kings. It has been heard that the great Ramayana account originates in this lineage. From the beginning to the end, everything will be recounted. It is full of dharma, *kama* and *artha*[93] and must be heard without any censure.

There was the great kingdom[94] of Kosala, prosperous and happy. It possessed a lot of wealth and grain and was located on the banks of the Sarayu. The city of Ayodhya,[95] famous in the worlds, was situated there. Manu, Indra among men, himself constructed that city. That great city was twelve yojanas long and three yojanas wide. It was beautiful and spread out, divided by highways. The beautiful and large royal roads were laid out well. They were always sprinkled with water and flowers were strewn on them. The king there was Dasharatha, an extender of the great kingdom. He made that city his abode, like the king of the gods in heaven. There were gates and arches and the interiors of the buildings were laid out well. There were machines and implements of war everywhere, constructed by all manner of artisans. There were bards and minstrels everywhere. That handsome city was infinite in splendour. There were tall walls with standards, surmounted by hundreds of *shataghni*s.[96] Everywhere, that city was also full of large numbers of dancers and actors. There were mango groves and a giant wall formed a girdle around the city. There were moats

---

[91] Implying Manu.

[92] The king's name is Sagara and the ocean is named *saagara* after him.

[93] These are regarded as the three objectives (*trivarga*) of human existence. Kama is the pursuit of the senses and artha is the pursuit of wealth. The goal of *moksha* (emancipation) transcends these three.

[94] The text uses the word *janapada*.

[95] The capital of Kosala.

[96] A shataghni is a weapon that can kill one hundred at one stroke.

that were difficult to cross. Thus, the fortification was impossible for others to breach. It was populated by horses, elephants, cattle, camels and donkeys. Large numbers of vassal kings came from the frontiers to offer tribute. Merchants and residents of many countries came there. The palaces were embedded with jewels and were as beautiful as mountains. There were secret residences[97] and the place was like Indra's Amaravati.[98] The city was full of large numbers of beautiful women and was wonderfully laid out, like an *ashtapada* board.[99] It was encrusted with gems everywhere and the mansions were like celestial vehicles. The houses were densely constructed on level ground and there was no space between them. There were stores of *shali* rice[100] and the water was like the juice of sugar cane. There were drums, percussion instruments,[101] veenas and cymbals. They were sounded loudly, signifying that this was the best city on earth. Through their austerities, *siddhas*[102] obtain celestial vehicles in heaven. With extremely well-laid-out residences and populated by the best among men, this city was like one of those. The archers there were skilled and dexterous of hand. But they did not use their arrows to pierce someone who was alone, someone who was without heirs, or someone who was running away. Nor did they aim by sound alone.[103] Intoxicated lions, tigers and wild boars roared and roamed around in the forests. They killed these with their sharp weapons and even through the sheer strength of their arms. The place was full of thousands of such *maharathas*.[104] The city that was King Dasharatha's residence was like this. It was populated by those with qualities, those who offered oblations into the fire. There

---

[97] For women.

[98] Indra's capital.

[99] Ashtapada was a game, probably a precursor to chess.

[100] A fine rice.

[101] We have translated *mridanga* in this way and *dundubhi* as drum.

[102] Successful sages.

[103] *Shabdavedhyam*, shooting at a target on the basis of sound, rather than sight. Unlike the others, which are principles of fair fighting, this prohibition might have been because of Dasharatha's experience and curse, recounted later.

[104] Great warrior, more specifically, a maharatha is someone who can single-handedly fight ten thousand warriors.

were the best among brahmanas, accomplished in the Vedas and the Vedangas. There were thousands of great-souled ones, devoted to the truth. All of them were like sages and some were the equals of the great sages.

# Chapter 1(6)

K ing Dasharatha resided in that city of Ayodhya and collected those who knew about the Vedas around him. He was far-sighted and immensely energetic and loved by the residents of the city and the countryside. He was a great warrior from the Ikshvaku lineage who performed sacrifices. He controlled himself and was devoted to dharma. He was a *rajarshi* who was the equal of a *maharshi*.[105] He was famous in the three worlds. He was powerful and slew his enemies. He possessed friends and had conquered his senses. He accumulated wealth and other kinds of riches. He was like Shakra and Vaishravana.[106] Like the immensely energetic Manu, he protected the world. He ruled over the earth. Adhering to the truth, he pursued the three objectives.[107] He ruled over that best of cities, like Indra in Amaravati. There were extremely learned people in that best of cities, happy and with dharma in their souls. The men were satisfied with the riches they had obtained themselves. They were truthful in speech and not avaricious. In that supreme of cities, there was no one who had not accumulated some amount of riches. There was no household without riches in the form of cattle, horses, wealth and grain. There was no man who was lustful, ignoble or cruel. One was incapable of seeing an ignorant person or a non-believer in Ayodhya. All the men and women were extremely controlled and devoted to dharma. They were joyful and good in conduct, like unblemished maharshis. There was no one without an earring, without a headdress, without a garland and

[105] A maharshi is a great sage. A rajarshi is a royal sage.
[106] Respectively, Indra and Kubera.
[107] Dharma, artha and kama.

without some means of finding pleasure. There was no one who did not have a bath, nor anyone who did not smear the body with unguents and fragrances. There was no one who did not have the best of food. There was no one who was not generous, no one who did not decorate the body with ornaments. No one could be seen without ornaments on the hands, nor one who was heartless. There was no one who did not light the sacrificial fire. There were thousands of brahmanas who performed sacrifices. There was no one in Ayodhya who was without a means of subsistence, nor anyone of mixed varna. The brahmanas had conquered their senses and were always engaged in their own tasks. They were devoted to donating and studying. They were controlled and received gifts. There was no one who was a non-believer, no one who was a liar, nor anyone who was not extremely learned. There was no one who was jealous or incapable. There was no one who was not learned. There was no one who was distressed or disturbed in mind, no one who was miserable. There was no man or woman who was poor or ugly. In Ayodhya, one was incapable of seeing a person who was not devoted to the king. All the four varnas worshipped gods and guests. All the men possessed long lifespans and were devoted to dharma and the truth. The kshatriyas placed brahmanas ahead of them and the vaishyas followed the kshatriyas. The shudras were devoted to their own dharma and served the other three varnas. That city was guarded extremely well by that lord of the Ikshvaku lineage, just like the intelligent Manu, Indra among men, in ancient times. The accomplished warriors were intolerant and were like the touch of fire. They had completed all their training and were like lions in caves. There were the best of horses, born in the kingdoms of Kamboja and Bahlika. It was full of other horses born in mountainous regions and riverine tracts.[108] They were like Indra's horse. The place was full of extremely strong and crazy elephants that were like mountains, born in the Vindhya mountains and the Himalayas. These elephants were descended from Anjana

---

[108] Instead of mountainous region, Vanayu might also refer to the name of a specific country, such as Arabia. Riverine tract might mean the region of the five rivers, especially the area around the Sindhu.

and Vamana.[109] The city's elephants were *bhadra-mandra, bhadra-mriga* and *mriga-mandra*.[110] The city was always full of crazy elephants that were like mountains. Making true its name, the city extended for another two yojanas beyond.[111] With firm gates and ramparts, it was true to its name. With colourful houses, it was auspicious and beautiful. There were thousands of men in the city of Ayodhya. Like Shakra, the king ruled it.

## Chapter 1(7)

There were eight brave and illustrious advisers. They were pure and devoted and were always engaged in the king's tasks—Dhrishti, Jayanta, Vijaya, Siddhartha, Arthasadhaka, Ashoka, Mantrapala—and Sumantra was the eighth. There were two officiating priests, supreme among rishis—Vasishtha and Vamadeva. There were other ministers too. They were prosperous and great-souled, learned in the sacred texts and firm in their valour. They were controlled and the performers of deeds, acting just as they said they would. They possessed energy, forgiveness and fame. They smiled before they spoke. Because of anger, desire or wealth, they never spoke false words. There was nothing that was unknown to them, in their own kingdom, or in that of others, whether it had been done, was being done, or was being thought of. This was ensured through spies. They were skilled in administration and their affections had been tested.[112] At the right time, the appropriate punishment was imposed, even on

---

[109] The Critical Edition excises half a shloka, where Iravata and Mahapadma are also mentioned. Eight elephants stand in the eight directions and their names are Airavata, Pundarika, Vamana, Kumuda, Anjana, Pushpadanta, Sarvabhouma and Suprateeka. All that is meant is that Ayodhya's elephants had divine ancestry.

[110] There were four classes of elephants, classified according to complexion, tusk and belly—*bhadra, mandra, mriga* and *mishra*. The first three are mentioned here, Ayodhya's elephants interbred from these three classes.

[111] Ayodhya means something that cannot be assailed. The sense is that the fortifications extended for another two yojanas, beyond the city's perimeter.

[112] By the king, so that they did not yield to nepotism and other relationships.

their own sons. They were devoted to accumulating the treasury and the army. They caused no violence to even men who were unfriendly, as long as they were blameless. They were brave and always full of enterprise, devoted to the science of governing. They were pure and always protected those who resided in the kingdom. In an attempt to fill up the treasury, they did not cause violence to brahmanas and kshatriyas. After examining a man's strengths and weaknesses, they imposed extremely stiff punishments. Pure and single-minded, all of them governed together. In the city or in the kingdom, there was no man who was a liar. There was no man who was wicked, addicted to another person's wife. Everything in the kingdom was peaceful and the city was also like that. All of them[113] were well attired and well decorated, excellent in conduct. For the sake of the king, their eyes of good policy were always open. They obtained their good qualities from their preceptors and were renowned for their valour. Because of their intelligence and decisions, they were famous in foreign countries too. These were the qualities that the advisers possessed. With their aid, the unblemished King Dasharatha ruled the earth. Using spies, he kept an eye on what happened. He delighted the subjects through dharma. There was no one who was his superior or equal. Nor did he have any enemies. Those ministers were devoted to providing advice that brought welfare. They were devoted, accomplished and skilled, and surrounded him. The king thus gained radiance. He was like the rising sun, illuminating with its blazing rays.

# Chapter 1(8)

He knew about dharma, was great-souled and was powerful. However, he did not have a son who would extend the lineage and he was tormented because of the lack of a son. While he reflected on this, a thought occurred to the great-souled one. 'For the sake of a son, why don't I perform a horse sacrifice?' The intelligent

---

[113] The ministers.

one made up his mind to undertake such a sacrifice and consulted with all his pure ministers. The king told Sumantra, supreme among ministers, 'Quickly summon the priests and all my seniors.'

Having heard this, the *suta*,[114] Sumantra, spoke to the king in secret. 'I have heard an ancient account that was instructed by the officiating priests. O king! In an assembly of sages, the illustrious Sanatkumara had earlier recounted this tale about how you would obtain sons.[115] Kashyapa has a son who is famous by the name of Vibhandaka. He will have a son who will be renowned by the name of Rishyashringa.[116] That sage will always be reared in the forest and will always roam around in the forest. That Indra among brahmanas will not know anyone else and will always follow his father. That great-souled one will observe both kinds of *brahmacharya*.[117] O king! He will be famous in the world and will always be spoken about by brahmanas. The illustrious one will tend to the sacrificial fire and his father. The time will come for him to be brought here. At that time, there will also be an extremely strong, powerful and famous king named Romapada in Anga. Because of a transgression committed by the king, there will be an extremely terrible period of drought. It will be so terrible that all the creatures will face fear. Because of the onset of the drought, the king will be overcome by grief. He will summon brahmanas and those who are aged in learning and address them. "All of you know the sacred texts of dharma and also know about the nature of the worlds. Instruct me about the rituals and about the atonement I should perform." The brahmanas, learned in

---

[114] The sutas were charioteers and bards, but were sometimes, advisers to kings.

[115] Sanatkumara, Sanaka, Sanatana and Sanandana were four sages who were created through Brahma's mental powers.

[116] This is being foretold as something that will happen in the future. Literally, Rishyashringa means the rishi who possesses horns. Since *shringa* also means peak, this can also be interpreted as a lofty sage.

[117] The word brahmacharya is usually translated as celibacy, but that's a simplification. Brahmacharya means conduct along the path of the *brahman*. In the four stages (*ashramas*) of life, brahmacharya is the first, followed by *garhasthya*, *vanaprastha* and *sannyasa*, in that order. Brahmacharya is the stage when one is a student and follows celibacy. Hence, this is the first kind of ashrama. On attaining the stage of a householder (garhasthya), brahmacharya is not interpreted as celibacy. Instead, it means intercourse at prescribed times and for prescribed purposes. This is the second kind of brahmacharya.

the Vedas, will tell the king, "O king! Vibhandaka's son provides all the means. Bring him here. O king! Bring Rishyashringa and honour him extremely well. Control yourself, follow the rituals and bestow your daughter, Shanta, on him." Hearing their words, the king will begin to think. Through what means will I be able to bring the valiant one here? Having consulted with his ministers, the king will make up his mind. With the requisite honours, he will dispatch his priests and advisers. On hearing the king's words, they will be distressed and will lower their faces. "O king! We entreat you. We are scared of the rishi[118] and cannot go there. Having thought about it, we will tell you of a means whereby he can be brought here. We will be able to bring the brahmana here and no taint will result." Hence, the lord of Anga will employ a courtesan to bring the rishi's son there. The god[119] will shower down and he will bestow Shanta on him. This son-in-law, Rishyashringa, will also ensure sons for you.[120] I have told you everything that Sanatkumara had said.'

At this, Dasharatha was delighted and replied, 'How can Rishyashringa be brought here? You should tell me in detail.'

## Chapter 1(9)

Urged by the king, Sumantra replied in these words. 'With your ministers, hear about how Rishyashringa can be brought here. The advisers and priests told Romapada, "We have thought of a means so that there is no harm. Devoted to austerities and studying, Rishyashringa wanders around in the forest. He is inexperienced about women, worldly matters and pleasure. Excessive addiction to the senses causes turbulence in the minds of men. We must make efforts to bring him to the city quickly. Let beautiful and ornamented

---

[118] Vibhandaka.

[119] The rain god.

[120] There is another aspect to the expression son-in-law. According to some accounts, before he had sons, through Kousalya, Dasharatha had a daughter named Shanta, who became King Romapada's adopted daughter.

courtesans go there. Let them honour and seduce him in many kinds of ways and bring him here." On hearing this, the king agreed to what the priests had said. Accordingly, the priests and ministers made the arrangements. Hearing the instruction, the best among courtesans entered that great forest. They stationed themselves close to the hermitage and made efforts to show themselves. The rishi's patient son always resided in the hermitage. He was always content with his father and never ventured outside the hermitage. Since his birth, the ascetic had never seen anyone else, woman, man, or any other being, from either the city or the countryside. Wandering around as he willed, on an occasion, he arrived at that spot.[121] Vibhandaka's son arrived there and saw the courtesans. The women were splendidly attired and were singing in melodious voices. All of them approached the rishi's son and spoke these words. "O brahmana! Who are you? Why do you conduct yourself like this? We wish to know this. You are roaming around alone in this desolate and terrible forest? Tell us." In that forest, those women possessed desirable forms and these were forms he had not seen earlier. Affection was generated in him and he desired to tell them about his father and himself. "My father is Vibhandaka and I am his son. I am known as Rishyashringa because of an act that happened on earth.[122] O beautiful ones! Our hermitage is not far from here. I wish to honour all of you there, following the prescribed rites." Hearing the words of the rishi's son, all of them desired to see the hermitage and all of them went there with him. When they had gone there, the rishi's son worshipped them. "Here are arghya, padya, roots and fruits for you." All of them eagerly accepted this worship. However, they were scared of the rishi and made up their minds to depart quickly. "O brahmana! Take these best of fruits from us. May you be fortunate. Accept them and eat them, without any delay." Full of delight, all of them embraced him. They gave him many kinds of wonderful sweetmeats to eat. The energetic one

[121] Where the courtesans were.

[122] There are different stories about Rishyashringa's birth, such as he being the son of Vibhandaka and Urvashi. In some, not all, of these accounts, he is born from a doe, which explains the horns. Vibhandaka was descended from the sage Kashyapa.

ate them, taking them to be fruits. Having always resided in the forest, he had never tasted anything like this before. They told the brahmana that they had their vows to tend to and took his leave. The women were terrified of the father and desired to leave the spot. When they had all left, the brahmana who was Kashyapa's descendant was miserable and did not feel well. His heart was in a whirl. After some time, the valiant one went to the spot where the delightful and ornamented courtesans could be seen. On seeing the brahmana arrive, they were delighted in their minds. All of them surrounded him and spoke these words. "O amiable one! Come to our hermitage. There will be special and wonderful rituals there." He heard all their words, pleasing to the heart. He made up his mind to go and the women took him away. When the great-souled brahmana was thus brought,[123] the god suddenly showered down and delighted the world. When the brahmana arrived in his kingdom with the rains, the king[124] advanced to worship the sage, bowing his head down on the ground. Controlled, as is proper, he offered him arghya. He sought the favour of that Indra among brahmanas, in particular from the anger the brahmana[125] would be overwhelmed with. He made him enter the inner quarters and following the prescribed rites, bestowed his daughter Shanta on him. The king obtained peace of mind.[126] In this way, the immensely energetic Rishyashringa resided there, with his wife, Shanta, worshipped extremely well and with all his desires satisfied.'

## Chapter 1(10)

'O Indra among kings![127] Listen yet again to my beneficial words. This is what the intelligent one, foremost among

---

[123] To Anga.
[124] Romapada.
[125] Meaning Vibhandaka.
[126] Since peace is *shanti,* there is a bit of a pun.
[127] Sumantra is still speaking.

gods,[128] had said. "A king named Dasharatha will be born in the
lineage of Ikshvaku. He will be extremely devoted to dharma. He
will be handsome and truthful to his vows. That king will be friendly
with the king of Anga. He will have an extremely fortunate daughter
named Shanta.[129] Anga's[130] son will be a king who will be spoken
of as Romapada. The immensely illustrious King Dasharatha will
go to him and say, 'O one with dharma in your soul! I am without
a son. For the sake of my sacrifice, grant me Shanta's husband. For
the sake of a son and for the sake of the lineage, he will preside
over the sacrifice.' The king who will be controlled will hear these
words and think about them in his mind, about granting Shanta's
husband for the sake of obtaining a son. He will grant him, and
devoid of anxiety, the king[131] will receive the brahmana. Delighted
in his mind, he will make arrangements for the sacrifice. Desiring
to perform the sacrifice, King Dasharatha, knowledgeable about
dharma, will join his hands in salutation and request Rishyashringa,
foremost among brahmanas. For the sake of the sacrifice, for the
sake of sons and for the sake of heaven, the lord of men and the
lord of the earth will have his desires satisfied by that foremost
among brahmanas. He will have four sons, infinite in valour. They
will establish lineages and will be famous in all the worlds." This is
what the illustrious lord Sanatkumara, foremost among gods, told
in an account in an ancient time, during *deva yuga*.[132] O great king!
Let that tiger among men be honoured well and brought here. You
should yourself go, with your army and mounts.'

Having heard the suta's words and having obtained Vasishtha's
permission, he[133] left for where that brahmana was, with the residents
of his inner quarters and his advisers. They gradually passed over
forests and rivers. They entered the country where that bull among

[128] Sanatkumara.

[129] The text leaves this vague enough for the 'he' to be interpreted as either Dasharatha
or Romapada.

[130] This Anga means Romapada's father.

[131] Dasharatha.

[132] Obviously, another name for krita yuga.

[133] Dasharatha.

sages was. He approached that best among brahmanas, seated near
Romapada. He saw the rishi's son, who blazed like a fire. On seeing
the king, the king[134] followed the proper rites and worshipped him,
especially because of their friendship. He was delighted in his mind.
Romapada told the intelligent rishi's son and about their friendship
and relationship and he also worshipped him.[135] Honoured
extremely well in this way, the bull among men spent some time
there. After having spent seven or eight days there, the king told the
king, 'O king! O lord of the earth! Let your daughter, Shanta, and
her husband come to my city. There is the task of a great sacrifice
to be performed.' Hearing this, the intelligent king agreed to the
idea of their travelling there and spoke these words. 'O brahmana!
Go there with your wife.' The rishi's son agreed with what the
king had said. Having taken the king's permission, he left with his
wife. The valiant Dasharatha and Romapada were delighted. They
joined their hands in salutation and affectionately embraced each
other. Having taken leave of his well-wisher,[136] the descendant of
the Raghu lineage departed. He sent along swift messengers ahead,
to inform the citizens. 'Swiftly make arrangements for the city to be
decorated in every possible way.' The citizens were delighted to hear
that the king was arriving. They made all the arrangements, as the
king's messengers had conveyed. Placing the bull among brahmanas
ahead of him and to the sound of the blaring of conch shells and the
beating of drums, the king entered the ornamented city. On seeing
the brahmana, everyone in the city was delighted. When the Indra
among men,[137] with deeds to rival those of Indra, entered, he was
honoured extremely well. He made him[138] enter the inner quarters
and following the sacred texts, worshipped him. Having brought
him there, he thought that his task had already been accomplished.
All those in the inner quarters saw that the large-eyed Shanta had
arrived there, with her husband. They were filled with joy. She was

[134] Dasharatha and Romapada respectively.
[135] Rishyashringa also worshipped Dasharatha.
[136] Romapada.
[137] Dasharatha.
[138] Rishyashringa.

honoured by them, especially by the king. With the brahmana, she
happily resided there for a while.

## Chapter 1(11)

After several days had passed, the extremely pleasant season
of spring presented itself and the king made up his mind
to undertake the sacrifice. He bowed his head down before
the brahmana,[139] whose complexion was like that of the gods,
and sought his favours. For the sake of sons and the lineage, he
requested him to be the officiating priest at the sacrifice. Honoured
extremely well, he agreed to the king's words. 'Let the requisite
objects be brought and let the horse be released.'[140] The king spoke
the following words to Sumantra, supreme among ministers. 'O
Sumantra! Quickly invite officiating priests who are knowledgeable
about the *brahman*.'[141] Sumantra, swift in his valour, departed
quickly. He brought all the brahmanas who were accomplished
in the Vedas—Suyajna, Vamadeva, Javali, Kashyapa, the priest
Vasishtha and other supreme brahmanas. King Dasharatha, with
dharma in his soul, worshipped them. He gently spoke these words,
full of dharma and artha. 'My mind is not at peace. There is no
happiness without a son. That is the reason I have made up my mind
to undertake a horse sacrifice. I wish to perform that sacrifice in
accordance with the rites laid down in the sacred texts. Through the
powers of the rishi's son,[142] I hope to accomplish my desire.' All the
brahmanas, with Vasishtha at the forefront, praised the undecaying
words that had emerged from the king's mouth and honoured the

[139] Rishyashringa.

[140] Spoken by Rishyashringa. In a horse sacrifice, a horse is released, left free to wander
around. When the horse wanders into another king's kingdom, that king seizes the horse
and provokes a battle, or accepts vassalage. When the triumphant horse eventually returns,
it is sacrificed.

[141] The brahman or *paramatman* is the supreme soul. Though Rishyashringa was the
chief officiating priest, there were other officiating priests too.

[142] Rishyashringa.

king back. With Rishyashringa at the forefront, they told the king,
'Let all the necessary objects be brought and let the horse be released.
By all means, you will obtain four infinitely valorous sons. Because
your mind has turned towards dharma, those sons will arrive.'
On hearing the words that the brahmanas had spoken, the king
was delighted. Filled with joy because of those auspicious words,
the king told the advisers, 'Obeying the words of the preceptors,
let all the necessary objects be brought quickly. Let the horse be
released, guarded adequately and followed by preceptors. Let the
sacrificial arena be marked out on the northern banks of the Sarayu.
Following the ordinances laid down in the sacred texts, let peace
prosper. This is the supreme sacrifice. If all the kings are capable of
performing this sacrifice without any hindrances, they do not suffer
from any hardships. The learned *brahma-rakshasas*[143] always seek
out weaknesses. If the ordinances are not observed, the performer
of a sacrifice is always destroyed. Therefore, let the sacrifice be
completed in accordance with the prescribed ordinances. All of you
are capable of acting in accordance with the ordinances.' All the
ministers agreed to this and honoured him back. They followed the
king's words, exactly as they had been instructed. All the brahmanas
also granted permission to that bull among kings, who knew about
dharma, and returned to wherever they had come from. When the
brahmanas had departed, the lord of men also allowed the ministers
to leave. The immensely radiant one entered his own abode.

## Chapter 1(12)

After an entire year had passed, it was spring again.[144] Following
the rites, he[145] greeted Vasishtha and worshipped him. To
obtain sons, he spoke these humble words to that supreme among
brahmanas. 'O brahmana! O bull among sages! Please perform

---

[143] Brahmanas who become rakshasas after death.
[144] The horse returned after wandering around for a year.
[145] Dasharatha.

the sacrifice properly. Let impediments not be caused to any part
of the sacrifice. You are extremely affectionate towards me and
you are my supreme preceptor. The sacrifice that I am about to
undertake is a burden and you are capable of bearing that load.'
The supreme among brahmanas agreed to what the king had
said and replied, 'I will do everything that you have asked.' He
accordingly instructed all the aged brahmanas who were familiar
with sacrificial rites, accomplished architects, those who were
aged and extremely devoted to dharma, artisans who could see
everything through until completion, carpenters, those who dug,
astrologers, craftsmen, actors, dancers and extremely learned
men acquainted with the unsullied sacred texts, 'Following the
king's command, engage yourselves in tasks connected with the
sacrifice. Quickly bring several thousand bricks. For the kings,
construct many structures that possess all the qualities. You must
build hundreds of auspicious residences for the brahmanas. They
must be properly stocked with many kinds of food and drink. For
the residents of the city and the countryside, there must be many
beautiful abodes that are stocked with diverse kinds of food and all
the objects of desire. Food must be given properly and with honour,
not indifferently. All the varnas must be worshipped, respected
well and given this. Nothing must be offered with disrespect, or
with sentiments of desire and anger. Men and artisans who are
eagerly engaged in tasks connected with the sacrifice must be
specially worshipped, in the due order. If no one is disrespected,
then they will perform their tasks properly. All of you act in this
way, pleasantly and with affection.' Vasishtha summoned all of
them and told them this and they promised that they would all act
in this way, with nothing being ignored.

Vasishtha summoned Sumantra and spoke these words. 'Invite
all the kings on earth who are devoted to dharma and thousands of
brahmanas, kshatriyas, vaishyas and shudras. Respectfully summon
men from all the countries and the brave Janaka, lord of Mithila,
for whom truth is his valour. He is devoted to all the sacred texts
and devoted to the Vedas. Honour that immensely fortunate one
well and bring him here yourself. It is because I know about the

earlier alliance that I am mentioning him first.[146] Then there is the
gentle king of Kashi, always pleasant in speech. His conduct is
like that of a god. Bring him yourself. The aged king of Kekaya is
extremely devoted to dharma. He is the father-in-law of this lion
among kings. Bring him, together with his son. The illustrious and
immensely fortunate Romapada, lord of Anga, is a friend to this
lion among kings. Honour him well and bring him here. Bring all
the kings from the east, Sindhu, Souvira and the kings from the
southern regions. Bring all the other virtuous and pleasant kings on
earth. Bring all of them swiftly, with their followers and relatives.'
Hearing Vasishtha's words, Sumantra quickly instructed men to
act in accordance with the king's auspicious words. Following the
sage's instructions, Sumantra, with dharma in his soul, himself
departed quickly to invite the kings.

Everyone came and informed the intelligent Vasishtha that the
designated tasks had been completed. All of them told him that
the objects needed for the sacrifice had been brought. Delighted,
the foremost among brahmanas again told all of them, 'Even in
jest, nothing should be given with any mark of disrespect. There
is no doubt that if something is given without respect, the giver is
destroyed.' After some days and nights, the kings started to arrive.
They brought many kinds of gems for King Dasharatha. Extremely
joyful, Vasishtha told the king, 'O tiger among men! Following
your command, the kings have arrived. As each one deserved, I have
honoured those best among kings. O king! Disciplining themselves,
the men have made arrangements for the sacrifice. So that the
sacrifice can be performed, you should now go to the sacrificial
ground. In every direction, it has been stocked with all the objects
of desire.' Following the words of Vasishtha and Rishyashringa,
on an auspicious day and nakshatra, the lord of the earth left.
With Vasishtha leading the way and placing Rishyashringa at the
forefront, the supreme among brahmanas started the process for
the sacrifice.

---

[146] This probably means earlier friendship. At a stretch, this might also mean that
Vasishtha knew about the future matrimonial alliance.

# Chapter 1(13)

After an entire year was over, the horse returned. The king's sacrifice started on the northern bank of the Sarayu. Placing Rishyashringa at the forefront, the bulls among brahmanas started the rites for the great horse sacrifice of the extremely great-souled king. Learned in the Vedas, the officiating priests performed the required rites. In due order, they followed the ordinances and policies of the sacred texts. The brahmanas followed the sacred texts in observing the *pravargya* and *upasad* rites.[147] In accordance with the sacred texts, they performed all the other tasks. Delighted, all the bulls among the sages worshipped and, following the rites, performed all the rituals that have to be performed in the morning. In no way was there any deviation in any of these. The brahmana[148] checked that everything was properly performed. No one who was exhausted or hungry could be seen there. There was no ignorant brahmana present, nor one without hundreds of followers. The brahmanas incessantly ate. The ascetics ate. The mendicants ate. The aged, the diseased, women and children incessantly ate and were still not satisfied. Many urgings of 'give', 'give food and different kinds of garments' were heard there. Many heaps of food could be seen, as large as mountains and every day, they were cooked in the proper way. The brahmanas praised the tasty food that had been prepared in the proper way. 'I am content. We are fortunate.' These are the words Raghava[149] heard. Ornamented men served the brahmanas. They were aided by others wearing polished and bejewelled earrings. In gaps between the rituals, the brahmanas indulged in many kinds of debates. Wishing to defeat each other, those patient and extremely eloquent ones spoke to each other. From one day to another day, those accomplished brahmanas performed all the rites, urged on by the sacred texts. There was no one there who did not know the six Vedangas. There

---

[147] Specific rites connected with a *soma* sacrifice.
[148] Rishyashringa.
[149] Dasharatha.

was no one without vows, or without learning. As an assistant priest, the king had no brahmana who was not skilled.

When the time came to erect the sacrificial posts, there were six each made out of *bilva*, *khadira* and *parnina*. There was one constructed from *shleshmataka* and two from *devadaru*, these two being laid out like two outstretched arms.[150] All of these were erected by those who were learned about the sacred texts and about sacrifices. To bring beauty to the sacrifice, these were ornamented and embellished in gold. In accordance with the ordinances, all of these were firmly laid out by accomplished artisans. Each possessed eight smooth sides. They were covered with garments and decorated with flowers and fragrances. They were radiant, like the *saptarshi*s in heaven.[151] Bricks were properly measured and laid out and brahmanas knowledgeable about *shulba* rites readied the place for the fire.[152] Eighteen bricks were laid out on three sides[153] and it looked like Garuda[154] with golden feathers. As instructed by the sacred texts, animals, serpents, birds, horses and aquatic creatures were tethered to sacrificial stakes, as offerings to the gods. Following the sacred texts, the officiating priests sacrificed these. Three hundred animals were tethered to sacrificial stakes, including King Dasharatha's supreme horse. In great joy, Kousalya worshipped the horse and used three swords to kill it.[155] With a peaceful mind and wishing to obtain dharma, Kousalya then spent a single night with that

[150] In a horse sacrifice, stretching from the north to the south, twenty-one sacrificial posts are laid out. The horse is tied to the main one and this is made out of the *rajjudala* (shleshmataka) tree. Two posts made out of devadaru are to the north and south of this. There are six posts each from bilva, khadira and *palasha* (parnina).

[151] The saptarshis are the seven great sages. The list varies, but the standard one is Marichi, Atri, Angira, Pulastya, Pulaha, Kratu and Vasishtha. In the sky, the saptarshis are identified with the constellation of Ursa Major (Great Bear).

[152] Shulba rites are those connected with the construction of the altar for the sacrifice. The associated sacred texts are known as *Shulba Sutras*.

[153] In the shape of a triangle.

[154] The king of the birds, Vishnu's mount.

[155] Or three strokes of the sword.

horse. The *hotri*s, *adhvaryu*s and *udgatri*s[156] united the *mahishi*,
*parivritti* and *vavata* with the horse.[157] The extremely controlled
officiating priests, controlled in their senses, extracted the horse's
entrails, and following the sacred texts, offered this as oblation
into the fire. At the appropriate time, following the rituals and
desiring to cleanse himself of sins, the lord of men inhaled the
fragrance of the smoke from the entrails. Sixteen brahmanas who
were officiating priests observed the rituals and offered all the
limbs of the horse into the fire. In other sacrifices, oblations are
offered using the branch of a *plaksha* tree.[158] However, in the
case of a horse sacrifice, the sacrifice is conducted with a single
reed. According to the *Kalpa Sutra*s and the *Brahmana* texts,[159]
the horse sacrifice numbers three days. The first day after that
has been thought of as *chatushtoma*, the second has been counted
as *uktha* and the third is known as *atiratra*.[160] Thereafter, other
great sacrifices like *jyotishtoma*, *ayushtoma*, atiratra, *abhijit*,
*vishvajit* and *aptoryama* were performed. The king, the extender
of his own lineage, gave away the eastern direction to the hotri,
the western direction to the adhvaryu, the southern direction
to the brahmana and the northern direction to the udgatri as
*dakshina*.[161] In ancient times, Svayambhu had performed a great
horse sacrifice. Having properly completed the sacrifice, the king,

---

[156] There were four classes of priests, though the classification varied over time.
The hotri is the chief priest and is accomplished in the Rig Veda. The adhvaryu is the
assistant priest and is accomplished in the Yajur Veda, though later, the udgatri came to be
identified with the Sama Veda. In addition, there was the brahmana or *purohita*.

[157] Mahishi is the chief queen, the one who has been consecrated. Parivritti or *parivrikti*
is a queen who was earlier favoured, but is now neglected. Vavata is a favourite wife. *Palagali* is
mentioned as the most inferior wife, a king being entitled to four wives. Sometimes, mahishi
is said to be the kshatriya wife, vavata is said to be the vaishya wife and parivritti is said to be
the shudra wife. In this case, the former meaning is appropriate.

[158] The holy fig tree.

[159] *Kalpa Sutra*s are sacred texts that describe rituals, *Brahmana*s are sacred texts, not
to be confused with the varna of brahmana.

[160] These are days on which soma sacrifices are offered, chatushtoma also being known
as *agnishtoma*.

[161] Sacrificial fee. These were donated symbolically.

bull among men and extender of sacrifices, donated the earth to
the officiating priests. With the king cleansed of all his sins, all the
officiating priests told him, 'You alone are capable of protecting
the entire earth. We have nothing to do with the earth. We are
incapable of ruling it. O lord of the earth! We are always engaged
in studying. Instead, give us something that has an equivalent
value.' The king gave them one million cows, ten crore gold coins
and forty crore silver coins. Collectively, all the officiating priests
gave those riches to the sage Rishyashringa and the intelligent
Vasishtha. Each of those supreme among brahmanas received
his proper share. All of them were supremely delighted and said
that they were satisfied. Having performed that supreme sacrifice,
which destroyed sins and conveyed one to heaven, the king was
delighted. It was a sacrifice that was extremely difficult for kings
to perform. King Dasharatha then told Rishyashringa, 'O one
who is excellent in his vows! You should act so that my lineage
is extended.' The supreme among brahmanas told the king that it
would indeed be that way. 'O king! You will have four sons who
will extend your lineage.'

# Chapter 1(14)

The intelligent one[162] reflected for some time on what he should
say. Having regained his senses, the one who knew about the
Vedas told the king, 'So that you can have sons and daughters, I will
perform a sacrifice.[163] I will observe the ordinances and *mantras*
decreed by *Atharvashirasa*[164] and they will be successful.' He then
performed the sacrifice that generates sons and daughters. Chanting
mantras and following the indicated rites, the energetic one offered

---

[162] Rishyashringa.

[163] The horse sacrifice has only removed the sins. A specific ceremony now has to be
performed, to obtain offspring.

[164] While this clearly refers to the Atharva Veda, many *Atharvashirasa* texts are of
much later vintage.

oblations into the fire. As is appropriate, the gods, the gandharvas, the siddhas[165] and the supreme rishis assembled there to receive their shares.

In the proper way, the gods who had gathered in that assembly spoke these great words to Brahma, the creator of the worlds. 'O illustrious one! Through your favours, the rakshasa named Ravana is using his valour to obstruct us in every possible way. We are incapable of subjugating him. O illustrious one! In ancient times, because of your affection, you granted him a boon. Since then, we have had to respect him in every way and have had to tolerate him. The evil-minded one shows his enmity against all those who rise up and oppresses the three worlds. As he wills, he torments Shakra, the king of the gods. He is invincible and confused because of the boon he has received. He acts against the rishis, the *yakshas*,[166] the gandharvas, the asuras and the brahmanas. The sun god cannot torment him. The wind god cannot blow against his flanks. On seeing him, the god of the ocean, with his turbulent waves, cannot make him tremble. There is great fear from that rakshasa, who is terrible to look at. O illustrious one! You should think of a means to bring about this death.' He[167] was thus addressed by all the gods. He thought for a while and said, 'The means of countering that evil-souled one and slaying him has been decided. He had asked that gandharvas, yakshas, gods, *danavas*[168] and rakshasas should be incapable of slaying him and I had agreed to his desire. Because of his disrespect towards them, the rakshasa had not mentioned humans. Therefore, a man will bring about his death. His death cannot occur in any other way.' On hearing the agreeable words Brahma spoke, all the gods and maharshis were delighted. At that time, the immensely radiant Vishnu arrived there. He approached Brahma, who was still meditating. All the gods bowed down before him and said, 'O Vishnu! For the sake of the welfare of the worlds, we wish

---

[165] Term used for successful sages who have become semi-divine.

[166] Yakshas are semi-divine species, described as companions of Kubera, the lord of riches.

[167] Brahma.

[168] Demons.

to invoke you. The lord King Dasharatha is the king of Ayodhya. He knows about dharma and is talked about. His energy is like that of a maharshi. His three wives are virtuous, prosperous and famous.[169] O Vishnu! Divide yourself into four parts and become their sons. You will be born as men. The gods find him to be invincible. He is a like a growing thorn that the worlds face. Defeat Ravana in a battle. The rakshasa Ravana is stupid. However, because his valour has been ignited, he obstructs gods, the gandharvas, the siddhas and the supreme rishis. The terrible Ravana is fierce in his energy. His enmity and intolerance towards the lord of the gods has increased. He is like a thorn to the virtuous ascetics and makes them scream.[170] Save the ascetics from that great fear.'

## Chapter 1(15)

Narayana Vishnu was thus engaged by the supreme gods, though he knew all this. He spoke these gentle words to the gods. 'O gods! What is the means to bring about the death of the lord of the rakshasas? How will I slay the one who is a like a thorn to the rishis?' Thus addressed, all the gods replied to the undecaying Vishnu. 'Assume a human form and slay Ravana in a battle. O destroyer of enemies! Over a long period of time, he has tormented himself through fierce austerities. Brahma, the creator of the worlds and worshipped by the worlds, was satisfied at this. Content, the lord granted a boon to that rakshasa. With the exception of humans, he will not face fear from any other creature. Because of disrespect, in those ancient times, he ignored humans at the time of the boon. O scorcher of enemies! Therefore, it is evident that his death can only come about through men.' The compassionate Vishnu heard the words spoken by the gods. The idea of choosing King Dasharatha as his father appealed to him. The king was without a son and at that

---

[169] It is possible to identify Kousalya with virtue, Sumitra with prosperity and fame with Kaikeyee.

[170] There is a pun. The word *rava* means to scream or shriek.

time, the immensely radiant destroyer of enemies was performing a
sacrifice with a desire to obtain sons.

A great being manifested himself from the sacrificial fire. He
was immensely valorous and immensely strong, infinitely radiant.
He was dark and attired in red garments. His face was red and
his voice was like the rumbling of a drum. His eyes were tawny.
However, his body, with an excellent beard and hair, was pleasant.
He possessed all the auspicious signs and he was adorned with
celestial ornaments. He was as tall as the peak of a mountain and
his valour was like that of a proud tiger. His form was like that
of the sun, blazing like the flames of a fire. He held a vessel made
of molten gold, covered with a lid made out of silver. It looked as
agreeable as a beloved wife and was full of celestial *payasam*.[171]
He held it himself in his extended hands and it seemed to be like
some maya. On seeing King Dasharatha, he spoke these words. 'O
king! Know me to be a being who has been sent here by Prajapati.'
The king joined his hands in salutation and addressed the supreme
one. 'O illustrious one! Welcome. What can I do for you?' The
being sent by Prajapati again spoke these words. 'O king! You have
worshipped the gods and have now obtained this. O tiger among
men! This payasam has been made by the gods and gives rise to
progeny. It is blessed and increases good health. Accept it. Give it to
your deserving wives and make them eat it. O king! Through them,
you will obtain the sons you performed the sacrifice for.' The king
was delighted. He bowed his head down and accepted the golden
vessel given by the gods, filled with food that the gods ate. He
worshipped that extraordinary being, so agreeable to behold. He
was filled with great delight and circumambulated him. Dasharatha
obtained the payasam, prepared by the gods. He was overcome by
great delight, like a poor person who has obtained riches. Having
accomplished his task, the supremely radiant being, extraordinary
in form, instantly vanished.

The inner quarters seemed to be bathed in rays of delight,
like the pleasant autumn sky when it is enveloped by the moon's

---

[171] A dish made out sweetened milk and rice.

beams. He entered the inner quarters and told Kousalya, 'For the sake of obtaining a son, accept this payasam. The king gave half of the payasam to Kousalya. The king gave half of what remained to Sumitra. For the sake of obtaining a son, he gave half of what remained to Kaikeyee. Having thought about it, the lord of the earth again gave what remained of the payasam, which was like amrita,[172] to Sumitra.[173] In this way, the king gave separate shares of the payasam to his wives. The supreme wives of the king obtained the payasam and all of them thought this was a great honour. Their hearts were full of joy.

## Chapter 1(16)

After Vishnu had become the son of the great-souled king, the illustrious Svayambhu[174] spoke these words to all the gods. 'The valiant Vishnu is devoted to the truth and all of you are his well-wishers. Assume forms that you desire and create powerful aides for him. Let these be accomplished in maya and bravery, with a speed that is like that of the wind. Let them know about policy and possess intelligence. Let them be like Vishnu in valour. Let them be indestructible and let them know about all the means. Let their bodies be divine. Let them know about all weapons, like those who subsist on amrita. Let them be born from the bodies of the best among apsaras and gandharva women.[175] Let them be born through yaksha, pannaga, riksha and vidyadhara maidens.[176] Let them be born from the limbs and bodies of kinnara and vanara

---

[172] Nectar or ambrosia.

[173] Thus, Kousalya obtained ½, Kaikeyee obtained ⅛, Sumitra obtained ¼ + ⅛ = ⅜.

[174] The one who created himself, Brahma.

[175] Apsaras are celestial dancers, while gandharvas are celestial musicians. Both are semi-divine.

[176] Pannagas or nagas are semi-divine. We have translated them as serpents. Nagas are not snakes (sarpas). Unlike sarpas, nagas have special powers and can assume any form at will. They also have specific habitats, such as in the nether regions. Rikshas are bears. Vidyadharas are semi-divine, occupying the region between heaven and earth.

ladies.[177] Create sons who are your equals in valour. Create them
in the form of apes.' Thus addressed by the illustrious one, they
agreed to adhere to his instructions. They gave birth to sons who
were like apes in form. The great-souled rishis, the siddhas, the
vidyadharas, the serpents and *charanas*[178] created brave sons who
roamed around in the forest. They created many thousand, who
would rise up to slay Dashagriva.[179] They were brave and valiant,
immeasurable in strength. They could assume any form at will.
Those immensely strong ones possessed bodies that were like
elephants and mountains. They swiftly took birth as rikshas, vanaras
and *gopuchchhas*.[180] Each god had a different kind of form, attire
and valour and the sons who were separately born mirrored these
from the father. Some born from golangula women were superior
in valour. There were others born to riksha, vanara and kinnara
women. All of them fought with rocks. All of them used trees as
weapons. All of them fought with nails and teeth. All of them were
knowledgeable about all kinds of weapons. They were capable of
dislodging the greatest of mountains. They could shatter and uproot
large trees. With their speed, they were capable of agitating the
ocean, the lord of the rivers. They were capable of shattering the
ground with their feats. They could leap over the great ocean. They
were capable of seizing the clouds in the sky. They could capture
crazy elephants when these roamed around in the forest. With the
sound of their roars, they could make birds fall down. Such were
the apes that were born and they could assume any form at will.
The number of such great-souled ones was in millions. Brave ones
were born as leaders of troops of apes. There were thousands who
departed, to dwell on the slopes of Mount Rikshavat. There were
many others who resided in other mountains and groves. Sugriva

[177] Kinnara, also known as *kimpurusha*, is a semi-divine species, described as Kubera's
companions. Vanaras are apes, at least we have translated it in that way. There is no
consensus on the identification of vanaras. Etymologically, the word means those who
roam around in the forests.

[178] Celestial bards.

[179] Ravana.

[180] With a tail like that of a cow, langur. Also known as *golangula*.

was the son of Surya and Vali was the son of Shakra. All the lords among apes served these two brothers. Their bodies were like large masses of clouds. The leaders among the herds of vanaras were immensely strong. They arrived on earth, assuming terrible forms. They assembled so as to help Rama.

## Chapter 1(17)

When the great-souled one's horse sacrifice was over, the gods accepted their respective shares and returned to wherever they had come from. With the consecration and rituals over, the king entered the city with his servants, soldiers and mounts, and accompanied by his wives. The king honoured the other kings, in accordance with what they deserved. Bowing down before that bull among sages,[181] they joyfully returned to their own countries. When the kings had departed, placing the supreme brahmanas at the forefront, the prosperous King Dasharatha again entered his own city. Honoured well, Rishyashringa left, with Shanta. Having taken his leave, the intelligent king[182] also left with his followers.

Born as a portion of Vishnu, Kousalya gave birth to the immensely fortunate Rama, the extender of the Ikshvaku lineage and one who possessed all the divine signs.[183] With the infinitely energetic son, Kousalya was radiant. She was like Aditi, after having given birth to the supreme god, the one with the *vajra* in his hands.[184] Kaikeyee gave birth to Bharata, for whom truth was his valour. He was like a fourth portion of Vishnu himself and possessed all the qualities. Sumitra gave birth to the sons Lakshmana and Shatrughna. All of them were brave and skilled in all the weapons.

[181] Vasishtha.

[182] Romapada.

[183] The Critical text excises the shloka which gives the positions of the nakshatras at the time of Rama's birth.

[184] Aditi, Kashyapa's wife, is the mother of the gods, who are known as the Adityas. Indra is the wielder of the vajra.

They were born as Vishnu's portions. The king's four great-souled
sons were born separately. They possessed all the qualities and were
as resplendent as Proshthapada.[185] When eleven days were over, the
ceremony for giving names was undertaken. The eldest was the
great-souled Rama. Kaikeyee's son was Bharata. Sumitra's sons
were Lakshmana and Shatrughna. Extremely delighted, Vasishtha
gave them their names. He also performed the rites connected with
birth and all the other sacraments. The eldest one, Rama, was like
a standard and brought great pleasure to his father. He appeared to
all creatures as if he was the revered Svayambhu. All of them knew
about the Vedas. All of them were brave and devoted to the welfare
of creatures. All of them were learned and all of them possessed
all the qualities. Among them, Rama, with truth as his valour, was
immensely energetic. Since childhood, Lakshmana, the extender of
prosperity, was extremely pleasant.[186] He was always devoted to
his eldest brother, Rama, one who brought delight to the worlds.
With body and soul, he always did what brought Rama pleasure.
Lakshmana possessed prosperity. Though his body was different,
his breath of life was like Rama's. Without him, Purushottama[187]
was unable to go to sleep. Without him, he[188] would not eat any
delicious food that was brought to him. When Raghava[189] rode a
horse and went out on a hunt, he[190] wielded a bow and protected
him from the rear. Shatrughna, Lakshmana's younger brother, was
thus attached to Bharata. He was always dearer than his[191] own
life and remained devoted to him. Dasharatha loved these four

---

[185] Proshthapada is a nakshatra. More accurately, it is a collective name for two
nakshatras, Purva Bhadrapada and Uttara Bhadrapada. These are stars in the constellation
Pegasus, which partly consists of a quadrilateral, with four stars at four vertices. The four
stars are probably being compared with the four sons.

[186] Lakshmana's name is derived in that way, someone who has Lakshmi in him, or
makes Lakshmi prosper. Rama means someone who causes delight. Bharata is someone
who bears a burden and Shatrughna is someone who destroys the enemy.

[187] Rama.

[188] Rama.

[189] Rama.

[190] Lakshmana.

[191] Bharata's.

extremely fortunate sons. He was extremely delighted with them, like the grandfather[192] with the gods. All of them possessed learning. All of them possessed all the qualities. They possessed humility and were renowned. They knew everything and were far-sighted.

With his priests and relatives, the great-souled King Dasharatha started to think about their marriages. In an assembly of his ministers, the great-souled one reflected on this. At that time, the immensely energetic and great sage, Vishvamitra, arrived there. He told the gatekeeper that he wished to meet the king. 'Quickly tell him that Koushika, Gadhi's son, has arrived.' Hearing this and frightened in their minds,[193] they were urged by these words and rushed towards the king's residence. They went to the king's abode and told the king who was descended from the Ikshvaku lineage that rishi Vishvamitra had arrived. Hearing these words, he was delighted. He controlled himself and, with his priests, headed for the place, like Vasava[194] towards Brahma. The ascetic, firm in his vows, was radiant. On seeing him, with a cheerful face, the king offered him arghya. Following the rituals instructed in the sacred texts, he accepted arghya from the king and asked about the king's welfare. When Vasishtha arrived, the immensely fortunate one asked about the welfare of that bull among sages and also that of the other rishis. Worshipped and cheerful in their minds, all of them entered the king's residence. Each sat down on the seat he deserved. The extremely generous king was delighted in his mind. He cheerfully worshipped the great sage, Vishvamitra, and said, 'Your arrival here is like the receipt of amrita, like rain in a place that is without water, like a barren wife giving birth and like getting back riches that have been destroyed. O great sage! I think that your arrival here signifies joy like that. Welcome. I am delighted. What can I do for you? What is your great desire? O brahmana! O one who follows dharma! You are a worthy recipient and it is good fortune that you have come here. Today, my birth has been rendered successful and it is as if I have indeed lived a successful

---

[192] Brahma.
[193] Vishvamitra was known for his rage.
[194] Indra.

life. You were earlier known as a rajarshi and blazed in radiance because of your austerities. You then became a brahmana rishi.[195] You should be worshipped by me in several ways. O brahmana! Your arrival here is supremely sacred and wonderful. O lord! Merely by looking at you, it is as if I have visited an auspicious spot. Please tell me what you desire and the reasons for your coming here. If I can ensure the fruition of your desires, I will be greatly blessed. O Koushika! You are like a god to me. Unless I do not deserve to be told, you should tell me about the task that needs to be performed and I will accomplish it completely.' The supreme rishi heard these words, which were pleasant to hear about and brought happiness to the heart. They were uttered with humility by someone who possessed all the qualities and was famous for his qualities. He was greatly delighted.

## Chapter 1(18)

On hearing the wonderful words of that lion among kings, expounded in detail, the immensely energetic Vishvamitra's body hair stood up and he said, 'O tiger among kings! It is befitting that you, and no one else on earth, should speak these words. You have been born in a great lineage and have been instructed by Vasishtha. I will tell you what is in my heart and you can decide on your course of action accordingly. O tiger among kings! You are true to your pledges. Act in accordance with that. O bull among men! To become successful, I am now engaged in some rituals. Two rakshasas are causing obstacles along that path and they can assume any form at will. I am nearing the completion of my vows. However, those two rakshasas, Maricha and Subahu, are valiant and well trained. They shower down torrents of flesh and blood on the sacrificial altar. With the advent of this obstruction, the completion of the rituals is uncertain. Though I had exerted myself, I have lost

---

[195] Born as a kshatriya, because of his austerities, Vishvamitra became a brahmana.

all interest and have left that place. O king! My intelligence should
not be excited and fall prey to anger. When one is practising rituals
of that kind, one should not come under the influence of rage. O
tiger among kings! Rama is your own son and truth is his valour.
He is brave and the eldest. The sidelocks of his hair are like a crow's
wings.[196] Give him to me. He will be protected by me and is also
celestial in his own energy. He is capable of countering the rakshasas
and destroying them. There is no doubt that I will also confer many
kinds of objects on him and they will be beneficial. Through those,
he will obtain fame in the three worlds. Those two are incapable of
standing before Rama in any way. No man other than Raghava[197]
is capable of killing them. Intoxicated by their valour, those two
wicked ones have been bound by the noose of destiny. O tiger among
kings! They are incapable of withstanding the great-souled Rama. O
king! Just because he is your son, you should not display excessive
affection. I am assuring you. Know that those two rakshasas are as
good as slain. I know the great-souled Rama. Truth is his valour. The
immensely energetic Vasishtha knows this and so do all the ascetics
who are stationed here. O Indra among kings! If you desire to obtain
dharma and constant and supreme fame on earth, you should give
Rama to me. O Kakutstha![198] If your ministers grant you permission
and so do the others, with Vasishtha at the forefront, grant him
to me and let go of Rama. Without any attachment towards him,
you should grant me your desired son, the lotus-eyed Rama. The
sacrifice will only last for ten nights. O Raghava! Act so that the
designated time for my sacrifice is not in vain. You should not have
any unnecessary sorrow in your mind. Act so that there is good
fortune.' The one with dharma in his soul spoke these words, which
were full of dharma. Then the great sage, the immensely energetic
Vishvamitra, stopped speaking. The lord of men heard these words
and they shattered his heart and mind. He was distressed in his mind
and, suffering from great fear, was dislodged from his throne.

---

[196] A mark of beauty, *kaka* (crow) *paksha* (wing).

[197] Rama.

[198] Kakutstha was an ancestor. Hence, both Dasharatha and Rama are addressed as
his descendants.

# Chapter 1(19)

Hearing the words spoken by Vishvamitra, for some time, the tiger among kings lost his senses. Having regained his senses, he said, 'My lotus-eyed Rama is still less than sixteen years of age.[199] I do not see him as being capable of fighting against the rakshasas. Here is an entire *akshouhini* and I am its lord and commander.[200] Surrounded by them, I will go there and fight against those who roam around in the night.[201] These servants are brave and valiant and accomplished in the use of weapons. They are capable of fighting against large numbers of rakshasas. You should not take Rama. In the forefront of the battle, I will protect you with a bow in my hand. As long as I have life, I will fight against those who roam around in the night. Thus protected well, you will face no obstructions in the completion of your vows. I will go there. You should not take Rama. He is a child. He has not completed his education. He does not know about strengths and weaknesses.[202] He does not possess the strength of weapons. Nor is he accomplished in fighting. There is no doubt that the rakshasas will resort to deceitful methods of fighting and he cannot counter that. O brahmana! O tiger among sages! Separated from Rama, I am not interested in remaining alive, not even for an instant. You should not take Rama. O brahmana! O one who is excellent in his vows! However, if you do wish to take Raghava, take me with him, with the four kinds of forces.[203] O Koushika! Sixty thousand years have passed since my birth. He has been born after a lot of misery. You should not take Rama. I am extremely affectionate towards my four sons. According to dharma, the eldest is the most important. You should not take Rama. What valour do those rakshasas possess? Whose sons are they? O bull

---

[199] For several purposes, sixteen is a threshold and all that is known is that Rama was younger than that.

[200] An akshouhini is an army, consisting of 21,870 chariots, 21,870 elephants, 65,610 horse riders and 1,09,350 foot soldiers.

[201] That is, rakshasas.

[202] Of the enemy.

[203] Chariots, elephants, cavalry and infantry.

among sages! What is their size and who protects them? How
will Rama be able to act against those rakshasas? O brahmana!
They will fight in deceitful ways and I alone possess the strength to
counter them. O illustrious one! Instruct me everything, about how
I can fight against them in the battle. Those rakshasas are full of
valour and base themselves on evil sentiments.'

Hearing his words, Vishvamitra replied, 'There is a rakshasa
named Ravana, born in Poulastya's lineage. Thanks to a boon
obtained from Brahma, he oppresses and obstructs the three
worlds. He is immensely strong and immensely valorous. He is
surrounded by a large number of rakshasas. It has been heard that
the immensely valorous Ravana, lord of the rakshasas, is the brother
of Vaishravana[204] himself and the son of the sage Vishravasa. The
immensely strong one does not cause obstructions to sacrifices
himself. He urges two immensely strong rakshasas named Maricha
and Subahu and they cause obstructions to sacrifices.'

The king was thus addressed by the sage and told the sage, 'In an
encounter, I am myself incapable of standing before that evil-souled
one. O one who knows about dharma! You should show your
favours towards me and towards my young son.[205] We are limited
in fortune. You are our god and our preceptor. The gods, danavas,
gandharvas, yakshas and pannagas are incapable of standing before
Ravana in an encounter. What can humans do? In an encounter,
that brave rakshasa sucks away the valour of his adversaries. O best
among sages! I am incapable of fighting against him and his army,
even with my soldiers and even if I am with my sons. My son is
said to be an equal of the immortals. But he does not know about
fighting. O brahmana! My son is but a child. Grant him to me. In
addition, those two are the descendants of Sunda and Upasunda[206]
and are like Death in a battle. They may obstruct sacrifices, but I
will not give you my son. Maricha and Subahu are full of valour and

[204] Kubera.

[205] And not ask either of us to fight against Ravana.

[206] Famous demons. Deceived by Vishnu, they ended up fighting against each other
and killing each other.

are extremely well trained. In an extremely terrible battle, I will fight against one or the other of those two.'

# Chapter 1(20)

K oushika heard what he had said, his words were full of affection. Filled with anger, he answered the king in these words. 'You have been born in Raghava's lineage and will bring destruction to the line. Having pledged earlier, you now wish to deviate from your promise. O king! Pardon me. I will go to wherever I came from. O Kakutstha! Having taken a false pledge, may you be happy with your relatives.' The intelligent Vishvamitra was thus filled with rage and the entire earth trembled. The gods were terrified. The great and patient rishi, Vasishtha, excellent in his vows, discerned that the form of the entire universe was scared. He addressed the king in these words. 'You have been born in the Ikshvaku lineage and are like another Dharma[207] yourself. You possess fortitude and are excellent in your vows, and prosperous. You should not abandon dharma. Raghava[208] is famous in the three worlds as one who has dharma in his soul. Follow your own dharma and do not resort to adharma. O Raghava! If a person has taken a pledge and then transgresses it, he destroys the fruits of all the sacrifices he has performed earlier. Therefore, let Rama go. Whether he is accomplished in the use of weapons or unaccomplished in the use of weapons, the rakshasas cannot harm him. He will be protected by Kushika's son, like amrita by the fire.[209] He[210] is supreme among valiant ones and is the personified form of Dharma. In intelligence and strength of austerities, there is no one in this world who is superior to him. He is the only one in the three worlds of mobile and immobile objects who knows about all the weapons. There is no

[207] The god of dharma.
[208] An oblique way of referring to Dasharatha himself.
[209] Amrita is protected by a circle of fire that surrounds it.
[210] Vishvamitra.

other man who knows about these, or for that matter, gods, rishis,
asuras, rakshasas, gandharvas, the best among yakshas, kinnaras
and the giant serpents. Krishashva's sons were supremely devoted
to dharma and while he ruled his kingdom, in ancient times, he gave
all these weapons to Koushika.[211] Krishashva's sons were the sons
of Prajapati's[212] daughters. They[213] were not similar in form. They
were immensely valorous, resplendent and brought victory. The
slender-waisted Jaya and Suprabha were Daksha's daughters. They
generated hundreds of thousands of supremely radiant weapons. In
ancient times, Jaya gave birth to five hundred supreme sons. They
were capable of adopting many different forms and were designed
to slay the soldiers of the asuras.[214] Then again, Suprabha gave
birth to another five hundred sons. They were strong, impossible
to withstand and invincible, designed to destroy.[215] Kushika's
son knows about these weapons. He knows about dharma and is
capable of also creating many other weapons that have not been
known earlier. Vishvamitra is immensely energetic and a great
ascetic. Such is his valour. O king! You should not harbour any
doubts about Rama going.'

# Chapter 1(21)

When he was thus addressed by Vasishtha, with a cheerful face,
King Dasharatha summoned his sons, Rama and Lakshmana.
Their mothers, their father, Dasharatha, and Vasishtha and the
other priests pronounced benedictions and chanted auspicious
mantras. Extremely delighted in his mind, King Dasharatha

---

[211] That is, Krishashva gave these weapons. Krishashva is described as a famous king.
He is also described as one of the original Prajapatis (guardians or rulers of the world) who
married Daksha's daughters.

[212] Daksha's.

[213] The sons.

[214] The sons were weapons.

[215] These sons were also weapons.

inhaled the fragrances of the heads of his beloved sons and handed
them over to Kushika's son. A fragrant breeze, pleasant to the
touch, began to blow, when it was seen that the lotus-eyed Rama
approached Vishvamitra. The drums of the gods were sounded and
a great shower of flowers rained down. Those great-souled ones
departed to the sounds of conch shells and drums. Vishvamitra was
at the front and the immensely illustrious Rama, with sidelocks
like a crow's wing and wielding a bow, followed him. He was
followed by Sumitra's son. With quivers and bows in their hands,
they illuminated the ten directions. They were with the great-souled
Vishvamitra, thus resembling a three-headed serpent. It was as if the
two Ashvins followed the grandfather,[216] protecting him.

After having travelled for half a yojana, they reached the
southern banks of the Sarayu and Vishvamitra addressed Rama in
these sweet words. 'O son! Accept some water and do not allow any
more time to pass. With the respective set of mantras, accept Bala
and Atibala.[217] As a result of these, there will be no exhaustion, no
fever and no destruction of form. Even if you are asleep or distracted,
the *nairritas*[218] will not be able to assail you. There will be no one
on earth who will be your equal in valour or in the strength of
your arms. O Rama! There will be no one in the three worlds who
will be your equal. O unblemished one! In this world, there will
be no one who will be your equal in fortune, generosity, wisdom,
intelligence, determination and ability to respond. The mothers of
Bala and Atibala are the sources of all learning and having obtained
these two kinds of knowledge, there will be no one who will be
your equal. O Rama! O best among men! You will not suffer from
hunger and thirst. O Raghava! Along the way, study Bala and
Atibala. Having studied these two kinds of knowledge, one obtains
unsurpassed fame on earth. These two kinds of knowledge are full

[216] Brahma.
[217] Water has to be touched and ablutions performed before any auspicious act. Bala
and Atibala are the divine weapons. Divine weapons are invoked through the use of
mantras.
[218] Demons.

of energy and were generated from the grandfather's daughters.[219]
O Kakutstha! Because you are full of dharma, you are worthy of
receiving these. There is no doubt that you will also reap all the
objects of desire that have many qualities, the treasure that is only
the outcome of many kinds of austerities.' At this, with a cheerful
face, Rama touched water and purified himself. He then accepted
the knowledge from the maharshi with the cleansed soul. Suffused
with that knowledge, Rama became radiant in his great valour.
Kushika's son, who was like a preceptor, was ready to engage them
in various tasks. In great happiness, the three of them spent the
night on the banks of the Sarayu.

## Chapter 1(22)

When night was over, Vishvamitra addressed Kakutstha,
who was lying down on a bed of leaves. 'O excellent son
of Kousalya! O Rama! It is dawn. O tiger among men! Arise and
perform rites for the gods.' The two princes heard the words
of the extremely generous rishi. They bathed and performed
ablutions in the water. Those two brave ones chanted supreme
mantras. Having performed their ablutions, those two extremely
valorous ones cheerfully bowed down before Vishvamitra, store
of austerities, and made arrangements for departure. Those two
extremely valorous ones departed and saw the sacred confluence
of the Sarayu with the divine river that has three flows.[220] The
sacred hermitages of fierce and energetic rishis were there, those
who had tormented themselves through supreme austerities for
many thousand years. On seeing that sacred hermitage,[221] the two
descendants of Raghava were greatly delighted. They spoke these
words to the great-souled Vishvamitra. 'Whose sacred hermitage
is this and which man resides here? O illustrious one! We are

[219] In an extended sense, since Daksha was born from Brahma.
[220] The Ganga has three flows, in heaven, on earth and in the nether regions.
[221] In the singular.

overcome by great curiosity and wish to know this.' On hearing
their words, the bull among sages laughed. He said, 'O Rama!
I will tell you whom this hermitage belonged to earlier. Listen.
Kandarpa[222] used to have a body earlier. The learned ones also
speak of him as Kama. Sthanu[223] was controlled in his rituals and
performed austerities here. Having married, the lord of the gods
left, accompanied by large numbers of Maruts. At that time, the
great-souled one was afflicted by the one with evil intelligence[224]
and uttered the sound of *humkara*.[225] O descendant of the Raghu
lineage! All the limbs and body of that evil-minded one were
burnt down and destroyed by Rudra's eyes. The great-souled one
scorched him and destroyed his body. Because of the great god's
rage, Kama was rendered without a body. O Raghava! That is
the reason he came to be known as Ananga.[226] The place where
he released his handsome body came to be known as the land
of Anga. His ancient hermitage came to be frequented by sages
who were his disciples.[227] Since they were supremely devoted to
dharma, there is no evil in this place. O Rama! O one who is
auspicious to behold! We will spend the night here. Tomorrow,
we will again proceed along this sacred river.' While they were
conversing, the sages, who were far-sighted because of their
austerities, realized that they were there. They were greatly
delighted and arrived happily. They offered arghya and padya to
the guest who was Kushika's son. After this, they also tended to
Rama and Lakshmana as guests. Having been honoured well, they
cheerfully resided in Kamashrama[228] and delighted themselves in
all kinds of conversation.

[222] The god of love, also known as Kama, Ananga or Madana. He was burnt down by
Shiva's rage and ceased to have a body.

[223] Shiva.

[224] Kandarpa.

[225] Humkara means to utter the sound 'hum', a sound believed to possess special
powers.

[226] The one without a body (*anga*).

[227] Shiva's hermitage, the sages were Shiva's followers.

[228] The hermitage (ashrama) associated with Kama.

## Chapter 1(23)

When the morning sparkled, the two scorchers of enemies performed their ablutions. Placing Vishvamitra at the forefront, they arrived at the banks of the river. All those great-souled sages, rigid in their vows, also went there. They prepared an excellent boat and spoke to Vishvamitra. 'Placing the princes in the front, ascend this boat without any delay, so that you can proceed along your path without any hindrances.' Honouring those rishis, Vishvamitra agreed. Taking those two with him, he went to the river that was heading towards the ocean. When they were in the middle of the river, Rama asked the bull among sages, 'What is this tumultuous sound that seems to be shattering the waters?' Raghava's words were full of curiosity. On hearing them, the one with dharma in his soul told him about the reason for the sound. 'O Rama! O tiger among men! In Mount Kailasa, Brahma created a lake through the powers of his mind and that is the reason the lake is known as Manasa.[229] The sacred Sarayu originates from that lake, from the lake created by Brahma. Emerging from that lake, it flows past Ayodhya. That tumultuous sound results when it unites with Jahnavee,[230] from the friction caused by the two flows of water. O Rama! Control yourself and bow down.' Those two were extremely devoted to dharma and bowed down. At that time, they approached the southern bank and dexterous in their valour, alighted.

Those two supreme sons of the king saw a forest that was terrible in form. Having alighted, the descendant of the Ikshvaku lineage asked the bull among sages about this. 'This forest is impenetrable and resounds with the sound of crickets. It is populated by ferocious predatory creatures and the noise of horrible birds can be heard. There are many kinds of predatory birds that shriek in fierce tones. It is populated by lions, tigers, wild boars and elephants. It is full of *dhava, ashva, karna, kakubha,* bilva, *tinduka, patala* and *badari*

---

[229] From *mana* (mind).
[230] Ganga.

trees.[231] What a terrible forest this is!' The immensely energetic and
great sage, Vishvamitra, replied, 'O son! O Kakutstha! Listen to the
reason why this forest is so terrible. O supreme among men! Earlier,
this habitation used to be extremely prosperous. Two countries
created by the gods, named Malada and Karusha, used to be here.[232]
In ancient times, the one with the one thousand eyes killed Vritra
and the sin of having killed a brahmana penetrated him.[233] The
gods and the rishis, stores of austerities, therefore bathed Indra.
When they bathed him with pots of water, the filth was released.
The filth was released on the ground, the muck was released on the
ground.[234] When these were released from his body, the great Indra
was delighted. Cleansed of the filth and muck, Indra became pure.
Greatly delighted, the lord granted those two countries a supreme
boon. "Malada and Karusha have borne the filth that was released
from my body. Therefore, these two countries will be prosperous and
will be famous in the world." When the chastiser of Paka[235] spoke in
this way, the gods praised him, on seeing that the intelligent Shakra
had honoured the countries in this way. O destroyer of enemies! For
a long time, those two countries, Malada and Karusha, were happy
and prosperous places, full of wealth and grain. After some time,
a female yaksha was born and she could assume any form at will.
She possessed the strength of one thousand elephants. O fortunate
one! Her name is Tataka and she is the intelligent Sunda's wife.
Her son is the rakshasa Maricha, who is like Shakra in his valour.
O Raghava! The evil-acting Tataka has incessantly destroyed these
two countries, Malada and Karusha. She obstructs the path here
and dwells half a yojana away. Using the strength of your arms,
slay that evil-acting one. On my instructions, remove this region
of its thorn. O Rama! Uproot this terrible female yaksha who is

[231] Dhava is the axle-wood tree, ashva can't be identified, karna is the Indian laburnum,
kakubha is the Arjuna tree, bilva is wood apple, tinduka is ebony, patala is *Bignonia
suaveolens* and badari is the jujube tree.

[232] Malada and Karusha are in the Baghelkhand-Mirzapur-Shahabad region.

[233] The one with the one thousand eyes is Indra. Vritra was the son of a brahmana.

[234] *Mala* means filth or dirt, hence Malada. Karusha is not that easy to derive, though
*karisha* means dung.

[235] Indra, Indra having killed a demon named Paka.

so difficult to withstand, so that she is incapable of destroying this region in this way. I have told you everything about how this forest came to be terrible. The female yaksha does not refrain and still continues to destroy everything.'

## Chapter 1(24)

Hearing the words of the immeasurable sage, the tiger among men replied in auspicious words. 'O bull among sages! It has been heard that the yakshas are limited in valour. How can this weak one[236] bear the strength of a thousand elephants?' Vishvamitra spoke these words. 'Hear how she came to bear great strength. This weak one bears valour and strength because of a boon that was bestowed on her. Earlier, there was a great and valiant yaksha named Suketu. He was without offspring. Therefore, he followed auspicious conduct and tormented himself through great austerities. O Rama! Thus, the grandfather[237] was extremely pleased with that lord among yakshas and bestowed a gem of a daughter on him. Her name was Tataka. The grandfather also bestowed the strength of one thousand elephants on her. The immensely illustrious Brahma did not give that yaksha a son.[238] Having been born, she grew up and possessed beauty and youth. He[239] bestowed the illustrious one on Sunda, Jambha's son, as a wife. After some time, the female yaksha gave birth to a son. He was invincible and his name was Maricha. However, because of a curse, he became a rakshasa. O Rama! When Sunda was slain by Agastya, the supreme rishi, Tataka and her son wished to take revenge. He[240] cursed Maricha that he

---

[236] The word used is *abala*, meaning weak one, or woman. Yakshas are limited in valour and a female yaksha must be even more so.

[237] Brahma.

[238] Anticipating that a strong daughter would be less dangerous than a strong son.

[239] Suketu.

[240] Agastya.

would become a rakshasa.[241] In great rage, Agastya also cursed Tataka. "You will give up this form and assume a terrible form. O great yaksha! You will become a maneater. You will become deformed, with a distorted visage." Thus cursed, Tataka became intolerant and senseless with anger. Agastya roamed around in this sacred region and she started to destroy it. O Raghava! This female yaksha is extremely terrible and wicked in conduct. She is evil in her valour. For the welfare of cattle and brahmanas, slay her. O descendant of the Raghu lineage! She is so enveloped in the curse that in the three worlds, no man except you is capable of standing up to her. O supreme among men! You should not be revolted at the prospect of killing a woman. O son of a king! This is what must be done for the welfare of the four varnas. This is eternal dharma for someone who has been entrusted with the burden of a kingdom. O Kakutstha! Slay the source of adharma. There is no dharma in her. O king! We have heard that, in ancient times, Shakra destroyed Manthara, Virochana's daughter, when she desired to devastate the earth. O Rama! Bhrigu's wife and Kavya's[242] mother was firm in her vows. However, when she desired to remove Indra from the worlds, Vishnu crushed her. O prince! The great-souled ones have performed many such tasks. Those supreme beings have slain women who were devoted to adharma.'

# Chapter 1(25)

On hearing the sage's words, the son of the supreme among men, lost all despondency. Raghava, firm in his vows, joined his hands in salutation and replied, 'On my father's instructions, to honour my father's words and to follow Koushika's words, I will dispel all doubt and undertake this task. In the midst of my superiors, my father, the great-souled Dasharatha, commanded me

---

[241] The Critical text excises a shloka where Tataka and Maricha attack Agastya.
[242] Kavya is Shukra or Shukracharya.

in Ayodhya and his command cannot be disregarded. I have heard
my father's words and the instructions of one who knows about
the brahman.[243] Without a doubt, I will undertake the supreme task
of killing Tataka. For the welfare of cattle and brahmanas, for the
happiness of the country and to follow your immeasurable words,
I will engage myself in this task.' Having said this, the destroyer of
enemies grasped the middle of his bow with his fist. He twanged
his bow and filled the directions with this terrible sound. Tataka,
the resident of the forest, was terrified at this sound. Tataka was
confounded by this sound, but was also enraged. Senseless with
rage, the *rakshasi*[244] determined where that sound had come
from. Having heard the sound, she swiftly dashed towards the
direction from where it had emerged. Raghava saw that enraged
one, malformed, distorted in visage and extremely gigantic in size.
He spoke to Lakshmana. 'Behold Lakshmana! This female yaksha
possesses a fierce and terrible body. On seeing her, the hearts
of cowards will be shattered. Behold her. She is invincible and
possesses the strength of maya. I will now make her withdraw by
severing her ears and the tip of her nose. Since she is protected by
her nature of being a woman, I do not wish to kill her. It is my view
that one should only destroy her valour and her speed.' When Rama
said this, Tataka became senseless with rage. Raising her arms, she
roared and rushed towards Rama. She descended with great force
and valour, like a bolt of thunder. However, he pierced her body
and she fell down, dead. Her form was terrible. On seeing that she
had been slain, the lord of the gods uttered words of praise. The
gods worshipped Kakutstha. Extremely delighted, the thousand-
eyed Purandara[245] spoke these words. Extremely happy, all the gods
also spoke to Vishvamitra. 'O sage! O Koushika! O fortunate one!
Indra, and all the large numbers of Maruts, are satisfied at this task.
Display your affection towards Raghava. The sons of Prajapati and
Krishashva have truth for their valour. They possess the strength
of austerities. O brahmana! Offer them to Raghava. O brahmana!

[243] Vishvamitra.
[244] Female rakshasa.
[245] Indra, the destroyer of cities.

He is a worthy recipient and is steadfast in following you. This is your task. This son of a king will perform a great task for the gods.' All the gods said this. After worshipping Vishvamitra, delighted, they returned to wherever they had come from. Evening had set in. The supreme among sages was happy and content at Tataka having been killed. He inhaled the fragrance of Rama's head and spoke these words. 'O Rama! O one with an auspicious face! We will spend the night here. Tomorrow, when it is morning, we will go to my hermitage.'

## Chapter 1(26)

The immensely illustrious Vishvamitra spent the night there. He smiled at Raghava and spoke these sweet words. 'O fortunate one! O prince! O greatly illustrious one! I am satisfied with you. I am extremely delighted and will give you all the weapons. With these, you will be able to pacify, subjugate and defeat large numbers of gods, asuras, gandharvas, serpents and enemies. O fortunate one! I will bestow all those divine weapons on you. O Raghava! I will give you the extremely divine *dandachakra*.[246] O brave one! I will give you *dharmachakra* and *kalachakra*.[247] I will give you Vishnu's fierce chakra and Indra's chakra too. O best among men! I will give you the vajra weapon and Shiva's supreme trident. O Raghava! I will give you the *brahmashira* and *aishika* weapons. O mighty-armed one! I will give you Brahma's supreme weapon. O Kakutstha! I will give you both the Modaki and Shikhari clubs. O tiger among men! O son of a king! O Rama! I will give you the blazing weapons, Dharma's noose and Death's noose. I will give you the supreme weapon that is Varuna's net. O descendant of the Raghu lineage! I will give you two vajra weapons, one that dries up and one that wets. I will give you the Painaka weapon and the Narayana weapon. I will

---

[246] *Chakra* which acts like a staff of chastisement.
[247] Respectively, chakra which ensures dharma and chakra which drives time/destiny.

give you Agni's beloved weapon, the one that is named Shikhara.
O Raghava! I will give you Vayu's weapon, known as Prathama. I
will give you the weapon Hayashira and the weapon Krouncha. O
Kakutstha! I will give you two spears, Kapala and Kankana, and
the terrible mace, Kankala. I will give you everything that the asuras
wield. I will give you the great weapon of the vidyadharas, named
Nandana. O mighty-armed one! O son of supreme among men! I
will give you a jewel among swords. I will give the beloved weapon
of the gandharvas, known by the name of Manava. O Raghava! I
will give you Prasvapana, Prashamana, Soura, Darpana, Shoshana,
Santapana and Vilapana.[248] I will give you Kandarpa's[249] beloved
and invincible weapon, Madana. I will give you the weapon loved
by the *pishachas*,[250] named Mohana.[251] O tiger among men! O
prince! O greatly illustrious one! Accept these. O tiger among men!
O prince! O mighty-armed one! There are Tamasa, the immensely
strong Soumana, Samvarta, the invincible Mousala, the weapon
known as Satya, the supreme weapon that wields maya, the terrible
weapon named Tejaprabha that saps away the energy of others,
Soma's weapon Shishira, Tvashtra's weapon Sudamana, Bhaga's
Daruna and Manu's Shiteshu. O Rama! O mighty-armed one!
These are extremely strong and are capable of assuming any form at
will. O prince! Swiftly accept these extremely pervasive ones.' Then,
the supreme among sages purified himself and stood, facing the
east. Extremely delighted, he gave Rama those supreme mantras.[252]
The intelligent sage, Vishvamitra, chanted the mantras and all those
extremely revered weapons presented themselves before Raghava.
All of them joined their hands in salutation and joyfully addressed
Rama. 'O greatly generous one! O Raghava! We are your servants.'
Kakutstha extended his hands and accepted them. He urged them,

---

[248] Prasvapana puts to sleep, Prashamana pacifies, Shoshana dries up, Santapana scorches
and Vilapana causes lamentations. Soura is a weapon identified with the sun. Darpana causes
vanity.

[249] Kandarpa, or Kama or Madana, is the god of love.

[250] Malevolent beings.

[251] Something that confounds and intoxicates.

[252] Divine weapons were invoked, released and withdrawn through the use of mantras.

'May you remain in my mind.' Rama was delighted and worshipped the immensely energetic and great sage, Vishvamitra. He got ready to leave.

## Chapter 1(27)

Kakutstha purified himself. He accepted the weapons with a cheerful face. Ready to go, he spoke to Vishvamitra. 'O illustrious ones! I have accepted weapons that are difficult for even the gods to withstand. O bull among sages! I also wish to know about how these weapons can be countered.' Thus addressed by Kakutstha, the great sage, Vishvamitra, full of patience, excellent in his vows and pure, instructed him about countering and withdrawing. 'O Raghava! O fortunate one! O Raghava! These radiant ones are known as Bhrishashva's[253] sons and can assume any form at will. You are a worthy recipient. Accept them—Satyavanta, Satyakirti, Dhrishta, Rabhasa, the one named Pratiharatara, Paranmukha, Avanmukha, Laksha, Alaksha, Vishama, Dridanabha, Sunabha, Dashaksha, Shatavaktra, Dashashirsha, Shatodara, Padmanabha, Mahanabha, Dundunabha, Sunabha,[254] Jyotisha, Krishana, Nairashya, Vimala, Yougandhara, Haridra, Daitya-pramathana, Pitrya, Soumanasa, Vidhutama, Makara, Karavirakara, Dhana, Dhanya, Kamarupa, Kamaruchi, Mohama, Avarana, Jrimbhaka, Sarvanabha, Santana and Varanou.' Cheerful in his mind, Kakutstha accepted the pleasant and embodied forms of those radiant and divine ones. Having manifested themselves before Rama, they joined their hands in salutation and addressed him in sweet voices. 'O tiger among men! We are here. Instruct us about what we can do for you.' The descendant of the Raghu lineage replied, 'Remain in my mind, so that you can assist me when the opportune moment presents itself. Till then, as you wish, leave.' They agreed to what Kakutstha had

---

[253] This should probably read Krishashva.
[254] Sunabha is mentioned twice.

said. They circumambulated Rama and taking his leave, went away to wherever they had come from.

Having got to know about them, as they proceeded, Raghava addressed the great sage, Vishvamitra, in soft and gentle words. 'What is that, located not far from the mountain? This clump of trees is as radiant as a cloud. I am supremely curious. It is beautiful and a sight to see. It is full of many kinds of animals. It is ornamented with birds that possess melodious tones. O best among sages! We have clearly emerged from the desolate forest that makes the body hair stand up. We are headed towards a region that is agreeable. O illustrious one! Tell me everything. Whose hermitage is this? Is this the place where those wicked ones of evil conduct, the slayers of brahmanas, come?'

# Chapter 1(28)

When the immeasurable one asked about the grove, the greatly energetic Vishvamitra started to explain. 'O Rama! Earlier, this used to be the hermitage of the great-souled Vamana. This was famous as Siddhashrama, because the great ascetic obtained success here.[255] At this time, King Bali, Virochana's son, conquered the large numbers of gods, with Indra and the arrays of Maruts. The famous one ruled over the kingdom of the three worlds. Bali performed a sacrifice. With Agni at the forefront, the gods approached Vishnu himself in this hermitage.[256] They said, "O Vishnu! Bali, Virochana's son, is undertaking a supreme sacrifice. Our own sacrifice, which will accomplish all our tasks, is yet incomplete. Whichever supplicant arrives before him, from whatever direction he may come, he[257] gives all of them everything, regardless of what they ask for. For the welfare of

[255] To become a siddha is to obtain success in one's austerities/meditations.

[256] This makes it clear that Vishnu observed austerities in this hermitage, prior to assuming his vamana (dwarf) incarnation.

[257] Bali.

the gods, resort to your maya and present yourself before him. O Vishnu! Assume the form of a vamana and perform this supremely beneficial act. Through your favours, this spot will assume the name of Siddhashrama. O lord of the gods! O illustrious one! Arise and accomplish this task." At this, the greatly energetic Vishnu generated himself through Aditi.[258] He assumed the form of a dwarf and presented himself before Virochana's son. He asked for three strides and respectfully received the gift.[259] Engaged in the welfare of all creatures, the soul of the worlds, encompassed all the worlds. He controlled Bali's energy and again gave the three worlds back to the great Indra. The greatly energetic one again brought them under Shakra's subjugation. This hermitage was inhabited by him earlier, in his vamana form, and is the destroyer of all exhaustion. Because of my devotion, I enjoy it now. The rakshasas, the creators of obstructions, arrive at this hermitage. O tiger among men! This is where the ones of evil conduct will be killed by you. O Rama! We will now head for the supreme Siddhashrama. O son![260] This hermitage belongs to you, just as it does to me.'

On seeing him, all the sages who were residents of Siddhashrama quickly presented themselves before Vishvamitra and worshipped him. As he deserved, they worshipped the intelligent Vishvamitra. They then performed the rites for the two princes, who were the guests. The princes, the scorchers of enemies, rested for a short while. The descendants of the Raghu lineage then joined their hands in salutation and addressed the bull among sages. 'O fortunate one! O bull among sages! Please consecrate yourself today. Let this Siddhashrama bring about success and may your words come true.' The immensely energetic and great sage, Vishvamitra, was addressed in this way. He controlled himself, controlled his senses and consecrated himself.[261] Having slept in the night, when it

---

[258] Kashyapa's wife, the mother of the gods.

[259] Vishnu asked for the region that could be covered in three strides. He covered the earth with one stride, heaven with another and the nether regions (alternatively, Bali's head) with the third, so that Bali was driven down to the nether regions.

[260] The word used is tata.

[261] Consecration is *diksha*, a preparatory to the main rite.

was morning, the princes arose. They controlled themselves and worshipped Vishvamitra.

# Chapter 1(29)

The two princes, destroyers of enemies, knew about the time and the place. Conscious of what should be said at the right time and the right place, they spoke these words to Koushika. 'O illustrious one! O brahmana! We wish to hear when those dwellers of the night present themselves. When must this place be protected? Let the moment not pass.' Hastening to fight, the two Kakutsthas spoke in this way. All the sages were pleased and praised the two princes. 'O Raghavas! From today, you will have to protect this spot for six nights. Having consecrated himself, the sage[262] is observing a vow of silence.' Having heard their words, the two illustrious princes dispensed with sleep for six days and six nights and protected the hermitage. The brave ones were supreme archers and roamed around. Those two destroyers of enemies protected the supreme sage, Vishvamitra.

Time passed and the sixth day arrived. Rama told Soumitri,[263] 'Be attentive and alert.' Having said this, Rama quickly readied himself for the fight. The priests and assistant priests kindled the fire on the sacrificial altar. As is proper, mantras were uttered and the sacrifice proceeded. At that time, a great and terrible sound was heard in the sky. It was as if clouds had enveloped the sky during the monsoon. Resorting to maya, the rakshasas attacked. There were Maricha and Subahu and their followers. They arrived, fierce in form, and showered down torrents of blood. The lotus-eyed one saw that they were violently descending. Glancing towards Lakshmana, Rama said, 'O Lakshmana! Behold these rakshasas. They are evil in conduct and eat raw flesh. I will use the Manava

---

[262] Vishvamitra.
[263] Sumitra's son, Lakshmana.

weapon to drive them away, like clouds dispelled by the wind.' The Manava weapon was extremely powerful and supremely resplendent. Supremely angry, Raghava hurled this at Maricha's chest. He was struck by that supreme weapon, Manava, and hurled one hundred yojanas away, amidst the waves of the ocean. He was whirled around and became unconscious, oppressed by the strength of Shiteshu.[264] On seeing that Maricha had been repulsed, Rama told Lakshmana, 'O Lakshmana! Behold. Shiteshu and Manava are suffused with dharma. They have confounded him and carried him away, but have not deprived him of his life. However, I do wish to slay these abhorred ones, who are evil in conduct.[265] The rakshasas are wicked in conduct. They destroy sacrifices and subsist on blood.' The descendant of the Raghu lineage affixed the extremely great Agneya weapon and hurled it at Subahu's chest. Thus pierced, he fell down on the ground. The immensely illustrious one seized the Vayavya weapon and killed the remaining ones. The extremely powerful Raghava brought delight to the sages. The descendant of the Raghu lineage slew all the rakshasas who sought to destroy the sacrifice. He was worshipped by the rishis, as the victorious Indra was in earlier times. When the sacrifice was completed, the great sage, Vishvamitra, saw that the directions were free of all difficulties. He told Kakutstha, 'O mighty-armed one! I have become successful and you have accomplished your preceptor's words. O Rama! O immensely illustrious one! You have made the name of Siddhashrama come true.'

# Chapter 1(30)

Having been successful, the brave Rama and Lakshmana rejoiced in their heart of hearts. Cheerfully, they spent the night there. When night turned into morning, they performed

---

[264] The Manava and Shiteshu weapons are probably being used partly synonymously.
[265] The other rakshasas.

their morning ablutions. They then approached Vishvamitra, who was with the other rishis. They greeted that best among sages, who was like a blazing fire. Gentle in speech, those generous ones spoke these sweet words to him. 'O tiger among sages! We, your servants, are present before you. Instruct us about what is beneficial. Command us what we must do.' When they spoke in this way, all the maharshis, with Vishvamitra at the forefront, spoke these words to Rama. 'O best among men! Janaka of Mithila is devoted to dharma and will undertake a supreme sacrifice. We will go there. O tiger among men! You should also come with us. There is an extraordinary gem of a bow there and you should see that. It is fierce and is immeasurable in strength. It is supremely radiant in a battle. O best among men! In an assembly, the gods gave it to him earlier.[266] The gods, the gandharvas, the asuras and the rakshasas are incapable of raising it, not to speak of men. Many kings wished to test the energy of that bow. However, those supremely strong princes were incapable of raising it. O tiger among men! That bow belongs to the great-souled lord of Mithila. O Kakutstha! You will be able to see it and witness the extraordinary sacrifice. O tiger among men! The bow possesses an excellent grip. The lord of Mithila had sought this supreme bow as the fruit of a sacrifice from all the gods.' Having said this, the supreme among sages[267] prepared to leave with the large number of rishis and Kakutstha, having taken his leave of the gods of the forest. 'I have become successful in Siddhashrama. May I be safe in the course of my journey. I will leave for the Himalaya mountains, located on the northern banks of the Jahnavee.' Having circumambulated the supreme Siddhashrama, he got ready to leave for the northern direction. The supreme among sages departed, accompanied by his followers. One hundred carts followed the one who knew about the brahman. The birds and animals that resided in Siddhashrama also followed the great-souled and great sage, Vishvamitra.

---

[266] Gave it to Janaka.
[267] Vishvamitra.

When the sun stretched out,[268] the large number of sages had proceeded some distance. They controlled themselves and rested on the banks of the Shona river. When the sun set, they bathed and kindled a fire. They seated themselves in front of the infinitely energetic Vishvamitra. Rama and Soumitri worshipped the sages. They too seated themselves in front of the intelligent Vishvamitra. The infinitely energetic Rama was full of curiosity. He asked the great sage, Vishamitra, tiger among sages. 'O illustrious one! What is this place, prosperous with forests? O fortunate one! I wish to hear. You should tell me the truth about this.' Thus urged by Rama's words, in the midst of the rishis, the great ascetic, excellent in his vows, told him everything about that region.

## Chapter 1(31)

'There was a great ascetic named Kusha, descended from the great Brahma. Through the princess of Vidarbha, he had four sons who were exactly like him—Kushamba, Kushanabha, Adhurtarajas and Vasu. They were radiant and great in enterprise, interested in observing the dharma of kshatriyas. The sons were devoted to dharma and truthful in speech. Kusha told them, "O sons! Rule properly, so that you may obtain all the fruits of dharma." Having heard Kusha's words, those best among men, revered in the worlds, sought to create four cities. The immensely energetic Kushamba constructed the city of Koushambi.[269] Kushanabha, with dharma in his soul, constructed the city of Mahodaya. O Rama! King Adhurtarajas constructed Dharmaranya and King Vasu constructed Girivraja,[270] supreme among cities. O Rama! This is the dominion of the great-souled Vasu, known as Vasumati. In every direction, five great mountains can be seen. This beautiful river,

---

[268] Was ready to set.

[269] Identified with Kannauj, or the village of Kosam, on the banks of the Yamuna and near Allahabad.

[270] Identified with Rajagriha or Rajgir.

Sumagadhi,[271] flows towards the famous land of Magadha. In the midst of those five great mountains, it is as radiant as a garland. O Rama! Sumagadhi[272] flows eastwards through the great-souled Vasu's land. O Rama! The area is garlanded by excellent fields that yield a lot of grain. O descendant of the Raghu lineage! Through Ghritachi,[273] the great-souled royal sage, Kushanabha, with dharma in his soul, had one hundred supreme daughters. They were young and beautiful. Once, ornamented, they went to a grove and were like one hundred flashes of lightning during the monsoon. O Raghava! They sang, danced and played on musical instruments. Adorned in excellent ornaments, they were in a paroxysm of delight. Their limbs were beautiful and their beauty was unmatched on earth. They went to that grove and were like stars amidst clouds. Having seen them, Vayu, who pervades everything, told them, "I desire all of you. Become my wives. Abandon your human forms and obtain long lifespans instead." They heard the words of Vayu, unsullied in his deeds. However, those one hundred maidens laughed at his words and replied, "O supreme among gods! You roam around inside all creatures. All of us know about your powers. But why are you slighting us? O supreme among gods! All of us are Kushanabha's daughters and are capable of dislodging you from your status. It is just that we want to preserve our store of austerities. O evil-minded one! Our father is truthful in speech. The time will never come when we will cross our father, transgress dharma and resort to *svayamvara*.[274] Our father is our lord. He is our supreme divinity. Our husband will be the one to whom our father bestows us." Hearing their words, Vayu was greatly enraged. The illustrious lord entered their bodies and disfigured their limbs. Mangled by Vayu, those maidens entered the king's residence. On seeing that they had been mangled, the king was terrified and spoke these words. "O daughters! How did this happen? Who has shown

---

[271] A name for the Shona.
[272] The text says Magadhi, but we have used Sumagadhi to avoid confusion.
[273] The name of an apsara.
[274] When a maiden chooses her own husband.

disrespect towards dharma? Who has made your bodies crooked? Why are you trembling and not saying anything?"'

## Chapter 1(32)

'Hearing the words of the intelligent Kushanabha, the one hundred daughters touched his feet with their heads and said, "O king! Vayu pervades everything and desired to dishonour us. He did not pay heed to dharma and resorted to an inauspicious path. We told the fortunate one that we are not independent and are devoted to our father's words. He should ask our father and our father will decide whether we should be bestowed on him or not. However, addicted to evil, he did not accept our words. Vayu has severely afflicted us." All of them told him this. The king, supremely devoted to dharma, heard their words. The extremely energetic one replied to those one hundred supreme maidens. "O daughters! Forgiveness is the trait of the forgiving and you have observed that great duty. You have remembered my lineage and all of you have united in acting in this way. Whether it is a woman or a man, forgiveness is the true ornament. It is extremely difficult to be forgiving, especially when the gods are involved. O daughters! This is particularly true of the kind of forgiveness you have exhibited. Forgiveness is generosity. Forgiveness represents sacrifices. O daughters! Forgiveness is truth. Forgiveness is fame. Forgiveness is dharma. The universe is established on forgiveness." O Kakutstha! The king, who was like the gods in his valour, gave his daughters permission to leave. He knew about good policy and consulted his ministers about who they should be bestowed on. What would be the time and the place for the bestowal? Which groom would be their equal?

'At that time, there was a great sage named Chuli. He held up his seed and was auspicious in conduct. He had attained the brahman. While the rishi was engaged in austerities, a gandharva lady served him. The fortunate one's name was Somada and she was Urmila's daughter. Devoted to serving him, she prostrated herself before him. She was devoted to dharma. After she had spent some time there, her preceptor was satisfied with her. O descendant of the Raghu lineage! When the time was right, he told her, "O fortunate one! I am satisfied with you. What can I do to please you?" Knowing that the sage was satisfied, the gandharva lady spoke to him in sweet words. She was accomplished in speech and was conversant with the use of words. Supremely delighted, she replied, "O great ascetic! The brahman is in you and pervaded by the brahman, prosperity is manifest in you. I desire a son who is devoted to dharma, one who is united with the brahman and with austerities. O fortunate one! I do not have a husband. I am no one's wife. I have come here because you are suffused with the brahman. You should grant me a son." Pleased with her, the brahmana rishi gave her a supreme son. This son was born through Chuli's mental powers and was famous as Brahmadatta. King Brahmadatta resided in the supremely prosperous city of Kampilya,[275] like the king of the gods in heaven.

'O Kakutstha! King Kushanabha, extremely devoted to dharma, made up his mind that he would bestow his one hundred daughters on Brahmadatta. The immensely energetic king invited Brahmadatta. Extremely happy in his mind, he bestowed the one hundred daughters on him. O descendant of the Raghu lineage! In due order, King Brahmadatta, who was like the lord of the gods, accepted their hands. As soon as he touched them with his hands, their deformations disappeared and they became devoid of anxiety. The one hundred maidens were united with supreme beauty. On seeing that they had become free of Vayu, King Kushanabha was supremely delighted and rejoiced repeatedly. When the marriage was over, the king sent King Brahmadatta on his way, with his wives and with large numbers of priests. Somada was also extremely happy at seeing the act that her son had accomplished. As is proper, the gandharva lady found delight in her daughters-in-law.'

[275] Described as the capital of Panchala, specifically, South Panchala. Identified with Kampil, in Farrukhabad district of Uttar Pradesh.

# Chapter 1(33)

'O Raghava! After the marriage was over, Brahmadatta departed. Since he was without a son, King Kushanabha thought of performing a sacrifice so that he might have a son. While the sacrifice was going on, Kusha, Brahma's son, was extremely happy and spoke these words.[276] "O son! There will be a son who will be extremely devoted to dharma, like you. His name will be Gadhi and he will obtain eternal fame in this world. O Rama! Kusha spoke in this way to King Kushanabha. He then went up into the sky and entered Brahma's eternal abode. After some time, the intelligent Kushanabha had a son named Gadhi, who was supremely devoted to dharma. O Kakutstha! Gadhi, supremely devoted to dharma, is my father. O descendant of the Raghu lineage! I have been born in Kusha's lineage and am Koushika. O Raghava! Earlier, I had a sister who was excellent in her vows. Her name was Satyavati and she was bestowed on Richika. Following her husband, she went to heaven in her own physical body. The extremely generous one started to flow as the great river Koushiki.[277] She is divine, with sacred waters. She is beautiful and flows through the Himalayas. For the welfare of the worlds, my sister flowed as a river. That is the reason I always dwell happily on the slopes of the Himalayas. O descendant of the Raghu lineage! This is because of the affection I bear towards my sister, Koushiki. Satyavati is sacred and is established in true dharma. The immensely fortunate one is devoted to her husband and is Koushiki, supreme among rivers. O Rama! Because of my vows, I left her and came to Siddhashrama. Because of your energy, I have obtained success. O Rama! This is my origin and I have recounted my lineage and about this region. O mighty-armed one! That is what you had asked me about. O Kakutstha! Half the night has passed in telling you about my account. O fortunate one! We should sleep now. We have come half the way and let there be no hindrances. O descendant of the Raghu lineage! Everything is quiet

---

[276] To Kushanabha.
[277] The river Koshi.

and the birds and animals are resting. The darkness of the night has
pervaded all the directions. Evening has slowly crept away and the
sky is covered with nakshatras and planets that look like eyes. Their
radiance illuminates everything. The moon, the dispeller of darkness
from the worlds, has arisen, with its cool beams. O lord! With its
radiance, it gladdens the worlds and the minds of creatures. Here
and there, the creatures of the night are roaming around. There are
large numbers of yakshas and rakshasas. They are terrible and feed
on raw flesh.'

Having spoken in this way, the immensely energetic and great
sage ceased. All the other sages praised him and worshipped him.
Rama and Soumitri were somewhat astounded. They also praised
the tiger among sages and went to sleep.

## Chapter 1(34)

With the maharshis, Vishvamitra spent the rest of the night on
the banks of the Shona. When night turned into an excellent
morning, he said, 'O Rama! The night has turned into an excellent
morning and the first *sandhya* has commenced.[278] Arise. O fortunate
one! Arise. You should get ready for departure.' On hearing his
words, he[279] performed the morning ablutions. He prepared to
leave and replied in these words. 'The Shona possesses auspicious
waters. It is full of sandbanks and can be crossed. O brahmana!
What mode should we use to cross over it?'[280] Thus addressed by
Rama, Vishvamitra said, 'I instruct that we should follow the path
that the maharshis have travelled along.'[281] After having travelled
some distance, for half a day, they saw Jahnavee, best among rivers,
frequented by the sages. On seeing the sacred waters, populated by
swans and cranes, all the sages, together with the two Raghavas,

[278] Sandhya is any conjunction of day and night. Hence, it is dawn, as well as dusk.
[279] Rama.
[280] That is, boats are not necessary. Should one use a boat or should one walk across?
[281] That is, walking across.

were delighted. They set up residence along the banks. They bathed there. As is proper, they offered water to the ancestors and the gods. They rendered offerings into the *agnihotra* fire and those oblations were like amrita. Pure and cheerful in their minds, they resided on the banks of the Jahnavee. In every direction, they surrounded the great-souled Vishvamitra.

Delighted in his mind, Rama spoke to Vishvamitra. 'O illustrious one! I wish to hear about the Ganga, the river with the three flows. How does she flow through the three worlds and reach the lord of the male and female rivers?'[282] Urged by Rama's words, Vishvamitra, the great sage, started to describe the birth and progress of Ganga. 'The Himalayas, Indra among mountains, is a great store of minerals. O Rama! He had two daughters and their beauty was unmatched on earth. O Rama! Their mother was the slender-waisted daughter of Mount Meru. Her name was Mena. That beautiful one was the beloved wife of the Himalayas. Her daughter Ganga was the elder daughter of the Himalayas. O Raghava! There was a second daughter and her name was Uma. All the gods wished that the elder daughter should accomplish a task for the gods. They asked the Indra among mountains and she became a river with three flows. Following dharma, the Himalayas donated his daughter, for the sake of purifying the worlds. For the welfare of the three worlds, Ganga started to flow as she willed. For the benefit of the three worlds, those who desired the welfare of the three worlds[283] accepted Ganga and returned, successful at their inner wishes having been met. O descendant of the Raghu lineage! The mountain had another daughter. That store of austerities resorted to fierce vows and asceticism. That daughter of the supreme among mountains engaged in terrible austerities. The unmatched Uma, revered in the worlds, was bestowed on Rudra. These daughters of the king of mountains are worshipped by the worlds. O Raghava! Ganga is best among rivers and Uma is a goddess. I have told you everything about the river that has

---

[282] The ocean is the lord of the rivers.
[283] The gods.

three flows. O son!²⁸⁴ The one with the best of flows first flowed
in the sky.'

## Chapter 1(35)

When the sage said these words, the brave Rama and
Lakshmana applauded the account and spoke to the bull
among sages. 'O brahmana! You have recited a supreme account
that is full of dharma. You should tell us about the elder daughter of
the king of the mountains in detail. You are capable of recounting
divine and human origins in detail. What is the reason why the
purifier of the worlds has three flows? Why is Ganga, the one
with the three flows, known as the best among rivers? O one who
knows about dharma! What are the tasks that she has performed
in the three worlds?'

When the two Kakutsthas addressed him in this way, in
the midst of all the rishis, Vishvamitra, the store of austerities,
narrated the entire account. 'O Rama! In ancient times, the great
ascetic, Shitikantha,²⁸⁵ married. Having seen the goddess,²⁸⁶ he
desired to have intercourse with her. One hundred divine years
passed for the god Shitikantha.²⁸⁷ O Rama! O scorcher of enemies!
However, he still did not have a son. At this, with the grandfather
at the forefront, all the gods were anxious. "When an offspring
is born, who will be able to sustain him?"²⁸⁸ All the gods went
and prostrated themselves before him. They said, "O Mahadeva!
O god of the gods! O one who is engaged in the welfare of the
worlds! The gods have prostrated themselves before you. You
should show them your favours. O supreme among the gods!
The world will not be able to sustain your energy. Resort to the

---

²⁸⁴ The word used is tata.
²⁸⁵ The one with the blue throat, Shiva.
²⁸⁶ Uma.
²⁸⁷ 360 human years equal one divine year.
²⁸⁸ Because the offspring would be extremely energetic.

austerities of the brahman. Unite with the goddess in that kind of austerity.[289] For the welfare of the three worlds, withdraw your semen and energy. Protect all these worlds. You should not destroy the worlds." Maheshvara, the lord of all the worlds, heard the words of the gods. He agreed to this. He again told all of them, "I will restrain my semen and my energy within Uma. The gods and the earth will be secure. However, the part of my energy that has already been stirred cannot be restrained. O supreme among the gods! Tell me who is going to sustain this." Thus addressed, the gods replied to the one who has a bull on his banner.[290] "The earth will bear the energy that has already been dislodged." Thus addressed, the lord of the gods released it on the surface of the ground. The earth, with its mountains and groves, was pervaded by this energy. At this, the gods again spoke to the fire god. "Aided by Vayu, enter Rudra's great energy." It again pervaded Agni and created Mount Shveta. There was a celestial clump of reeds that was like the fire and the sun in complexion. Created from Agni, the greatly energetic Kartikeya was born there. The gods, with the large number of rishis, were greatly delighted and wholeheartedly worshipped Uma and Shiva. O Rama! However, the daughter of the mountain[291] was enraged and her eyes turned red with anger. Full of intolerance, she cursed the gods and told them, "I desired to have intercourse for the sake of a son, but you restrained me. Because of that, you will never be able to obtain offspring through your own wives. From today, your wives will remain infertile." Having spoken in this way to all the gods, she also cursed the earth. "O earth! You will never possess one single form and will always be the wife to many. You will be tainted through my rage and will never know any affection towards your sons. O extremely evil-minded one! You obtained my son, though you never wished for him." The lord of the gods saw that all the gods were ashamed. He prepared to leave for the direction that is protected by Varuna.[292]

[289] That is, do not have physical offspring.

[290] Shiva has a bull on his banner.

[291] Uma.

[292] Varuna rules over the western direction.

He went to the slopes of the northern mountains[293] and performed austerities there. Through the powers of Maheshvara and the goddess, a summit was created there, in the Himalayas. O Rama! I have told you in detail about the daughter of the mountain. With Lakshmana, now hear about the origin of the Ganga.'

## Chapter 1(36)

'In ancient times, the gods performed austerities in this way.[294] At that time, the gods, with large numbers of rishis, went to the grandfather, desiring a general. All the gods, with Indra and Agni at the forefront, bowed down before the illustrious grandfather and spoke these auspicious words. "O illustrious one! In earlier times, you gave us a general.[295] However, with Uma, he is now resorting to supreme austerities and is scorching himself. Desiring the welfare of the worlds, you must decide on what should be done now. O one who knows about what must be done! You are our supreme refuge and must decide on a course of action." The grandfather of all the worlds heard the words of the gods. He comforted the gods and spoke these sweet words to them. "The mountain's daughter has said that you will not have offspring through your wives. There is no doubt that her unsullied words will come true. However, through Ganga, who flows in the sky, Agni can have a son and that destroyer of enemies will be the general of the gods.[296] The eldest daughter of the Indra among mountains will welcome this son. There is no doubt that this will also find great sanction with Uma." O descendant of the Raghu lineage! On hearing his words, all the gods thought that they had obtained success. They bowed down and worshipped the grandfather. O Rama! All the gods went to Mount Kailasa, which is decorated with minerals. There, they urged

---

[293] Obviously the Himalayas.
[294] This is still Vishvamitra speaking.
[295] Referring to Shiva.
[296] Since Ganga is not married to Agni, the curse will not be violated.

Agni to produce a son. "O god! O fire god! Accomplish the task
of the gods. The great energy has so far been contained in Ganga,
the daughter of the mountain. Release that energy." Pavaka[297] gave
his pledge to the gods and approached Ganga. "O goddess! To
bring pleasure to the gods, please bear this in your womb." Hearing
these words, she assumed a divine form. On seeing her great form,
he[298] spread throughout her person. Pavaka spread throughout the
goddess and sprinkled her.[299] O descendant of the Raghu lineage!
All of Ganga's flows became full. At this, Ganga spoke to the
priest of the gods.[300] "O god! Your energy is extremely potent and
I am incapable of bearing it. I am being scorched by the fire and
my senses are distressed." All the gods and the fire god spoke to
Ganga. "Deposit the embryo on the foothills of the Himalayas."
O unblemished one! Hearing Agni's words, Ganga released that
radiant embryo in torrents of great energy. Wherever that flow,
with the complexion of molten gold, was released in the Himalayas,
the sacred ground became sparkling and golden. From the friction
between the gods,[301] copper and iron ore were also generated. The
residue that was left became tin and lead. It is from this that the
earth obtained many kinds of minerals. As soon as that embryo was
flung down, the sparkling energy created a golden grove everywhere
in that mountain. O Raghava! O tiger among men! Since then,
with a complexion like that of the fire, gold has been known as
Jatarupa.[302]

'When the son was born, Indra, with the large number of
Maruts, engaged the Krittikas to provide milk for him.[303] As soon
as he was born, they[304] took an excellent pledge. "He is our son."
Having decided this, all of them gave him milk. Because of this, all

[297] The one who purifies, one of Agni's names.
[298] Agni.
[299] With the seed.
[300] Agni is being described as the priest of the gods.
[301] Shiva and Agni.
[302] Literally, something that obtains form from birth.
[303] There are various stories about Kartikeya's birth. For example, he was found in a
clump of reeds and reared by the Krittikas (the Pleiades).
[304] The Krittikas.

the gods said, "This son will be known as Kartikeya and there is no doubt that he will be famous in the three worlds." The embryo that had been dislodged from the womb was exceedingly beautiful and blazed like the fire. On hearing these words, they[305] bathed it. O Kakutstha! The immensely fortunate Kartikeya was like the fire. Since he had been secreted from the womb, the gods called him Skanda.[306] Excellent milk began to ooze out from the breasts of the six Krittikas and assuming six faces, he fed on this. Having fed on this milk, he grew up to be a boy in a single day. Because of the lord's valour, the soldiers of the *daityas*[307] found him to be invincible. With Agni at the forefront, the large number of gods assembled and consecrated the unblemished and radiant one as the general of the soldiers of the gods. O Rama! I have thus told you about Ganga in detail and about the blessed and sacred account of Kumara's birth.'

## Chapter 1(37)

In a sweet voice, Koushika told Rama about that account. He again addressed the following words to Kakutstha. 'There was a brave king who was earlier the lord of Ayodhya. His name was Sagara and he possessed dharma in his soul. However, since he did not have any offspring, he desired offspring. In her beauty, Arishtanemi's daughter was unmatched on earth. She was known as Sumati and she was Sagara's second wife.[308] With those two wives, the king went to the Himalayas, to the mountain known as Bhriguprasravana.[309] There, he tormented himself through austerities. After the sage

---

[305] The Krittikas.

[306] From *skanna*, which means to be secreted out.

[307] Demons who are descendants of Diti.

[308] In a shloka excised from the Critical Edition, we are told that the first wife's name was Keshini.

[309] This is also known as Bhrigutunga and is identified as a mountain in Nepal, on the banks of the Gandaki.

Bhrigu, supreme among those who uphold the truth, had been worshipped with austerities for one hundred years, he gave a boon to Sagara. "O unblemished one! You will obtain extremely great offspring. O bull among men! You will obtain unsurpassed fame in this world. O son![310] One of your wives will give birth to a son who will extend the lineage. The other will give birth to sixty thousand sons." Having shown his favours to the king's wives, this is what he told that tiger among men. Extremely delighted, they joined their hands in salutation and said, "O brahmana! Who will have a single son and who will give birth to many? O brahmana! We wish to learn this. May your words come true." Having heard their words, Bhrigu, extremely devoted to dharma, spoke these supreme words. "This will be decided by you, independently. Who wants a son who will extend the lineage? Who wants many sons who are extremely strong, famous and great in endeavour? Who wants which boon?" O descendant of the Raghu lineage! O Rama! Hearing the sage's words, in the presence of the king, Keshini desired a son who would extend the lineage. Sumati, Suparna's[311] sister, wished for sixty thousand sons who would be great in endeavour and famous. O descendant of the Raghu lineage! With his wives, the king bowed his head down before the rishi, circumambulated him and returned to his own city. After some time had passed, the elder wife, Keshini, gave birth to a son. This son of Sagara came to be known by the name of Asamanja. O tiger among men! Sumati gave birth to a gourd. When this gourd was shattered, sixty thousand sons emerged. Nursemaids nurtured them in pots filled with *ghee* and reared them there. After a long period of time, they became youths. After another long period of time, these sixty thousand of Sagara's sons became handsome adults. O best among men! O descendant of the Raghu lineage! The eldest of Sagara's sons[312] used to grab children and hurl them into the waters of the Sarayu. Having hurled them there, seeing them drown, he always used to laugh. Since he was engaged in injuring the citizens, his father

[310] The word used is tata.
[311] Garuda's name is Suparna.
[312] Asamanja.

banished him from the city. However, Asamanja had a valiant son named Amshumat. He was respected by all the worlds and spoke pleasantly to everyone. O best among men! After a long period of time, Sagara reflected and made up his mind about performing a sacrifice. Having thus made up his mind, the king, who knew about the Vedas, told his preceptors to begin the rites for undertaking a sacrifice.'

## Chapter 1(38)

Hearing Vishvamitra's words, the descendant of the Raghu lineage was supremely delighted. When the account was over, he spoke to the sage, who blazed like the fire. 'O fortunate one! I wish to hear about this account in detail. O brahmana! How did my ancestor complete the sacrifice?'

Vishvamitra seemed to smile at Kakutstha and said, 'O Rama! Hear in detail about the great-souled Sagara. Shankara's father-in-law is the supreme mountain, known as Himalayas. He approaches Mount Vindhya and the two glance at each other. O supreme among men! O best among men! The land that extends between them is a region that is praised for performing sacrifices. O Kakutstha! O son![313] Following Sagara's words, maharatha Amshumat, the firm archer, tended to the horse.[314] On the auspicious day when the sacrificer was going to undertake the sacrifice, Vasava assumed the form of a female rakshasa and stole the sacrificial horse. O Kakutstha! When the great-souled sacrificer's horse was stolen, all the large number of preceptors spoke to the sacrificer. "This is the auspicious time. Quickly fetch the sacrificial horse. O Kakutstha! Slay the thief and bring the horse. If there is a lacuna in the sacrifice, all of us will face something inauspicious. O king! Therefore, act so

---

[313] The word used is tata.

[314] In a horse sacrifice, a horse is left free to roam around. Kings who allow the horse unimpeded access agree to pay tribute to the king who is undertaking the horse sacrifice. Those unwilling to do so, seize the horse and a battle ensues.

that there is no weakness in the sacrifice." Hearing the words of the preceptors in that assembly, the king spoke these words to his sixty thousand sons. "O sons! O bulls among men! I do not perceive any means for rakshasas to make an entry. Extremely fortunate ones have sanctified this great sacrifice with mantras. O sons! Therefore, go and search. May you be safe. Go to everywhere on earth, right up to the garland of the ocean. O sons! Each of you search for the expanse of one yojana. Until you see the horse, dig up the earth. On my command, seek out the horse and the thief. I have been consecrated with my grandson.[315] O fortunate ones! Until I see the horse, I will remain here with all the preceptors." Thus addressed, the extremely strong princes were cheerful in their minds. O Rama! Urged by their father's words, they penetrated the surface of the earth. O tiger among men! With arms that were like the touch of the vajra, they dug it up. They used extremely terrible ploughs and spears that were like the vajra. O descendant of the Raghu lineage! Thus shattered, the earth began to shriek. O Raghava! The serpents and the asuras were slaughtered and so were rakshasas and other invincible beings. There was a tumultuous roar. O descendant of the Raghu lineage! Those brave ones penetrated the earth for sixty thousand yojanas, right up to the excellent *rasatala*.[316] O tiger among kings! Jambudvipa[317] is girded by mountains and those princes dug it up everywhere. At this, all the gods, gandharvas, asuras and serpents were terrified in their minds and went to the grandfather. With distressed faces, they sought the favours of the great-souled one. Extremely scared, they spoke these words to the grandfather. "O illustrious one! Everywhere, Sagara's sons are digging up the earth. Many great-souled aquatic creatures are being killed. 'The one who has stolen the horse is destroying our sacrifice.' Thinking this, Sagara's sons are slaughtering all the creatures.'"

[315] Amshumat. Therefore, they cannot search for the horse.

[316] Generally, the nether regions. There are actually seven nether regions—*atala, vitala, sutala, rasatala, talatala, mahatala* and *patala*.

[317] Jambudvipa is one of the seven continents (*dvipa*) that surround Mount Meru and Bharatavarsha is in Jambudvipa. Jambudvipa is named after *jambu* (*jamun*) trees that grow there.

## Chapter 1(39)

'The gods were extremely terrified and confounded by the strength of those destroyers. The illustrious grandfather replied to them. "The entire earth is owned by the intelligent Vasudeva and he eternally holds up the earth. He has assumed the form of Kapila. A long time ago, the shattering of the earth was foreseen and so was the destruction of the sons of Sagara, who will not live for a long time." Hearing the grandfather's words, the thirty-three gods, the scorchers of enemies, were extremely happy and returned to wherever they had come from.[318]

'When Sagara's great-souled sons shattered the earth, a great sound was heard, like that of thunder. Having penetrated the earth, they circled it everywhere. All of Sagara's sons then went to their father and spoke these words. "We have travelled through the entire earth and destroyed all the creatures—gods, danavas, rakshasas, pishachas, serpents and kinnaras. However, we have not been able to see the horse, or the thief who stole the horse. O fortunate one! What will we do now? It is necessary to reflect on this." O descendant of the Raghu lineage! Hearing the words of his sons, Sagara, supreme among kings, was overcome by rage and spoke these words. "O fortunate ones! Dig the earth again and penetrate the surface of the earth. Search out the horse and the thief. Return only when you are successful." Hearing the words of their father, the great-souled Sagara, the sixty thousand sons rushed to rasatala. They dug there and saw the *dishagaja* Virupaksha.[319] He was like a mountain and held up the earth. O descendant of the Raghu lineage! The great elephant, Virupaksha, held up the entire earth, with its mountains, on his head. O Kakutstha! When the great elephant is tired and wishes

---

[318] The thirty-three gods are the eight Vasus, the eleven Rudras, the twelve Adityas and the two Ashvins. Sometimes, instead of the two Ashvins, Indra and Prajapati are included.

[319] Four (sometimes eight) elephants are believed to hold up the four (or eight) directions. They are known as *diggajas* or *dishagajas*, from *gaja* (elephant) and *dig/disha* (direction). The names differ. Virupaksha holds up the eastern direction.

to rest, it moves its head and earthquakes result. O Rama! They circumambulated the great elephant, the guardian of the direction. Having showed it honours, they penetrated the earth and went to rasatala. They penetrated the eastern direction and again penetrated the southern direction. They saw a great elephant in the southern direction too. This was the great-souled Mahapadma and he was like an extremely gigantic mountain, holding up the earth on his head. They were extremely astonished. Having circumambulated him, Sagara's great-souled sixty thousand sons penetrated the western direction. In the western direction too, those extremely strong ones saw the dishagaja Soumanasa, who was like a gigantic mountain. They circumambulated him and asked him about his welfare. They continued to dig and reached the northern direction.[320] O best among the Raghu lineage! In the northern direction, they saw Bhadra, holding up the earth. He was as white as snow and his form was auspicious. All of them touched him and circumambulated him. Those sixty thousand sons then penetrated the surface of the earth. Sagara's sons then went to the famous north-east direction. In great rage, Sagara's sons dug up the entire earth. They saw Kapila, the eternal Vasudeva, there. The horse was also wandering around there, not very far from the god.[321] Taking him to be the one who had destroyed the sacrifice, their eyes dilated with rage. Asking him to wait, they angrily dashed towards him. "You are the one who has stolen our horse and destroyed the sacrifice. O evil-minded one! You should know that we, the sons of Sagara, have arrived." O descendant of the Raghu lineage! Hearing their words, Kapila was overcome by great anger and uttered the sound of humkara. O Kakutstha! The immeasurable and great-souled Kapila reduced all of Sagara's sons to ashes.'

---

[320] The text states, the Somavati direction. Soma is another name for Kubera and Kubera is the guardian of the north. Soma is also a name for the moon and the moon's direction is the north.

[321] To destroy Sagara's sons, Indra hid the horse there.

# Chapter 1(40)

'O descendant of the Raghu lineage! When King Sagara saw that his sons had been gone for a long time, he spoke to his grandson,[322] who was radiant in his own energy. "You are brave and accomplished in learning. In energy, you are an equal of your ancestors.[323] Go and search for your fathers[324] and for the person who has stolen the horse. There are great and valiant beings in the bowels of the earth. To repulse their attacks, take your sword and your bow. Honour the ones that deserve honour and slay the ones who cause obstructions. Return when you have ensured the success of the sacrifice, or cross over to the other side."[325] Amshumat was thus properly addressed by the great-souled Sagara. He grasped his bow and sword and departed, dexterous in his valour. He proceeded along the path that had been dug up in the earth by his great-souled fathers. O best among men! He proceeded, urged on by the king's words. He saw the immensely energetic dishagaja, worshipped by the daityas, danavas, pishachas, birds and serpents. He circumambulated him and asked him about their welfare. He asked him about his fathers and about the person who had stolen the horse. On hearing this, the dishagaja was pleased and replied in these words. "O Amshumat! O son of Asamanja! You will be successful and will swiftly return, with the horse." As is proper, in due order, he then asked all the other dishagajas. Hearing his words, all the guardians of the directions,[326] who were accomplished in speech, honoured and urged him with words and said, "You will return with the horse." Hearing their words, he proceeded, dexterous in his valour. He reached the spot where his fathers, Sagara's sons, had been reduced to ashes. At this, Asamanja's son was overcome by grief. Extremely miserable and severely afflicted that they had been killed, he wept. He saw the sacrificial horse wandering around, not very far away. Full of sorrow

---

[322] Amshumat.
[323] That is, the uncles.
[324] By extension, meaning the uncles.
[325] Die in the process.
[326] The dishagajas.

and misery, the tiger among men saw it. To perform the water rites
for the princes, the immensely energetic one searched for water, but
could not find a store of water. Casting his trained eye around, he
saw the lord of the birds.[327] O Rama! Suparna was like the wind and
was the maternal uncle of his fathers.[328] Vinata's extremely strong
son spoke these words to him. "O tiger among men! Do not sorrow.
This slaughter has been sanctioned by the worlds. The immeasurable
Kapila has burnt down these extremely strong ones. O wise one!
Therefore, you should not offer them water through the normal
water rites. O bull among men! Ganga is the eldest daughter of the
Himalayas. That purifier of the worlds will purify these mounds of
ashes. When the ashes of these sixty thousand sons are sprinkled by
the waters of the Ganga, beloved by the worlds, they will be conveyed
to the world of heaven. O immensely fortunate one! O bull among
men! Seizing the horse, leave this spot. O brave one! Return, so that
your grandfather's sacrifice can be carried out." Hearing Suparna's
words, the valiant and immensely illustrious Amshumat quickly
seized the horse and returned. O descendant of the Raghu lineage! He
went to the king who had been consecrated and reported what had
happened. He also recounted Suparna's words. Hearing Amshumat's
terrible words, the king performed the sacrifice, following the rites
and observing the rituals. Having completed the desired sacrifice, the
king returned to his own city. However, the king could not make
up his mind about how Ganga was to be brought. Even after a long
period of time, the king could not arrive at a decision. Having ruled
the kingdom for thirty thousand years, he went to heaven.'

# Chapter 1(41)

'O Rama! When Sagara departed, following the rule of time,
the ordinary people wished to make Amshumat, who was

---

[327] Garuda.
[328] Garuda was Sumati's brother and Vinata's son.

extremely devoted to dharma, the king. O descendant of the Raghu lineage! Amshumat was an extremely great king. He had a great son, who was famous by the name of Dileepa. O descendant of the Raghu lineage! Having handed over the kingdom to Dileepa, he[329] went to a beautiful summit in the Himalayas. There, he tormented himself through extremely terrible austerities.[330] The extremely illustrious king performed austerities in the hermitage for thirty-two thousand years. The store of austerities then went to heaven. The immensely energetic Dileepa heard about the slaughter of his grandfathers. Though he was afflicted by grief, he could not make up his mind about what should be done. "How will Ganga be brought down? How will water rites be performed for them? How will they be saved?" These were the profound thoughts he pondered about. With his mind immersed in dharma, he always thought about this. He had a son named Bhageeratha, who was supremely devoted to dharma. The immensely energetic Dileepa performed many desired sacrifices. The king ruled over the kingdom for thirty thousand years. However, the king could not make up his mind about how they should be saved. O tiger among men! Following the dharma of time, the king succumbed to disease. Because of the deeds that he had himself performed, the king went to Indra's world, after the bull among men had instated his son, Bhageeratha, in the kingdom.

'O descendant of the Raghu lineage! Bhageeratha was a royal sage who was devoted to dharma. The immensely energetic one was without offspring. He didn't possess any sons and desired sons. O descendant of the Raghu lineage! For a long period of time, the king performed austerities in Gokarna.[331] He conquered his senses. He raised up his hands and ate only once, at the end of the month. He observed the vow of the five fires.[332] He engaged in these fierce austerities for one thousand years. The illustrious Brahma, the lord and god of all subjects, was extremely pleased. Accompanied by a large number of gods, the grandfather appeared before the

---

[329] Amshumat.

[330] So as to bring Ganga down.

[331] Gomukha, near Gangotri.

[332] To meditate amidst four fires on four sides, with the sun above one's head.

great-souled Bhageeratha, who was tormenting himself through austerities, and said, "O Bhageeratha! O immensely fortunate one! O lord of men! I am pleased with you. You have tormented yourself with excellent austerities. O one who is great in vows! Accept a boon." The immensely energetic and immensely fortunate Bhageeratha joined his hands in salutation and spoke to the grandfather of all the worlds. "O illustrious one! If you are pleased with me and if my austerities have borne fruit, let all of Sagara's sons obtain water through me. With their ashes sprinkled with the water of the Ganga, let all my great-souled great grandfathers find their ultimate objective in heaven. O god! Grant me offspring. There is no one in our lineage, in this lineage of the Ikshvakus. This is the next boon that I ask for." Having been thus addressed, the grandfather of all the worlds replied in auspicious and sweet words, which were full of sweet syllables, to the king. "O Bhageeratha! O maharatha! This desire of yours is great. O fortunate one! O extender of the lineage of the Ikshvakus! It shall be this way. Ganga, who flows through the Himalayas, is the eldest daughter of the Himalayas. O king! The earth is incapable of withstanding the descent of the Ganga. O king! Hara[333] has been given the task of bearing her burden. O brave one! With the exception of the wielder of the trident, I do not see anyone else who can take on that burden." Speaking in this way to the king, the creator of the worlds addressed Ganga. With the large number of gods, the god then went to heaven.'

## Chapter 1(42)

'O Rama! When the god of the gods[334] had departed, he[335] pressed down on the earth with his big toe and stood there, performing austerities for one year. When one year had passed, Pashupati, Uma's consort, worshipped by all the worlds, spoke to the king. "O best

---

[333] Shiva.
[334] Brahma.
[335] Bhageeratha. He performed austerities in that way, standing on his toe.

among men! I am pleased with you. I will do what is agreeable to
you. I will bear the daughter of the king of the mountains on my
head. O Rama! The eldest daughter of the Himalayas is worshipped
by all the worlds. She assumed an extremely great form, with a force
that is difficult to withstand. She descended from the sky, on Shiva's
auspicious head. Having been released from there, she was confused
by that mass of matted hair. The goddess roamed around there for
a large number of years. O descendant of the Raghu lineage! Hara
was extremely delighted at this and eventually released Ganga in the
direction of Vindusara.[336] The gods, the rishis, the gandharvas, the
yakshas and the large number of siddhas witnessed the progress of
Ganga from the sky to that spot. The gods were stationed on celestial
vehicles that were like cities, yoked to the best of horses and elephants.
These mounts staggered at the sight. The supreme descent of Ganga
on the earth was extraordinary. All the infinitely energetic gods who
had assembled witnessed this. As they were surprised, the ornaments
fell down from the bodies of these infinitely energetic gods and it was
as if one hundred suns glittered amidst the clouds in the sky. Large
numbers of porpoises, serpents and fish were agitated. It was as if
flashes of lightning were streaked throughout the sky. Thousands of
flows of foam from the water were splashed around. It was as if a
flock of swans was stretched out against clouds in the autumn sky. In
some places, the flow coursed speedily. In other places, it meandered
along curves. In some places, the flow was humble and slow. In other
places, it proceeded faster and faster. In some places, water dashed
against water and rose up in torrents. It rose up in an instant and then
fell down on the earth again. Dislodged once,[337] it was dislodged once
again from Shankara's head on to the surface of the earth. Devoid
of all taints, the sparkling water roamed freely. The large number of
rishis, gandharvas and the residents of earth touched the sacred water
released from Bhava's[338] body. There were those who were cursed and
had fallen down from the sky to earth. They were sprinkled with this
water and cleansed of all sin. With their sins cleansed by the water,

---

[336] A lake near Gangotri.
[337] From the sky.
[338] Shiva's name.

they regained their radiant forms. They again headed towards the sky and regained their own respective worlds. Cheerfully, the world sprinkled itself with that resplendent water. Cleansed of sin, everyone was delighted. Bhageeratha, the royal sage, was on a celestial chariot. As the immensely energetic one proceeded in front, Ganga followed him at the rear. O Rama! The gods, the rishis, all the daityas, danavas and rakshasas, the best of gandharvas and yakshas, kinnaras and giant serpents and all the apsaras followed Bhageeratha's chariot. All the aquatic creatures also cheerfully followed Ganga. Wherever King Bhageeratha went, the illustrious Ganga, best among rivers and the cleanser of all sins, followed.'

## Chapter 1(43)

'The king went to the ocean and penetrated the surface of the ground where the mounds of ashes were, followed by Ganga. O Rama! The ashes were sprinkled with the waters of the Ganga. Brahma, the lord of all the worlds, spoke these words to the king. "O tiger among men! Sagara's sixty thousand great-souled sons have been saved and will go to heaven, like gods. O king! As long as there is water in this ocean on earth, till then, Sagara's sons will reside in heaven, like gods. This Ganga will be known as your eldest daughter. Because of your deeds, she will be famous on earth through your name. The divine Ganga, with three flows, will be known as Bhageerathee. Since she has three flows, she will be known as Tripathaga.[339] O lord of men! Perform the water rites for all your ancestors here. O king! You will thus accomplish your pledge. O king! Your ancestors were exceedingly illustrious. However, even though they were supremely devoted to dharma, they could not achieve what you have. O son![340] In that way, Amshumat was infinitely energetic in this world. However,

[339] The one with three courses.
[340] The word used is tata.

even he could not accomplish the pledge of bringing Ganga down. Your father, Dileepa, was immensely fortunate and infinite in his energy. He was a royal sage, but like a maharshi in his qualities. Though he was established in the dharma of kshatriyas, he was like me in austerities. O unblemished one! Even he was unable to accomplish his desire of bringing Ganga down. O bull among men! However, you have been able to accomplish your pledge. You will obtain supreme worlds and fame and will be greatly revered. O destroyer of enemies! You have accomplished the task of bringing Ganga down. Because of this, you have obtained a great deal of dharma. O supreme among men! O tiger among men! You will always be able to bathe yourself in these waters and purify yourself, thus obtaining sacred fruits. Now go and perform the water rites for all your ancestors. O king! May you be fortunate. I will now go to my own world and so should you." The lord of the gods, the grandfather of all the worlds, spoke in this way. After this, the immensely illustrious one went away to the world of the gods, which is where he had come from. The royal sage, Bhageeratha, performed the excellent water rites for the immensely illustrious sons of Sagara, as is proper, and following the due order. Having purified himself by bathing in the water, the king entered his own city. O best among men! O Raghava! For the sake of prosperity, he ruled his own kingdom well and the people were delighted to get their king back. He was devoid of sorrow and devoid of anxiety. He was prosperous and wealthy. O Rama! I have thus told you about Ganga in detail. O fortunate one! May you be safe. The time for sandhya has passed. This account of Ganga's descent, recounted by me, is blessed and brings fame, long life, heaven and sons.'

# Chapter 1(44)

On hearing Vishvamitra's words, Rama and Lakshmana were overcome by great wonder. Rama told Vishvamitra, 'O brahmana! The account recited by you, about Ganga's sacred descent and the filling up of the ocean, is wonderful. With Soumitri, I spent the entire night thinking about the auspicious account that you had told us.' When a sparkling morning dawned, after having performed the morning ablutions, Raghava, the destroyer of enemies, spoke these words to Vishvamitra, the great sage. 'While we heard this supreme account, the illustrious night has passed. O great ascetic! It is as if the entire night passed in a single instant, as we reflected on everything that you have told us. We now have to cross this best of rivers, the sacred river with the three flows. O illustrious one! On knowing that you have come, the rishis, the performers of auspicious deeds, have swiftly come here and have brought boats with comfortable spreads.' On hearing Raghava's words, the great-souled one,[341] made arrangements for crossing over, with Raghava and with the large number of rishis. Having reached the northern bank, they worshipped all the rishis. They saw the city of Vishala,[342] situated on the banks of the Ganga. With Raghava, the supreme among sages quickly proceeded towards the beautiful city of Vishala, which was as divine as heaven.

The immensely wise Rama joined his hands in salutation and asked Vishvamitra, the great sage, about the supreme city of Vishala. 'O great sage! To which royal lineage does Vishala belong? O fortunate one! I am supremely curious and wish to hear about this.' Hearing Rama's words, the bull among sages started to recount the ancient tale about Vishala. 'O Rama! Listen to what I have heard. This is an auspicious account about Shakra. O Raghava! Hear the truth about what happened in this region. O Rama! Earlier, in krita yuga, there were the extremely strong sons of Diti. Aditi had immensely fortunate and brave sons who were extremely devoted to dharma.[343] O tiger among men! Those great-souled

---

[341] Vishvamitra.

[342] Vaishali, in Bihar.

[343] Diti and Aditi were the daughters of Daksha and married the sage Kashyapa. Diti's sons were the daityas, loosely, the demons. Aditi's sons were the *adityas*, the gods. Diti was older, so the daityas were elder brothers of the gods. Daksha had another daughter named Danu, also married to Kashyapa. Danavas are her sons. However, daityas, danavas and asuras (the counter to *suras* or gods) are words often used synonymously.

ones began to think about how they might be immortal, about
how they might be without old age and without disease. O Rama!
Reflecting on this, those learned ones arrived at a conclusion. They
would churn the ocean and obtain juices from this.[344] Having made
up their minds to churn, they made Vasuki the rope to be used
for churning. With Mount Mandara as the churning road, those
infinitely energetic ones started to churn. Dhanvantari[345] arose and
so did the extremely radiant apsaras.[346] O best among men! Since
those supreme women were generated when the juices of the water
were churned, they came to be known as apsaras. Sixty crores of
such immensely radiant apsaras arose. O Kakutstha! The number
of their attendants was infinite. None of the gods or the danavas
wished to accept them. Since they were not accepted, they came to
be known as general women.[347] O descendant of the Raghu lineage!
The immensely fortunate Varuni,[348] Varuna's daughter, arose and
began to search for the path that she should follow. O Rama! Diti's
sons did not accept her, Varuna's daughter. O brave one! Aditi's
sons accepted that unblemished one. Thereby, the daityas came
to be asuras and Aditi's sons became suras.[349] Having accepted
Varuni, the suras were delighted and rejoiced. O best among men!
Uchchaishrava, best among horses, arose, and so did the jewel
Koustubha. O Rama! So did the supreme amrita and there was a
great destruction of the lineage because of that. The sons of Aditi
devastated the sons of Diti. The brave sons of Aditi slaughtered
Diti's sons in that great, terrible and fierce battle that raged between
the daityas and the adityas. When Diti's sons were slain, Purandara
obtained the kingdom. Delighted, he ruled over the worlds, with
large numbers of rishis and charanas.'

---

[344] The juices mean amrita, the nectar that confers immortality.

[345] The physician of the gods. The Critical Edition excises shlokas about poison
emerging and Shiva drinking the poison.

[346] Etymologically, apsara means someone created from the water.

[347] That is, apsaras were never married to anyone.

[348] The goddess of liquor.

[349] Sura means liquor and the gods became suras because they accepted Varuni.
Rejecting Varuni, the daityas became asuras, those without liquor.

# Chapter 1(45)

'When her sons were killed, Diti was extremely miserable.
O Rama! She went to her husband Kashyapa, the son of
Marichi, and said, "O illustrious! Your immensely strong sons[350]
have killed my sons. Through a long period of austerities, I wish
to obtain a son who will kill Shakra. I will observe austerities and
you should grant me such a conception. I seek your permission
to obtain a son who will be Indra's slayer." Hearing her words,
the immensely energetic Kashyapa, Marichi's son, replied to Diti,
who was supremely afflicted by grief. "O fortunate one! O store
of austerities! This will indeed be the case if you remain pure.
You will give birth to a son who will kill Shakra in an encounter.
However, you will have to remain pure for the entire duration of
one thousand years. Through me, you will then give birth to a son
who will destroy the three worlds. Having said this, the immensely
energetic one touched her with his hand and embraced her. Saying,
"May you be safe," he left for his own austerities. O best among
men! When he had departed, Diti was greatly delighted. She went
to Kushaplavana[351] and tormented herself through extremely
terrible austerities. O best among men! While she observed these
austerities, the thousand-eyed one,[352] full of supreme qualities,
tended to her. The thousand-eyed one supplied her with whatever
she desired—fire, *kusha* grass, kindling, water, fruits, roots and
everything else. To remove her exhaustion, he massaged her body.
Through the entire period, Shakra tended to Diti. O descendant of
the Raghu lineage! Only ten years were left for the thousand years
to be completed. Extremely happy, Diti told the one with the one
thousand eyes, "O supreme among valiant ones! Only ten years
are left for my austerities to be complete. O fortunate one! When
those are over, you will be able to see your brother. O son! It is for
your sake that I will rear him as someone who wishes for victory. O

---

[350] The gods.
[351] A hermitage to the east of Vishala.
[352] Indra.

son! He will conquer the three worlds and you will be able to enjoy
them with him, without any anxiety." As Diti spoke in this way,
the sun reached the midpoint of the sky. The goddess went to sleep,
with her feet placed where her head should have been.[353] Since her
feet were where her head should have been, Shakra saw that she
had become impure. He was delighted to see that her head was
where her feet should have been and laughed. O Rama! Through
that weakness, Purandara entered her body. The supremely brave
one split her embryo into seven parts. He shattered the embryo
with a vajra that possessed one hundred joints. O Rama! Diti woke
up at the sound of the weeping and lamenting. Shakra addressed
the embryo, "Do not cry! Do not cry!" However, having been
shattered by the immensely energetic Vasava, it continued to cry.
Diti exclaimed, "Do not kill it. Do not kill it." To show respect
to his mother's[354] words, Shakra fell out of the body. Still holding
the vajra, Shakra joined his hands in salutation and told Diti, "O
goddess! You are impure. You slept with your head in the direction
that your feet should have been in. I got the chance to strike at the
one who would kill Shakra in an encounter. O goddess! I shattered
it into seven fragments. You should pardon this act."'

## Chapter 1(46)

'When the embryo was shattered into seven fragments, Diti
was extremely miserable. She entreated the invincible
and thousand-eyed one in these words. "The embryo has been
shattered into seven fragments because of my crime. O lord of the

---

[353] Indra didn't really want to help and serve her. He didn't want the son to be born
and was in close attendance to spot for a weakness in Diti. Obviously, Diti shouldn't have
slept in the afternoon. In addition, when sleeping, the head should be in a certain direction,
usually east or south, and the feet should face the opposite direction. In her carelessness,
Diti did the opposite.

[354] Stepmother.

gods! O slayer of Bala![355] No sin attaches to you because of this. Though my embryo has been destroyed, I wish that you should do something agreeable for me. Let the seven times seven Maruts become guardians of different places.[356] Let these seven sons of mine roam around in the firmament, on the shoulders of the wind. Let these sons of mine be divine in form and let them be famous as Maruts. Let one of them roam around in Brahma's world and another in Indra's world. Let the third and immensely illustrious one be known as the wind that blows through the firmament. O best among the gods! Let the fourth follow your command and roam around in the directions. Let the name Maruts be given by you and let them be known as this." Hearing her words, the thousand-eyed Purandara joined his hands in salutation. Bala's slayer spoke the following words to Diti. "There is no doubt that everything will occur exactly as you have spoken. O fortunate one! Your sons will roam around in the form of gods." This is what mother and son decided in that hermitage. O Rama! Having become successful, we have heard that they[357] proceeded to heaven. O Kakutstha! In ancient times, this is the country where the great Indra used to reside. This is where Diti obtained success in her austerities and he tended to her.

'O tiger among men! Ikshvaku had a son who was supremely devoted to dharma. His mother was Alambusha and he was famous as Vishala.[358] In this spot, he is the one who constructed the city of Vishala. O Rama! Vishala's son was the immensely strong Hemachandra. After this, Hemachandra's son was the famous Suchandra. O Rama! Suchandra's son was famous by the name of Dhumrashva. Dhumrashva had a son named Srinjaya.

---

[355] Indra killed a demon named Bala.

[356] The Maruts are wind gods and the word is derived from do not (*ma*) cry (*ruda*). The Maruts are Indra's companions. They are usually said to be seven in number. But sometimes, each of the seven is divided into another seven, so that there are forty-nine Maruts. The Maruts are rarely named individually. One possible listing of the seven Maruts is Avaha, Pravaha, Samvaha, Udvaha, Vivaha, Parivaha and Varavaha.

[357] Diti and Indra.

[358] The son was named Vishaala (Vishala), while the city was named Vishaalaa. This Ikshvaku is clearly different from the Ikshvaku of Ayodhya.

Srinjaya's son was the handsome and powerful Sahadeva. Kushashva was Sahadeva's son and he was extremely devoted to dharma. Kushashva had a greatly energetic and powerful son, Somadatta. Somadatta's son was known as Kakutstha. His son is greatly famous and invincible. That immensely energetic one is named Sumati and he is the one who now resides in this city. Through Ikshvaku's favours, all the kings of Vishala are great-souled, valiant and extremely devoted to dharma. They have long lives. O Rama! We will happily spend the night here. O best among men! Tomorrow, when it is morning, we should see Janaka.' The immensely energetic and greatly illustrious Sumati heard that Vishvamitra had come. On hearing this, the best among men came out to welcome him. With his priests and relatives, he worshipped him in excellent ways. Asking about his welfare, he joined his hands in salutation and told Vishvamitra, 'O sage! I am blessed that you have shown me your favours by coming to my kingdom. I have now seen you. There is no one who is more fortunate than I am.'

## Chapter 1(47)

Having met, they asked about each other's welfare. After the conversation was over, Sumati addressed the great sage in these words. 'O fortunate one! These two young ones are like the gods in their valour. These brave ones possess the strides of elephants and lions. They are like tigers and bulls. Their eyes are large, like the petals of lotuses. They hold swords, quivers and bows. They are about to become adults and are as handsome as the Ashvins. They are like immortals from the world of the gods, who have followed their will and come down to earth. Why have they come here? O sage! What is the reason? Whose sons are they? They are ornaments for this kingdom, like the moon and the sun in the sky. The proportions of their limbs and signs are just like each other's, identical. What is the reason why these best of men have traversed this difficult path?[359] These brave ones wield the best of weapons. I wish to hear the truth about this.' Hearing his words, Vishvamitra told him about what had happened—the residence in Siddhashrama and the slaughter of the rakshasas. Hearing Vishvamitra's words, the king was greatly delighted. Dasharatha's sons had arrived there, as great guests. He worshipped them in the proper way and tended to the two extremely strong ones. The two Raghavas were honoured extremely well by Sumati. After having spent a night there, they left for Mithila.

On seeing Janaka's sacred city, all the sages had words of commendation and praise for Mithila and worshipped it. Raghava saw that there was a hermitage in a grove near Mithila. 'This looks like a beautiful hermitage. Why has it been abandoned by the sages? O illustrious one! I wish to hear about it. Whose hermitage was it earlier?' Hearing the words spoken by Raghava, the immensely energetic and great sage, Vishvamitra, eloquent in the use of words, replied. 'O Raghava! I will tell you with pleasure. Hear the truth about whose hermitage this was and which great-souled one cursed it in rage. O best among men! Earlier, it belonged to the great-souled Goutama. This hermitage was divine and it was worshipped even by the gods. Earlier, he practised austerities here, together with Ahalya. O prince! The immensely illustrious one spent innumerable years here. Discerning that there was an opportunity,[360] the thousand-eyed one, Shachi's husband,[361] assumed the garb of a sage. He came to Ahalya and addressed her in these words. "O one who is well proportioned! Those who seek pleasure[362] do not wait for the time of conception to arrive. O slender-waisted one! I desire to have intercourse with you." O descendant of the Raghu lineage! She knew that it was the one with the one thousand eyes in the garb of a sage. However, because of her curiosity, the evil-minded one acceded to what the king of the gods wanted. Satisfied in her heart of hearts, she

[359] They could have used other means to come there.
[360] Goutama was away.
[361] Shachi is Indra's wife.
[362] As opposed to those who seek progeny.

told the best of the gods, "O best among the gods! I have been
satiated. O lord! However, leave this spot quickly. O lord of the
gods! O one who shows honours! Always protect me and your
own self." Indra laughed at these words and told Ahalya, "O one
with the excellent hips! I am also satiated. I will go back to where
I have come from." After the act of intercourse, he emerged from
the cottage. O Rama! He was terrified and scared that Goutama
might return. He saw that the great sage, Goutama, was entering.
He was full of the strength of austerities and the gods and danavas
found him impossible to withstand. He blazed like the fire and
was wet with water from various tirthas. The bull among sages
arrived there, after collecting kindling and kusha grass. On seeing
him, the lord of the gods was terrified. His face bore the marks of
distress. Seeing the one with the one thousand eyes, attired in the
garb of a sage, the sage, full of good conduct, became angry. He
spoke these words to the one with evil conduct. "O evil-minded
one! You have assumed my form[363] and have done this. Since
you have done what should not have been done, you will become
infertile." The great-souled sage, Goutama, said this in rage and
instantly, the testicles of the thousand-eyed one fell down on the
ground. Having cursed Shakra, he also cursed his wife. "You
will reside here for many thousands of years. Subsisting on air
and without food, you will torment yourself through austerities.
You will sleep on ashes. You will live in this hermitage, unseen
by all creatures. When the invincible Rama, Dasharatha's son,
arrives in this terrible forest, you will be purified. O one who is
evil in conduct! When he becomes your guest, you will lose your
avarice and confusion. You will then regain your own form and
find delight with me." The extremely energetic Goutama spoke
in this way to the one who was evil in conduct. He abandoned
this hermitage, once frequented by siddhas and charanas. The
great ascetic performed austerities on a beautiful summit in the
Himalayas.'

[363] The earlier shlokas didn't make it clear that Indra hadn't assumed the form of any
sage. He had specifically assumed Goutama's form.

# Chapter 1(48)

'Having been rendered infertile, with Agni at the forefront and with a distressed face, Shakra spoke to the gods and large numbers of rishis and charanas. "I have caused an obstruction in the austerities of the great-souled Goutama and have ignited his rage, but I have accomplished a task for the gods.[364] In his rage, he has rendered me infertile and has banished her. Because he released that great curse, I have been able to rob him of his store of austerities.[365] I have helped the cause of the gods. O best among the gods! O large numbers of rishis! O charanas! Therefore, all of you should strive to render me potent again." Hearing Shatakratu's words, the gods, with all the Maruts and with Agni at the forefront, went to the ancestors[366] and spoke these words. "This ram has testicles and Shakra has lost his testicles. Quickly take away the testicles from this ram and give them to Shakra. To cause you delight, if humans offer you rams without testicles, even then, you will grant them supreme satisfaction."[367] Hearing Agni's words, the assembled ancestors severed the ram's testicles and gave them to the thousand-eyed one. O Kakutstha! Since then, the assembled ancestors enjoy rams without testicles and discard the testicles if those are offered.[368] O Raghava! Since then, Indra possesses the testicles of a ram. This is as a result of the power of austerities of the great-souled Goutama. O immensely energetic one! Therefore, enter the hermitage of the performer of auspicious deeds.[369] Save the immensely fortunate Ahalya, who has the form of a goddess.'

---

[364] This requires explanation. Austerities confer power. Sometimes, austerities and consequent powers can be used to dislodge Indra from his status. Therefore, Indra always sought to prevent anyone from successfully completing austerities.

[365] Any curse takes away from the store of austerities/merit accumulated by the one who is doing the cursing.

[366] The *pitris*, usually translated as manes. These are the original ancestors, born through Brahma's mental powers. They are not gods. They are also the souls of dead human ancestors.

[367] Henceforth, ancestors can be offered castrated rams.

[368] If a ram with testicles is offered, they ignore the testicles.

[369] Goutama.

Hearing Vishvamitra's words, with Vishvamitra at the forefront, Raghava entered the hermitage, accompanied by Lakshmana. He saw the immensely fortunate one, radiant in complexion because of her austerities. He approached the one who could not be seen by the worlds, not even by gods and asuras. She had been carefully crafted by the creator, using divine maya. Her limbs were covered in smoke and she was like the blazing flames of a fire. She was like a cloud covered in snowy mist, with a radiance like that of the full moon. She was unapproachable, with the complexion of the blazing sun, amidst a store of water. Because of Goutama's words, she had been rendered invisible to the three worlds, until she had seen Rama. The two Raghavas approached her and touched her feet. Remembering Goutama's words, she received them. Extremely controlled, she treated them as guests and offered padya and arghya. Following the prescribed rites, Kakutstha accepted this hospitality. A great shower of flowers descended from above and the drums of the gods were sounded. There was a large assembly of gandharvas and apsaras. The gods worshipped Ahalya and uttered words of praise. She had followed Goutama's instructions and had purified her limbs through the strength of austerities. The immensely energetic Goutama was happy with Ahalya. Following the prescribed ordinances, the great ascetic worshipped Rama. Rama also worshipped the great sage, Goutama, in excellent ways. Having met him in the proper way, he then moved on to Mithila.

## Chapter 1(49)

With Vishvamitra at the forefront and with Soumitri, Rama then travelled towards the north-east and arrived at the sacrificial arena. With Lakshmana, Rama spoke to the tiger among sages. 'The sacrifice of the great-souled Janaka is auspicious and prosperous. O immensely fortunate one! There are many thousand brahmanas who have come here. There are the residents of many countries and are accomplished in studying the Vedas. The

residences of the rishis can be seen and there are hundreds of carts.
O brahmana! We should identify a proper spot for us to dwell.'
Hearing Rama's words, Vishvamitra, the great sage, instructed
that an abode should be constructed in an uninhabited spot that
had water.

Hearing that Vishvamitra, the best among sages, had arrived,
the great king came, with his unblemished priest, Shatananda, at
the forefront. With arghya, the great-souled officiating priests also
arrived. Following dharma, they offered this and water sanctified
with mantras to Vishvamitra. The great-souled one accepted
Janaka's worship. He asked about the king's welfare and about
whether all was well with the sacrifice. As is proper, the sage
cheerfully asked about the priests and the preceptors and about
all those who had arrived. The king joined his hands in salutation
and spoke to the best among sages. 'O illustrious one! With all the
excellent sages, please be seated.' Hearing Janaka's words, the great
sage sat down. With his officiating priest[370] at the forefront, and
with his ministers, so did the king. On seeing that everyone had
properly sat down on seats in different directions, the king spoke to
Vishvamitra. 'Today, the gods have ensured that my sacrifice will
be successful. O illustrious one! Now that I have seen you, I will
obtain the fruits of the sacrifice. I am blessed. I am favoured. O
bull among sages! O brahmana! With all the sages, you have come
to this sacrificial arena. O brahmana rishi! The learned ones have
said that only twelve days remain for the sacrifice to be concluded.
O Koushika! You should remain here, to see the gods receive their
shares.' With a cheerful face, the king addressed the tiger among
sages in this way.

Controlling himself, he joined his hands in salutation and
asked, 'O fortunate one! These two young ones are like the gods in
their valour. These brave ones possess the strides of elephants and
lions. They are like tigers and bulls. They have large eyes that are
like the petals of lotuses. They hold swords, quivers and bows. They
are like the Ashvins in beauty and are about to become adults. They

[370] Shatananda.

are like immortals from the world of the gods, who have voluntarily come down to earth. O sage! Why have they come here on foot? What is the reason? Whose sons are they? O great sage! These brave ones wield the best of weapons. Whose sons are they? They are ornaments for this country, like the moon and the sun in the sky. They are identical to each other, in the proportion of their limbs and in their bodily signs. These brave ones possess sidelocks that are like the wings of a crow. I wish to hear the truth about this.' Hearing the words of Janaka, the great-souled one told him that these two were Dasharatha's great-souled sons. He also recounted the residence in Siddhashrama, the slaughter of the rakshasas, their subsequent sight of Vishala, the meeting with Ahalya, Goutama's arrival and their decision to come there, to examine the great bow. Vishvamitra, the great sage, told all this to the great-souled and immensely energetic Janaka. He then stopped.

## Chapter 1(50)

Hearing the words of the intelligent Vishvamitra, the body hair of the immensely energetic and great sage, Shatananda, stood up. He was Goutama's eldest son and was extremely radiant because of his austerities. Having seen Rama, he was supremely astounded. Those two princes were happily seated, with their heads bowed. On seeing them, Shatananda spoke to Vishvamitra, best among sages. 'O tiger among sages! After having performed austerities for a long period of time, my illustrious mother[371] showed herself to these two princes. Using forest fare, my illustrious mother worshipped the immensely energetic Rama, who deserves to be worshipped by all creatures that have bodies. You have told Rama about the ancient account, whereby my mother was treated badly by that immensely energetic god.[372] O Koushika! O fortunate

---

[371] Ahalya was Shatananda's mother.
[372] Indra.

one! O best among sages! After having met Rama, my mother has been united with my senior.[373] O descendant of Kushika! My senior has been worshipped by Rama. The immensely energetic and great-souled one has now arrived here and deserves to be worshipped. O descendant of Kushika! Before coming here, did Rama honour my father with a peaceful and controlled state of mind?' The great sage, Vishvamitra, was accomplished in the use of words and eloquent in speech. Hearing Shatananda's words, he replied, 'O best among sages! I have not neglected anything that I could have done. The sage has been united with his wife, just as Bhargava was with Renuka.'[374]

Hearing the words of the intelligent Vishvamitra, the immensely energetic Shatananda spoke these words to Rama. 'O best among men! Welcome. O Raghava! It is good fortune that you have come here, with Vishvamitra, the unvanquished maharshi, leading the way. The brahmana rishi is infinite in his splendour and austerities and has accomplished unthinkable deeds. The immensely energetic Vishvamitra has to be recognized as the supreme destination. O Rama! The truth is that there is no one on earth who is more blessed than he is. You have been protected by Kushika's son, who tormented himself through great austerities. Listen. I will tell you about the great-souled Koushika, about his strength and his conduct. Listen attentively. For a long time, this destroyer of enemies used to be a king, with dharma in his soul. He knew about dharma and was accomplished in learning. He was devoted to the welfare of the subjects. There was a king named Kusha and he was Prajapati's son. Kusha's son was the powerful Kushanabha, who was extremely devoted to dharma. Kushanabha's son was the famous Gadhi. The immensely energetic and great sage, Vishvamitra, is Gadhi's son. The immensely energetic Vishvamitra ruled over the earth. He was a king and ruled the kingdom for many thousand years. On one occasion, the immensely energetic

[373] His father, Goutama.

[374] Goutama has been united with Ahalya. Bhargava means a descendant of the Bhrigu lineage. Here, Bhargava means Jamadagni, Parashurama's father. Jamadagni's wife was Renuka. On Jamadagni's instructions, Parashurama beheaded Renuka. However, subsequently, Renuka was reunited with Jamadagni.

one arrayed an army. Surrounded by an akshouhini, he roamed around the earth. The king progressively travelled through cities, kingdoms, rivers and mountains and arrived at a hermitage. This was Vasishtha's hermitage and there were trees with many kinds of flowers and fruit there. There were diverse kinds of animals and the place was frequented by siddhas and charanas. It was adorned by gods, danavas and gandharvas and those who were in the form of kinnaras. It was populated by peaceful deer and large numbers of birds dwelt there. It was full of a large number of brahmana rishis and inhabited by *devarshi*s.[375] There were siddhas who practised austerities and those great-souled ones were like the fire. There was prosperity everywhere and there were great-souled ones who were like Brahma. Some lived on water, others survived on air. There were others who subsisted on dry leaves. There were self-controlled ones who lives on fruits and roots. They had conquered anger and had conquered their senses. There were *valakhilya* rishis,[376] devoted to chanting and the offering of oblations. Vasishtha's hermitage was like Brahma's world. The immensely strong Vishvamitra, best among victorious ones, saw that.'

# Chapter 1(51)

'Seeing this, the immensely strong Vishvamitra was greatly delighted. In humility, the brave one bowed down before Vasishtha, supreme among those who meditate. The great-souled Vasishtha said, "Welcome." The illustrious Vasishtha requested him to take a seat. When the intelligent Vishvamitra had seated himself, as is proper, the supreme among sages offered him roots and fruits. The supreme among kings accepted the honour Vasishtha showed him. The immensely energetic Vishvamitra asked him about the well-being of austerities, the agnihotra, his disciples

---

[375] Divine sages.
[376] 60,000 sages who were the sizes of thumbs. They preceded the sun's chariot.

and the trees. Vasishtha told the supreme among kings that all was
well, everywhere. King Vishvamitra was seated comfortably. The
great ascetic, Vasishtha, Brahma's son[377] and best among those who
meditate, then asked, "O king! Is everything well with you? Do you
take delight in dharma? O king! O one who follows dharma! Are you
upright in ruling over your subjects? Are your servants well trained?
Do they adhere to your commands? O slayer of enemies! Have you
defeated all your enemies? O scorcher of enemies! O tiger among
men! O unblemished one! Is everything well about your army,
treasury, friends and your sons and grandsons?" The king told
Vasishtha that all was well, everywhere. The immensely energetic
Vishvamitra behaved in a humble way towards Vasishtha. Devoted
to dharma, they spent a long period of time in conversing about
auspicious accounts. They were supremely delighted and behaved
affectionately towards each other. O descendant of the Raghu
lineage! When the conversation was over, the illustrious Vasishtha
smiled and spoke these words to Vishvamitra. "O greatly strong
one! I wish to show my hospitality towards you and your army.
O immeasurable one! Accept the honours that you deserve. I wish
to behave properly towards you. Please accept what I am about to
render. O king! You are the best of guests and I will make efforts
to show you worship." When Vasishtha spoke in this way, the
immensely intelligent King Vishvamitra replied, "You have already
shown me hospitality. You have given me honours through your
words. O illustrious one! I have received the fruits and roots that
can be obtained in the hermitage. O illustrious one! I have received
padya and achamaniya and I have seen you. O immensely wise one!
You have worshipped me well in every possible way of worship.
I bow down before you. I will depart now. Please look on me
with eyes of affection."[378] The king spoke in this way. However,
Vasishtha, with dharma in his soul, invited him again and repeatedly
entreated him. At this, Gadhi's son agreed and replied to Vasishtha,
"O illustrious one! O supreme sage! Then, so be it—whatever

---

[377] Through Brahma's mental powers.

[378] Vishvamitra was conscious that a hermitage couldn't have offered proper hospitality
to a king and his army.

brings you pleasure." Thus addressed, the immensely energetic Vasishtha, supreme among those who meditate, was delighted. The one who was cleansed of sin summoned his speckled cow. "O Shabala![379] Come here quickly and listen to my words. I wish to make all the arrangements to treat this royal sage and his army. Make all the arrangements for an extremely expensive banquet. Let every desirable food be brought, characterized by the six kinds of flavour.[380] O divine one! O one who yields every object of desire! For my sake, shower all of this down. Let the food be succulent. Let there be drink. Let there be *lehya* and *choshya*.[381] O Shabala! Swiftly create a store of every kind of food."'

## Chapter 1(52)

'O slayer of enemies! Vasishtha spoke to Shabala in this way. The cow that can be milked for every object of desire brought everything that had been wished for. There were sugar cane, honey, parched grain, *maireya*, the best of *asava*,[382] expensive kinds of drink and diverse kinds of food to eat. There were heaps of hot food, piled as high as mountains. There were sweetmeats, liquids and flows of curds. There were many kinds of succulent juices, with the six kinds of flavours. The vessels were full with thousands of products made out of cane. All the people there were satisfied. They ate well and were cheerful. O Rama! Vasishtha made Vishvamitra's army content. The royal sage, Vishvamitra, rejoiced at having been fed so well. Those who were in the king's inner quarters[383] and the brahmanas and the priests were also fed well.

---

[379] *Shabala* means speckled or spotted. This was a *kamadhenu*, a cow that could yield every object of desire.

[380] Caustic, acidic, sweet, salty, bitter and alkaline.

[381] The four types of food are those that are chewed (*charvya*), sucked (*choshya* or *chushya*), licked (*lehya*) and drunk (*peya*).

[382] Both maireya and asava are kinds of liquor. Specifically, maireya is made from molasses or grain and asava is made through a process of distillation, not mere fermentation.

[383] The royal ladies.

The advisers, ministers and servants were also honoured in this way. Filled with great delight, he[384] spoke to Vasishtha. "O brahmana! You deserve to be worshipped. Yet, you have honoured us well and worshipped us. O one who is eloquent in speech! Hear my words now. Give me Shabala in exchange for one hundred thousand cows. O illustrious one! She is a jewel and a king is the one who should accumulate jewels. O brahmana! Give me Shabala. According to dharma, she belongs to me." The illustrious Vasishtha, supreme among sages, was addressed in this way. The one with dharma in his soul replied to Vishvamitra, the lord of the earth. "O king! In exchange for one hundred thousand cows, one billion cows, or large amounts of silver, I am incapable of giving you Shabala. O destroyer of enemies! I should not abandon her, nor should she be separated from me. Shabala is eternally inseparable from me, like deeds are from one's own self. She is the one who provides *havya*, *kavya*,[385] the means of sustaining my life and undertaking agnihotra and the source of sacrificial offerings and oblations. She is the source of utterances of *svaha* and *vashatkara*[386] and different kinds of learning. O royal sage! There is no doubt that all of these are obtained because of her. In truth, she represents everything for me and she always satisfies me. O king! There are many kinds of reasons why I cannot give you Shabala." Vasishtha was eloquent in speech and spoke these words. However, Vishvamitra became exceedingly angry and said, "I will give you fourteen thousand elephants that have golden harnesses and are decorated with golden necklaces and golden goads. I will give you eight hundred golden chariots that are ornamented with tinkling bells, each yoked to four white horses. O one who is excellent in vows! I will give you eleven thousand extremely energetic horses, born in noble lineages from the best of countries. I will give you ten million adult cows, classified into different complexions. Give me this single cow, Shabala." When the

---

[384] Vishvamitra.

[385] Offerings to gods are havya, offerings to ancestors are kavya.

[386] Vashatkara is the exclamation *'vashat'* made at the time of offering an oblation. *Svadha* is said at the time of offering oblations to the ancestors and svaha is said at the time of offering oblations to the gods.

intelligent Vishvamitra spoke in this way, the illustrious one replied,
"O king! Under no circumstances will I give you Shabala. She alone
is my gem. She alone represents my treasure. She is everything to
me. She is truly my life. When sacrifices are performed at the time
of the new moon and the full moon, she is the one who supplies the
dakshina. O king! She is the one who ensures the performance of
many kinds of rites. O king! There is no doubt that all my rites have
her as the foundation. There is no need to speak any more. I will not
give the one who can be milked for every object of desire.'"

## Chapter 1(53)

'The sage Vasishtha refused to give up the kamadhenu. O Rama!
Vishvamitra then started to drag Shabala away. O Rama!
As Shabala was dragged away by the great-souled king, she was
miserable. Afflicted by grief and thinking about this, she wept.
"Why have I been abandoned by extremely great-souled Vasishtha?
I am distressed and extremely miserable, being thus seized by the
servants of the king. What injury have I done to the maharshi with
the cleansed soul? I have committed no crime. I am devoted to him
and love him. Why is the one who is devoted to dharma abandoning
me?" She thought in this way and sighed repeatedly. With great
speed, she dashed towards the supremely energetic Vasishtha. O
destroyer of enemies! She flung away the hundreds of servants.
With the speed of the wind, she rushed towards the feet of the great-
souled one. She wept and lamented. Stationed before Vasishtha, in
a voice that was like the rumbling of the clouds, Shabala said, "O
illustrious one! O son of Brahma! Why am I being abandoned by
you? How is it that the servants of the king are dragging me away
from your presence?" The brahmana rishi was thus addressed by
the one whose heart was grief-stricken. She was grieving and was
like his own sister. He said, "O Shabala! I am not abandoning you,
nor have you caused me any injury. The immensely strong king is
dragging you away from me by force. I do not possess the strength

that is equal to his. In particular, he is a king. A king is powerful. The kshatriyas are like the lords of the earth. This akshouhini is full of horses and chariots. There are many elephants and standards. His strength is superior to mine." The brahmana rishi was infinite in his splendour. Thus addressed by Vasishtha, the one who knew about the use of words, humbly replied in these words. "It has been said that the strength of kshatriyas is not superior in power to that of brahmanas. Brahmanas possess the divine strength of the brahman. They are superior to kshatriyas. Your strength is immeasurable. He is not stronger than you. Vishvamitra may be immensely valiant. However, your energy is impossible to withstand. You possess the power of the brahman. Invoke your great energy in me. I will destroy the insolence and strength of that evil-souled one." O Rama! The greatly illustrious Vasishtha then said, "Create an army that will overcome the army of the enemy." O king! With her bellow, she created Pahlavas in hundreds. While Vishvamitra looked on, they destroyed his entire army. The king became extremely angry and his eyes dilated with rage. Using superior and inferior weapons, he destroyed the Pahlavas. On seeing that the hundreds of Pahlavas were afflicted by Vishvamitra, she again created a mixed and terrible force consisting of Shakas and Yavanas. The earth was completely covered by this mixed army of Shakas and Yavanas. They were brave and exceedingly valiant. They blazed like golden filaments in a flower. They wielded long swords and javelins. Their golden complexion seemed to envelop the sky. Like a blazing fire, they burnt down his[387] entire army. At this, the immensely energetic Vishvamitra released his weapons.'

## Chapter 1(54)

'Vasishtha saw that they were being devastated, confounded by Vishvamitra's weapons. He invoked the powers of *yoga*

---

[387] Vishvamitra's.

and urged the kamadhenu to create more forces. Through her bellowing, she created Kambojas who were like the sun in their complexion. The Pahlavas, wielding weapons in their hands, were generated from her udders, the Yavanas from the region around her vagina, the Shakas from the region around her rectum and the *mlechchhas*[388] from her body hair. There were also Haritas and Kiratakas. O descendant of the Raghu lineage! In an instant, they devastated Vishvamitra's army of soldiers, the infantry, the elephants, the cavalry and the chariots. On seeing that the soldiers had been destroyed by the great-souled Vasishtha, one hundred of Vishvamitra's sons attacked Vasishtha, supreme among those who meditate. They wielded many kinds of weapons. With his humkara, the great rishi burnt all of them down. In an instant, the great-souled Vasishtha reduced Vishvamitra's sons to ashes, with their horses, chariots and foot soldiers. The extremely illustrious Vishvamitra saw that the army of his sons was destroyed. He was ashamed and immersed in thought. It[389] was like an ocean without force, like a defanged serpent and like a sun without colour, having just lost its radiance. With his sons slain, he was distressed, like a bird that has lost its wings. His insolence was destroyed, his enterprise was destroyed and he didn't know what to do.

'Engaging the single son who was left to rule over the kingdom and the earth, following the dharma of kshatriyas, he resorted to the forest. He went to the slopes of the Himalayas, frequented by kinnaras and serpents. To obtain the favours of Mahadeva, the great ascetic tormented himself through austerities. After a long period of time, the lord of the gods, the granter of boons who has the bull on his banner, showed himself to Vishvamitra, the great sage. "O king! Why are you engaged in these austerities? Tell me what you desire. I am the one who grants boons. What boon do you wish for? Let it be known." Thus addressed by the god, the great ascetic, Vishvamitra, prostrated himself and spoke these words to Mahadeva. "O Mahadeva! O unblemished one! If you

---

[388] Barbarians, non-Aryans, those who did not speak Sanskrit.
[389] The army.

are satisfied with me, bestow on me dhanurveda and its various
limbs and the Upanishads with their different limbs and mysteries.
O unblemished one! Let all the weapons that are known to gods,
danavas, maharshis, gandharvas, yakshas and rakshasas manifest
themselves before me. O god of the gods! Through your favours,
may I obtain what I desire." Saying that he agreed to this, the lord
of the gods went away to heaven. The immensely strong royal sage,
Vishvamitra, obtained these weapons. He was filled with great
insolence. He was full of pride. His valour increased, like that of
the ocean on the day of the full moon. He thought that the supreme
rishi, Vasishtha, was already dead. The king went to the hermitage
and released these weapons. He burnt down the entire hermitage
with the energy of these weapons. On seeing that the place was
devastated because of the weapons released by the intelligent
Vishvamitra, all the sages were terrified and fled in hundreds of
directions. Vasishtha's disciples and the birds and animals were
frightened. Scared, they fled in thousands of directions. The great-
souled Vasishtha's hermitage became deserted. In an instant,
it became as silent as a cremation ground. Vasishtha repeatedly
said, "Do not be frightened. I will destroy Gadhi's son, like the
sun dispels the mist." The immensely energetic Vasishtha, supreme
among those who meditate, said this. Angrily, he spoke these words
to Vishvamitra. "I have nurtured this hermitage for a long time
and you have destroyed it. You are foolish and evil in conduct.
Therefore, you will no longer survive." Saying this, in great rage,
he quickly raised his staff. It was like the fire of destruction, devoid
of smoke, and was just like the other staff.'[390]


## Chapter 1(55)

'The immensely strong Vasishtha spoke in this way to
Vishvamitra. Asking him to wait, he raised the Agneya

---

[390] A reference to Yama's rod or staff.

weapon.[391] In anger, the illustrious Vasishtha spoke these words. "O worthless kshatriya! Stay there and show me whatever strength you possess. O son of Gadhi! I will destroy your insolence and your weapons. What is the strength of kshatriyas when it faces the great strength of brahmanas? O worst of kshatriyas! Behold my divine strength, one that comes from being a brahmana." With the supreme Agneya weapon, invoked on the brahmana's rod, he pacified the weapon of Gadhi's son, like a flood of water douses a fire. In rage, Gadhi's descendant hurled *varuna*, roudra, *aindra*, *pashupata* and aishika weapons and *manava*, *mohana*, *gandharva*, *svapana*, *jrimbhana*, *mohana*, *santapana* and *vilapana*.[392] There were *shoshana* and *darana* and the vajra weapon, which is extremely difficult to withstand. There was Brahma's noose, Kala's[393] noose and Varuna's noose. There was the beloved weapon *pinaka*,[394] the weapon that dries up, the weapon that wets and the weapon that is like thunder. There were the weapons *danda*, *paishacha* and *krouncha*.[395] There were the chakras of Dharma, Kala and Vishnu. There were the weapons *vayavya*, *mathana* and *hayashira*.[396] He hurled two spears known as *kankala* and *musala*. There was the extremely great weapon of the Vidyadharas and Kala's terrible weapon. There was the terrible trident and *kapala* and *kankana*.[397] O descendant of the Raghu lineage! He hurled all these different weapons. Vasishtha is supreme among those who meditate and

[391] The rod was invoked with this weapon.

[392] Varuna, roudra, aindra and pashupata are divine weapons respectively associated with Varuna, Rudra, Indra and Shiva. Aishika is a weapon invoked on a blade of grass. Manava means a human weapon, mohana causes confusion, gandharva is associated with the gandharvas, svapana puts to sleep, jrimbhana causes yawning, santapana scorches and vilapana causes lamentations. The Critical text uses the word mohana twice. Non-Critical versions have *madana* in place of the second mohana, meaning a weapon that causes intoxication. Shoshana dries up and darana shatters.

[393] Time or Destiny.

[394] Shiva's bow or trident.

[395] Danda punishes and paishacha is associated with pishachas. In this context, krouncha probably means a weapon tinged with poison.

[396] Vayavya is associated with Vayu, it is a weapon that uses the wind to blow away. Mathana churns and hayashira is a weapon that is in the form of a horse's head.

[397] Kapala is a skull and kankana is something that twirls.

what transpired was extraordinary. The son of a brahmana used
his staff to devour all of these. When all these were pacified, in
anger, Gadhi's descendant invoked *brahmastra*.[398] On seeing that
weapon, on seeing that brahmastra had been invoked, all the gods,
with Agni at the forefront, the divine rishis, the gandharvas, the
giant serpents and all the three worlds were terrified. However,
even that extremely terrible brahmastra was devoured by the
brahmana's energy. O Raghava! Vasishtha devoured everything
through the brahmana's staff. The great-souled Vasishtha devoured
brahmastra and assumed an extremely terrible and fierce form that
confounded the three worlds. From the great-souled Vasishtha's
body hair, flames seemed to emerge and those fiery rays seemed to
be tinged with smoke. The brahmana's staff flamed as it was held
in his hand. It was like the fire of destruction, devoid of smoke, and
was like Yama's rod. The large number of sages praised Vasishtha,
supreme among those who meditate. "O brahmana! Your strength
is invincible and so is the energy you bear and ignite. O brahmana!
You have countered the great ascetic, Vishvamitra. O supreme
among those who meditate! Show your favours. Let the distress of
the worlds be dispelled." Thus addressed, the immensely strong and
great ascetic was calmed. Countered, Vishvamitra sighed and spoke
these words. "Shame on the strength of kshatriyas. The strength of
a brahmana's energy is indeed the strength that is most powerful.
A single staff of a brahmana has destroyed all my weapons. On
examining the matter, my mind and senses are pleased. I will resort
to great austerities so that I can become a brahmana.'"

# Chapter 1(56)

'His heart was tormented,[399] remembering the subjugation
he had been subjected to. Because of the enmity with the

[398] Brahma's weapon.
[399] Vishvamitra's.

great-souled one,[400] he sighed repeatedly. O Raghava! With his wife, he headed for the southern direction. Vishvamitra, the great ascetic, subjected himself to supreme austerities. He followed self-control, practising those supreme austerities and subsisting on fruits and roots. He had sons who were devoted to truth and dharma— Havishpanda, Madhushpanda, Dridhanetra and Maharatha. After a full one thousand years, Brahma, grandfather of the worlds, spoke these sweet words to Vishvamitra, the store of austerities. "O son of Kushika! Through your austerities, you have conquered the worlds meant for rajarshis. Because of your austerities, we will know you as a rajarshi." Having said this, with the other gods, the immensely energetic Brahma, the supreme lord of the worlds, went to heaven and to Brahma's world. Hearing this, Vishvamitra was somewhat ashamed and crestfallen. Full of great misery and intolerance, he said, "Despite my having practised great austerities, all the gods and the large number of rishis have only come to know me as a rajarshi. I think all my austerities have been fruitless." O Kakutstha! Having made up his mind in this way, the supreme-souled and great ascetic undertook supreme austerities again. At that time, there was the famous Trishanku, a descendant of the lineage of the Ikshvakus. He was truthful in speech and had conquered his senses. O Raghava! His mind turned towards undertaking a sacrifice whereby, in his own physical body, he could go to the supreme destination of the gods.[401] Having thought of this, he invited Vasishtha.[402] However, the great-souled Vasishtha expressed his inability. Having been refused by Vasishtha, he left for the southern direction, where Vasishtha's sons had been tormenting themselves through austerities for a long time. Trishanku saw one hundred of Vasishtha's supremely radiant, extremely energetic and illustrious sons, tormenting themselves. He approached all those great-souled sons of his preceptor.[403] He first greeted them, somewhat ashamed and with a downcast face. He joined his hands in salutation and addressed all those greatly

---

[400] Vasishtha.
[401] That is, heaven.
[402] To be the officiating priest at the sacrifice.
[403] Vasishtha.

energetic ones. "I have come here to seek refuge with you. You
are the ones who grant refuge and I am one who seeks refuge. O
fortunate ones! I have been refused by the great-souled Vasishtha.
I wish to perform a great sacrifice and you should grant me your
permission. I have bowed down before all the sons of my preceptor,
seeking their favours. O brahmanas! You have based yourselves in
austerities and I bow down my head and worship you. I desire that
you self-controlled ones should ensure the success of my sacrifice,
so that I can reach the world of the gods in my own physical body.
O stores of austerities! Refused by Vasishtha, I do not see any other
refuge anywhere, with the exception of all the sons of my preceptor.
For all those who belong to the Ikshvaku lineage, priests are the
supreme destination. Therefore, thereafter,[404] all of you are like
gods to me."'

## Chapter 1(57)

'O Rama! On hearing Trishanku's words, the one hundred
sons of the rishi were enraged. They addressed the king
in these words. "O evil-minded one! You have been refused by
your preceptor, who is truthful in speech. How can you cross him
and approach a different branch?[405] In every situation, priests are
the supreme destination for those of the Ikshvaku lineage. We
are incapable of negating the words of the one who is truthful in
speech. The illustrious rishi, Vasishtha, has conveyed his inability.
How can you then think of inviting us to undertake such a sacrifice?
O best among men! You are foolish. You should go back to your
own city. O king! In the three worlds, that illustrious person[406] is
the only one who can undertake such a sacrifice." Hearing their
words, the king's eyes dilated in rage. He again addressed them in
these words. "I have been refused by my preceptor and by the sons

[404] After Vasishtha's refusal.
[405] Vasishtha is being compared to a tree.
[406] Vasishtha.

of my preceptor. O stores of austerities! May you be fortunate. I will find another destination." Hearing those terrible words, the sons of the rishi became extremely angry. They cursed him, "You will become a *chandala*."[407] Saying this, those great-souled ones entered their own respective hermitages. When the night was over, the king became a chandala. He was dark and was attired in dark-blue garments. His form was harsh and his hair stood up, like a standard. He was smeared in paste and adorned with garlands from funeral pyres. His ornaments were made out of iron. Seeing this, all the ministers abandoned the person who now had the form of a chandala. O Rama! The citizens who followed him also fled. O Kakutstha! Alone, the king went to the supreme-souled Vishvamitra, the store of austerities who was scorching himself, day and night. O Rama! Vishvamitra saw that the king had been unsuccessful. Seeing his form of a chandala, the sage was overcome by compassion. Overcome by compassion, the extremely energetic one, supremely devoted to dharma, spoke these words to the king, who was terrible in form. "May you be fortunate. O prince! O immensely strong one! What task has brought you here? O brave one! The lord of Ayodhya has been cursed and has attained the state of a chandala." He was addressed in these words by one who was eloquent in speech. Hearing these words, the king, who had become a chandala, joined his hands in salutation and said, "I have been rebuffed by my preceptor and by the sons of my preceptor. I have not accomplished my wish and am now confronted by this catastrophe. O one who is amiable to behold! I desire to go to heaven in my own physical body. I have performed one hundred sacrifices, but have not obtained that fruit. I have never uttered a lie in the past, nor will I ever utter a falsehood. O amiable one! Following the dharma of kshatriyas, I vouch that this is the reason for this catastrophe. Curse me if it is otherwise. I have performed many kinds of sacrifices. I have followed dharma and ruled over the subjects. I have satisfied my great-souled preceptors with my good conduct. I sought and desired

---

[407] Chandala has different nuances and a chandala is not necessarily a shudra. A chandala is also of mixed parentage, with a shudra father and a brahmana mother. More generally, chandalas are outcastes, while shudras are within the caste fold.

to perform a sacrifice in accordance with dharma. O bull among
sages! However, my preceptors are not content at this. I think that
destiny is supreme and human endeavour is futile. Destiny cannot
be crossed. In every way, destiny is the supreme refuge. That is the
reason I am supremely afflicted and seek your favours. O fortunate
one! My deeds have been countered by destiny. You should do what
needs to be done. There is no other destination for me. There is
no other refuge for me. You should counter destiny through your
human endeavour.""

# Chapter 1(58)

'Full of compassion, Kushika's descendant spoke these sweet
words to the king, who presented himself in the form of
a chandala. "O son![408] O descendant of the Ikshvaku lineage!
Welcome. I know that you are extremely devoted to dharma. O bull
among sages! Do not be scared. I will be your refuge. I will invite
all the maharshis who are auspicious in their deeds, so that they
can assist in the sacrifice. O king! You will perform the sacrifice
that was foiled. You will go to heaven in your own physical body,
in your original form, as well as in the form obtained because of
the curse of your preceptors. O lord of men! I think that heaven is
as good as in your hands. You have approached and sought refuge
with Koushika, who is the one who grants refuge." Having said
this, the immensely energetic and immensely wise one instructed
his sons, who were supremely devoted to dharma, to make all the
arrangements for the sacrifice. He summoned all his disciples and
spoke these words to them. "O sons! Following my instructions,
bring all the rishis and their disciples. Bring their well-wishers and
the extremely learned assistant priests. If anyone ignores these
words, or inflamed by the strength of their words, speaks anything
against them, and also everything that is left unsaid, let all that be

---

[408] The word used is tata.

reported to me." Hearing these words and following his command, they left in different directions. All those who knew about the brahman started to assemble from different countries. The disciples returned to the sage, who blazed in his energy, and reported all the words spoken by those who knew about the brahman. "On hearing your words, all the brahmanas have arrived from different countries, or are coming. However, Mahodaya[409] ignored them. Also, all those one hundred sons of Vasishtha dilated their eyes in rage. O bull among sages! You should hear everything that they said. 'A kshatriya[410] is the officiating priest for a chandala who is undertaking a sacrifice. In such an assembly, how can the gods and the rishis partake of the oblations? Having enjoyed the food of a chandala, how will the great-souled brahmanas go to heaven, even if they are protected by Vishvamitra?' O tiger among sages! Their eyes dilated with rage, all the sons of Vasishtha, together with Mahodaya, uttered these harsh words." Hearing all their words, the eyes of that bull among sages dilated with rage. He angrily said, "I am established in my fierce austerities. All those evil-souled ones who revile an unblemished one like me will be reduced to ashes. There is no doubt about this. Right now, the noose of time will convey them to Yama's eternal abode. For seven hundred births, all of them will be those who feed on corpses. They will be known as *mushtika*s.[411] They will be shunned and will always feed on the flesh of dogs. They will roam around in the worlds, deformed and disfigured. The evil-minded Mahodaya has abused someone as unblemished as me. He will be abhorred by all the worlds and will become a nishada. He will always be engaged in taking the lives of others and will always be cruel. Because of my rage, he will face this catastrophe for a long period of time." The great ascetic, Vishvamitra, spoke these words. After this, in the midst of the rishis, the immensely energetic and great sage stopped.'

[409] The name of a priest.

[410] Vishvamitra.

[411] A variety of chandala. Vasishtha's sons became this.

# Chapter 1(59)

'In the midst of the sages, through the strength of his austerities, the immensely energetic Vishvamitra said that he would slay Mahodaya and the sons of Vasishtha. He said, "This heir of the Ikshvaku lineage is known by the name of Trishanku. He is generous and is devoted to dharma. He has sought refuge with me. He wishes to conquer the world of the gods in his own physical body. With me, all of you undertake this sacrifice, so that he can go the world of the gods in his own physical body." All those maharshis knew about dharma. Hearing his words, all of them consulted with each other and spoke words that were full of dharma. "The sage who is an heir of the Kushika lineage is extremely prone to anger. There is no doubt that we must completely act in accordance with his words. The illustrious one is like the fire. He will curse us in his rage. Therefore, let us undertake this sacrifice, so that the heir of the Ikshvaku lineage can go to heaven in his own physical body, thanks to Vishvamitra's energy." Thus, all of them engaged themselves in undertaking that sacrifice. Having spoken those words, all the maharshis initiated the rites. The immensely energetic Vishvamitra became the officiating priest for the sacrifice. The officiating priests, accomplished in the use of mantras, chanted mantras. Following the prescribed ordinances, they performed all the rituals. After a long period of time, Vishvamitra, the great ascetic, invited all the gods to accept their shares in the sacrifice. However, all the gods did not arrive to accept their shares in the sacrifice. At this, Vishvamitra, the great sage, was infused with rage. He angrily raised a sacrificial ladle and spoke to Trishanku. "O lord of men! Behold the strength of the austerities I have earned for myself. Through my own energy, I will convey you to heaven in your physical body. It is extremely difficult to go to heaven in one's own physical body. O lord of men! Go there. O king! Even if I have earned a little bit of merit through my own austerities, through that energy, go to heaven in your own physical body." O Kakutstha! When the sage spoke in this way, while the sages looked on, the lord of men went to heaven in his own physical body.

'When he saw that Trishanku had soared to the world of the gods, with all the other large number of gods, the chastiser of Paka addressed him in these words. "O Trishanku! Leave this place. You have not done anything to make heaven your abode. O foolish one! You have been cursed by your preceptor. Fall down to earth, with your head facing downwards." Thus addressed by the great Indra, Trishanku started to fall down again. He screamed out to Vishvamitra, the store of austerities, "Save me." Hearing his loud wails, Koushika became extremely angry and said, "Stay there. Stay there." He was like another Prajapati.[412] In the midst of the sages, along the southern direction, the energetic one created another group of saptarshis.[413] Senseless with rage, in the midst of the sages, the extremely illustrious one then started to create garlands of nakshatras, located in the southern direction. Tainted by his rage, he created generations of nakshatras. "I will create another world with an Indra, or perhaps it doesn't need an Indra." In his anger, he started to create another set of gods. The large number of rishis and the bulls among the gods were extremely terrified at this. They entreated the great-souled Vishvamitra in these words. "O immensely fortunate one! This king is blemished because of the curse imposed by his preceptor. O store of austerities! He does not deserve to go to heaven in his own physical body." Hearing the words of the gods, Koushika, bull among sages, spoke these extremely great words to all the gods. "O fortunate ones! I have promised King Trishanku that he will ascend there in his own physical body. I am not interested in ensuring the falsity of that pledge. In his own physical body, let Trishanku enjoy heaven for eternity. Let all my fixed nakshatras also be there. As long as the worlds exist, let all of them remain there. For my sake, all of you gods should agree to this." Thus addressed, all the gods replied to the bull among sages. "O fortunate one! It shall be that way and all of them will remain there. Many of them will be there, but will be outside

---

[412] Meaning Brahma.
[413] Ursa Major.

Vaishvanara's path.[414] O best among sages! Trishanku will also
be there, amidst the radiance of the blazing nakshatras, like an
immortal, but with his head hanging downwards." In the midst
of the rishis, worshipped by all the gods, the immensely energetic
Vishvamitra, with dharma in his soul, agreed to what the gods
had said. O supreme among men! After this, at the conclusion
of the sacrifice, all the gods and the great-souled sages, stores of
austerities, returned to wherever they had come from.'

## Chapter 1(60)

'O tiger among men! The immensely energetic Vishvamitra
saw that the rishis had left. He spoke to all the residents
of the forest. "A great obstruction has now arisen in the southern
direction.[415] We will head for another direction and perform
austerities there. O great-souled ones! There is the extensive
region of Pushkara in the western direction. We will happily
practise austerities in the supreme hermitages there." Having said
this, the immensely energetic, invincible and great sage performed
fierce austerities in Pushkara. He subsisted on roots and fruit. At
that time, there was a king who was the lord of Ayodhya. He
was famous as Ambareesha and he started to perform a sacrifice.
However, Indra seized the animal the sacrificer had earmarked.
When the animal was destroyed, the brahmanas spoke to the
king. "O king! Because of your carelessness, the animal has been
seized and destroyed. If objects belonging to the king are left
unprotected and are destroyed, the sin devolves on the king. O
bull among men! A great rite of atonement must be performed.
Let a man or an animal be quickly brought, so that the ritual
can continue." O bull among men! Hearing the words of the
preceptors, the immensely intelligent king offered thousands of

[414] Vaishvanara has several meanings. The sense is that these new creations will be in
a parallel galaxy/universe.

[415] Because of Trishanku's ascent to heaven there.

cows in exchange, so that he might obtain an animal. The lord
of the earth searched in countries, habitations, cities, forests and
even in sacred hermitages. O descendant of the Raghu lineage! O
son![416] He saw Richika seated in Bhrigutunda, with his son and
his wife. The infinitely radiant rajarshi bowed his head down and
worshipped the immensely energetic brahmana rishi, who blazed
in the radiance of his austerities. In every possible way, he asked
about Richika's welfare and then spoke these words. "O immensely
fortunate one! O descendant of the Bhrigu lineage! If you give
me your son in exchange for one hundred thousand cows, I will
obtain a sacrificial animal and will be successful. I have visited
all the countries, but have not obtained an appropriate sacrificial
animal. In exchange for that price, you should grant me one of
your sons."[417] Thus addressed, the immensely energetic Richika
replied in these words. "O best among men! I will never sell my
eldest son." Hearing those words, the ascetic mother of those
great-souled ones spoke to Ambareesha, tiger among men. "O
king! Know that the youngest son is my beloved.[418] O best among
men! It is often the case that the eldest is loved by fathers and the
youngest by mothers. Therefore, I am protecting the youngest." O
Rama! When the sage spoke those words and the sage's wife spoke
similar words, the son in the middle, Shunahshepa,[419] himself said,
"My father has said that the eldest cannot be sold and my mother
has said the same about the youngest. O king! I therefore think
that the son in the middle can be sold. Take me." O descendant
of the Raghu lineage! Extremely happy, the lord of men gave one
hundred thousand cows, accepted Shunahshepa and left. Rajarshi
Ambareesha swiftly ascended his chariot. The immensely energetic
and greatly illustrious one left quickly with Shunahshepa.'

---

[416] The word used is tata.

[417] So far, only a single son has been mentioned.

[418] The Critical text uses the word *shunaka*, though non-Critical versions don't always
have this word. We have translated this as youngest son. But shunaka actually means young
dog or puppy.

[419] Shunahshepa should be translated as dog's penis, though it can also be translated
as dog's tail.

# Chapter 1(61)

'O best among men! O descendant of the Raghu lineage! Having taken Shunahshepa, when it was noon, the immensely illustrious king rested in Pushkara. While he was resting, the immensely illustrious Shunahshepa also came to the excellent Pushkara and saw Vishvamitra. He showed distress in his face. He was miserable because of thirst and exhaustion. He fell down on the sage's lap and spoke these words. "I do not have a mother, nor a father. Where are my kin and relatives? O amiable one! O bull among sages! Following dharma, you should save me. O best among sages! You alone are the protector, the preserver of everything. Let the king be successful, but let me also have an undecaying and long life. Let me torment myself through the best of austerities and obtain the world of heaven. Using your intelligence become a protector to one who is without a protector. O one with dharma in his soul! Like a father, you should save me from all difficulty." Hearing his words, Vishvamitra, the great ascetic, comforted him in various ways. He spoke these words to his sons. "Fathers give birth to sons for the sake of welfare and benefit in the world hereafter. That time has come to pass. This child, the son of a sage, desires refuge with me. O sons! We should bring him pleasure by ensuring his life. All of you are the performers of excellent deeds. All of you are devoted to dharma. Satisfy Agni by offering one of your own selves, like a sacrificial animal, to the Indra among kings. Then Shunahshepa will have a protector and there will be no obstructions to the sacrifice. The gods will be satisfied and I will also adhere to my pledge." O best among men! On hearing the sage's words, Madhushyanda and the other sons were insolent. They dismissively said, "O lord! How can you abandon your own sons and protect the son of another? We perceive this as something that should not be done, it is like an act of eating dog meat." When he heard the words of his sons, the eyes of that bull among sages became red with rage. He said, "You have foolishly uttered these words and have thereby censured dharma. You have transgressed me in words that are terrible. They make the body hair stand up. Like the sons of Vasishtha, all of you will be reborn as those who subsist on dog meat. For a full one thousand years, you will roam around on the earth in that way." Having cursed his sons in that way, the supreme sage then sought to protect the afflicted Shunahshepa and ensure his welfare. "When you are tied to the Vaishnava sacrificial altar with sacred bonds and adorned with red garlands and paste, address these eloquent words to Agni. O son of a sage! At Ambareesha's sacrifice, chant these two divine hymns and you will obtain success." Controlled in his mind, Shunahshepa accepted those two chants. He quickly went to Ambareesha and said, "O lion among kings! O great spirit! Let us quickly go to the assembly. O Indra among kings! Let your consecration take place." On hearing the words of the rishi's son, the king was eager and happy. Without deviating, he swiftly went to the sacrificial arena. With the permission of the assistant priests, he dressed the sacrificial animal[420] in red garments, marked him out with auspicious signs and tied him to the altar. When he had been tied there, the sage's son pleased the two gods, Indra and Indra's younger brother[421] with those two chants. The thousand-eyed one was pleased at that secret chanting. O Raghava! He granted a long life to Shunahshepa. O best among men! O Rama! The king completed his sacrifice and through the favours of the thousand-eyed one, obtained a multitude of fruits. O best among men! The great ascetic, Vishvamitra, with dharma in his soul, performed austerities in Pushkara for another one thousand years.'

## Chapter 1(62)

'One thousand years were over. After the vow was over, the great sage bathed and all the gods assembled to grant him the fruits he desired from the austerities. The greatly energetic Brahma spoke these extremely agreeable words to him. "O fortunate

[420] Shunahshepa.
[421] Vishnu.

one! Through your own auspicious deeds, you have now become
a rishi." Having said this, the lord of the gods again returned to
heaven. The immensely energetic Vishvamitra performed great
austerities again. O best among men! After a long period of time,
the supreme apsara, Menaka, arrived and started to bathe in
Pushkara. Kushika's greatly energetic son saw Menaka. She was
unmatched in her beauty and was like a flash of lightning in a cloud.
On seeing her, the sage came under the subjugation of Kandarpa
and spoke these words. "O apsara! Welcome. Reside here, in my
hermitage. O fortunate one! Show me your favours. I am extremely
confounded by Madana." Thus addressed, the beautiful one started
to dwell there. Vishvamitra was confronted with a great obstruction
in his austerities. O Raghava! O amiable one! While she happily
dwelt there, in Vishvamitra's hermitage, ten years passed. After
this time had passed, the great sage, Vishvamitra, became ashamed.
He was overcome by sorrow and started to think. O descendant
of the Raghu lineage! The sage had intolerant thoughts. "All the
gods have done this, to rob me of my great austerities. Ten years
have passed, like only a day and a night. Because I was overcome
by desire and confusion, this obstruction has presented itself." The
supreme among sages sighed. He sorrowed with repentance. He
saw that the apsara was terrified and trembling, her hands joined
in salutation.[422] Using sweet words, Kushika's son asked Menaka to
leave. O Rama! Vishvamitra then went to the northern mountains.[423]
Wishing to conquer desire, the immensely illustrious one turned
to devotion. On the banks of the Koushiki, he tormented himself
through extremely difficult austerities. O Rama! In the northern
mountains, he practised terrible austerities for one thousand years
and the gods were scared. All the large number of rishis and gods
assembled and consulted, deciding that Kushika's son should be
successful in obtaining the appellation of "maharshi". Hearing the
words of the gods, the grandfather of all the worlds spoke these
sweet words to Vishvamitra, the store of austerities. "O son! O

[422] In case she was cursed.
[423] Presumably the Himalayas.

maharshi! Welcome. I am satisfied by your fierce austerities. O
Koushika! I grant you the title of maharshi." Hearing Brahma's
words, Vishvamitra, the store of austerities, bowed down, joining
his hands in salutation. He replied to the grandfather, "O illustrious
one! If I have accumulated unsurpassed merit through my own
auspicious deeds, if I have conquered my senses, you should address
me as *brahmarshi*."[424] Brahma told him, "O tiger among sages!
You have still not conquered your senses and need to strive more."
Saying this, he returned to heaven. The gods also departed. The
great sage, Vishvamitra, stood with his hands raised up, without any
support. Subsisting only on air, he performed austerities. During the
summer, he observed the five fires. During the monsoon, the open
sky was his shelter. During the winter, during night and day, the
store of austerities slept in the water. In this way, he performed
fierce austerities for one thousand years. While Vishvamitra, the
great sage, tormented himself in this way, Vasava and the other
gods were extremely frightened. With the large number of Maruts,
Shakra spoke words that were beneficial to him, but not beneficial
to Koushika, or to the apsara Rambha.'

# Chapter 1(63)

' "O Rambha! You have to perform an extremely great
task for the gods. You have to seduce Koushika,
confounding him with desire." O Rama! Thus addressed, the
apsara spoke to the intelligent and thousand-eyed one. She joined
her hands in salutation and replied to the lord of the gods. "O
lord of the gods! The great sage, Vishvamitra, is terrible. O god!
There is no doubt that he will unleash his terrible rage on me. O
god! I am frightened on that account and you should show me
your favours." The thousand-eyed one replied to the one who was
trembling, her hands joined in salutation. "O Rambha! Do not be

---

[424] A sage with knowledge of the supreme being (brahman).

scared and act according to my instructions. I will become a cuckoo
that sings in beautiful and agreeable tones in the trees during the
spring. With Kandarpa, I will be at your side. Assume an extremely
radiant form that is beautiful in many ways. O Rambha! Create
conflict in that rishi and ascetic, Koushika." Hearing these words,
she assumed a form that was supreme in beauty. The sweet-smiling
and beautiful one tempted Vishvamitra. He heard the melodious
tones of the cuckoo singing and with a gladdened heart, he glanced
towards her. However, on hearing the unmatched tones of the
song and on seeing Rambha, the sage was suspicious. The bull
among sages discerned that this was the work of the thousand-
eyed one. Overcome with rage, Kushika's son cursed Rambha.
"O Rambha! I have been trying to conquer desire and anger, but
you have tempted me. O unfortunate one! For ten thousand years,
you will become a rock. O Rambha! You have been tainted by
my rage. An extremely energetic brahmana, full of the strength of
austerities, will eventually save you."[425] Vishvamitra, the extremely
energetic and great sage, spoke in this way. However, because he
was incapable of controlling his anger, he also repented. Because of
that great curse, Rambha became a rock. On hearing these words,
Kandarpa fled from the maharshi. Having succumbed to rage, the
immensely energetic one was divested of his store of austerities. O
Rama! Having not been able to conquer his senses, he could not
find any peace in his mind.'

# Chapter 1(64)

'O Rama! The great sage abandoned the direction of the
Himalayas. He resorted to the eastern direction and
practised extremely terrible austerities. He observed a supreme vow
and did not speak for one thousand years. O Rama! He performed
extremely difficult and unmatched austerities. For one thousand

---

[425] Meaning Vasishtha.

years, the great sage was like a block of wood. Though confronted
with many kinds of obstructions, anger did not enter his heart. The
gods, the gandharvas, the serpents, the asuras and the rakshasas were
confounded by his energy. His austerities dulled their own radiance.
Since this was like a taint, all of them addressed the grandfather.
"We have sought to tempt the great sage, Vishvamitra, in many
kinds of ways. But because of his austerities, he has not allowed his
rage to increase. Not even a subtle sign of weakness can be seen in
him. If he is not granted what is in his mind, through his austerities,
he will destroy the three worlds and all their mobile and immobile
objects. All the directions are anxious and nothing can be seen. All
the oceans are turbulent and the mountains are being shattered. The
earth is trembling and an extremely tumultuous wind is raging. O
god! O illustrious one! The immensely radiant one has a form like
that of Agni. The great sage should be shown favours, before he
makes up his mind to destroy everything. In earlier times, the fire
of destruction destroyed everything in the three worlds. Even if he
desires the kingdom of the gods, it is our view that he should be
granted that." All the gods, with the grandfather at the forefront,
approached the great-souled Vishvamitra and addressed him in these
sweet words. "O brahmarshi! Welcome. We are extremely satisfied
with your austerities. O Koushika! Through your fierce austerities,
you have obtained the status of a brahmana. O brahmana! With
the large number of Maruts, I grant you a long life. O fortunate
one! O amiable one! May you be fortunate! You can now return
to wherever you came from." Hearing the grandfather's words and
those of all the residents of heaven, the great sage was delighted.
He bowed down before them and said, "Since I have obtained
the status of a brahmana and have also received a long life, may
*oum*,[426] vashatkara and the Vedas reveal themselves to me. O gods!
Vasishtha is Brahma's son. May he also acknowledge me as the
best among those who possess the knowledge of the kshatriyas and
the knowledge of the brahmanas. O bulls among the gods! Depart
only after you have accomplished this supreme desire of mine." The

---

[426] The sacred akshara, also written as *om* or *aum*.

gods showed him their favours. Vasishtha, supreme among those who meditate, also arrived, made his friendship and said, "You are a brahmarshi. Since you are now a brahmarshi, there is no doubt that everything will now manifest itself before you." After this was said, all the gods went away to wherever they had come from. Vishvamitra, with dharma in his soul, obtained the supreme status of being a brahmana. He worshipped brahmarshi Vasishtha, supreme among those who meditate. Having obtained his wish, he based himself on austerities and roamed around the entire earth. O Rama! This is how the great-souled one obtained the status of being a brahmana. O Rama! He is the best among sages. He is the embodiment of austerities. He is always devoted to supreme dharma and valour.'

In the presence of Rama and Lakshmana, Janaka heard Shatananda's words. He joined his hands in salutation and spoke these words to Kushika's son. 'O bull among sages! O one who follows dharma! I am blessed that you have shown me your favours and have come to this sacrifice with Kakutstha. O brahmana! O great sage! Your mere sight has purified me. By beholding you, I have obtained many kinds of qualities. O brahmana! I, and the immensely energetic and great-souled Rama, have heard the detailed recital of your great austerities. The assistant priests in this assembly have also heard about your many qualities. Your austerities are immeasurable. Your strength is immeasurable. O Kushika's son! Your qualities are always immeasurable. O lord! Creatures are never satisfied at hearing about your extraordinary account. O best among sages! However, the solar disc is elongated[427] and it is time for the rituals. O immensely energetic one! Tomorrow morning, I will see you again. O best among ascetics! Welcome. You should grant me permission to leave now.' The best among sages was thus addressed by the lord of Videha and Mithila, who circumambulated him, together with his priests and relatives. Worshipped by the maharshis, with Rama and Lakshmana, Vishvamitra, with dharma in his soul, left for his own residence.

[427] It is evening.

# Chapter 1(65)

When it was sparkling morning, the king performed the morning rituals and invited the great-souled Vishvamitra and Raghava. Following the ordinances laid down in the sacred texts, he worshipped the great-souled one[428] and the two great-souled Raghavas. He then spoke these words. 'O illustrious one! O unblemished one! Welcome. What can I do for you? O illustrious one! Command me. I am ready to be commanded by you.' The one with dharma in his soul was thus addressed by the great-souled Janaka. The sage, eloquent in the use of words, replied in these words to the valiant one. 'These two are the sons of Dasharatha. They are kshatriyas and are famous in the worlds. They wish to see the supreme bow that is in your possession. O fortunate one! If they can see the bow, the wishes of these two princes will be satisfied. Having seen the bow, as they wish, they can then return.'

Thus addressed, Janaka replied to the great sage. 'Hear about the bow and about why it is kept here. There was a king famous by the name of Devarata and he was the sixth in line from Nimi.[429] The illustrious and great-souled one[430] left it in his hands in trust. Earlier, at the time of the destruction of Daksha's sacrifice, the valiant Rudra angrily raised the bow and playfully spoke to the gods. "O gods! I desired a share of the sacrifice, but you did not think of a share for me. Therefore, I will severe your heads with this extremely revered bow." O bull among sages! At this, all the gods were distressed. They sought the favours of the lord of the gods and Bhava was pleased. Happy, he bestowed his favours on those great-souled ones. O lord! After this, the great-souled god of the gods handed over this gem of a bow in trust to our ancestor. Later, I was ploughing and purifying my field. From the field, my upraised plough brought up the one who has become famous by the

---

[428] Vishvamitra.

[429] Nimi was the king who established the dynasty in Mithila. He was Janaka's ancestor.

[430] Shiva.

name of Sita.[431] Having been raised from the surface of the ground, she was reared as my daughter. She was not born from a womb and this maiden will be bestowed as *viryashulka*.[432] Having been raised from the surface of the ground, she has grown up as my daughter. O bull among sages! These kings have come to seek her hand. O illustrious one! I have not bestowed my daughter on any of the kings who have come. I will bestow my daughter through the mode of viryashulka. O bull among sages! That is the reason all these kings have assembled here. They have arrived in Mithila to test their valour. Their valour will be tested by their ability to raise the bow. However, none of them have been able to grasp the bow or raise it. O great sage! I got to know that those valiant ones possess little valour. O store of austerities! Listen. I therefore refused all those kings. O bull among sages! At this, the kings were extremely enraged. Since their valour was being doubted, all of them laid siege to Mithila. O bull among sages! They thought that they had been slighted. Therefore, prey to great rage, they oppressed the city of Mithila. After an entire year passed everything began to suffer and the supplies were exhausted. O best among sages! That is the reason I became extremely miserable. After this, I pleased the large number of gods through my austerities. Extremely pleased, the gods gave me armies with four kinds of forces.[433] Through these, those evil-acting and cowardly kings, who doubted my valour, were routed, killed and driven away in different directions, together with their advisers. O tiger among sages! O one excellent in vows! I will show that extremely radiant bow to Rama and Lakshmana too. O sage! If Rama is capable of stringing that bow, I will bestow my daughter Sita, who was not born from a womb, on Dasharatha's son.'

[431] The word *sita* means the furrow caused by a plough.

[432] Viryashulka is not the same as a svayamvara. Svayamvara is a ceremony where the maiden herself (*svayam*) chooses her husband (*vara*) from assembled suitors. Viryashulka is when the maiden is offered to the suitor who shows the most valour (*virya*), *shulka* meaning price.

[433] Chariots, elephants, horses and foot soldiers.

# Chapter 1(66)

Having heard Janaka's words, the great sage, Vishvamitra, told the king, 'Show Rama the bow.' At this, King Janaka instructed his advisers, 'Bring the divine bow, decorated with fragrances and garlands, here.' Commanded by Janaka, the advisers entered the city. Following the king's command, they emerged, placing the bow at the front. There were five thousand tall and great-souled men. Together, they somehow managed to tug it along on a casket with eight wheels. Having brought the iron casket with the bow, the ministers informed the king, who was like a god. 'O king! This is the supreme bow that is worshipped by all the kings. O lord of Mithila! O Indra among kings! This is what you wished to be shown.' Hearing their words, the king joined his hands in salutation and addressed the great-souled Vishvamitra and Rama and Lakshmana. 'O brahmana! This is the supreme bow, worshipped by those of the Janaka lineage. Extremely valiant kings have not been able to use it to take aim. Nor have the large numbers of gods, asuras, rakshasas, gandharvas, the best of yakshas, kinnaras, or the giant serpents. How can men raise the bow, string it, affix an arrow and take aim with it? O bull among sages! O immensely fortunate one! The best among bows has been brought so that it can be shown to the two princes.' Vishvamitra, with dharma in his soul, heard Janaka's words. He told Raghava, 'O Rama! O son! Behold the bow.'

Hearing the maharshi's words, Rama opened the casket where the bow was kept. He saw the bow and said, 'O brahmana! I wish to touch this supreme bow with my hands. I want to try to raise it and take aim with it.' The king and the sage said, 'Go ahead.' Hearing the sage's words, he playfully grasped the bow at the middle. While many thousands of men looked on, the descendant of the Raghu lineage, with dharma in his soul, playfully strung the bow. The valiant one, immensely illustrious and best among men, strung the bowstring and took aim. The bow snapped at the middle. A great sound arose, like the roar of a storm. It was as if there was an extremely giant earthquake that made the

mountains shatter. Confounded by that sound, all the men, with
the exception of the supreme among sages, the king and the two
Raghavas, fell down unconscious. When the men regained their
senses, having got his composure back, the king joined his hands
in salutation and spoke these words to the bull among sages, who
was eloquent with words. 'O illustrious one! I have witnessed the
valour of Rama, Dasharatha's son. This is extremely wonderful
and unthinkable. This is something that has not even been talked
about. If Sita gets Rama, Dasharatha's son, as her husband, my
daughter will bring fame to the lineage of the Janakas. O Koushika!
My truthful pledge is that she will be bestowed as viryashulka. My
daughter Sita is worth many of my lives and it is my view that she
should be given to Rama. O brahmana! With your permission, let
my ministers quickly go. O Koushika! O fortunate one! Let them
go to Ayodhya on chariots. With diligent words, let them bring
the king[434] to my city. Let them tell him everything and about the
bestowal through viryashulka. They will also tell the king that
the two Kakutsthas are under the protection of the sage.[435] With
affectionate words, they will bring the king extremely swiftly.'
When Koushika agreed to this, the king addressed his ministers.
The one with dharma in his soul commanded them and sent them
to Ayodhya.

## Chapter 1(67)

Following Janaka's instructions, the messengers used mounts
that did not get exhausted. Resting for three nights along the
way, they entered the city of Ayodhya. Following the instructions
of the king, they entered the royal residence and saw the aged King
Dasharatha, who was like a god. All the messengers showed their
reverence by joining their hands in salutation. Controlled, they

[434] Dasharatha.
[435] Vishvamitra.

spoke words with sweet syllables to the king. 'O one who follows
the agnihotra rites! King Janaka of Mithila asks about your welfare
and that of your preceptors and priests. O great king! Repeatedly
using sweet words that are full of affection, Janaka also asks about
the welfare of your servants. The lord of Videha and Mithila first
eagerly asks about your welfare. With Koushika's permission, he
then addresses you in the following words. "My former pledge
is known, that I will offer my daughter as viryashulka. Those
intolerant kings were seen to be devoid of valour and were refused.
O king! With Vishvamitra at the forefront, your brave sons[436] have
come and have won my daughter. O great king! In a great assembly
of people, the great-souled Rama has shattered the divine bow in
the middle. As viryashulka, I must bestow Sita on the great-souled
one. That is my pledge and I desire that you should grant me your
permission. O great king! O fortunate one! With the priest[437] at
the forefront, you should quickly come with your preceptors and
see the two Raghavas. O Indra among kings! You should display
your affection towards me. You will also be delighted at seeing both
your sons." These are the sweet words that the lord of Videha has
spoken. This has Vishvamitra's permission and Shatananda holds
the same view.' On hearing the words of the messengers, the king
was greatly delighted. He addressed Vasishtha, Vamadeva and
the other ministers. 'The one who extends Kousalya's delight has
been protected by Kushika's son. With his brother, Lakshmana,
he now resides in Videha. The great-souled Janaka has witnessed
Kakutstha's valour. He wishes to bestow his daughter on Raghava.
If all of you find the great-souled Janaka's intentions desirable, let us
quickly go to that city, without wasting any time on reflection.' The
ministers, and all the maharshis, agreed to this. Extremely happy,
the king told his ministers, 'We will leave tomorrow.' Honoured
well, the king's[438] ministers, all of whom possessed all the desired
qualities, happily spent the night there.

---

[436] Though Rama is meant, the plural is being used as a mark of respect.
[437] Vasishtha.
[438] Janaka's.

# Chapter 1(68)

When the night was over, with his preceptors and his relatives, King Dasharatha happily spoke to Sumantra. 'Let all the superintendents of treasuries collect large quantities of riches. Prepared well, let them advance in front, with many kinds of jewels. Following my instructions, let excellent carriages be yoked at the same time and let an army with the four kinds of forces quickly advance.[439] Vasishtha, Vamadeva, Jabali, Kashyapa, Markandeya and Katyayana—let these brahmanas with long lives advance in the front. Let my chariot be yoked. The messengers are asking me to speed up and not delay.' Following the king's words, half of the army, consisting of the four kinds of forces, proceeded with the king and the rishis. The other half followed at the rear. After travelling for four days along the road, they reached the extremities of Videha. On hearing this, the prosperous King Janaka arranged for all the honours to be shown. On meeting King Janaka, the aged King Dasharatha was delighted. The king[440] was also supremely delighted. Happy, the best of men spoke to the best of men.[441] 'O great king! O Raghava! Welcome. It is good fortune that you have come here. You will obtain happiness through your two sons, who have triumphed because of their valour. It is good fortune that the greatly energetic and illustrious rishi, Vasishtha, has come here with all the other supreme brahmanas, like Shatakratu with the gods. It is good fortune that all obstructions have been conquered. It is good fortune that my lineage has been honoured. I will have this matrimonial alliance with the Raghavas, who are great-souled and the best among those who are brave. O Indra among kings! You should begin the arrangements tomorrow morning. O best among kings! After the conclusion of the sacrifice, with the permission of the rishis, the marriage ceremony will be held.' In

---

[439] Instead of the four kinds of forces that characterize an army, since this is a marriage, the four can also be understood as riches, gold, equipment and vehicles.

[440] Janaka.

[441] Janaka and Dasharatha respectively.

the midst of the rishis, the lord of men[442] heard his words. The one
who was best among those who are eloquent with words replied to
the lord of the earth.[443] 'The nature of a gift is determined by the
donor. This is what I have heard in earlier times. O one who knows
about dharma! We will do exactly what you have said.' He[444] was
devoted to dharma and famous. He was truthful in speech. On
hearing his words, the lord of Videha was greatly astounded. All
the sages were greatly delighted at having met each other.[445] They
spent the night happily. The king was greatly delighted at having
spoken to his sons, the two Raghavas. Honoured extremely well by
Janaka, he resided there. The greatly energetic Janaka, who knew
the truth about the rituals, followed dharma and performed them.
Having performed sacrifices for his two daughters, he spent the
night there.[446]

## Chapter 1(69)

When it was morning, Janaka had the rituals performed by
the maharshis. The one who was eloquent with the use
of words then spoke these words to the priest, Shatananda. 'My
greatly energetic younger brother is extremely devoted to dharma.
He is famous by the name of Kushadhvaja and lives in an auspicious
city that has moats all around it. This sacred city of Samkashya
seems to drink the waters of the river Ikshumati.[447] This city is like

[442] Dasharatha.
[443] Janaka.
[444] Dasharatha.
[445] Those on Janaka's side and those on Dasharatha's side.
[446] This causes a problem of translation. The word can be translated as two sons or
two daughters. It makes perfect sense if one is talking about Dasharatha. However, one is
talking about Janaka. Therefore, it has to be two daughters, though we have not yet been
told anything about Janaka having a second daughter.
[447] Literally, Ikshumati means a river whose water tastes like sugar cane juice. Elsewhere,
it is said that Ikshumati flowed near Kurukshetra and Ikshumati has also been identified
with the river Sarasvati.

Pushpaka vimana.[448] I wish to see him and it is my view that he should arrange for this sacrifice. With me, that extremely energetic one will be delighted to participate in this.' On the instructions of the king, who was a tiger among men, like Vishnu following Indra's command, messengers on swift steeds were dispatched. On the king's command, Kushadhvaja arrived. He saw the great-souled Janaka, who was devoted to dharma. He greeted Shatananda and the king who was devoted to dharma. He ascended a supremely divine seat that befitted kings. Those two infinitely energetic brothers seated themselves. The brave ones then sent for Sudamana, best among ministers. 'O lord of ministers! Quickly go to the infinitely resplendent descendant of Ikshvaku. Invite the invincible one here, with his sons and his ministers.' He went to the place meant for guests and saw the extender of the lineage of Raghu. Bowing his head down and greeting him, he said, 'O brave one! O lord of Ayodhya! The lord of Mithila and Videha is waiting to see you, with his preceptors and priests.' Hearing the words of the best among ministers, the king, with the large number of rishis and his relatives, went to the place where Janaka was. With his ministers, his preceptors and his relatives, the king, best among those who are eloquent with words, spoke these words to the lord of Videha. 'O great king! It is known to you that the illustrious rishi, Vasishtha, is like a god to the lineage of the Ikshvakus and can speak on our behalf about our conduct. With the permission of Vishvamitra, and that of all the maharshis, Vasishtha, with dharma in his soul, will speak about my ancestry.'

When Dasharatha was silent, the illustrious rishi, Vasishtha, eloquent in the use of words, spoke these words to the lord of Videha and his priest. 'Brahma's powers are not manifest. He is eternal, everlasting and without decay. He had a son named Marichi[449] and Marichi's son was Kashyapa. Vivasvan[450] was Kashyapa's son and Manu is said to be Vivasvan's son. Manu was the first Prajapati

---

[448] A vimana is a celestial vehicle. Pushpaka belonged to Kubera and was later seized by Ravana.

[449] Through Brahma's mental powers.

[450] The sun.

and Ikshvaku was Manu's son. Know that Ikshvaku was the first king of Ayodhya. Ikshavku had a prosperous son, Vikukshi. The greatly energetic Vikukshi's son was the powerful Bana. The greatly energetic Bana's son was the powerful Anaranya. Anaranya had a son named Prithu and Prithu's son was Trishanku. Trishanku had an immensely illustrious son named Dhundumara. Dhundumara's son was the immensely energetic maharatha, Yuvanashva. Yuvanashva's son was the handsome King Mandhata. Mandhata's son was the handsome Susandhi. Susandhi had two sons—Dhruvasandhi and Prasenjit. Dhruvasandhi had an illustrious son named Bharata. The immensely energetic Bharata had a son named Asita. Since he was born with poison, he came to be known as Sagara.[451] Sagara had a son named Asamanja and Asamanja's son was Amshumat. Dileepa was Amshumat's son and Dileepa's son was Bhageeratha. Bhageeratha's son was Kakutstha and Kakutstha's son was Raghu. Raghu had an energetic son named Pravriddha, but he grew up to be an eater of human flesh. He thus became Kalmashapada and his son was Shankana.[452] Sudarshana was Shankana's son and Sudarshana's son was Agnivarna. Agnivarna's son was Sheeghraga and Sheeghraga's son was Maru. Maru's son was Prashushruka and Ambareesha was born through Prashushruka. Ambareesha's son was Nahusha, lord of the earth. Yayati was Nahusha's son and Yayati's son was Nabhaga. Nabhaga's son was Aja and Aja's son is Dasharatha. The brothers, Rama and Lakshmana, are Dasharatha's sons. Right from the beginning, this lineage of kings is pure and is extremely devoted to dharma. There are brave ones who have been born in the lineage of Ikshvaku and they are truthful in speech. O king! Your daughters should be bestowed on Rama and Lakshmana. O best among men! They are equal[453] and bestowal must always be on equals.'

[451] The Critical Edition excises some shlokas and this breaks the continuity. While Sagara was still in his mother's womb, his stepmother tried to unsuccessfully poison him. Hence, he was *sa* (with) *gara* (poison).

[452] Vasishtha cursed Pravriddha that he would be an eater of human flesh. Pravriddha wished to curse Vasishtha in turn and held some sanctified water in his hand. However, he was dissuaded by his wife, Madayanti. The sanctified water fell on his feet. He was thus known as Kalmashapada, because his feet (pada) had a blemish (*kalmasha*).

[453] In lineage.

# Chapter 1(70)

Thus addressed, Janaka joined his hands in salutation and replied, 'O fortunate one! You should now hear the supreme account of our lineage. O best among sages! At the time of bestowal, a person born in a noble lineage should recount everything about his lineage. O great sage! Listen. There was a king named Nimi who was famous in the three worlds because of his own deeds. With dharma in his soul, he was supreme. He was greatest among spirited ones. His son was named Mithi and Mithi's son was Janaka.[454] This was the first one by the name Janaka and Udavasu was Janaka's son. Nandivardhana was born from Janaka and he had dharma in his soul. Nandivardhana's son was known by the name of Suketu. Suketu's son was the extremely strong Devarata, who had dharma in his soul. It has been heard that rajarshi Brihadratha was born from Devarata. Brihadratha's son was the extremely brave, intelligent and powerful Mahaveera. Sudhriti, with truth as his valour, was Mahaveera's son. Sudhriti's son was Dhrishtaketu, who was extremely devoted to dharma and had dharma in his soul. Dhrishtaketu's son was the famous rajarshi Haryashava. Haryashava's son was Maru and Maru's son was Prativandhaka. Prativandhaka's son was King Kirtiratha, who had dharma in his soul. Kirtiratha's son is known as Devamidha. Devamidha's son was Vibudha and Vibudha's son was Maheedhraka. Maheedhraka's son was the extremely strong King Keertirata. Rajarshi Keertirata gave birth to Maharoma. Maharoma's son was Svarnaroma, who had dharma in his soul. Rajarshi Svarnaroma's son was Hrasvaroma, who was great-souled and knew about dharma. He had two sons. I am the elder and my younger brother is the brave Kushadhvaja. Since I am elder, the king, my father, instated me in the kingdom. Having entrusted the task of looking after Kushadhvaja on me, he went to the forest. When my aged father went to heaven, I have followed dharma in bearing this burden and have affectionately reared my brother Kushadhvaja, who is like a god. After some time,

[454] This was an earlier Janaka.

the brave King Sudhanva came from the city of Samkashya and laid siege to Mithila. He asked me to give him Shiva's supreme bow. He also said, "Bestow on me your lotus-eyed daughter, Sita." O brahmana rishi! When I did not give him these, he fought with me. In the battle, I killed Sudhanva, who had acted against me. O best among sages! When King Sudhanva was slain, I instated my brave brother, Kushadhvaja, in Samkashya. O great sage! I am the elder and he is younger to me. O bull among sages! Extremely delighted, I will give you these two fortunate daughters-in-law, Sita for Rama and Urmila for Lakshmana. My daughter Sita is like a daughter of the gods and is offered as viryashulka and Urmila is the second. O descendant of the Raghu lineage![455] There is no doubt that extremely cheerfully, I will bestow these two daughters-in-law. I state this in three ways.[456] O king! Let the *godana* ritual be performed for Rama and Lakshmana.[457] O fortunate one! Let rites for the ancestors be performed next. After that, let the marriage ceremony be undertaken. O lord! The nakshatra Magha is in the ascendant now and three days from now, it will be Uttaraphalguni.[458] O king! Arrange for the ceremony then. So that Rama and Lakshmana enjoy happiness, let donations be made.'

## Chapter 1(71)

When the lord of Videha spoke in this way, the great sage, Vishvamitra, together with Vasishtha, spoke these words to the brave king. 'O bull among men! These two lineages are unthinkable and immeasurable. There is no other lineage that is a

---

[455] This is directed at Dasharatha.

[456] Through thoughts, words and deeds.

[457] Though godana literally means the donation of a cow, it has a symbolic connotation here. Since Rama and Lakshmana enter the householder (garhasthya) stage, they go through a sacrament (*samskara*).

[458] Some nakshatras are regarded as auspicious for marriage, but that list includes both Magha and Uttaraphalguni.

match for the Ikshvakus and the Videhas. O king! These marriages
are among those who are equal in dharma, equal in beauty and
equal in prosperity—Rama and Lakshmana, and Sita and Urmila.
O best among men! I have something to say. Listen to me. Your
younger brother, King Kushadhvaja, knows about dharma. O king!
He has two daughters who are devoted to dharma and their beauty
is unmatched on earth. Bestow them as wives on Prince Bharata
and the intelligent Shatrughna. O king! For the sake of those two
great-souled ones, we will accept these daughters. In their beauty
and youth, all of Dasharatha's sons are like the guardians of the
worlds and are like the gods in valour. O Indra among kings! Let
these two excellent lineages, auspicious in deeds, yours and that of
the Ikshvakus, be closely tied to each other through an alliance.'
Having heard Vishvamitra's words, which were in agreement
with Vasishtha's views, Janaka joined his hands in salutation and
addressed those bulls among sages. 'As you have commanded, I
also think this alliance is between two lineages that are equal. O
fortunate ones! Let it be that way. Let Kushadhvaja's daughters
tend to Shatrughna and Bharata as their wives. O great sage! Let
the four princesses accept the hands of the four extremely strong
princes on the same day. O brahmana! The learned ones have
praised a marriage on the day of Uttaraphalguni, when Bhaga is the
presiding lord.'[459] Having spoken in this way, the amiable one arose
and joined his hands in salutation. King Janaka spoke these words
to those two supreme sages. 'You have performed a supreme act of
dharma for me. I will always be your disciple. O bulls among sages!
Seat yourselves on these excellent seats. In the way they are ruled,
there is no difference between my kingdom and Dasharatha's city
of Ayodhya. You should therefore act so that everything is properly
undertaken.'

When the lord of Videha said this, King Dasharatha, descendant
of the Raghu lineage, cheerfully replied to King Janaka in these
words. 'O lords of Mithila! You two brothers are immeasurable

---

[459] The presiding deity of Uttaraphalguni (Denebola) is Bhaga, the god of marital
bliss and prosperity. In fairness, there is scope for interpretation here, with the word *uttara*
also being interpreted as the latter part of the day.

in your qualities. You have honoured the rishis in this assembly
of kings. O fortunate one! May everything be well with you. I will
now go to my own abode and undertake the funeral rites for the
ancestors.' Having said this, King Dasharatha took his leave of the
two kings, placing those two Indras among sages at the forefront.
The immensely illustrious one swiftly departed. Having gone to his
abode, the king followed the ordinances and performed the funeral
rites. When it was morning, he arose and performed the excellent
rite of godana. The king donated one hundred thousand cows to
brahmanas. Following dharma, the king donated these in the names
of each of his sons. The horns of these cows were encrusted with
gold. They were donated with their calves and with brass vessels
for milking them. The bull among men gave away four hundred
thousand cows.[460] The descendant of the Raghu lineage gave away
many other kinds of riches to brahmanas. Devoted to his sons, he
undertook godana in the names of his sons. Having undertaken
godana in the names of his sons, the king was as radiant as the
agreeable Prajapati,[461] surrounded by the guardians of the worlds.

# Chapter 1(72)

On the day when the king performed the excellent godana rite,
on that very same day, the brave Yudhajit arrived. He was
the son of the king of Kekaya and Bharata's own maternal uncle.
Having met the king, he asked about his welfare in these words.
'Affectionately, the king of Kekaya has inquired about your welfare.
You will also be interested in the welfare of those who are there
and as of now, they are well. O Indra among kings! O descendant
of the Raghu lineage! The king wished to see my sister's son[462] and
that is the reason I was sent to Ayodhya. I heard in Ayodhya that

---

[460] For each son, one hundred thousand cows were donated.
[461] Brahma.
[462] Bharata.

you had left for the marriage, with your sons.[463] O king! That is the reason I have come here to Mithila, to meet you. To see my sister's son, I have quickly come here.' King Dasharatha saw that his beloved guest had arrived. On seeing this, he honoured the one who deserved honours with great worship.

When the night was over, with his great-souled sons, and placing the rishis at the forefront, he arrived at the sacrificial arena. At the appropriate hour, when all the auspicious signs for victory were present, adorned in ornaments, Rama and his brothers performed the sacred rites. They placed Vasishtha and the other maharshis ahead of them. The illustrious Vasishtha addressed the lord of Videha. 'O king! King Dasharatha has performed all the auspicious rites. With his sons, the supreme one among the best among men now desires a donor. All forms of prosperity result when the receiver accepts from the donor. Following your own dharma, now perform the excellent wedding rites.' He was addressed in these words by the great-souled Vasishtha. The extremely generous and immensely energetic one, supremely devoted to dharma, replied in these words. 'Who is preventing entry?[464] Whose instructions are you waiting for? This is your own house. What are you thinking about? This kingdom is like your own. O best among sages! Having performed the auspicious rites, my daughters have arrived at the sacrificial altar. They are like the flames of a blazing fire. I have prepared everything and am waiting for you at the sacrificial altar. There are no obstructions. What is the king waiting for?' Hearing Janaka's words, with his sons and with the large number of rishis, Dasharatha entered. King Janaka spoke to the one who extended Kousalya's delight. 'This is my daughter Sita and she will perform every act of dharma with you. O fortunate one! If you also desire her, accept her hand with your hand. O Lakshmana! O fortunate one! Come here. I have earmarked Urmila for you. If you also desire her, accept her hand. You should not waste any time in thinking.' Having spoken to him, Janaka addressed

---

[463] Bharata and Shatrughna.
[464] These are ceremonial and rhetorical questions, not meant to be answered.

Bharata. 'O descendant of the Raghu lineage! Accept Mandavi's hand with your hand.' Lord Janaka, with dharma in his soul, also spoke to Shatrughna. 'O mighty-armed one! Accept Shrutakeerti's hand with your hand. All of you are agreeable. O Kakutsthas! With your wives, all of you will be excellent in the observance of vows. You should not waste time in thinking.' Hearing Janaka's words and with Vasishtha's sanction, the four accepted the hands of those four with their hands. With their wives, those excellent ones, born in Raghu's lineage, progressively circumambulated the fire, the sacrificial altar, the king[465] and the rishis. They acted as they had been asked to. Following the ordinances, the marriages were concluded. A great shower of radiant flowers rained down from the sky. Divine drums were sounded and there were the sounds of singing and musical instruments. Large numbers of apsaras danced and gandharvas sang in melodious tones. At the marriages of the best among the Raghus, this was the wonderful spectacle. While this was going on, trumpets were sounded. With their wives, those greatly energetic ones circumambulated the fire thrice. After this, with their wives, the descendants of the Raghu lineage went to the residences meant for guests. While the large number of rishis looked on, the king[466] followed them, with his relatives.

## Chapter 1(73)

When night was over, taking his leave of the kings, Vishvamitra, the great sage, left for the northern mountains. After Vishvamitra had left, the king[467] took his leave of the lord of Videha and Mithila. King Dasharatha swiftly left for his own city. The king of Videha gave his daughters many kinds of riches. The lord of Mithila gave them hundreds of thousands of cows, the best of

[465] Janaka.
[466] Dasharatha.
[467] Dasharatha.

blankets, crores of silken garments, elephants, horses, chariots and foot soldiers. The father also gave his daughters excellent male and female servants, adorned in ornaments that seemed divine. There were gold, silver, pearls and coral. Extremely happy, he gave his daughters these supreme riches. Having given these many kinds of riches, the king took the king's permission.[468] The lord of Mithila entered his own residence in Mithila.

With his great-souled sons, the king and lord of Ayodhya proceeded. All the rishis were at the forefront and he was followed by his forces. The tiger among men proceeded, with the large number of rishis and the Raghavas. At this time, in every direction, a terrible sound of birds was heard. On earth too, all the animals circled leftwards.[469] On seeing this, the tiger among kings asked Vasishtha, 'The birds are distracted and behaving in a terrible way. The animals are also circling leftwards. Why is this? My heart is trembling and my mind is distressed.' Hearing Dasharatha's words, the great rishi replied sweetly. 'Hear what these portend. A terrible and divine fear presents itself and this is being voiced from the mouths of the birds. The animals will be pacified and this torment will pass.' While they were conversing, a wind began to rage. It made the earth tremble and brought down the auspicious trees. The sun was enveloped in darkness and none of the directions could be discerned. Everything was covered in ashes and the army was confounded. Vasishtha and the other sages and the king and his sons remained stationed there. Though all of them were in their senses, they seemed to be unconscious. The army was shrouded in that terrible darkness and the ashes. At that time, a form was seen. He was terrible in appearance, with circles of matted hair. He was as unassailable as Kailasa and he was extremely difficult to withstand, like the fire of destruction. He seemed to blaze in his energy and ordinary people found it impossible to look at him. A battleaxe was slung on his shoulder and he wielded a bow that was like a flash of lightning. He held the best of arrows, like Hara at the time

---

[468] Janaka and Dasharatha respectively.
[469] The left is regarded as inauspicious.

of the destruction of Tripura.[470] They saw him, terrible in form, like a blazing fire. Vasishtha and the best among brahmanas were devoted to meditations and oblations. All those assembled sages began to discuss among themselves. 'He became intolerant because of his father's death and destroyed the kshatriyas.[471] Having killed the kshatriyas earlier, his intolerance and fever were dispelled. Is he again interested in destroying the kshatriyas?' Having said this, they offered arghya to Bhargava, who was terrible to behold. The rishis addressed him in these sweet words. 'O Rama![472] O Rama!' Having accepted the honours from the powerful rishi,[473] the Rama who was Jamadagni's son spoke to the Rama who was Dasharatha's son.

## Chapter 1(74)

'O Rama! O Dasharatha's son! O brave one! I have heard about your extraordinary valour. I have heard everything about how you shattered the bow. That shattering of the bow is wonderful and unthinkable. On hearing this, I have come here, with another auspicious bow. This is the great bow received from Jamadagni and it is terrible in form. String it and affix a bow. Show me your own strength. I will witness your strength in your ability to string this bow. If you can do this, you can pride yourself on being valiant and I will then grant you a duel.' Hearing these words, King Dasharatha's face became downcast. Distressed, he joined his hands in salutation and said, 'O brahmana! Your anger against the immensely illustrious kshatriyas has been pacified. My sons are children. You should grant them freedom from fear. You have been

---

[470] The demons had a city named Tripura and Shiva (Hara) destroyed this with a single arrow.

[471] Parashurama destroyed the kshatriyas twenty-one times, because Kartavirya Arjuna (a kshatriya) killed his father, Jamadagni. Jamadagni was descended from Bhrigu. Hence, Parashurama is called Bhargava.

[472] Meaning Parashurama. Parashurama means the Rama with the battleaxe (parashu).

[473] Vasishtha.

born in the lineage of the Bhargavas. You are engaged in studying
and are devoted to your vows. You promised the one with the one
thousand eyes that you would cast aside your weapons. Devoted to
dharma, you then gave the earth away to Kashyapa. Having given
him that, you went to the forest, becoming like a standard to Mount
Mahendra. O great sage! Have you decided to destroy all of us?
While all of us are alive, it is not possible for you to kill Rama
alone.' While he was speaking in this way, Jamadagni's powerful son
ignored Dasharatha's words and spoke to Rama instead. 'There are
two supreme bows. They are divine and famous in the worlds. They
are firm and excellent and have been crafted well by Vishvakarma.
O best among men! O Kakutstha! The gods gave one of these to
Tryambaka, when he wished to fight and destroy Tripura. This is
the one that has been shattered by you. The best among the gods
gave the second invincible one to Vishnu. O Kakutstha! This is
innately equal to Rudra's bow. Once, all the gods reflected on the
strengths and weaknesses of Shitikantha and Vishnu and asked
the grandfather. The grandfather, supreme among those who are
truthful, ascertained that the gods wished to engender a conflict.
There was a great encounter between Shitikantha and Vishnu, as
they sought to defeat each other. This made the body hair stand up.
Through his[474] yawn and humkara, Shiva's terrible and excellent
bow was countered. The three-eyed Mahadeva was rendered
motionless. The gods, with large numbers of rishis and charanas,
assembled. They sought pacification and those two supreme among
gods desisted. On seeing that Vishnu's powerful yawn had rendered
Shiva's bow powerless, the gods, and the large number of rishis,
deduced that Vishnu was superior. The immensely illustrious Rudra
was enraged and gave his bow, with the arrow still held in his hand, to
rajarshi Devarata from Videha. O Rama! This is Vishnu's excellent
bow, capable of vanquishing the cities of enemies. Vishnu gave it
to Richika Bhargava, to be held in trust. The immensely energetic
Richika gave this divine bow to his great-souled son Jamadagni,
who cannot be countered in his deeds and who was my father. My

[474] Vishnu's.

father, full of the strength of austerities, cast aside his weapons and was killed by Arjuna,[475] whose intelligence was inferior. I heard about the extremely terrible and unrivalled account of my father's death. Because of the anger that resulted, I exterminated a large number of kshatriyas. O Rama! Having obtained the entire earth, I handed it over to the great-souled Kashyapa, as an auspicious act of dakshina at the end of a sacrifice. Having given it away, full of the strength of austerities, I made my abode on Mount Mahendra. Having heard about the shattering of the bow, I have quickly come here. O Rama! This supreme and great Vaishnava bow has come to me through my father and grandfather. Placing the dharma of kshatriyas at the forefront, wield it. String it and affix an arrow to this bow, which is the conqueror of enemy cities. O Kakutstha! If you are capable of doing this, I will thereafter grant you a duel.'

## Chapter 1(75)

Hearing the words of Jamadagni's son, showing respect to his father, Rama, Dasharatha's son, addressed him in these words. 'O Bhargava! I have heard about the deeds that you have accomplished. O brahmana! I also applaud what you did to repay the debt to your father. O Bhargava! In following the dharma of kshatriyas, you deem me to be inferior in valour and incapable. You slight my energy. Therefore, witness my valour now.' Raghava's hands were dexterous in their valour. Having said this, he angrily seized Bhargava's supreme weapon and an arrow. Rama strung the bow and affixed an arrow to it. Rama then angrily spoke these words to Rama who was Jamadagni's son. 'You are a brahmana and deserve to be worshipped. There is also Vishvamitra to consider.[476] O Rama! Therefore, I am incapable of releasing this arrow, which can take away your life. O Rama! You can swiftly

---

[475] Kartavirya Arjuna.
[476] Jamadagni was married to Satyavati, Vishvamitra's sister.

travel wherever you want. You have also conquered and obtained unmatched worlds through the strength of your austerities. Of these two, I will destroy whichever one you wish. This is a Vaishnava bow and a divine arrow that can destroy the cities of enemies affixed to it. This destroys strength and insolence and its valour is inviolate.' Placing the grandfather at the forefront, large numbers of rishis and gods assembled to see Rama and the supreme weapon. There were gandharvas, apsaras, siddhas, charanas, kinnaras, yakshas, rakshasas and serpents, desiring to witness this great and extraordinary wonder. As Rama wielded that supreme bow, the worlds seemed to be senseless. Rama, who was Jamadagni's son, became devoid of his valour and glanced at Rama. Devoid of his energy and devoid of his valour, Jamadagni's son was benumbed.

Extremely gently and softly, he spoke to the lotus-eyed Rama. 'Earlier, I gave the earth to Kashyapa. Kashyapa told me, "Do not reside in my dominion." Following the words of my preceptor, I do not dwell on the earth at nights. O Kakutstha! This is the pledge I made to Kashyapa. O brave one! O Raghava! Therefore, you should not destroy my mobility. With the speed of thought, I will go to the supreme Mount Mahendra. O Rama! Through my austerities, I have conquered unmatched worlds. Do not waste time in thinking. With this supreme arrow, destroy those worlds. I know you to be the destroyer of Madhu, the one without decay.[477] You are the lord of the gods. I know this from your touch on the bow. O scorcher of enemies! May you be well. This large number of gods has assembled and is looking at you. Your deeds are unmatched and you cannot be countered in a fight. O Kakutstha! I should not be ashamed at this. You are the protector of the three worlds and I have been countered by someone like you. O Rama! O one excellent in vows! Release the unmatched arrow. When the arrow has been released, I will go to the supreme Mount Mahendra.' Jamadagni's son spoke in this way to Rama. The handsome Rama, Dasharatha's son, released the supreme arrow. The darkness was dispelled and all the directions could be seen. The gods and all the rishis praised Rama and the

---

[477] Vishnu, who killed a demon named Madhu.

upraised weapon. Rama who was Jamadagni's son praised the
Rama who was Dasharatha's son. Having circumambulated him,
the lord,[478] who no longer possessed any worlds, went away.

## Chapter 1(76)

When Rama had departed, Rama who was Dasharatha's son
became serene of soul. He handed over the bow and the
arrow to the immeasurable Varuna. Rama worshipped Vasishtha
and the other best of rishis. Seeing that his father was still distracted,
Rama, the descendant of the Raghu lineage said, 'Jamadagni's son
has departed. Protected by you, let the army with the four kinds
of forces proceed towards Ayodhya.' Hearing Rama's words,
King Dasharatha embraced his son with his arms and inhaled the
fragrance of Raghava's head. On hearing that Rama had departed,
the king was delighted. He urged the soldiers to quickly leave for
the city. There were beautiful flags and standards. Sounds could be
heard from the trumpets. The charming royal roads were sprinkled
with water and flowers were strewn on them. Citizens sounded
auspicious musical instruments at the gate of the royal palace.
As the king entered, the place was adorned and full with a large
number of people.

With other royal women, Kousalya, Sumitra and the slender-
waisted Kaikeyee engaged themselves in welcoming the daughters-
in-law. The immensely fortunate Sita, the illustrious Urmila and
Kushadhvaja's two daughters were received by the royal ladies.
Everyone was smeared with auspicious paste and adorned in silken
garments. All of them quickly went to the abodes meant for the
gods and performed worship there. All the princesses[479] worshipped
those who should be honoured. All of them found pleasure with
their husbands. They had obtained wives and weapons. They had

---

[478] Parashurama.
[479] Sita, Urmila, Mandavi and Shrutakeerti.

obtained riches and well-wishers. Those bulls among men engaged themselves in tending to their father.

Rama, with truth as his valour, obtained great fame in this world. Because of his superior qualities, he was like Svayambhu to all creatures. With Sita, Rama found pleasure for many seasons. The spirited one was devoted to her and her heart was also always devoted to him. Her father had bestowed her as a wife and she became Rama's beloved. His delight and qualities were enhanced by her qualities. Her husband's heartfelt devotion to her doubled because of this. Whatever was in the innermost portions of their hearts became manifest to each other. Maithilee Sita, Janaka's daughter, was special and was like the gods in her beauty. She was as beautiful as Shri.[480] The beautiful and supreme princess was united with the delightful son of a rajarshi. Rama was extremely radiant, like someone who is extremely desired. He was like the god Vishnu, the lord of the immortals, united with Shri.

*This ends Bala Kanda.*

[480] Lakshmi.

# CHAPTER TWO

# *Ayodhya Kanda*

# Chapter 2(1)

After some time, King Dasharatha, descendant of the Raghu lineage, spoke to his son Bharata, who was Kaikeyee's son.

'O son! Yudhajit is the brave son of the king of Kekaya. Your maternal uncle came to take you there and has been residing here.'[1] Hearing Dasharatha's words, Bharata, Kaikeyee's son, made arrangements to leave, along with Shatrughna. The brave one, best among men, took his leave of his father, Rama, the performer of unblemished deeds and his mother, and left with Shatrughna. Yudhajit was delighted. Taking Bharata and Shatrughna, the brave one entered his own city and his father rejoiced. With his brother, he[2] was treated with great honour. Like a son, he was affectionately reared by his uncle, who was a lord of horses. They resided there and enjoyed all the objects of desire. However, the brave brothers remembered their aged father, King Dasharatha. The immensely energetic king also remembered the two sons who were away, Bharata and Shatrughna, who were like the great Indra and Varuna. He loved those four bulls among men equally, as if they were four arms growing out of his own body.

Among them, the greatly energetic Rama brought great delight to his father. Endowed with superior qualities, he was like Svayambhu[3] to creatures. When Bharata had gone, Rama and the immensely strong Lakshmana tended to their father, who was like a god. Placing his father's instructions at the forefront, Rama, with dharma in his soul, performed all the agreeable and pleasant tasks required by the citizens. Supremely attentive, he tended to all the tasks required by their mothers. All the time, he took care of all the tasks required by the preceptors. In this way, because of Rama's good conduct, Dasharatha, the learned brahmanas and all the residents of the kingdom were delighted. He was also peaceful in his soul and spoke gently. He did not respond to harsh and loud words spoken by others. He was content with whatever good deed was done to him. Even if a hundred acts of injury were committed against him, he did not remember them. Whenever he found time while practising with weapons, he always conversed with those who were aged, whether they were aged in conduct or wisdom, and with virtuous people. His birth was fortunate. He was

[1] He stayed on because of the marriage.
[2] Bharata.
[3] Brahma.

virtuous and not distressed. He was truthful and upright. He was
instructed by aged brahmanas who were conversant with dharma
and artha. He knew about dharma, artha and kama.[4] He possessed
memory and innate intelligence. He was skilled and accomplished
in prevalent customs. He knew about the sacred texts and about
how they should be followed. He understood differences among
people. He was accomplished in policy and knew about whom to
reward and whom to punish. He knew about earning revenue and
was accomplished in the techniques of expenditure. He obtained
instructions about the best collections of sacred texts and about
the ancillary texts. He knew that artha should not be accumulated
through adharma. He was not lazy when pursuing pleasure. He
was acquainted with details about artisanship and the fine arts.
He knew how to control and ride elephants and horses. He was
best among those who knew about dhanurveda. The world revered
him as an *atiratha*.[5] He was accomplished in commanding armies
and could strike while advancing. The prince exhibited the best of
qualities while dealing with the subjects. He was revered in the three
worlds and his qualities of forgiveness was like those of the earth.
He was like Brihaspati[6] in his wisdom and like Shachi's consort[7] in
his valour. He was thus loved by all the subjects and brought joy
to his father. Rama was radiant in his qualities, like the sun with
its rays. He followed all the vows and his valour was unassailable.
The earth desired him as her protector, as if he was a guardian of
the world. Rama was endowed with many such supreme qualities.

On seeing this, Dasharatha, scorcher of enemies, started to
think. A great reason for delight began to circulate in his heart.
'When will I see my son instated as the heir? His prosperity in this
world is growing and he is compassionate towards all creatures.

---

[4] Dharma, artha and kama are the three objectives (purushartha) of human existence.
Artha is the pursuit of material prosperity, kama is the pursuit of sensual pleasure, it being
best not to translate dharma. Sometimes, moksha (emancipation) is added as a fourth
objective.

[5] Dhanurveda is the science of war. An atiratha is a great warrior, greater than a
maharatha.

[6] The preceptor of the gods.

[7] Indra.

Like Parjanya[8] showering down, he is loved more than me in this world. He is like Yama and Shakra in his valour and like Brihaspati in his wisdom. He is like the earth in patience and is superior to me in qualities. Will I see my son instated over this entire earth? As I age, will I behold this and then ascend to heaven?' The great king saw that he was endowed with all these qualities. With his advisers, he determined that he would be made the heir apparent. He summoned all the foremost kings on earth and all those who resided in different cities and habitations. All of them seated themselves in different seats earmarked by the king. Attentive, all those kings seated themselves and looked towards the king.[9] All the revered and humble kings and men from cities and habitations seated themselves. Surrounded by them, he looked like the one with one thousand eyes, surrounded by the immortals.

## Chapter 2(2)

The lord of men invited all the courtiers. He spoke these unmatched, beneficial and agreeable words. His voice was deep, like the rumbling of a drum. The king's voice was great, like the rumbling of the clouds. 'Kings from the Ikshvaku lineage have ruled here earlier. I wish that this entire earth, which deserves happiness, should be full of welfare. I have acted in accordance with and followed the path of my ancestors. To the best of my capacity, I have attentively protected the subjects. In ensuring the welfare of the world, this entire body of mine has decayed and has become pale from the shadow of the umbrella.[10] I have obtained a lifespan lasting for many thousand years. Since the body has decayed, I desire to rest. Regal power is extremely difficult to bear and can only be sustained by a person who has conquered his senses. I am exhausted from bearing the extremely heavy burden of dharma that

[8] The god of rain.
[9] Dasharatha.
[10] A white umbrella is held aloft a king's head.

holds up the world. Engaging my son in the welfare of the subjects, I desire to rest, after taking the permission of all the bulls among brahmanas who are nearby. My eldest son, Rama, the conqueror of enemy cities, possesses all the qualities. He is Purandara's equal in valour. He is supreme among those who uphold dharma. He is like the moon, in conjunction with Pushya nakshatra. I will cheerfully anoint that bull among men as the heir apparent. As a protector, Lakshmana's prosperous elder brother is like the protector of the three worlds. He will be the supreme protector. By entrusting this entire earth to such a son now, I will do what is beneficial and ensure that it suffers from no hardships.' Delighted, the kings loudly welcomed the words of the king, like peacocks crying in delight when they see a giant cloud showering down. All of them got to know the desire and sentiments of the aged King Dasharatha, who was accomplished in dharma and artha. 'O king! Having lived for many thousand years, you are aged. O king! Therefore, consecrate Rama as the heir apparent.' Hearing their words, the king got to know what was agreeable to their minds. He had not known this earlier and wished to test them. He spoke these words. 'I follow dharma and rule over this earth. Why do you then wish to see my son instated as the heir apparent?'

All the inhabitants of the city and the countryside replied to the great-souled one. 'O king! Your son possesses many auspicious qualities. Rama has truth for his valour. Invested with divine qualities, he is like Shakra. O lord of the earth! He is superior to all those in the Ikshvaku lineage. Rama is devoted to truth and dharma and is a virtuous man in this world. He knows about dharma and never wavers from the truth. He is good in conduct and suffers from no jealousy. He is patient and comforting. He speaks gently and is grateful. He has conquered his senses. He is mild and his mind is not fickle. He is always good in behaviour and does not suffer from envy. Towards all creatures, he is pleasant in speech. Raghava is truthful in speech. He worships the aged brahmanas who are extremely learned. His deeds and fame are infinite and are increasing. He is accomplished in all the weapons of gods, asuras and humans. With Soumitri, when he advances into a battle for the sake of a village or a city, he does not return without being victorious. When he returns from a battle, whether it is on an elephant or a chariot, he always asks about the welfare of the citizens and their relatives. Progressively, he asks about everything, their sons, their sacrificial fires, their wives, their servants and their disciples, like a father asking about his own biological sons. He attentively asks us whether our disciples are tending to our needs. This is what Rama, tiger among men, always asks us. He is extremely miserable when people suffer from hardships. In all festivals, he is as satisfied as a father. He is truthful and a great archer. He has conquered his senses and serves the aged. It is good fortune that Raghava has been born to you as an excellent son. It is good fortune that you have a son with such qualities, like Kashyapa was to Marichi. Rama's soul is known. All the people in the kingdom and in this supreme city, all the people who are inside and outside the city and the countryside, women, aged and young—morning and night, all of them attentively desire strength, freedom from disease and a long life for him. They bow down before all the gods, wishing fame for Rama. Through prayers to the gods they worship and through your favours, we will obtain prosperity. O king! We will see your son Rama, with the complexion of a dark lotus, the destroyer of enemies everywhere, instated as the heir apparent. Your son is like the god of the gods. He is engaged in the welfare of the worlds. O one who grants boons! For the sake of welfare, you should swiftly and cheerfully instate the one who is generous in qualities.'

# Chapter 2(3)

The king joined his hands, which were like lotuses, in salutation. He accepted their words. Having accepted them, he spoke these agreeable and beneficial words to them. 'I am extremely delighted and my power has become unmatched, now that you desire that my beloved eldest son should be instated as the heir apparent.'

The king worshipped the brahmanas Vasishtha and Vamadeva
and told them, 'Listen. This is the prosperous and sacred month
of Chaitra.[11] The groves are full of blossoming flowers. Let all the
arrangements be made for Rama to become the heir apparent.'
Delighted and full of joy, those two bulls among brahmanas told
the lord of the earth, 'Everything has been arranged as you had
instructed.' The radiant king spoke these words to Sumantra.
'Bring Rama, cleansed in his soul, here quickly.' Sumantra pledged
to do what the king had asked him to. He brought Rama, supreme
among charioteers, there in a chariot. King Dasharatha seated
himself. He was surrounded by kings from the east, the west, the
north and the south. There were mlechchhas and aryas and others
who resided in forests and extremities of mountains.[12] All of them
seated themselves there, like the gods around Vasava. The royal
sage was in their midst, like Vasava among the Maruts. From the
palace, he saw that his son had arrived on a chariot. He[13] was like
a king of the gandharvas. He was famous in this world because of
his manliness. He was long-armed and great in spirit. His stride
was like that of a crazy elephant. Rama's face was pleasant to
behold, like the moon. His beauty, generosity and qualities stole
the sight and hearts of men. Like rain, he gladdened subjects who
had been tormented by the summer. The king was not satisfied
from looking at him.

Raghava descended from the supreme chariot. Hands joined
in salutation, he approached his father, Sumantra following at the
rear. To see the king, along with the charioteer, Raghava, bull
among men, climbed up to the palace, which was like the summit
of Kailasa. Having approached his father, he joined his hands in
salutation. He worshipped at his father's feet and recited his own
name.[14] On seeing him bow down, join his hands in salutation
and stand near him, the king embraced his beloved son. The king

---

[11] March–April.

[12] Arya means a noble one and is used for those who speak Sanskrit.

[13] Rama.

[14] This is a customary form of greeting. It is not as if Dasharatha did not know who
Rama was.

gave Rama a beautiful and supreme seat. It was tall and beautiful, adorned with gems and gold. Having ascended that supreme seat, Raghava dazzled with his own resplendence, like the sparkling and rising sun atop Meru. His radiance made the assembly shine, like the resplendence of the moon amidst planets and nakshatras in a clear autumn sky. On seeing his beloved son, the king was delighted, just as one is happy to see one's ornamented person reflected in a mirror. The king, supreme among those who have sons, smiled and spoke these words to his son, like Kashyapa to Indra of the gods.[15] 'You have been born to my eldest wife and are a son who is just like me. O Rama! You have been born with the best of qualities and are the most beloved of my sons. You have delighted the subjects with your qualities. Therefore, at the conjunction of Pushya, you will be instated as the heir apparent. Your nature is extremely humble. You possess the qualities. O son! Though you possess the qualities, out of affection for you, I will tell you something for your welfare. Be even more humble. Always conquer your senses. Cast aside any distractions that arise because of desire and anger. Use direct and indirect means of examination to keep all the advisers and ordinary people happy. If you protect the earth in that way, the ordinary people will be satisfied and devoted. Your friends will rejoice, like the immortals having obtained amrita. O son! Therefore, act towards them as towards one's own self."

On hearing this, Rama's well-wishers, who wished to do him well, quickly went to Kousalya and told her what had happened. Kousalya, supreme among women, gave her friends gold, cattle and many kinds of jewels. Raghava honoured the king and ascended his chariot. Worshipped by large numbers of people, he went to his radiant house. Having heard, the citizens had obtained what they had wished for. They worshipped the king. Obtaining the king's permission, they went to their own houses and joyfully offered worship to the gods.

[15] The gods, including Indra, are Kashyapa's sons.

# Chapter 2(4)

When the citizens had left, the king, who was firm in taking decisions that needed to be taken, consulted with his ministers. 'There is a conjunction of Pushya tomorrow. My son, lord Rama, with eyes that are as coppery red as a red lotus, will be instated as heir apparent tomorrow.' After this, King Dasharatha entered the inner quarters of his residence and again instructed the charioteer that Rama should be brought. Obeying these words, the charioteer swiftly left for Rama's residence again, so as to bring Rama. The gatekeepers informed Rama that he had arrived again. On hearing that he had come, Rama was worried. Having allowed him to enter, Rama addressed him in these words. 'Tell me completely the reason for your arrival.' Thus addressed, the charioteer replied, 'The king wishes to see you. On hearing this, you have to decide whether to go or stay.' Hearing the charioteer's words, Rama swiftly left for the king's residence, so as to see the king. On hearing that Rama had arrived, King Dasharatha instructed that he should enter the house. He wished to speak some agreeable and supreme words. The handsome Raghava entered his father's residence. On seeing his father from a distance, he joined his hands in salutation and prostrated himself. The king raised the one who was prostrate and embraced him. He offered him a beautiful seat and again spoke, 'O Rama! I am aged and have lived for a long time. I have enjoyed all the desired objects of pleasure. I have performed hundreds of sacrifices at which I have offered food and copious quantities of dakshina. I have had the desired offspring and you are unmatched on earth. O supreme among men! I have donated and studied, as I wished. O brave one! I have felt the desired happiness. I have repaid the debts due to gods, rishis, ancestors, brahmanas and towards my own self. No other task remains, but for you to be consecrated. Therefore, I am engaging you in undertaking what needs to be done. Now, all the ordinary people desire that you should be the king. O son! Therefore, I wish to instate you as the heir apparent. O Rama! In my sleep, I see many kinds of terrible portents. Showers of giant

meteors descend from the sky and they make a loud noise. Those
who know about portents tell me that terrible planets, the sun,
Angaraka and Rahu, are approaching the nakshatra.[16] Whenever
such evil portents present themselves, the king dies, or confronts
a terrible catastrophe. O Raghava! Therefore, before my senses
are confounded, you need to be instated. The intelligence of living
beings is fickle. Today, the moon is in Punarvasu, which comes
before Pushya. Those who think about the portents have said that
the conjunction of Pushya is tomorrow. Your consecration will
be during the conjunction of Pushya. My mind is urging me to
hurry. O scorcher of enemies! I wish to instate you as the heir
apparent tomorrow. Therefore, control your soul and observe the
vows. Fast with your wife and sleep on the ground, on a mat made
of darbha grass. Your well-wishers will attentively protect you
from all directions. Whenever a task presents itself, there are many
kinds of obstructions. Bharata is not in this city and is far away. It
is my view that this is the right time for you to be consecrated. It is
indeed true that your brother, Bharata, is virtuous. He has dharma
in his soul and follows his elder brother. He is compassionate
and has conquered his senses. However, it is my view that the
minds of men are fickle. O Raghava! Even those who are virtuous
and always devoted to dharma may act impetuously.' Having
thus told him about the consecration the following day, he gave
Rama permission to leave. Worshipping his father, he left for his
own house.

After this, he left for his mother's residence, in the inner
quarters. He saw his mother worshipping there, clad in silken
garments. He saw her silently meditating in the abode meant for
the gods, worshipping Shri.[17] On hearing the agreeable news about

---

[16] Angaraka is another name for Mangala (Mars). Though the text leaves it implicit,
the nakshatra presumably means Dasharatha's natal nakshatra. There is an anomaly that
caught Rama unawares too. Dasharatha decided that Rama should be made the heir
apparent. He subsequently decided that it needed to be done instantly, though Bharata
was still away in his maternal uncle's kingdom. A charioteer was sent to fetch Rama. We
have kept this as charioteer (suta), though most translations interpret this as Sumantra.
Since that equation is not obvious, we retained charioteer.

[17] Lakshmi, the goddess of wealth and prosperity.

Rama's consecration, Sumitra and Lakshmana arrived there, even before Sita was brought. At that time, Kousalya's eyes were closed and she was meditating. Sumitra was seated there, along with Sita and Lakshmana. On hearing that her son would be instated at the time of Pushya's conjunction, she was engaged in *pranayama*[18] and meditating on the supreme being, Janardana. While she was engaged in these vows, he approached and greeted her. Rama spoke these words to her, causing her joy. 'O mother! My father has engaged me in the task of protecting the subjects. Following my father's command, my consecration will be tomorrow. With me, Sita must fast throughout the night. My father, along with his preceptors, have told me this. Let all the auspicious rites, for me and Vaidehi, be performed in preparation for the consecration tomorrow.' Kousalya had desired this for a long time. Hearing this, her eyes filled with tears of joy and she spoke these words to Rama. 'O Rama! May you live for a long time and let those who cause obstructions in your path be destroyed. Let my kin and that of Sumitra's find delight at your prosperity. O son! You were born to me at the time of an auspicious nakshatra. That is the reason you have surpassed your father, Dasharatha, in your qualities. My austerities before the lotus-eyed being[19] are inviolate. O son! Hence, the prosperity of this kingdom of the Ikshvakus will find a refuge in you.' His brother was humbly seated nearby, hands joined in salutation. Hearing his mother's words, he glanced towards him, smiled and spoke these words. 'O Lakshmana! You will rule over this earth with me. You are like my second self and this prosperity will also find a refuge in you. O Soumitri! Enjoy all the desired objects of pleasure and the fruits of this kingdom. I wish to remain alive and desire this kingdom for your sake.' Having addressed Lakshmana in these words, Rama greeted his two mothers and took their permission. With Sita, he left for his own residence.

---

[18] Yoga has eight elements—*yama* (restraint), *niyama* (rituals), asana (posture), pranayama (control of the breath), *pratyahara* (withdrawal), *dharana* (retention), *dhyana* (meditation) and *samadhi* (liberation). That's the reason the expression *ashtanga* (eight-formed) yoga is used.

[19] Vishnu.

# Chapter 2(5)

After instructing Rama, the king summoned his priest, Vasishtha, and told him about the consecration the next day. 'O store of austerities! Go to Kakutstha and make him fast. For the sake of prosperity, fame and the kingdom, make him observe the rites, together with his wife.' The one who was supreme among those who knew about the Vedas agreed to what the king had said. The illustrious Vasishtha himself went to Rama's residence. He reached Rama's residence, with the pale radiance of a thick cloud. The supreme among sages passed through the three chambers on his chariot.[20] Showing respect, Rama quickly came forward to greet the rishi. He emerged from his residence to show honours to the one to whom honours were due. He swiftly approached the learned one's chariot and himself grasped him and helped him descend from the chariot. On seeing Rama, the one who brought pleasure, the priest spoke these words, bringing him joy and delight. 'O Rama! Your father is pleased with you and you will become the heir apparent. With Sita, you must fast today. When it is morning, the king will anoint you as the heir apparent. Your father, Dasharatha, is pleased with you, as Nahusha was with Yayati.'[21] Having said this, the sage made Rama, together with Vaidehi, observe the vows of fasting, accompanied by the associated mantras. Rama worshipped the royal preceptor. Having taken Kakutstha's leave, he[22] left Rama's residence. Seated there, Rama spoke pleasant words to his well-wishers and was congratulated by them. Taking their permission, he entered his own house. Rama's residence was radiant, full of delighted men and women. It was like a lake populated by herds of crazy elephants and blooming lotuses.

Vasishtha emerged from Rama's residence, which was like the royal palace. He saw that the roads were full of people. In every direction, Ayodhya's royal roads were crowded with large numbers

---

[20] The sense is that ordinary people would have got down from the chariot at the outer gate and proceeded through the three chambers on foot.

[21] Nahusha was Yayati's father.

[22] Vasishtha.

of people. Large numbers of curious people created a melee. As those large crowds met, there were sounds of joy. The royal roads were resplendent and seemed to roar like the ocean. All the roads, flanked by garlands of trees, were sprinkled with water.[23] Flags were raised in all the houses in the city of Ayodhya. All the people who resided in Ayodhya, women, children and disabled, wished that the sun would rise, so that Rama's desired consecration could take place. People were anxious to witness that great festival in Ayodhya, which would be like an adornment for the subjects and would increase the delight of people. Those crowds and large masses of people along the royal roads created obstructions, like a vyuha.[24] Slowly, the priest reached the royal residence. He ascended up to the palace, which was like the summit of a mountain, tinged by a white cloud. He went and met the king, like Brihaspati meeting Shakra. On seeing that he had come, the king got down from his throne. He asked him and was told that all the rituals had been observed. Taking his preceptor's permission and that of the large number of people, the king left them and entered his inner quarters, like a lion entering a cave in a mountain. That best of residences was full of a large number of women. The residence was like the great Indra's abode. As the king entered the beautiful residence, it seemed to become even more resplendent, like the moon in the firmament, surrounded by a large number of stars.

## Chapter 2(6)

When the priest had left, Rama controlled his mind and bathed. With his large-eyed wife, he approached Narayana.[25] As is recommended in the ordinances, he placed the vessel of oblations on his head. He then rendered these oblations into the blazing fire, as offerings to the great god. For his own good, he then partook of

---

[23] These were avenues, lined with trees.
[24] A vyuha is a battle formation.
[25] Figuratively.

the remainder of the oblations. Meditating on the god Narayana, he lay down on a mat of kusha grass. Vaidehi was controlled in her speech and controlled in her mind. With her, the son of the supreme among men slept in Vishnu's beautiful shrine.[26] He awoke when one *yama* of the night was still left.[27] He arranged that all the decorations should be made in his house. He heard the pleasant words of sutas, *magadha*s and *vandi*s.[28] Seated, and controlled in his mind, he meditated on the chants for the morning sandhya. He bowed his head down and praised Madhusudana. Attired in clean and silken garments, he made brahmanas utter words of praise. Those sacred chants were deep and sweet. Ayodhya was filled with the sounds of trumpets being sounded. With Vaidehi, Raghava had fasted.

On hearing this, all the people who resided in Ayodhya rejoiced. All the residents of the city had heard that Rama would be consecrated. On seeing that night had turned into morning, they again arranged for excellent decorations—on the summits of temples that looked like peaks with clouds around them, at crossroads, along roads, in sanctuaries and in mansions, in the shops of traders, filled with many expensive objects, in the handsome houses of prosperous families, in all the assembly halls and all the visible parts of trees. Colourful flags and pennants were raised. Large numbers of dancers danced. Singers sang. Words that were pleasant to the mind and the eyes were heard. On the occasion of Rama's consecration, people conversed with each other. As Rama's consecration approached, they did this in squares and houses. Large numbers of children were playing at the entrances to the houses. They too spoke to each other about Rama's consecration. On the occasion of Rama's consecration, the citizens made the royal roads

[26] There was such a shrine inside the palace. This image is now believed to be in Srirangam.

[27] A yama is a period of three hours. Since it is made up of three yamas, the night is known as *triyama*.

[28] A suta is a bard, a magadha is a minstrel and a vandi is one who sings words of praise. Vandis probably did not compose anything themselves, while sutas and magadhas did, the former focusing on stories and the latter on rendering these into songs.

look splendid. They sprinkled flowers there and burnt incense and fragrances. Just in case night wasn't over, they had arranged for means of illumination, placing lamps in all the trees that lined all the roads. All the residents of the city decorated the city in this way. All of them desired Rama's consecration. Large numbers of them gathered in the squares and the assembly halls. They spoke to each other there, praising the king. 'This king, the delight of the Ikshvaku lineage, is great-souled. He knows himself to be aged. Therefore, for the sake of the kingdom, he wishes to anoint Rama in the kingdom. Rama, who is favoured by all of us, will become the lord of the earth. He can see what is inside and outside people and will be our protector for a long period of time. His mind is not insolent. He is learned and has dharma in his soul. He is devoted to his brothers. Raghava is as gentle towards us as he is towards his brothers. Let the unblemished King Dasharatha, with dharma in his soul, live for a long time. It is through his favours that we have been able to witness Rama's consecration.' These were the kinds of words that could be heard among the citizens. The people who came from different directions, and those who were from the countryside, heard them. People came to the city from different directions to witness Rama's consecration. On the occasion of Rama's consecration, the city was filled with people from the countryside. Large numbers of people moved around and a sound could be heard, like the roar of the ocean when it is time for the full moon. The city resembled Indra's residence. In a desire to witness the spectacle, people arrived from the countryside. In every direction, there was a loud roar, like that of the ocean, filled with aquatic creatures.

# Chapter 2(7)

Kaikeyee had a maid who lived with her. She had come to her from the household of her kin.[29] Roaming around as she willed,

---

[29] From her father's household.

she climbed up to the palace, which looked like the moon. From the palace, Manthara looked at Ayodhya, with all the royal roads sprinkled with water and strewn with lotuses and lilies. The entire place was decorated with expensive flags and standards. It was full of people who had washed their heads and anointed themselves with sandalwood paste. On seeing a nursemaid nearby, Manthara asked her, 'Why is Rama's mother filled with supreme delight? Despite being attached to riches herself, why is she giving away riches to the people? Why are the people extremely joyous? Tell me. Has the king done something to cause such delight?' The nursemaid was extremely happy and seemed to be bursting with joy. Rejoicing, she told Kubja[30] about Raghava's great prosperity. 'Raghava has conquered anger and tomorrow, when it is the conjunction of Pushya, King Dasharatha will instate the faultless Rama as the heir apparent.' On hearing the nursemaid's words, Kubja was filled with anger.

She quickly descended from the palace that was like the summit of Kailasa. Manthara, evil in her thoughts, was consumed by rage. Kaikeyee was lying down. She went to her and spoke these words. 'O foolish one! Arise. You confront a great fear and are going to be submerged in a flood of calamity. Why are you sleeping? Why don't you yourself realize what is going to happen? You pride yourself as someone who is fortunate,[31] but harm is going to be caused to your fortune. Fortune is fickle, like the flow of a river during the summer.' Kaikeyee heard these angry and harsh words spoken by Kubja, whose thoughts were evil. Overcome by great misery, Kaikeyee spoke these words to Kubja. 'O Manthara! Why are you not at peace? One can see that your face is distressed and that you are extremely miserable.' Manthara heard Kaikeyee's words, expressed in sweet syllables. Accomplished in the use of words, she spoke words that were full of rage. Desiring her[32] welfare, Manthara spoke words that enhanced her unhappiness. She sought

[30] *Kubja* means humpbacked and this is how Manthara is described. However, kubja also means a class of housemaids and Manthara need not have been humpbacked.

[31] Because Dasharatha loved her more.

[32] Kaikeyee's.

to create dissension between the miserable one and Raghava. 'O extremely great queen! You are no longer at peace and a miserable catastrophe confronts you. King Dasharatha will instate Rama as the heir apparent. I am submerged in fathomless fear and am full of grief and misery. I am being scorched, as if by a fire. I have come here for the sake of your welfare. O Kaikeyee! My misery has become greater because of your misery. There is no doubt that my prosperity lies in your prosperity. You have been born in a lineage of kings and are queen to a lord of the earth. O queen! How can you not realize that there is a ferocity in the dharma of kings? Your husband speaks about dharma, but is deceitful. Though he speaks gently, he is terrible. Because you are pure in your sentiments, you do not know that you are being gravely cheated by him. He approaches you and unites with you. He comforts you with futile words. Wherever there is a prospect of prosperity, your husband passes that on to Kousalya. The evil-souled one has sent Bharata away to your relatives. With the obstruction out of the way, at the opportune time, he will establish Rama in the kingdom. Like a mother, you desire his welfare. However, in the garb of a husband, he is your enemy. O foolish one! You have nourished a venomous serpent in your lap. King Dasharatha has acted towards you and your own son just as a snake or an ignored enemy does. O child! Though you always deserve happiness, he has comforted you with wicked and false words. With Rama established in the kingdom, you and your relatives will be destroyed. O Kaikeyee! The time has come. To ensure your own welfare, act quickly. O one who is amazing to behold! Save your son and your own self.'

Hearing Manthara's words, the one with the beautiful face arose from her bed. She gave a beautiful ornament to Kubja. Having given that ornament to Kubja, Kaikeyee, supreme among women, again spoke these cheerful words to Manthara. 'O Manthara! What you have told me brings me great delight. You have recounted something agreeable. What can I do for you next? I do not see any difference between Rama and Bharata. Therefore, I am content that the king is instating Rama in the kingdom. Thus, you deserve to be given something again. These supreme words bring happiness. They

are agreeable and cause pleasure. You cannot possibly say anything
that is more agreeable than this. Ask for a boon and I will grant it
to you next.'

# Chapter 2(8)

Full of jealousy, Manthara cast aside that ornament. Overcome
with anger and rage, she spoke these words. 'O foolish one!
Why are you filled with delight? You are immersed in an ocean
of grief, but are incapable of comprehending it yourself. Kousalya
is indeed fortunate that her son will be consecrated. Tomorrow,
at the conjunction of Pushya, the supreme among brahmanas will
confer greatness on him by making him the heir apparent. With
his enemies destroyed, he will obtain great delight and fame. Like
a maid, you will have to join your hands in salutation and present
yourself before Kousalya. Rama's women[33] will certainly be filled
with great joy. However, your daughters-in-law will be unhappy
at Bharata's destruction.' On seeing that Manthara spoke these
extremely unpleasant words, Queen Kaikeyee praised Rama's
qualities. 'He knows about dharma. His preceptors have trained him
in being controlled. He is grateful. He is truthful in words and pure.
Rama is the king's eldest son. He deserves to be the heir apparent.
He will have a long life. Like a father, he will protect his brothers
and servants. O Kubja! On hearing about Rama's consecration,
why are you tormented? After Rama has ruled for one hundred
years, it is certain that Bharata, bull among men, will obtain the
kingdom of his father and grandfathers. O Manthara! A beneficial
occasion has presented itself now. Why are you tormented? Does he
not tend to me more than he does to Kousalya?' Hearing Kaikeyee's
words, Manthara was extremely miserable. Her sighs were long
and warm. She addressed Kaikeyee in these words. 'You do not
see the catastrophe. Because of your stupidity, you do not realize

---

[33] His wife and mother.

it yourself. You are going to be submerged in an ocean of grief
that is full of misery and hardship. If Raghava becomes the king,
his son will succeed him. O Kaikeyee! Bharata will be excised
from the royal lineage. O beautiful one! All of a king's sons do not
inherit the kingdom. If all of them are instated in this way, there
will be great anarchy. O Kaikeyee! Therefore, kings pass on the
various elements of the kingdom to the eldest son. O one with the
unblemished limbs! They are instated, even though others may be
superior in qualities. This son of yours will be completely shattered
and dislodged from this royal lineage. O devoted one! He will
be miserable and without a protector. I have come here for your
sake, but you do not understand me. When your co-wife becomes
prosperous, you desire to give me something. Shorn of thorns,
when Rama obtains this kingdom, it is certain that he will banish
Bharata to some other country, or perhaps remove him from this
world. Even when Bharata was a child, you sent him to his maternal
uncle's house. Affection is generated through proximity, even if it is
towards an immobile object.[34] Rama is protected by Soumitri and
Raghava protects Lakshmana. Their fraternal love is as famous in
the worlds as that of the two Ashvins. Therefore, Rama will not
perform any wicked deed towards Lakshmana. However, there is
no doubt that Rama will act in a wicked way towards Bharata.
Therefore, it is best that your son should go to the forest from the
royal residence.[35] This appeals to me and it will bring great benefit
to you. Even if Bharata were to obtain his father's kingdom through
dharma, that would be better for your relatives.[36] That child[37]
deserves happiness and he is Rama's natural enemy. With one's
own prosperity destroyed, how can one live under the subjugation
of another person who has obtained prosperity? Like a lion chasing
a herd of elephants in the forest, Rama is enveloping Bharata and
you should save him. Earlier, because of your good fortune and

[34] Thus, Dasharatha never developed affection towards Bharata.
[35] From his uncle's royal residence.
[36] Bharata going to the forest.
[37] Bharata.

pride, you slighted Rama's mother.[38] Why will your co-wife not pursue that enmity? When Rama obtains the earth, it is certain that Bharata will be destroyed. Therefore, think of a means to obtain the kingdom for your son and of a reason to exile the enemy.'

## Chapter 2(9)

Thus addressed, Kaikeyee's face blazed with anger. With a long and warm sigh, she spoke these words to Manthara. 'Right now, I will quickly dispatch Rama to the forest. I will swiftly instate Bharata as the heir apparent. O Manthara! Now think of a means whereby Bharata, and not Rama, gets the kingdom.' Manthara, wicked in her thoughts, was addressed in this way by the queen. Desiring to cause injury and violence to Rama, she spoke to Kaikeyee. 'O Kaikeyee! I will tell you. Listen to me. This is the means whereby your son, Bharata, alone can obtain the kingdom.' On hearing Manthara's words, Kaikeyee arose a bit from her well-laid-out bed and said, 'O Manthara! Tell me the method and the reason. How can Bharata obtain the kingdom and never Rama?' Manthara, wicked in her thoughts, was addressed in this way by the queen. Desiring to cause injury and violence to Rama, Kubja spoke these words. 'There was a battle between the gods and the asuras. The rajarshi, your husband, went to help the king of the gods and took you along with him. O queen! He advanced in a southern direction, towards Dandaka.[39] He went to the city of Vaijayanta, where Timidhvaja was. He was famous by the name of Shambara.[40] That great asura was conversant with one hundred different kinds of maya.[41] In the battle, he fought with

[38] The details are not known.

[39] The forest of Dandaka, known as Dandakaranya. The word *dandaka* means that people were exiled there, as punishment (*danda*).

[40] Timidhvaja was one of Shambara's names. Timidhvaja means one who had a whale on his standard.

[41] The power of illusion.

Shakra and vanquished the army of the gods. King Dasharatha
fought in that great battle. O queen! When he lost his senses in
the battle, you removed him from the spot. Your husband was
mangled by weapons and you saved him from that spot. O one
with the beautiful face! Satisfied with you, he gave you two boons.
O queen! Your husband offered to grant you two boons. However,
you told the great-souled one that you would ask for the boons
when the time came and he agreed. O queen! I did not know
about this. But on an earlier occasion, you yourself told me. Ask
for those two boons from your husband—Bharata's consecration
and Rama's exile for a period of fourteen years. O Ashvapati's
daughter! Go and enter the chamber earmarked for you to exhibit
anger. Without any spreads, lie down on the bare ground, attired in
dirty garments. Do not arise and do not say anything to him. There
is no doubt that your husband always loves you. For your sake,
the great king will even enter a fire. He is incapable of being angry
with you. He cannot even glance at you in rage. To bring pleasure
to you, the king will even give up his own life. The great king will
be incapable of transgressing your words. O one who is foolish in
nature! Comprehend your own good fortune and strength. King
Dasharatha will offer you many kinds of gems, pearls, gold and
jewels. But let your mind not be fruitlessly attracted to these. At
the time of the battle between the gods and the asuras, Dasharatha
gave you two boons. O immensely fortunate one! Remind him of
those and do not get diverted from your own prosperity. Raghava
will himself make you rise and give you those boons. When the
great king is steady, seek those two boons from him. Rama must
be exiled to the forest for fourteen years and the bull among kings
must make Bharata the king of this earth. Having exiled Rama
in this way, he will not obtain peace. However, with the enemies
destroyed, Bharata will become the king. By the time Rama returns
from the forest, your son will have obtained enough time to create
a foundation for himself. He will have accumulated men and
well-wishers on his own side. I think the time has come for you
to prepare yourself and cast aside fear. Persuade him to withdraw
from his intention of consecrating Rama.'

What was undesirable appeared to Kaikeyee as something that was desirable. She happily responded to Manthara in these words. 'O Kubja! You speak about what is best. So far, I have not understood what is best. In using the intelligence to determine what should be done, you are the best among all kubjas on earth. You are the one who has always been engaged in my welfare and have sought what brings me benefit. O Kubja! In determining what the king desires, my intelligence is not equal to yours. There are many kubjas who are badly placed. They are extremely wicked and crooked.[42] However, you are beautiful to behold, like a lotus bent by the wind. Your chest is proportionate, right up to your lofty shoulder. Below that, the stomach stretches out, with a shy navel. Adorned with a golden belt, your hips make a sound. Your thighs are extremely plump and your feet are long. O Manthara! O one attired in silken garments! As you walk before me on your long thighs, you are as radiant as a swan. Your tall hump is as large as the front of a chariot. The intelligence of kshatriyas and of maya reside in you. O Kubja! When Bharata has been consecrated and Raghava has gone to the forest, I will adorn you with a golden garland. O beautiful one! When I am happy and obtain what I desire, I will decorate your hump with that well-crafted ornament made out of molten gold. I will adorn your face with auspicious and colourful marks that are made out of molten gold. O Kubja! I will have auspicious ornaments constructed for you. Adorned in beautiful garments, you will walk around like a god. Your unmatched face will be like the face of the moon. Priding yourself above your enemies, you will walk around, chief among the best. O Kubja! Adorned in all kinds of ornaments, the kubjas will always serve at your feet, just as they do at mine.

Kaikeyee was still lying down on a sparkling bed, like the flame of a fire on a sacrificial altar. Praised in this way, she replied to her.[43] 'O fortunate one! There is no point to constructing a dam when the water has left. Arise. Act so as to show the king what

---

[42] This still doesn't make it obvious that the crookedness is physical, though the succeeding shlokas do suggest this.

[43] Manthara replied to Kaikeyee.

is beneficial.' The large-eyed one was proud of her good fortune. Thus urged, the queen went with Manthara to the chamber where she showed her anger. The beautiful one took off the necklace that had hundreds and thousands of pearls and also many other beautiful and expensive ornaments. Kaikeyee was like a golden rod. Succumbing to the words of Kubja, she lay down on the ground and told Manthara, 'O Kubja! Let it be known to the king that unless Raghava goes to the forest and Bharata obtains the earth, I will die here.' She spoke these extremely terrible words. The beautiful one cast aside all the ornaments. Like a kinnara lady who has fallen down, she lay down on the bare and uncovered ground. Having cast aside the garlands and ornaments, her face was only enveloped in anger. Despite being the wife of a king, she was distracted. She was like a star in the sky, enveloped in darkness.

## Chapter 2(10)

Having instructed that the arrangements should be made for Raghava's consecration, the great and powerful king entered the inner quarters to tell the one who should be loved about the good news. She was lying down on the ground there, in a state that did not befit her. On seeing her in this state, the lord of the earth was tormented by grief. He was aged, but his wife was young. She was dearer to him than his own life. She should be sinless, but her resolution was wicked. He saw her lying down on the ground. She was like a female elephant in the forest, struck by a poisoned arrow in the course of a hunt. He touched her, like a giant elephant touching that female elephant in the forest. Scared and bereft of his senses, he engulfed her in his arms. Desiring the lotus-eyed woman, he spoke these words. 'I do not know why there is this anger in you. O queen! Who has accused you or insulted you? O fortunate one! Your lying down in the dust causes me grief. O fortunate one! Why are you lying down on the ground, as if you are unconscious? You are the one who disturbs the senses, yet your senses seem to have been possessed by a demon. There are plenty of accomplished and praised physicians. O beautiful one! Tell me what ails you and they will cure you. Whom do you desire something agreeable to be done to? Whom do you desire something disagreeable to be done to? To whom shall I do something agreeable and to whom shall I do something extremely disagreeable? Will I kill someone who should not be killed? Whom will I kill and whom will I free? Who shall be made poor? Who shall be made rich? Who shall be given riches? Whose riches will be taken away? I, and all those who are subservient to me, are under your control. I am not interested in countering any of your wishes. Even if it concerns my own life, tell me what you wish for. The earth belongs to me, wherever the wheel of the chariot goes.'

Addressed and comforted in this way, she desired to say what was disagreeable. She readied herself to make her husband suffer. 'O king! No one has insulted me. No one has shown me disrespect. There is something that I desire and it can be accomplished by you. When you know what I wish for, do it, if you so desire. After you give me your pledge, I will tell you what I wish for.' The king was completely under the control of his beloved wife and was addressed in this way. The greatly energetic one smiled a little and told Kaikeyee, 'O proud one! With the exception of Rama, tiger among men, do you not know that there is no other human I love more than you? O fortunate one! My heart is sinking, energize it through your touch. O Kaikeyee! Discerning this, tell me what virtuous act have you thought of? You know about your own strength. Therefore, you should not harbour any suspicions. I will do what causes you pleasure. I take a pledge on all my good deeds.' Delighted at his words, she told him about the desire that was in her mind, extremely terrible, like the news of a sudden death. 'With Indra at the forefront, let the thirty gods progressively hear about the boons you have pledged to bestow on me. Let the moon, the sun, the sky, the planets, the night, the day, the directions, the universe, the earth, gandharvas, rakshasas, the roamers of the night, the living beings in houses, the gods in houses and all the creatures hear the words you have spoken. He does not waver from the truth.

He is extremely energetic and knows about dharma. He is extremely
controlled. He is granting me a boon. Let the gods hear about it.'
The queen seized the great archer, who was ready to grant boons,
but had promised excessively, confounded by desire. Thereafter, she
spoke these words. 'O lord! O great king! You had granted me two
boons earlier. I am asking you to grant those to me now. Listen
to my words. All the arrangements have been made for Raghava's
consecration. I desire that these arrangements should be used for
Bharata's consecration. Rama will become an ascetic and will reside
in Dandakaranya for fourteen years. He will sport matted hair and
will be attired in rags and bark. Bereft of any thorns, Bharata must
be made the heir apparent. Right now, I wish to see Raghava leave
for the forest.'

The great king heard Kaikeyee's terrible words. He was
distressed and lost his senses, like a deer which has seen a tiger.
Bereft of his senses, he sank down on the bare ground and sighed
deeply. In rage, the king uttered the word, 'Shame!' With his senses
overtaken by sorrow, he again fell unconscious. After a long period
of time, the king regained his senses, but was extremely miserable.
He spoke angrily to Kaikeyee, as if he was going to burn her down
with his sight. 'O cruel one! O one who is wicked in conduct! O one
who destroys the lineage! What wicked act has Rama done towards
you? What evil have I done? Raghava's conduct towards you has
always been like that towards a mother. That being the case, why
are you engaged in causing this injury to him? You entered my own
house with a view to bring about my destruction. I did not know that
the daughter of a king was actually a snake with virulent poison. All
the living beings on earth extol Rama's qualities. What crime have I
committed that I have to cast aside my beloved son? I can abandon
Kousalya, Sumitra, my prosperity and my own life. But as long as I
am alive, how can I cast aside Rama, who is devoted to his father?
On seeing my eldest son, I am overcome by great delight. If I do
not see Rama, my consciousness is destroyed. The world can exist
without a sun and crops without water. However, without Rama,
there cannot be life in my body. O one who has made up her mind
about something wicked! Enough is enough, cast this resolution

aside. I will even touch your feet with my head, be pacified.' The lord of the earth lamented like one without a protector. Suffering exceedingly in his heart, he fell down before the extended feet of his wife, the queen, and seized them. He embraced them, like one who was afflicted.

# Chapter 2(11)

The great king did not deserve to lie down in this fashion. He was like Yayati, dislodged from the world of the gods after his store of good merits had been exhausted. Kaikeyee was in the form of something unpleasant, wishing to attain an undesirable objective. She was without fear and was causing fear instead. The beautiful one asked for the boons yet again. 'O great king! You pride yourself on speaking the truth and being firm in your vows. Why do you then wish to refuse the boon I asked for?' Thus addressed by Kaikeyee, for a while, King Dasharatha's anger made him lose his senses. He then replied, 'O ignoble one! You are my enemy. When Rama, bull among men, leaves for the forest and I am dead, you will accomplish your desire. May you be happy. If I tell the truth about banishing Rama to the forest in an attempt to cause pleasure to Kaikeyee, this will not be regarded as the truth. It is certain that my infinite ill fame in this world will destroy me.' His senses distracted, he lamented in this way. The sun set and night presented itself. Though it was adorned with the lunar disc, the night seemed to be afflicted. To the lamenting king, the night seemed to be dark. The aged King Dasharatha sighed long and warm sighs. With his eyes directed towards the sky, he lamented in his misery. 'I join my hands in salutation. I do not wish for a morning. Or pass swiftly.[44] I am shameless, since I am beholding Kaikeyee, who has brought about this great calamity.' After having said this, the king joined his hands in salutation and addressed Kaikeyee in these words. 'O Kaikeyee!

[44] Dasharatha is addressing the night.

Show me your favours. I am virtuous in conduct, but am distressed. I am devoted to you, but my lifespan is over. O queen! O fortunate one! You should show me your favours, especially because I am a king. O one with the beautiful hips! Everything that I have said has indeed been addressed to nothingness. O virtuous one! O child! You are kind-hearted. Show me your favours.' The king's coppery red eyes were full of tears and his sentiments were pure. However, she was wicked in her sentiments. Having heard the wonderful and piteous lamentations of her husband, the cruel one did not heed his words. At this, the king fell senseless again. His beloved one was not content and spoke against his words. On seeing that his son would be exiled, he was miserable and, bereft of his senses, fell down on the ground.

## Chapter 2(12)

Afflicted by sorrow on account of his son and bereft of his senses, he fell down on the ground and writhed there. Glancing towards the descendant of the Ikshvaku lineage, the wicked one said, 'What is this wickedness you are displaying by lying down on the ground? Having heard my words, you gave me your pledge. You should remain within the sanctioned bounds. People who know about dharma say that truth is the supreme dharma. I have adhered to the truth and have urged you to follow dharma. O king! Having given a pledge to a hawk, King Shaibya gave the bird a part of his own body and obtained a supreme end.[45] In that fashion, without faltering, the energetic Alarka offered his own eyes when he was asked by a brahmana accomplished in the Vedas.[46] Devoted to truth, the lord of the rivers[47] does not budge from his pledge to the

[45] King Shibi/Shaibya granted protection to a dove that was being chased by a hawk. When the hawk asked for its natural prey, King Shibi sliced off an equivalent portion of flesh from his own body and offered it to the hawk.

[46] King Alarka offered his eyes to a blind brahmana.

[47] The ocean.

slightest extent. Adhering to his pledge and the truth, he does not transgress the shoreline. O noble one! If you do not adhere to the pledge you have given me and act accordingly, I will be abandoned. In front of you, I will cast aside my life.' The king was thus addressed by Kaikeyee, who had no hesitation at all. He was incapable of freeing himself from the bond, like Bali was deprived by Indra.[48] His heart was disturbed and his face was pale. He was like a bull trembling in the yoke, caught between two wheels.[49] The king's eyes were clouded, as if he was unable to see. With great difficulty, he used his fortitude to calm himself and spoke to Kaikeyee. 'O wicked one! Before the fire and with the use of mantras, I accepted your hand. I abandon you and the son born to me through you.'[50] At this, Kaikeyee, wicked in her conduct, again spoke to the king. She was eloquent in the use of words and became senseless with rage. She spoke these harsh words. 'O king! Why are you uttering words that are like destructive poison? Without any hesitation, you should summon your son, Rama, here. Instate my son in the kingdom and make Rama a resident of the forest. Eliminate my enemies and do what needs to be done.' The king was like an excellent horse, fiercely struck by the whip. Thus goaded, he repeatedly spoke to Kaikeyee. 'I am tied down by the noose of dharma. My senses have been destroyed. I wish to see my eldest and beloved son Rama, who is devoted to dharma.'

Hearing the king's words, Kaikeyee herself told the suta, 'Go and fetch Rama here.' Miserable about his son and with his eyes red with sorrow, the prosperous king of the Ikshvaku lineage, devoted to dharma, also spoke to the suta. Sumantra heard the piteous words and saw that the king was distressed. He joined his hands in salutation and withdrew some distance away. Because of his distress, the great king was unable to say anything. Kaikeyee, who knew about the consultation, spoke to Sumantra. 'O Sumantra!

---

[48] In his dwarf (vamana) incarnation, Vishnu sought the three worlds from Bali and the generous Bali gave them.

[49] Of adhering to his pledge and love for Rama.

[50] The Critical Edition excises shlokas and this breaks the continuity. By abandoning, the king meant depriving Bharata of the right to offer funeral oblations to Dasharatha.

I wish to see the handsome Rama. Fetch him here quickly.' With delight in his heart, he paid heed to these auspicious words. Thus urged, Sumantra hurried. The one who knew about dharma thought it was evident that Rama was being brought for the consecration. Having made up his mind in this way, the suta was filled with great delight. The greatly energetic one departed, wishing to see Raghava. As he suddenly emerged, near the gate, he saw many kings who had assembled. He also saw many prosperous citizens. They too had arrived near the gate and were stationed there.

# Chapter 2(13)

Brahmanas, accomplished in the Vedas, had resided there during the night. With the royal priests, they also arrived at the spot. There were advisers, commanders of armies and the foremost citizens. Delighted at the prospect of Raghava's consecration, they assembled there. On the day of Pushya's conjunction, when a sparkling sun arose, the Indras among brahmanas had thought of Rama's consecration. There were golden pots of water and the auspicious seat was ornamented. The chariot was covered with shining tiger skin. Water was brought from the sacred conjunction of the Ganga and the Yamuna and also from other auspicious rivers, lakes, wells, ponds and rivulets. Water was brought from rivers that flowed eastwards, upwards, diagonally, those that merged together and from those that merged with the ocean from every direction. Honey, curds, clarified butter, parched grain, darbha grass, flowers and milk were gathered. Golden and silver pots were filled with parched grain and milk. They were filled with excellent water and shone with lotuses and lilies. An excellent whisk made of yak hair was kept ready for Rama. Pale, it spread out like the moon's beams and was decorated with jewels. There was a white umbrella, shaped like the lunar disc. It was beautiful and radiant and was kept ready for the consecration. A white bull was kept ready and a white horse was stationed there. A handsome elephant

was also there, ready to be mounted. There were eight auspicious
maidens, adorned in every kind of ornament. There were all kinds
of musical instruments and minstrels. All this had been collected
for a consecration in the kingdom of the Ikshvakus. All this had
been arranged for the prince's consecration. Following the king's
words, the kings had assembled. Unable to see him, they asked,
'Who will inform the king?'[51] We do not see the king and the sun has
arisen. Arrangements have been made for the intelligent Rama to be
consecrated as the heir apparent.' Sumantra, who was respected by
the king, spoke these words to the kings from various countries who
were conversing among themselves. 'I will convey your words and
ask the long-lived king, who must have awoken, about his welfare
and the reason for his not coming.'

Having said this, the one who knew about the ancient accounts,
entered the inner quarters. He pronounced words of benediction
and praised Raghava.[52] 'The illustrious night has passed and the
auspicious day has presented itself. O tiger among kings! Arise and
do what must be done next. O king! Brahmanas, commanders of
armies and merchants have arrived.' He was thus praised by the suta
Sumantra, who was accomplished in counselling. The king arose
and spoke these words. 'I am not asleep. Quickly bring Raghava[53]
here.' King Dasharatha again told the suta this. Hearing the king's
words, he bowed his head down and honoured him. Thinking about
the great joy that would follow, he left the king's residence. Happy,
he proceeded along the royal road that was decorated with flags
and standards. The suta heard words being spoken about Rama's
consecration. Sumantra saw Rama's beautiful residence, which was
as radiant as Kailasa and as resplendent as Shakra's residence. There
were large doors and it was adorned with hundreds of balconies.
The top was golden and the gates were decorated with jewels and
coral. It was as radiant as autumn clouds and was like a cave in
Meru. That gigantic place was decorated with the best of wreaths
and garlands. While the assembled men and the assembled kings

[51] About their arrival.
[52] Dasharatha.
[53] Rama.

looked on, the charioteer advanced on a chariot yoked to horses. Having reached the extremely expensive and extremely large residence, the charioteer was delighted and his body hair stood up. That excellent residence was like the summit of a mountain, like an immobile cloud and like a large vimana. With no one barring the way, the charioteer entered, like a *makara*[54] entering an ocean filled with a large number of jewels.

## Chapter 2(14)

Passing through that crowd of people, he approached the door to the inner quarters. The one who knew about ancient accounts entered the chamber. There were young guards with polished earrings, wielding shining spears and bows, devoted, attentive and not distracted in their duties. There were aged and ornamented ones, dressed in ochre garments and holding canes. He saw these self-controlled supervisors stationed there at the doors. They were engaged in doing what brought Rama pleasure and saw him arrive. He said, 'Go and quickly tell Rama and his wife that the suta wishes to enter, to convey his father's command.' Wishing to bring him pleasure, Raghava instructed that he should be brought in. Seated on an ornamented seat, he[55] looked like Vaishravana.[56] The suta saw him on that golden couch, covered with an excellent spread. The scorcher of enemies was smeared with sacred and fragrant sandalwood paste that had the complexion of the blood of a boar. With a whisk made of yak hair in her hand, Sita stood by his side. He was like the moon, with Chitra nakshatra by the side. Blazing in his own energy, he seemed to scorch like the sun. The minstrel was accomplished in humility. Humbly, he worshipped the granter of boons. Joining his hands in salutation, he asked about the welfare of the one who was reclining on the couch. Sumantra, who was

[54] A mythical aquatic creature, which can be loosely translated as shark or crocodile.
[55] Rama.
[56] Kubera.

respected by the king, spoke these words to the prince. 'O prince! O Kousalya's excellent son! Your father and Queen Kaikeyee wish to see you. Go there quickly.'

Thus addressed, the immensely radiant lion among men was delighted. Honouring him, he spoke to Sita. 'O queen! The king and the queen have summoned me to their presence. They have certainly thought of something connected with the consecration. It is evident that the extremely generous one with the maddening eyes[57] must intend to do something for me and has accordingly urged the king. A messenger befitting the assembly there has arrived. It is certain that the king will anoint me as the heir apparent today. I must quickly leave this place and go and see the king. You stay happily in this household and find your pleasure.' The black-eyed Sita honoured her husband. Thinking of auspicious things, she followed him up to the door. He greeted all those who had assembled there and ascended the supreme chariot, which was like a fire. Its radiance was golden and it stole the eyes. Supreme horses that were like baby elephants were yoked to it. It was as swift as the thousand-eyed Indra's chariot, yoked to tawny horses. Raghava, blazing in his prosperity, departed swiftly. Its clatter was like the roaring of clouds in the sky. As it emerged from the residence, its beauty was like that of the moon emerging from clouds. Raghava's younger brother, Lakshmana, ascended the chariot at the rear. He held a whisk and an umbrella in his hands and protected his brother. As the crowds of people emerged in every direction, a tumultuous roar arose. Raghava heard the conversation of the people who had assembled there. All the citizens of the city cheerfully spoke many things about his own prospective rule. 'Through the king's favours, Raghava is advancing towards great prosperity today. He will make all our dreams of prosperity come true, once he becomes our ruler. If he rules over this kingdom for a long time, the people will have everything to gain.' He proceeded amidst the noise created by the horses and elephants. Sutas and magadhas pronounced benedictions ahead of him. The best of musicians praised his greatness and he

[57] A reference to Kaikeyee.

proceeded like Vaishravana. The squares were full of large crowds of people and female elephants, male elephants, chariots and horses. There were shops with a lot of jewels and many commodities. As he went along, Rama saw the beautiful and large road.

## Chapter 2(15)

With his joyful well-wishers, Rama ascended the chariot. He saw the beautiful city, populated by crowds of people. Painted white, the houses were like clouds. Rama proceeded along the royal road, amidst incense from *agaru*.[58] The excellent royal road was adorned and was free of obstructions. There were many kinds of merchandise and diverse kinds of food. He heard the benedictions pronounced by many well-wishers and proceeded, honouring all the men as they deserved. 'Follow the conduct of your grandfathers and great-grandfathers. Get consecrated today. Rule according to the path they traversed. We were nurtured by his father and by his earlier ancestors. Once Rama becomes the king, all of us will reside even more happily. We have had enough of enjoying objects of pleasure and we have had enough of pursuing the supreme objective, now that we see Rama leave, to become established in the kingdom. There is nothing that will be more agreeable to us than that the infinitely energetic Rama should become consecrated in the kingdom.' The well-wishers uttered these and other auspicious words, honouring his own self. Hearing these, Rama proceeded along the royal road. No one could turn his sight away from that supreme among men. No man was capable of crossing Raghava. He had dharma in his soul and exhibited compassion towards all the four varnas and towards those who were aged. Therefore, they were devoted to him. He reached the royal palace, which was like the great Indra's residence. The prince entered his father's abode, which blazed in prosperity. Dasharatha's son passed through all

[58] Paste from the agallochum tree.

the chambers. Taken his leave of all the people, with a pure heart, he entered the inner quarters. All the people were delighted. The king's son entered and approached his father. They waited for him to emerge again, just as the lord of the rivers waits for the moon to rise.

## Chapter 2(16)

Rama saw his father seated on an auspicious seat. His face was distressed. He was with Kaikeyee, who was tending to him. Humbly, he first worshipped at his father's feet. Extremely controlled, he next worshipped at Kaikeyee's feet. With tears in his eyes, the miserable king only uttered the word 'Rama'. He was incapable of glancing at him, or saying anything more. He had never seen such a fearful form of the king earlier. Therefore, Rama was overcome with fear, like when one touches a snake with one's feet. The great king sighed, his senses miserable. He was afflicted by sorrow and torment. His mind was disturbed and grief-stricken. He was like an ocean that cannot be agitated, turbulent because of a garland of waves. He was like the sun during an eclipse, or like a rishi who has uttered a lie. On seeing the unthinkable, his father enveloped in sorrow, he was also agitated, like the ocean on the day of the full moon. Engaged in ensuring the welfare of his father, Rama began to think. 'Why has the king not greeted me back today? At other times, even when he is enraged, my father is pacified on seeing me. However, today, he seems exhausted on seeing me.' Rama became miserable and afflicted by sorrow. Greeting Kaikeyee, Rama spoke these words. 'Have I ignorantly committed a crime that my father is angry with me? Tell me and pacify him. His face is distressed and he is miserable. He is not speaking to me. Is something troubling him physically or mentally, making him suffer? It is rare to be happy always. Has something happened to Prince Bharata, handsome to behold, or the great-spirited Shatrughna? Has something inauspicious befallen my mothers? If the king is angry, I do not wish to remain alive even for an instant, causing dissatisfaction to the great king and not following my father's words. A great-souled man perceives him[59] as a divinity from whom he himself has emerged. That being evident, how can one act otherwise? I trust that in your rage, you have not uttered any harsh words, as a result of which, my father has been slighted and his mind is disturbed. O queen! I am asking you. Tell me the truth. Why is the lord of men suffering from an affliction that has not happened earlier? If the king's words lead to that, I will leap into the fire. I will consume fierce poison, or submerge myself in the ocean. The king is engaged in my welfare and I am devoted to my preceptor, my father. O queen! Therefore, tell me the king's words and what he desires. I promise to do that. Rama does not speak in two contrary ways.'

He was truthful in speech and upright. The ignoble Kaikeyee spoke these extremely terrible words to Rama. 'O Raghava! Earlier, in a battle between the gods and the asuras, your father was hurt by darts. When I protected him in that great battle, he granted me two boons. O Raghava! On that basis, I have asked the king for Bharata's consecration and for you to leave for Dandakaranya today. O best among men! If you desire that you and your father should stick to the pledge of truth, then hear my words. Adhere to your father's instructions and to what he has pledged. You must go to the forest for fourteen years. You will have to reside in Dandakaranya for fourteen years. You will have to forget about the consecration and wear bark and rags. Bharata will rule this earth, full of many jewels and with horses, chariots and elephants, from the city of Kosala.'[60] Rama, the slayer of enemies, heard these disagreeable words, which were like death. However, he was not distressed and spoke to Kaikeyee. 'It shall be that way. I shall depart from this residence to there, the forest. To ensure that the king's pledge is satisfied, I will wear bark and rags. But I wish to know why the invincible and great king, the scorcher of enemies, is unhappy with me. O queen! You should not be angry. You should be extremely happy. In front of you, I am telling you

[59] The father.
[60] Meaning the capital of Kosala, Ayodhya.

that I will go the forest in bark and rags. I am grateful to the king.
How can I not be engaged in the welfare of my preceptor, my father?
Engaged by him, I will faithfully do what is agreeable to him. But
something unpleasant is tormenting my mind and heart. Why has
the king not told me about Bharata's consecration himself? Without
being urged, I would have cheerfully given my brother, Bharata, Sita,
the kingdom, the desired riches and even my own life. To ensure
what brings you pleasure and to accomplish the pledge, why did
my father, Indra among men, not urge me himself? Therefore, you
should comfort him. Why is the lord of the earth sprinkling the earth
with tears from his eyes and releasing these inauspicious tears? On
the instructions of the king, let messengers on fleet-footed steeds
go to Bharata's maternal uncle's household and fetch him here. I
will hasten to leave for Dandakaranya, unthinkingly following my
father's words. I will reside there for fourteen years.'

On hearing Rama's words, Kaikeyee was delighted. Believing
them, she asked Raghava to hurry about his departure. 'Let it be
that way. Let messengers on fleet-footed steeds leave for Bharata's
maternal uncle's house and let those men bring him back. Since you
are so anxious, I think it is inappropriate that you should tarry.
O Rama! Therefore, you should quickly leave for the forest. It is
because of his shame that the king has not addressed you himself.
O best among men! This rage is nothing and it will pass. O Rama!
Until you leave for the forest and depart from this city, you father
will not bathe, or eat anything.' The king was overcome by sorrow.
He cried 'shame' and sighed. Losing his senses, he fell down on the
golden couch. Urged by Kaikeyee, Rama raised the king. Like a
horse goaded by a whip, he hastened to leave for the forest. Those
words were terrible, disagreeable and ignoble. Having heard them,
devoid of distress, Rama addressed Kaikeyee in these words. 'O
queen! I am not attached to artha. I am not interested in the ways
of the world. Know me to be the equal of a rishi, only interested
in being established in dharma. I will do whatever I am capable
of doing to ensure pleasure, even if it amounts to giving up my
own life. There is nothing greater than acting in accordance with
dharma, in the form of serving one's father or complying with his

words. Even though he has not told me, I will follow your words
and dwell alone in the forest for fourteen years. O Kaikeyee! Since
you have told the king and not me,[61] it is evident that you suspect
my qualities and take me to be inferior to my lord. After taking my
mother's leave and persuading Sita, today itself, I will leave for the
great forest of Dandaka. Bharata will rule the kingdom and tend to
our father. This is eternal dharma and it is your task to ensure this.'

On hearing Rama's words, his father was struck with extreme
grief. In a voice that choked with tears, he wept loudly. Rama
worshipped at the feet of his unconscious father. The immensely
radiant one also fell down at the feet of the ignoble Kaikeyee. Rama
circumambulated his father and Kaikeyee. He emerged from the
inner quarters and saw the well-wishers. Lakshmana, the extender
of Sumitra's delight, was extremely angry. With eyes full of tears,
he followed at the rear. Rama circumambulated the vessel meant
for the consecration. Glancing here and there, but without being
disturbed, he slowly left. The destruction of the kingdom did not
affect his great prosperity, like the onset of the night cannot touch
the one with the cool rays.[62] He was pleasant and was loved by the
people. Having cast aside the earth, he wished to leave for the forest.
He was beyond worldly pursuits and no mental disturbance could
be discerned. He controlled his senses and subdued the sorrow in
his mind. To inform his mother about the disagreeable tidings, he
entered his own house. He entered the house, which was filled with
great joy. On seeing them, he did not tell them about the calamity
that had struck. Suspecting the misery of his well-wishers, Rama did
not exhibit the least bit of disturbance.

# Chapter 2(17)

Rama was extremely hurt and sighed like an elephant. However,
he controlled himself and with his brother, went to his mother's

[61] About Kaikeyee's wishes.
[62] The moon.

inner quarters. He saw the extremely revered and aged man seated there, at the door to the house. He was stationed there, with many others.[63] He entered the first chamber and saw the second chamber. Aged brahmanas who were accomplished in the Vedas and honoured by the king were there. Bowing down before those aged ones, Rama saw the third chamber. Aged women and girls were engaged in guarding the door to that. As he entered the house, the joy of the women was enhanced. They quickly informed Rama's mother about the agreeable news.[64] Queen Kousalya had spent the night in a self-controlled way. In the morning, for the welfare of her son, she was worshipping Vishnu. She was cheerful and attired in silken garments. She was always devoted to her vows. To the sound of auspicious mantras, she was then offering oblations into the fire. Rama entered the auspicious inner quarters of his mother. He saw his mother there, offering oblations into the fire. Having seen that her son, whom she had not seen for a long time and who enhanced the delight of his mother, had arrived, she was happy, like a mare on seeing its colt. Kousalya, affectionate towards her son, spoke these agreeable and beneficial words to the invincible Raghava, her own son. 'May you obtain the lifespans of the aged who are devoted to dharma and of great-souled rajarshis. May you obtain fame and ensure the dharma of your lineage. O Raghava! Behold. Your father, the king, is devoted to the pledge of truth. Today, the one with dharma in his soul, will consecrate you as the heir apparent.'

Advancing a bit towards his mother, Raghava joined his hands in salutation. He was naturally humble and bowed down more, out of respect for her. 'O queen! It is certain that you do not know that a great calamity has presented itself. This will cause sorrow to you, Vaidehi and Lakshmana. I will have to live alone in the forest for fourteen years. Like a sage, I will have to forsake meat and live on honey, roots and fruits. The great king will make Bharata the heir apparent. As for me, like an ascetic, I will be exiled to Dandakaranya.' She did not deserve unhappiness.[65] On

[63] As guards.

[64] That he had come.

[65] The Critical Edition excises a shloka where Kousalya falls down, senseless.

seeing that his mother had fallen down like a plantain tree and
was unconscious, Rama raised her. He raised the distressed one,
who had fallen down like an overburdened horse. Her limbs were
covered with dust. He touched her with his hands. Rama seated
the one who was afflicted by grief, though she deserved happiness.
While Lakshmana heard, she addressed the tiger among men. 'O
Raghava! Had I not had a son, I would not have been this miserable.
My sorrow is greater, since I see that I will now be without a son.
Had I been barren, I would have had only one sorrow in my mind.
O son! There would have been no torment but for the fact that I
don't have a son. While my husband possessed his manliness, I did
not experience any benefit or happiness earlier. O Rama! All my
hopes were vested in my son. I have heard many disagreeable words
that shatter the heart. Though I am superior to them, I have heard
them from my inferior co-wives. What can bring greater grief to a
woman than that? Despite you being near me, I have been slighted
in this fashion. O son! On top of that, when you leave, it is certain
that death is better for me. When they see Kaikeyee's son, people
who serve me and follow me now will no longer speak to me. O
Raghava! Seventeen years have passed since your birth. That time
has elapsed, while I have expectantly waited for my sorrows to be
over. I have observed many fasts and exhausting yogas. In vain
have I nurtured you in my misery. My sorrows are insurmountable.
Since my heart has not been shattered, like the banks of a new river
overflowing with new water during the monsoon, I think that it is
still. It is certain that there is no death for me. Yama's abode has no
space for me. The Destroyer[66] doesn't want to carry me off either,
like a weeping deer carried by a lion. Since my still heart is not
pierced and shattered, it is certainly made of iron. This sorrow is
ingrained in my body and it is certain that I will not die before my
time. Because of this sorrow, my vows, donations and control have
clearly been futile. For the sake of offspring, I tormented myself
through austerities. That too has been futile, like seeds sown in
barren soil. I am afflicted by great distress. Without you, I will

[66] Yama.

be like a cow without its calf. Had one been able to obtain an untimely death through one's own wishes, I would have departed now and obtained the world hereafter.' She was extremely unhappy and angry. As Raghava looked on, she lamented a lot. Amidst that great hardship, she spoke in this way to her son, like a kinnara lady who had been tied.

## Chapter 2(18)

Kousalya, Rama's mother, was lamenting. Distressed, Lakshmana addressed her in words that were appropriate for the occasion. 'O noble lady! The prospect of Raghava abandoning the prosperous kingdom and going to the forest, because one is succumbing to the words of a woman, does not appeal to me. The aged king acts in a contrary way because he has been goaded by sensual pleasures. What can one say to a person excited by Manmatha? I do not see any taint in Raghava, or any sin that he has committed, that he should be exiled from the kingdom to the forest. In this world, I have not seen any man, whether he is an enemy or whether he has been banished, who points out any sin in him. He is like a god—upright, controlled and kind towards enemies. Looking towards dharma, who can unnecessarily cast aside such a son? The words of the king suggest that he has again become a child. Remembering the conduct of kings, how can one's heart act in such a way towards a son? Before any other man gets to know about what has happened, with my help, make this kingdom your own.[67] O Raghava! With a bow, I will protect you at your side, stationed like Yama. Who is capable of surpassing me? O bull among men! If anyone acts disagreeably against you, I will use sharp arrows to make Ayodhya devoid of all its men, those who are on Bharata's side and those who wish him well. I will slay all of them. It is indeed the mild who get vanquished.

[67] This is addressed to Rama.

O subjugator of enemies! Exhibiting great enmity towards you and me, who has the strength to give Bharata the prosperity? O queen! In truth, my sentiments are devoted to my brother. I truthfully pledge this on my bow and on whatever I have donated at sacrifices. O queen! Know that if Rama enters a blazing fire or the forest, before him, I will destroy myself there. Like a sun that rises, I will use my valour to dispel the darkness of your sorrow. O queen! Behold my valour. Let Raghava also witness it.' Hearing the great-souled Lakshmana's words, Kousalya completely abandoned her weeping and grief. She told Rama, 'O son! You have heard the words your brother, Lakshmana, has spoken. If it pleases you, you should next act in accordance with this. You have heard the words of adharma spoken to me by my co-wife. Leaving me in this tormented and grieving state, you should not go away from here. O one who knows about dharma! O one who acts according to dharma! If you wish to follow dharma, remain here and tend to me. Perform a supreme act of dharma. O son! Dwelling in his own house in a controlled way, Kashyapa served his mother. Thereby performing supreme austerities, he went to heaven. The king should be worshipped because of the respect he wields. But I am also like that. I am not giving you permission. You should not go to the forest. Separated from you, what will I do with my life or with happiness? It is better for me to be with you, even if I have to survive on grass. I am afflicted by misery. If you abandon me and go to the forest, without eating, I will give up my life. I will be incapable of remaining alive. I will then myself obtain the hell that is famous in the worlds, like the one obtained by the ocean, the lord of the rivers, on killing a brahmana.'[68] Distressed, his mother, Kousalya, lamented in this way.

With dharma in his soul, Rama addressed her in words that were in conformity with dharma. 'I do not possess the strength to act contrary to my father's words. I bow down my head and seek your favours. I wish to go to the forest. The learned rishi

---

[68] Suicide is a crime. The brahmana in question is Vritra. Indra acquired a sin from killing a brahmana and part of that sin was distributed to the ocean, the remainder was distributed among the earth, trees and women.

Kandu knew about dharma and followed his vows. Even then, obeying his father's words, he killed a cow. Earlier, in our lineage, following their father Sagara's instructions, his sons dug up the earth and faced a great destruction. In the forest, Rama,[69] Jamadagni's son, acted in accordance with his father's words and used his battleaxe to kill his mother, Renuka. Indeed, I am not the only one who is acting in accordance with his father's command. I am only following the path that has been agreed upon earlier. That is the way I must act. There is no other mode on earth. There is no ill fame from acting in accordance with a father's words.' Having spoken to his mother in this way, he next addressed Lakshmana. 'O Lakshmana! I know about your supreme affection for me. However, you do not understand the meaning of truth and tranquility. Dharma is supreme in the world. Truth is established in dharma. Our father's supreme words are also laced with dharma. O brave one! If one is established in dharma, if one has given one's word to a father, a mother, or a brahmana, one must not violate it. I am incapable of violating what my father has asked me to do. O brave one! Kaikeyee has urged me in this way because of my father's words. Therefore, cast aside this ignoble attitude of resorting to the dharma of kshatriyas. Follow dharma, not ferocity. Follow my inclination.' Lakshmana's elder brother spoke to his brother in this affectionate way. Joining his hands in salutation and bowing his head down, he again spoke to Kousalya. 'O Queen! Grant me permission to go to the forest. I am requesting you, on my life. Perform the benedictions. After accomplishing my pledge, I will again return to the city from the forest. My fame is only because of the kingdom. I cannot turn my back on this great glory. O queen! Following the dharma of those on earth, no one lives for a long time. Grant me the boon today.' The bull among men sought his mother's favours. Because of his prowess, he wished to go to Dandaka. He used the foresight of his heart to comfort his younger brother and circumambulated his mother.

[69] Parashurama.

## Chapter 2(19)

He[70] was like an Indra among elephants, miserable, distressed and extremely angry.[71] With his eyes dilated in rage, he seemed to be sighing. Rama resorted to the fortitude that was in his own inner self. He addressed his beloved brother, Soumitri, who wished him well. 'O Soumitri! You collected various objects for the consecration. Now that there will be no consecration, collect similar objects.[72] My mother's mind was tormented on account of my consecration. Act so that she does not harbour any suspicions.[73] O Soumitri! Not for an instant, can I tolerate misery and suspicion being generated in her mind, nor can I ignore it. Consciously or unconsciously, I cannot recall a single occasion when I have done anything disagreeable towards my mother or father. My father has always been truthful, unwavering from the truth. Truth is his valour. He is scared of what will happen in the world hereafter.[74] May he be fearless. If we do not refrain from this act,[75] his mind will be tormented that truth has not been followed and I will also be tormented. O Lakshmana! Therefore, refrain from this rite of consecration. Let me again say that I wish to leave for the forest. O son of a king! If I leave for the forest today, she[76] will be successful and will no longer have any anxiety about her son, Bharata's, consecration. If I attire myself in rags and bark and sporting matted hair, leave for the forest, Kaikeyee will be happy in her mind. I should not cause grief to the one who has given me intelligence and training and instructed me about great control of the mind.[77] I must leave quickly. O Soumitri! It remains to be seen whether Yama

---

[70] Lakshmana.

[71] Towards Kaikeyee.

[72] This can be interpreted in two ways—collect objects for departure to the forest or collect objects for Bharata's consecration. The latter is probably right.

[73] The mother means Kaikeyee, who may still have suspicions about Rama actually leaving for the forest.

[74] In case he doesn't keep his pledge.

[75] Of consecration.

[76] Kaikeyee.

[77] A reference to Dasharatha.

will grant me the kingdom once I return from my exile. But for destiny and the sanction of the gods, how could Kaikeyee's powers and my affliction have happened? O amiable one! You know that I have never exhibited any difference between my mothers, nor have I ever differentiated between their sons. However, to prevent my consecration and ensure my exile, she has used wicked words and fierce speech. This couldn't have occurred without the sanction of the gods. That lady is a princess and possesses the requisite qualities. Yet, in her husband's presence, she addressed me like an ordinary woman and caused me grief. Whatever is unthinkable is destiny and no being can transgress it. It is evident that this conflict between her and me has been caused by this. O Soumitri! Which man can fight against destiny? It is evident that nothing can be done, except to accept it. Happiness, unhappiness, fear, anger, gain, loss, what happens, what does not happen—all of these are indeed the work of destiny. I suffer no torment on account of the consecration not happening. Therefore, listen to me and still any torment. Quickly stop all the rites that have been arranged for the consecration. O Lakshmana! Let my younger mother[78] not harbour any suspicion about my standing in the way of the kingdom. She has spoken those undesirable words because of destiny. You know the power of destiny.'

# Chapter 2(20)

As Rama spoke again, Lakshmana lowered his head and heard, his mind filled with both misery and delight. The bull among men had his brows furrowed in a frown. Like an angry and large snake inside its hole, he sighed. With that frown, he was extremely difficult to behold. His angry visage was like that of a wrathful lion. He waved his forearm around, like an elephant waving its trunk around, when it bends its body and lowers its neck. With the upper

[78] Kaikeyee.

portions of his eyes he glanced sideways at his brother and said, 'There is a great deal of respect in you for what doesn't warrant it. In connection with dharma, you do not suspect that there are people who are wicked. O bull among kshatriyas! O valiant leader! How can a person like you be scared of destiny, which is powerless? Like a miserable person, why are you praising destiny, which is powerless? Why do you not harbour any suspicion about those two wicked ones?[79] O one who knows about dharma! Why do you not comprehend that there are those who deceive in the name of dharma? People will hate the idea of starting a consecration for someone else. O lord of the earth! I hate the fact that your intelligence is pulled in two opposite directions and that you are confused about the subject of dharma. You are of the view that this is the power of destiny. I do not like the idea that you are ignoring them[80] because of this. Impotent ones who lack valour follow destiny. Brave ones with self-respect do not serve destiny. A man who is capable of countering destiny through his manliness is not helpless and does not suffer from lassitude on account of destiny. Today, the difference between destiny and a man's manliness will be witnessed. The distinction between a man and his destiny will become manifest. Today, people will see that destiny has been crushed by my manliness. The destiny that has destroyed your instatement in the kingdom will itself be destroyed. Just as one uses a fierce goad on a crazy and rampaging elephant, I will use my manliness to counter and repel this destiny. Today, all the guardians of the worlds and all the three worlds will not be able to prevent Rama's consecration, not to speak of our father. O king! Those who futilely support the prospect of your exile in the forest will themselves have to dwell in the forest for fourteen years. I will thus shatter her[81] hopes and those of our father. For the sake of her son, she is seeking to create an obstruction to your consecration. The power of my fierce manliness will cause misery to those who seek to counter my strength, far more than the strength of destiny. O noble one! After having ruled over the subjects for

---

[79] Dasharatha and Kaikeyee.
[80] Dasharatha and Kaikeyee.
[81] Kaikeyee's.

more than one thousand years, you will leave for the forest and leave the kingdom for your sons. Residing in the forest has been recommended as proper conduct by former royal sages, but after having ruled over the subjects like sons and then handing them over to one's own sons. O one with dharma in his soul! O Rama! It is possible that you do not wish for the kingdom because you doubt that you will yourself be able to take care of it attentively as a king and will therefore not enjoy the worlds meant for the valiant. O brave one! Know that I will protect your kingdom, like the shoreline holds back the ocean. With all the auspicious objects, be consecrated. Because of my strength, I alone am sufficient to counter the kings.[82] These arms are not meant to be decorations and this bow is not an ornament. This sword is not intended for buckling and these arrows are not meant to be immobile. All these four[83] are meant for subduing enemies. I am not excessively affectionate towards someone I regard as an enemy. This sword is sharp at the edges and is as radiant as a flash of lightning. While I wield it, I do not respect any enemy, not even the wielder of the vajra. Elephants, horses, men, arms, thighs and heads will be severed by the sword and will be strewn on the earth, which will become desolate and impenetrable. Today, they will be shattered like mountains, struck by this sharp and blazing sword. Elephants will fall down on the ground, like clouds tinged with lightning. When I wear finger guards made out of the skin of lizards and wield my bow and arrow, which man, who prides himself on being a man, will be able to stand before me? I will use my arrows to strike at the inner organs of horses and elephants. Even if many strive against me, I alone am enough to take on many. O lord! Today, the power of my weapons will establish your prowess, remove the lordship from the king[84] and confer the lordship on you. O Rama! You should act. Your arms are meant for sporting sandalwood paste, wearing armlets, ensuring prosperity and protecting your well-wishers. Repulse the agents who seek to create obstructions towards your consecration.

[82] Those who oppose the consecration.
[83] Arms, bow, arrows and sword.
[84] Dasharatha.

Tell me. Which ill-wisher deserves to be deprived of his life, fame and well-wishers by me? I am your servant. Instruct me about how this earth can be brought under your subjugation.' The extender of the Raghava lineage[85] repeatedly wiped away Lakshmana's tears and comforted him. He said, 'I stand by my father's pledge. O amiable one! Listen to me. This is the path of virtue.'

# Chapter 2(21)

Kousalya saw that he was firm about following his father's command. Her voice choking with tears, she spoke words that were full of dharma. 'He[86] has never faced unhappiness earlier. He has dharma in his soul. He is pleasant in speech towards all creatures. He has been born from me and Dasharatha. How can he survive on *unchha*?[87] The dependents and servants will enjoy pleasant food. How will their protector survive on roots and fruits in the forest? On hearing that the qualified and beloved Raghava has been exiled by the king, who will believe this? Who will not be frightened? Separated from him, my misery will be like that of a great, unmatched and colourful fire which burns down dry kindling during the winter. How can a cow not follow her wandering calf? O son! Wherever you go, I will follow you.' The bull among men heard the words spoken by his mother, who was extremely miserable.

Having heard, Rama addressed his mother in these words. 'Kaikeyee has deceived the king. When I leave for the forest and he is also abandoned by you, it is certain that he will not remain alive. Only a cruel woman is capable of forsaking her husband and such a thought is reprehensible. You should not do this. Kakutstha, my father, is the lord of the earth. As long as he is alive, you should serve him. That is eternal dharma.' Kousalya, beautiful in appearance,

[85] Rama.

[86] Rama.

[87] There are grains left after a crop has been harvested, or after grain has been milled. If one subsists on these leftovers, that is known as *unchhavritti*.

was addressed by Rama in this way. Extremely pleased, she spoke to Rama, the performer of unblemished deeds, and agreed. Rama, supreme among the upholders of dharma, again spoke these words to his mother, who sorrowed greatly. 'It is my duty and yours to follow the instructions of my father. He is the king and master. He is the best among preceptors. Among all masters, he is the supreme lord. After wandering around in the great forest for fourteen years, I will be extremely happy to abide by your words.' She was thus addressed by her beloved son. Kousalya, extremely afflicted and devoted to her son, replied, her face overflowing with tears. 'I am incapable of residing in the midst of my co-wives. O Kakutstha! Looking towards your father, if you have made up your mind to leave for the forest, take me also with you, like a wild deer.' She wept as she said this. Rama told the one who was lamenting, 'As long as the husband is alive, he is a woman's master and god. Today, as our master, the king exercises his powers over you and me. Bharata has dharma in his soul and speaks pleasantly to all creatures. Always devoted to dharma, he will follow you. When I leave, the king will be afflicted by grief over his son. Be attentive towards him, so that he does not suffer from the slightest bit of exhaustion. Even if a supreme woman is devoted to vows and fasting, if she does not follow her husband, she comes to an evil end. She must serve her husband and be engaged in bringing him pleasure. Since ancient times, this dharma has been witnessed in the world and has been spoken about in the Vedas, shrutis and smritis.[88] O queen! For my sake, worship brahmanas who are excellent in their vows. Expectantly looking forward to my return, spend the time in this way. If the supreme upholder of dharma is still alive, when I return, you will obtain the supreme object of your desire.' In this way, Rama spoke to the one whose eyes were full of tears. Kousalya was afflicted by grief on account of her son. She addressed Rama in these words. 'O son! O lord! Go without any disturbance. May you always be fortunate.' The queen saw that

---

[88] Shrutis are sacred texts that have been revealed, they have no author. Smritis are sacred texts that have authors. They have been heard and memorized, and thus passed down the generations.

Rama had made up his mind to leave for the forest. Supreme in her intelligence, she addressed Rama in auspicious words, wishing to ensure that benedictions were pronounced.

## Chapter 2(22)

Rama's spirited mother cast aside her grief. To perform the auspicious rites, she purified herself and touched water. 'May the Sadhyas, Vishvadevas, Maruts and maharshis be favourable. May Dhatri, Vidhatri, Pusha, Bhaga and Aryama be favourable.[89] May the seasons, fortnights, months, years, nights, days and muhurtas always look favourably on you. O son! May the smritis, resolution, dharma, the illustrious god Skanda, Soma and Brihaspati protect you in every way. May the saptarshis and Narada protect you in every direction. While you intelligently wander around in the great forest in the garb of a sage, may the nakshatras, all the planets and gods also do this. As long as you are in that desolate forest, may monkeys, scorpions, gnats, mosquitoes, reptiles and insects not frequent those groves. O son! May giant elephants, lions, tigers, bears, those with fangs, and fierce and horned buffaloes not exhibit hostility towards you. O son! Worshipped by me, may spirited and fierce creatures that survive on human flesh not cause you injury. May your paths be auspicious. May your valour meet with success. O Rama! O son! Depart auspiciously, with all your prosperity. May those in the firmament and also those on earth be auspicious towards you. May all the gods and those who cause you impediments also be auspicious. As long as you reside in the forest, may the lord of all the worlds,[90] Brahma the creator, the preserver,[91] the rishis and all the remaining gods protect you.' The

---

[89] Dhatri and Vidhatri are often used synonymously. Dhatri has the sense of creator, while Vidhatri can be translated as ordainer. Pusha, Bhaga and Aryama are three of the twelve Adityas, the sons of Aditi. They can be regarded as different aspects of the sun god.

[90] Probably meaning Shiva.

[91] Vishnu.

illustrious and large-eyed one uttered these and other benedictions, with garlands and fragrances, worshipping the large number of gods. 'When Vritra was destroyed, the one with the one thousand eyes was worshipped by all the gods with auspicious portents. May those auspicious portents also occur for you. In ancient times, when Suparna[92] went in search of amrita, Vinata prayed for auspicious portents. May those auspicious portents occur for you.' To ensure success and protect him, Kousalya invoked mantras on the sacred herb *vishalyakarani*.[93] The illustrious one invoked the fragrance on his forehead and embraced him. She said, 'O son! O Rama! Go cheerfully and be successful. O son! I will see you return to Ayodhya, without disease and successful in every way. You will be happy and will reside in this palace then. Worshipped by me, the large number of gods, Shiva and the others, the maharshis, demons, giant asuras, serpents and the directions will wish for your welfare, when you spend a long time in the forest.' Her eyes full of tears, she thus completed the rites of benedictions in the decreed way. She circumambulated Raghava and repeatedly embraced him. Having thus been circumambulated by the queen, he repeatedly pressed his mother's feet. The immensely illustrious Raghava then went to Sita's abode, blazing in his own prosperity.

# Chapter 2(23)

Having bowed down before Kousalya, Rama was ready to leave for the forest. He was firmly established on the path of dharma and his mother had performed the rites of benediction. Surrounded by men, the prince entered the royal road. Because of his qualities and conduct, he crushed the hearts of the people. The ascetic Vaidehi had still not heard anything. Her heart was still set on his instatement as the heir apparent. Happy in

[92] Garuda. Garuda's mother was Vinata.

[93] Literally, something that removes arrows/weapons. The interpretation is that she fastened an amulet on him, with vishalyakarani in it.

her mind, she gratefully performed all the rites for the gods. Knowledgeable about the dharma of kings, she waited for the prince. Rama entered his own residence, which was decorated well. It was full of cheerful people. Humbly, he lowered his face a little.

On seeing that her husband was trembling, Sita stood up. She saw that he was tormented by grief and that his senses were distracted with thoughts. She saw that he was pale in face and sweating, as if he couldn't stand it. Tormented by sorrow, she asked, 'O lord! What has happened? O Raghava! Barhaspata Pushya is full of prosperity today.[94] That is indeed what the wise brahmanas have pronounced. Why are you distressed in your mind? Your beautiful face is covered. It does not shine like an umbrella with one hundred ribs, white like the foam in water. When fanned by a whisk, your lotus-eyed face is as radiant as the moon or a swan. But your face is not being fanned today. O bull among men! Delighted, the vandis, sutas and magadhas aren't singing praises today. Nor are they pronouncing the auspicious benedictions. After you have sprinkled your head,[95] nor are the brahmanas, accomplished in the Vedas, following the decreed rites and smearing your head with honey and curds. The ordinary people, all the ornamented leaders of the *shreni*s[96] and the inhabitants of the city and the countryside do not wish to follow you. The best *pushyaratha*[97] is yoked to four swift steeds with golden reins. Why is it not proceeding in front of you? O brave one! The handsome elephant is worshipped because it possesses the auspicious signs. It has the complexion of a dark cloud or a mountain. Why can't it be seen, proceeding before you? O handsome one! O brave one! Ahead of you, I do not see it bearing the golden and colourful throne. When arrangements have been made for the consecration, why is the complexion of your

[94] Brihaspati is the lord of Pushya nakshatra.

[95] Meaning, washed your hair.

[96] A shreni is like a guild, it is an association of traders or artisans who follow the same line of business. The word means a rank or line.

[97] A pushyaratha is a special chariot, ornamented and decorated, used not for fighting, but for pleasure.

face like this? This has never happened before. Why can no joy be discerned?'

She lamented in this way. The descendant of the Raghu lineage replied, 'O Sita! My father is exiling me to the forest. O one who knows about dharma! O one who follows dharma! You have been born in a great lineage! O Janakee! In due order, listen to what has befallen me. My father, King Dasharatha, is pledged to the truth. In earlier times, pleased in his mind, he granted two great boons to Kaikeyee. Now, the king has made arrangements for my consecration. Subduing him because of dharma, she has now held him to that pledge. I will have to dwell in Dandaka for fourteen years and my father will make Bharata the heir apparent. Before leaving for the desolate forest, I have come here to see you. When you are in Bharata's presence, you must never praise me. A prosperous person can never tolerate another one being praised. Therefore, in front of Bharata, you must never praise my qualities. You need not serve him in any special way. However, when you are near him, be kindly disposed. O spirited one! Observing the pledge given by my senior, I will leave for the forest today. Be steady. O fortunate one! O unblemished one! When I have left for the forest, frequented by sages, you can observe vows and fasting. You can wake at the appropriate time and following the ordinances, worship the gods. Worship my father, Dasharatha, lord of men. My mother, Kousalya, is aged and afflicted by grief. Placing dharma at the forefront, you should indeed show her respect. All my other mothers have always deserved worship. In their love, affection and fondness, all my mothers have been equal. In particular, I love Lakshmana and Shatrughna more than my own life. You should look on them as brothers or sons. Never do anything that is disagreeable to Bharata. He is the king and the lord, for the country and for the family. Kings are pleased when they are worshipped with good conduct and served carefully. If this is not done, they are enraged. If their own sons cause injury, kings cast them aside and accept other capable people. O beloved one! O beautiful one! I will leave for the great forest. Reside here. Never do anything injurious. Act in accordance with my words.'

## Chapter 2(24)

Vaidehi, who deserved to be loved and was pleasant in speech, was addressed in this way. However, because of her love, she became angry and addressed her husband in this way. 'O noble son! A father, a mother, a brother, a son and a daughter-in-law enjoy the fruits of their own auspicious deeds. They reap their own respective fortunes. O bull among men! However, the wife alone reaps her husband's fortune. Therefore, I have also been instructed to reside in the forest. In this world and in the next, for a woman, the husband is alone the refuge—not a father, not a son, not her own self, not a mother and not a friend. O Raghava! If you leave for the impenetrable forest today, I will proceed in front of you, trampling down kusha grass and thorns. Like water cast aside after a drink, abandon all jealousy and anger. O brave one! Have faith. There is no wickedness in me. In every situation, the shadow of a husband's feet is superior to being on the top of a palace or travelling in a celestial vehicle. My mother[98] and my father taught me about various situations. There is no need to tell me now about how to conduct myself. Without thinking about the three worlds and thinking only of my vow towards my husband, I will happily dwell in the forest, like residing in my father's residence. I will serve you always, devoted to the vow of brahmacharya. O brave one! I will reside with you in the forest that smells of honey. O Rama! In the forest, you are capable of protecting other people. O one who grants honours! Why not me? There is no doubt that I will always subsist on fruits and roots. I will dwell with you and not cause you any hardship. O intelligent lord! Fearless with you, I wish to see everything—rivers, mountains, lakes and groves. There will be beautiful and superb blossoming lotuses, populated by swans and ducks. O brave one! With you, I desire to happily see these. O large-eyed one! With you, I will be greatly delighted and find pleasure. I will be with you for a hundred thousand years. O Raghava! O tiger among men! Without you, even if I get to reside in heaven, that will

[98] Obviously, this refers to a stepmother.

not please me. I will go to the forest, which is extremely difficult to penetrate, full of many animals, monkeys and elephants. Clinging to your feet, I will live in the forest, as if it is my father's residence. Without any other thoughts, my mind is devoted to you. Without you, it is certain that I will be dead. Do what is virtuous. Grant me my wish and take me with you. Because of me, there will be no burden on you.' The one who was devoted to dharma spoke in this way. Not wishing to take her, the best among men said several things to restrain Sita and spoke about the difficulties of residing in the forest.

## Chapter 2(25)

Sita, who knew about dharma and was devoted to dharma, spoke in this way. To restrain her, the one who knew about dharma spoke these words. 'O Sita! You have been born in a great lineage. You are always devoted to dharma. Perform your own dharma here. That will bring pleasure to my mind. O Sita! O delicate one! I am telling you what you should do. There are many difficulties in the forest. Listen to what I say. O Sita! Abandon this intention of residing in the forest. It has been said that there are many hardships associated with dwelling in the desolate forest. Indeed, it is with your welfare in mind that I spoke those words of advice. I know that the forest is always fraught with misery, there is never any joy there. There are the sounds of waterfalls generated in the mountains and the roars of lions that reside in mountainous caverns. These are unpleasant to hear. Therefore, the forest has hardships. When one is exhausted at night, one has to sleep on the bare ground, on a bed of fallen leaves that one has made oneself. Therefore, the forest has great misery. O Maithilee! Depending on one's strength, one has to fast. One has to bear the burden of matted hair and wear garments made of bark. Strong winds, darkness and hunger are always there. There are many kinds of great fear. Therefore, the forest has greater misery. O beautiful one! There are many reptiles, diverse in form. These proudly roam around on the ground. Therefore, the forest has greater misery. There are snakes that make their abode in the rivers. These roam crookedly in the rivers and remaining there, make the rivers difficult to cross. Therefore, the forest has greater misery. There are flying insects, scorpions, insects, gnats and mosquitoes. O delicate one! These always cause annoyance. Therefore, in every way, the forest has greater misery. O beautiful one! There are trees with thorns and kusha grass and reeds. In every direction, these pervade the forest with their branches. Therefore, the forest has greater misery. Thus, enough about leaving for the forest. You will find the forest unbearable. Thinking about it, I see that the forest possesses many hardships.' The great-souled Rama couldn't consent to taking her to the forest. However, Sita did not accept these words. Extremely miserable, she told him the following.

## Chapter 2(26)

Hearing Rama's words, Sita was miserable. Her face overflowing with tears, she softly spoke these words. 'You have spoken about the hardships of living in the forest. Since your affection is more important, know that these are actually qualities. My seniors have instructed me that I should go with you.[99] O Rama! Separated from you, I will give up my life on earth. O Raghava! As long as I am near you, not even Shakra, the lord of the gods, is capable of oppressing me with his energy. A woman without a husband is incapable of remaining alive. O Rama! I have been taught by you about this being desirable. O immensely wise one! In earlier times, when I was in my father's house, I tell you truthfully that I heard from brahmanas that I was indeed going to live in the forest. O immensely strong one! In that house, I heard the words of the brahmanas that I possessed these

[99] At the time of marriage, not specifically about going to the forest.

signs. Therefore, I have always been ready to live in the forest.
That destiny of living in the forest must indeed be fulfilled by me.
O beloved one! I must go there with you. It cannot be otherwise.
Destiny will come true and I will go with you. The time has come
for the brahmana's[100] words to come true. Indeed, I know that
there are many kinds of hardships associated with residing in
the forest. O brave one! However, those are certainly faced by
men with uncleansed souls. As a maiden in my father's house, I
heard about living in the forest. In my mother's presence, a female
mendicant, with virtuous conduct, told me this. O lord! Earlier,
in many kinds of ways, I have given you pleasure. Therefore, with
you, I wish to leave for the forest. O fortunate one! O Raghava!
I am waiting for the time when I can go with you. The idea of
being brave and dwelling in the forest appeals to me. Because of
my pure soul and love, I will be without any taints. I will follow
my husband. My husband is my divinity. Even if I die, I will be
fortunate in remaining with you. O immensely wise one! In this
connection, the sacred words of the illustrious brahmanas have
been heard. "In this world, if a woman's father gives her away
with sanctified water, her own dharma is to be with her husband,
even after death." You desire this woman. She is excellent in
conduct and is devoted to her husband. That being the case, why
don't you wish to take me with you? I am faithful and devoted
to my husband. I am distressed. I share equally in your happiness
and unhappiness. O Kakutstha! Since I share equally in your joy
and misery, you should take me with you. I am miserable. If you
do not wish to take me to the forest, I will resort to poison, fire or
water, and thereby cause my death.' She wished to go, in this and
many other ways. However, the mighty-armed one did not agree
to take her to the desolate forest. Thus addressed, Maithilee was
overcome with thoughts. Warm tears issued from her eyes and
she seemed to be bathed in these. Vaidehi was full of rage and
immersed in thought. The self-controlled Kakutstha restrained her
and comforted her in many ways.

[100] The text uses the word in the singular.

# Chapter 2(27)

Maithilee, Janaka's daughter, was comforted by Rama about living in the forest. She spoke to her husband. Greatly agitated, Sita reproached the broad-chested Raghava in words full of love and pride. 'What will my father, the lord of Videha and Mithila think of himself? O Rama! He has obtained a son-in-law who is a woman in the guise of a man. In their ignorance, the people utter a falsehood about Rama's strength scorching like the rays of the sun. There is no great energy in you. Why are you distressed? What fear assails you? I have no other refuge. Why do you wish to forsake me? O brave one! Know me to be as devoted to you as Savitree, who followed Satyavan, Dyumatsena's son.[101] O unblemished one! With the exception of you, I do not wish to see anyone else, not even in my mind. I am not like others, who cause ill repute to their lineages. O Raghava! I will go with you. I am your own wife. Since I was a maiden, I have dwelt with you. O Rama! You now wish to give me away to others, as if I am a public dancer. Without taking me with you, you should not leave for the forest. Whether it is austerities, the forest or heaven, it should only be with you. I will follow behind you, whether you are sporting or sleeping. Along the road, I will not suffer from any exhaustion there. When I am on the path with you, kusha, reeds, cane, grass and thorns of trees will touch me. However, they will be like the touch of cotton or deer skin. Great storms will rise and will envelop me in dust. However, I will take pleasure in this, as if it is a supreme gift of sandalwood powder. While in the forest, at the extremities of the forest, I will lie down on green grass. Can lying down on a bed covered with spreads provide greater happiness than that? You will give me leaves, roots and fruits that you have collected yourself. Whether it is little or a lot, that will be like amrita to me. I will not remember the abodes of my mother and my father. I will enjoy the seasonal flowers and fruit. Having gone there, I will not see anything disagreeable. There

---

[101] Savitree was Satyavan's wife. When Satyavan died, she followed him to Yama's world, prayed to Yama and brought her husband back to life.

will not be any sorrow on my account. I will not be a great burden to bear. Being with you is heaven. Being without you is hell. O Rama! Knowing about my great love, go with me. I am anxious. Even after this, if you don't take me with you, I will drink poison. I will not come under the subjugation of the enemy. Therefore, I do not wish to live in misery. O beloved! If I am neglected by you, death is superior. Alone, I am incapable of tolerating this misery and grief for an instant, not to speak of fourteen years.' In this way, tormented, she lamented piteously in many ways. She embraced her husband and wept loudly. She was like a female elephant, pierced with the poisoned arrows of many words. Like a piece of kindling emitting a fire, she released tears that had been held back for a long time. As a result of her torment, tears flowed from her eyes. They were like crystal, like drops of water on lotuses.

In her misery, she seemed to be unconscious. Rama embraced her in his arms. Comforting her, he spoke these words. 'O queen! When you are in grief, even heaven does not appeal to me. Like Svayambhu, I do not have the slightest fear from any direction. O one with the beautiful face! I am capable of protecting you. However, without knowing all your intentions, I would not have liked to take you to the forest, to dwell there. O Maithilee! You have been created for the purpose of living in the forest with me. You are like my own deeds and I am incapable of abandoning you. O one with thighs like an elephant's trunk. In ancient times, virtuous ones observed dharma. You will follow me today, like Suvarchala[102] follows Surya. O one with excellent hips! Being obedient to the father and the mother is dharma. Therefore, transgressing their command, I am not interested in remaining alive. Established in the path of truth and dharma, my father has commanded me. I wish to act accordingly. That is eternal dharma. O timid one! Follow me. Be the one with whom I follow dharma.[103] Give jewels to brahmanas and food to mendicants. Grant them assurance. But be quick and do not delay.' Knowing that her husband was favourably inclined

[102] Surya's wife.

[103] The text uses the word *sahadharmachari*. The wife is *sahadharmini*, one with whom one follows dharma.

to the idea of her going, the queen was delighted. She quickly made arrangements for the donations. She was completely delighted in her mind. Hearing what her husband had said, the illustrious and beautiful lady made arrangements for giving away riches and jewels. The spirited one was one who upheld dharma.

## Chapter 2(28)

The immensely energetic Rama spoke to Lakshmana, who was in front of him. The brave one joined his hands in salutation. He was waiting there, desiring to proceed in front. 'O Soumitri! If you leave for the forest with me today, who will take care of Kousalya and the illustrious Sumitra? The immensely energetic king is bound by the noose of desire, as if Parjanya[104] is showering down desire on earth. After obtaining this kingdom, King Ashvapati's daughter[105] will not act properly and will cause grief to her co-wives.' Lakshmana was thus addressed by Rama, who knew about the use of words. The one who was accomplished in words replied in a gentle voice to Rama. 'O brave one! Because of your energy, Bharata will endeavour to worship Kousalya and Sumitra. There is no doubt about this. Because of the arrangements made, the noble Kousalya was given one thousand villages and those one thousand are enough to ensure her means of subsistence.[106] Wielding a bow, arrows, a spade and a basket, I will advance ahead of you, clearing and showing you the path. I will always collect roots and fruits and all the other food available in the forest, suitable for ascetics. You and Vaidehi will enjoy yourselves along the slopes of mountains. Whether you are awake or asleep, I will do everything.'

Rama was greatly delighted at these words and replied, 'O Soumitri! Go and take your leave from all your well-wishers. At

[104] The god of rain.

[105] Kaikeyee.

[106] When he married Kaikeyee, Dasharatha granted the income from one thousand villages to Kousalya.

Janaka's great sacrifice, the great-souled Varuna himself gave the king divine bows that are terrible to see. There are divine and impenetrable armour and quivers with inexhaustible stocks of arrows. There are two swords decorated with gold. They sparkle like the sun. All of those have been carefully kept in our preceptor's[107] residence. O Lakshmana! Collect those and return quickly.' Having made his mind up to reside in the forest, he[108] took his leave from the well-wishers. He took the permission of the preceptor of the Ikshvakus and took those supreme weapons. They were divine, maintained well and decorated with garlands. Soumitri, tiger among kings, showed Rama all those weapons. When Lakshmana returned, the self-controlled Rama cheerfully told him, 'O Lakshmana! O amiable one! You have returned at the time I wished for. O scorcher of enemies! With you, I desire to give away all my wealth to brahmanas and ascetics and to preceptors who are excellent brahmanas, residing here, firm in their devotion. I also wish to give to all those who are dependent on me for survival. Bring the noble Suyajna, Vasishtha's son, here. Also quickly bring the best among brahmanas. I wish to honour all the other excellent brahmanas and then leave for the forest.'

# Chapter 2(29)

His brother's command was auspicious and agreeable. Listening to this, he quickly went to Suyajna's residence. Lakshmana worshipped the brahmana, who lived in a house of fire,[109] and spoke to him. 'O friend! Come to the house of someone who is going to perform an extremely difficult task.' Having performed the sandhya rites, with Soumitri, he quickly went to Rama's large, prosperous and beautiful residence, populated by people. On seeing that the one

---

[107] Vasishtha.

[108] Lakshmana.

[109] This probably means that Suyajna performed austerities with fires around him on all four sides.

who knew about the Vedas had arrived, with Sita, Raghava joined his hands in salutation and honouring Suyajna, circumambulated the fire. Kakutstha offered him the best of sparkling earrings and armlets made out of molten gold, gems strung together on threads, bracelets to be worn on the upper arm and bracelets to be worn around the wrist. There were many other jewels too. He honoured them back. Urged by Sita, Rama spoke to Suyajna. 'O friend! O amiable one! For your wife, Sita now wishes to give a necklace, a golden thread and a girdle. Please accept them. Vaidehi desires to give you a couch strewn with the best of spreads and decorated with many kinds of jewels. My maternal uncle gave me an elephant named Shatrunjaya. O bull among brahmanas! I wish to give you that and one thousand other elephants.' Thus addressed by Rama, Suyajna accepted these and pronounced auspicious benedictions on Rama, Lakshmana and Sita.

Collected, Rama, who was pleasant in speech, spoke to his beloved brother Soumitri, like Brahma to the lord of the gods. 'O Soumitri! Both Agastya and Koushika are excellent brahmanas. Summon them and worship them with jewels, like pouring water on crops. There is a devoted preceptor who serves Kousalya and pronounces his benedictions on her. He knows about the Vedas and the rules that are in conformity with *Taittiriya*.[110] O Soumitri! Give that brahmana vehicles, female servants and silken garments, until he is content. The noble Chitraratha has been a charioteer and adviser for a very long time. Satisfy him with extremely expensive jewels, garments and wealth. Give him one thousand bullocks for carrying grain and two hundred bulls for ploughing. O Soumitri! Give him one thousand cows for sustenance.' At this, as addressed, Lakshmana, tiger among men, himself gave away those riches, like Kubera, to the best of brahmanas who had been named. He[111] gave away many kinds of objects to each person who was dependent on him. With tears choking his voice, he spoke to the dependents who were present there. 'Until my return, Lakshmana's house and my

---

[110] The *Taittiriya Upanishad*, associated with the Yajur Veda.
[111] Rama.

house should never be empty. In turn, each of you must ensure this.' Thus addressed, all those dependents were extremely unhappy. He instructed the treasurer, 'Bring my riches here.' At this, all the dependents brought the riches there. With Lakshmana, the tiger among men distributed those riches to brahmanas, children, the aged and those who were destitute.

There was a brahmana named Trijata. He was born in Gargya's lineage and was tawny in complexion. Till the fifth chamber, no one ever obstructed his path.[112] Trijata approached the prince and spoke these words. 'O immensely illustrious prince! I am poor and have many sons. Look at me. I always earn a subsistence through unchhavritti.' As if in jest, Rama replied, 'I have not given away even one thousand cows so far. Fling your staff. You will get as many as that expanse.' Anxious, he[113] girded his lower garment around his waist and flung the staff with as much strength and force as he could muster. Rama comforted Gargya's descendant and said, 'You should not be angry. I said this only in jest.' The great sage, Trijata, was delighted. He and his wife accepted a herd of cows. He pronounced benedictions for the extension of the great-souled one's fame, strength, joy and happiness.

# Chapter 2(30)

With Vaidehi, the two Raghavas gave away a lot of riches to brahmanas. With Sita, they then went to see their father. They took those blazing weapons, which were so difficult to look at. Sita adorned them with heaps of garlands. The mansions in the palace were like the tips of celestial vehicles. However, the prosperous and handsome people who ascended them seemed to be indifferent. The roads were full of many anxious people and it was

---

[112] In visiting royalty, one had to pass through successive gates and chambers, with guards at each gate. Usually, the third chamber is regarded as an exclusive preserve. This is superior to the third chamber.

[113] Trijata.

impossible to walk. Therefore, they climbed up to the palaces and distressed, glanced at Raghava. Those people saw Rama on foot, having cast aside his umbrella. With their senses distraught because of their sorrow, they uttered many kinds of words. 'He used to be followed by a large army with the four limbs.[114] He is now alone with Sita, followed by Lakshmana. He possessed riches. Though he knew about the essence of desire, he is the one who granted objects of desire. Because he revered dharma, he did not desire to make his father's words come false. The people who are on the royal road today can see Sita. Earlier, even creatures that flew through the sky were unable to see her. Sita applied unguents to her body and used red sandalwood paste. Rains, heat and cold will quickly render her pale. Truly, a spirit that has entered Dasharatha has spoken today. The king should not have exiled his beloved son. Even if a son is devoid of qualities, how can he be exiled, not to speak of a person who has conquered the world through his qualities? There are six qualities that adorn Raghava, best among men— non-injury, compassion, learning, good conduct, self-control and tranquility. The entire world is afflicted because this lord of the world is afflicted, just as a tree with flowers and fruit suffers when its foundation is destroyed. Like Lakshmana is following him, with our wives and our relatives, we will quickly go wherever Raghava is going. Abandoning the groves, fields and houses, we will follow Rama, who observes dharma, and endure the same kind of happiness and unhappiness. Treasures dug up,[115] desolate courtyards bereft of grains and riches, the best objects removed in every way, enveloped by dust and abandoned by the gods— let Kaikeyee enjoy those houses discarded by us. Since Raghava is going there, let the forest become a city. Since we are abandoning it, let the city become a forest. Since we have abandoned it, let fanged creatures in holes and animals and birds from the mountains inhabit this place. As long as we were here, they had abandoned it.' The large number of people uttered such diverse words. Though

---

[114] Chariots, elephants, horses and infantry.

[115] Meaning that the hidden treasures have been dug up and are no longer there.

he heard them, Rama's mind was not disturbed. Though he saw
that the people were distressed, his mind was not disturbed and he
seemed to be smiling. Wishing to follow his father's instructions
in the proper way, Rama went to see his father. The great-souled
Rama, the son of the descendant of Ikshvaku, saw that the suta
Sumantra was in front of him, miserable at the prospect of his
leaving for the forest. He waited, so that he could be announced
to his great-souled father. He was devoted to dharma and to
obey his father's command, had made up his mind to go to the
forest. On seeing Sumantra, Raghava told him, 'Tell the king that
I have come.'

## Chapter 2(31)

Sent by Rama, the suta entered quickly and saw the king, whose
senses were tormented. He was sighing. The immensely wise
one saw that his senses were greatly afflicted. He was grieving over
Rama. With hands joined in salutation, the suta approached. 'Your
son, tiger among men, is waiting at the door. He has given away all
his riches to brahmanas and the dependents. O fortunate one! Let
Rama, for whom truth is his valour, see you. Having taken his leave
of all the well-wishers, he wishes to see you now. O lord of the earth!
He will leave for the great forest. See him. He is surrounded by all
the royal qualities, like the sun with its rays.' That Indra among
men[116] was truthful in speech. He had dharma in his soul. He was
like the ocean in his gravity. He was like the sky in cleanliness and
replied, 'O Sumantra! Bring all my wives who are present. I wish
to see Raghava when I am surrounded by all my wives.' He passed
through to the inner quarters and addressed the women in these
words. 'O noble ones! The king has summoned you. You should
go there without delay.' Sumantra addressed all those women and
told them about the king's command. Knowing about the king's

---

[116] Dasharatha.

command, they went to their husband's residence. Three hundred and fifty women, with coppery red eyes and firm in their vows, surrounded Kousalya and went there slowly. When the wives had arrived, the king glanced at them. The king told the suta Sumantra, 'Bring my son here.'

Quickly, the suta brought Rama, Lakshmana and Maithilee and went to where the king was. From a distance, the king saw his son arriving, hands joined in salutation. Surrounded by the miserable women, he swiftly arose from his seat. On seeing Rama, the king speedily advanced towards him. However, before reaching him, afflicted by sorrow, he fell down on the ground, senseless. Rama and maharatha Lakshmana saw that the king had fallen down, afflicted by sorrow and grief. Mixed with the sound of the tinkling of ornaments, the wails of thousands of women suddenly arose from the palace, 'Alas, Rama! Alas!' With Sita, the weeping Rama and Lakshmana raised him with their arms and laid him down on a bed. Soon, the king regained his senses, though he was still submerged in an ocean of grief. Joining his hands in salutation, Rama told him, 'For all of us, you are the lord. O great king! I seek your leave. I am leaving for Dandakaranya. Look on me with kindly eyes. Permit Lakshmana and Sita to follow me to the forest. Despite being restrained by many kinds of reasons, they do not wish to remain here. O one who grants honours! Abandon grief and grant all of us permission, like Prajapati did to his sons.'[117] Rama waited anxiously for the king's permission to reside in the forest. The king glanced towards Raghava and replied, 'O Raghava! Because I had granted boons to Kaikeyee, I was confused. Imprison me and become the king of Ayodhya today.' The king addressed Rama, who was supreme among the upholders of dharma, in this way. The one who was eloquent in the use of words joined his hands in salutation and replied to his father. 'O king! May you be the lord of the earth for one thousand years. I will reside in the forest. I must

[117] Four sages who were created through Brahma's (Prajapati's) mental powers—Sanatkumara, Sanaka, Sanatana and Sanandana. They took Brahma's permission to go to the forest and practise austerities.

not act so as to make you false.' 'O son![118] For your benefit, advance fearlessly along the auspicious path, without any distractions, until you return. O son! However, it is night now, when one should never leave. Do not go today. Spend this night with your mother and me, so that we can see you. Having satisfied yourself with all the objects of desire, leave at the appropriate time tomorrow.' Hearing the words spoken by their miserable father, Rama, and his brother Lakshmana, were distressed. He[119] spoke these words. 'Even if we obtain these objects with qualities today, who will give them to us tomorrow? Therefore, without these objects of desire, I wish to leave this place. I have abandoned the earth and this kingdom, full of people, wealth and grain. May it be given to Bharata. Abandon this grief. Don't let your eyes overflow with tears. The ocean, the lord of the rivers, cannot be assailed and is not agitated. I do not wish for the kingdom, happiness, Maithilee, or you. O bull among men! Without any falsehood, I desire the truth. Forsaken by me, this city, kingdom and the entire earth should be given to Bharata. I will follow your instructions. I will go to the forest and dwell there for a long time. Forsaken by me, let this entire earth, with its mountains, boulders, cities, groves and frontiers, be given to Bharata, so that he can justly rule over it. Let it be the way you have pledged. O king! My mind does not hanker after great objects of desire or what brings pleasure to my own self. As is instructed by the virtuous, I will follow your command. O unblemished one! Do not be miserable on my account. O unblemished one! Therefore, right now, I do not desire the undecaying kingdom, happiness or Maithilee. When I am associated with falsehood, I do not wish to remain alive. I desire that the pledge of truth should come true. We will eat fruits and roots in the forest. We will see the mountains, rivers and lakes. We will enter the forest, with its wonderful trees. May you be happy. Let us withdraw.'[120]

---

[118] The Critical Edition excises some shlokas and this breaks the continuity. This is Dasharatha replying.

[119] Rama.

[120] The word used is *nivritti*, which therefore has the implied sense of withdrawal from the senses and objects of pleasure.

## Chapter 2(32)

The descendant of the Ikshvaku lineage[121] was afflicted because of the pledge he had himself given. Shedding tears, he sighed repeatedly and spoke to Sumantra. 'O suta! Let an army with the four kinds of forces be prepared. Let it be given all the jewels, so that it can quickly follow Raghava. Let the prince's army be extensive. Let it be adorned with courtesans who are good in conduct and extremely rich merchants. Engage all those dependents whose valour he takes delight in and give them many kinds of gifts. Once he kills deer and elephants, tastes honey from the forest and sees many rivers, he will not remember the kingdom. Let my store of grain and store of riches follow Rama, as he goes to reside in the desolate forest. He will then reside happily in the forest. He will be able to summon the rishis and perform sacrifices in auspicious spots, giving away the appropriate dakshina. The mighty-armed Bharata will rule over Ayodhya. However, let all the objects of desire be arranged for the prosperous Rama.'

When Kakutstha spoke in this way, Kaikeyee was overcome by fear. Her mouth went dry and her voice also choked. Pale and frightened, Kaikeyee spoke these words. 'All the virtuous people will leave the kingdom and it will be like a vessel from which the liquor has been drunk. It will be empty, bereft of all essence. Bharata will not accept it.' Kaikeyee discarded her shame and spoke these extremely terrible words. King Dasharatha spoke these words to the large-eyed one. 'Having imposed this unfortunate burden on me, why do you strike me when I am bearing the burden?' Kaikeyee became doubly angry and addressed the king. 'It is in your lineage that Sagara cast away his eldest son, known as Asamanja. He[122] should also leave in that way.' Thus addressed, King Dasharatha said, 'Shame.' All the people were ashamed, but she did not perceive this. There was an aged adviser who was virtuous and was greatly revered by the king. His name was Siddhartha and he addressed Kaikeyee. 'Asamanja

[121] Dasharatha.
[122] Rama.

seized children playing in the streets and flung them into the waters of the Sarayu. The evil-minded one took pleasure in this. On seeing this, all the citizens were angry and told the king, "O extender of the kingdom! You have to choose between us and Asamanja." At this, the king asked them, "What are you scared of?" Thus asked by the king, the ordinary people spoke these words. "When our sons are playing, the foolish one, confounded in his sense, seizes those children and flings them into the Sarayu. He obtains infinite delight from this." Hearing the words of the ordinary people, the king wished to bring pleasure to them and cast aside his inauspicious son. This is what King Sagara, extremely devoted to dharma, did. What wicked act has Rama perpetrated that he should be restrained?' The king heard Siddhartha's words. In a tired voice and afflicted by sorrow, he addressed Kaikeyee in these words. 'I will now follow Rama, forsaking the kingdom, happiness and riches. With King Bharata, you can happily enjoy the kingdom for a long period of time.'

## Chapter 2(33)

Rama knew about humility. On hearing the adviser's words, he humbly addressed Dasharatha in these words. 'O king! I have cast aside objects of pleasure, to dwell in the forest on forest fare. When I have cast everything aside, why should anyone follow me? If a person has given away the best of elephants, why will he turn his mind to the harness alone? If one has cast aside the best of elephants, why will he have affection only for the rope? O best among virtuous ones! O lord of the earth! In that way, what will I do with flags and all those who will follow me? Let tattered rags be brought for me. I am going to reside in the forest for fourteen years. As I leave, let a spade and a basket be brought for me.' At this, Kaikeyee herself brought tattered rags for Raghava. Despite the assembly, she wasn't ashamed and said, 'Wear these.' The tiger among men accepted those two[123]

---

[123] One as an upper garment, the second as a lower.

tattered rags from Kaikeyee. Casting aside his fine garments, he wore the garb of an ascetic. In front of his father, Lakshmana also cast aside his excellent clothes and covered himself in an ascetic's attire. Sita, attired in silken clothes, was alarmed, like a deer that sees a snare, on seeing the tattered rags that were meant to be worn by her. She was ashamed and distressed in her mind. She spoke to her husband, who was like a king of the gandharvas. 'How do sages, who reside in the forest, wear these rags?' She held one piece against her neck and the other in her hand. Janaka's daughter did not know how to wear these and was ashamed. Rama, supreme among those who uphold dharma, quickly came to her. He himself fastened the rags over Sita's silken garments.

She was attired in those tattered rags. Though she had a protector, she was like one without a protector. All the people were angry and said, 'Shame on Dasharatha.' The descendant of the Ikshvaku lineage[124] emitted warm sighs and addressed his wife. 'O Kaikeyee! Sita does not deserve to go, wearing kusha grass and rags. O wicked one! Exiling Rama should be sufficient for you. Why do you again wish to perform this wicked and cruel act?' Rama, about to leave for the forest, addressed his father, whose head was lowered down, though he was seated, in these words. 'My illustrious mother, Kousalya, is devoted to dharma. O king! She is aged. But her conduct isn't inferior and she won't censure you. O one who grants boons! Without me, she will be immersed in an ocean of grief. She has not confronted such a hardship earlier. You should respect her. O king who is like the great Indra! She has great affection for her son. When I am in the forest, she will be afflicted by grief. You should ensure that my mother remains alive and does not leave for Yama's eternal abode.'

## Chapter 2(34)

The king was bereft of his senses. With his wives, he heard Rama's words and saw that he was attired in a sage's garments.

---

[124] Dasharatha.

Tormented by grief, he was incapable of looking towards Raghava.
Distressed in his mind, he was incapable of glancing towards him,
or replying. However, though miserable, the great king regained
his senses in a moment. The mighty-armed one thought of Rama
and lamented. 'I think that in the past, I must have separated
several from their children. I must have caused injury to creatures.
That is the reason I am now confronted with this. Until the time
arrives, life is not separated from the body. Despite being afflicted
by Kaikeyee, I am not faced with death. I see my son stationed
before me and he is like a fire. However, abandoning his delicate
garments, my son is clad in the garb of an ascetic. Indeed, it is
because of Kaikeyee's deeds alone that all these people are
suffering. Driven by selfish motives, she has brought about this
act of deceit.' These are the words he spoke, his eyes overflowing
with tears. Afflicted by grief, he was incapable of saying anything
other than 'Rama!' After an instant, the great king regained his
senses. His eyes overflowing with tears, he addressed Sumantra
in these words. 'Arrange a chariot that can be driven and yoke it
to excellent steeds. Take this extremely fortunate one from here,
beyond the boundaries of the habitation. I think that these are
the fruits being reaped by someone with qualities, by virtue of his
qualities. A brave and virtuous person is being exiled to the forest
by his father and his mother.'

Following the king's command, Sumantra, swift in his valour,
yoked an ornamented chariot with horses and brought it there.
The suta prepared a chariot decorated in gold for the prince. He
joined his hands in salutation and reported that it had been yoked
to excellent steeds. The king knew about what should be done
at the right time and place and was also clear about everything
auspicious. He quickly summoned the person who was in charge of
accumulating riches and said, 'Remembering the number of years
that has to be spent, quickly bring extremely expensive garments
and excellent ornaments for Vaidehi.' Thus addressed by the Indra
among men, he went to the treasury. He quickly brought everything
and offered it to Sita. Vaidehi, born in a noble lineage and beautiful
in her limbs, was about to leave for the forest. She adorned her
limbs with those wonderful ornaments. Adorned in those excellent

ornaments, Vaidehi made the residence look radiant. She was like the sun with rays, arising at the right time and illuminating the sky with its resplendence. Her mother-in-law engulfed her in her arms. Maithilee never did anything that was inferior. She inhaled the fragrance of her head[125] and spoke these words. 'In this world, even though they are respected and loved, false women cease to honour their husbands when they face hardships. Do not disrespect my son, who is being exiled. Though he possesses riches, he is poor now. However, he is still your divinity.' Sita understood the words spoken, full of dharma and artha. She joined her hands in salutation and addressed her mother-in-law, who stood in front of her. 'O noble one! I will do everything that you had instructed me. I know how I should conduct myself towards my husband. I had heard this earlier too. O noble one! You should not equate me with wicked women. I am not capable of deviating from dharma, just as the moon cannot be separated from its radiance. Without chords, the veena doesn't make a sound. Without wheels, a chariot does not move. Even if she has one hundred sons, a woman doesn't obtain happiness without her husband. A father gives a limited amount. What a mother and a son give are also limited. What a husband gives is unlimited. Who does not worship a husband? O noble one! I have been instructed by the best, those who are supreme upholders of dharma. How can I disrespect him? To a woman, the husband is a divinity.' Sita's words penetrated Kousalya's heart and on hearing them, the one who was pure of heart, suddenly released tears, because they were a source of both misery and joy.

Rama was supreme in knowledge of dharma. Amidst all his mothers, he joined his hands in salutation and approached his own mother, who was most revered of all. He spoke these words. 'O mother! You should not be sad. Look towards my father. The period of dwelling in the forest will soon be over. The period of fourteen years will pass, as if you were sleeping. You will see me return here, surrounded by well-wishers. He spoke these words to his mother and they conveyed deep meaning. He then glanced at

---

[125] Kousalya and Sita respectively.

his three hundred and fifty mothers.[126] In a similar way, joining his hands in salutation, Dasharatha's son then spoke similar words, full of dharma and artha, to those distressed mothers too. 'While I resided here with you, if I said anything harsh, or if I did anything in ignorance, please pardon me. Now I seek my leave from all of you.' As Raghava spoke in this way, the sounds of lamentations arose from the king's wives, like those of curlews wailing. In former times, Dasharatha's residence used to resound with the sound of tambourines and drums, like the roar of thundering clouds. Because of the hardship, there was now the sound of extremely miserable wails and lamentations.

# Chapter 2(35)

The miserable Rama, Sita and Lakshmana joined their hands in salutation. They bowed down before the king and circumambulated him. Having taken his leave, Raghava, who knew about dharma, with Sita, bowed down before his mother, who was confounded by grief. Lakshmana followed his brother and bowed down before Kousalya. He next touched the feet of his mother, Sumitra. He worshipped his mother, who was weeping. For the sake of the mighty-armed one's welfare, she inhaled the fragrance of Lakshmana's head and addressed Soumitri. 'Because you are devoted to your well-wisher,[127] I have permitted you to reside in the forest. O son! Do not fail to take care of Rama, your brother who is leaving for the forest. O unblemished one! Whether it is prosperity or adversity, he is your refuge. In this world, that is the dharma of the virtuous, being obedient to an elder. This is the eternal appropriate behaviour for this lineage— donations, consecration for sacrifices and giving up one's body in battles. Know Rama to be like Dasharatha. Know Janaka's

---

[126] The stepmothers.
[127] Meaning Rama.

daughter to be like me. Know the forest to be Ayodhya. O son! Depart cheerfully.'

Knowledgeable about humility, Sumantra joined his hands in salutation and humbly spoke to Kakutstha, like Matali[128] to Vasava. 'O fortunate one! O immensely illustrious one! Ascend the chariot. O Rama! I will quickly take you to whichever place you tell me to. You will have to reside in the forest for fourteen years, as has been instructed by the queen. That period has commenced.' That chariot was like the sun. Having ornamented herself, the beautiful-hipped Sita ascended it with a cheerful mind. The brothers also ascended, with weapons and armour that they laid down on the firm leather seat of the chariot. On seeing that Sita, the third one, had also ascended, Sumantra urged the respected horses, which were as fleet as the speed of the wind. For many nights, Raghava departed for the great forest. It was as if the city's strength had been sapped, as if people had lost their senses. The city used to emit a great sound—because it was full of crazy, intoxicated and respected elephants and because of the neighing of the horses and the tinkling of their ornaments. That city was greatly afflicted.

Children and aged rushed towards Rama, like a person who is suffering in the summer rushes towards water. Their long and anxious faces could be seen at the rear and towards the sides. All of them were extremely miserable and their faces were overflowing with tears. They said, 'O suta! Hold back the reins of the horses and proceed slowly. We wish to see Rama's face, which will become extremely difficult for us to behold. There is no doubt that Rama's mother's heart is indeed made of iron. It has not got shattered despite her son, who is like a god, leaving for the forest. Vaidehi is doing what should be done and is following her husband like a shadow. She is devoted to dharma and does not abandon it, like Meru does not forsake the radiance of the sun. O Lakshmana! You are always pleasant in speech. Since you serve your brother, who is like a god, you have become successful in your objective. This is a great success and is a great accomplishment. Since you are following him, this is

[128] Indra's charioteer.

a path to heaven.' Incapable of restraining their tears, they spoke in this way.

The king was miserable in his mind and was surrounded by the grieving women. Saying that he wished to see his son, he emerged from his house. Ahead of him, the great sound of lamenting women could be heard. This was like the wailing of female elephants, when a large male elephant has been tied up. The father, King Kakutstha, used to be handsome. But he seemed shrunken, like the full moon when it has been enveloped in an eclipse. When the men saw that the king was distressed and extremely miserable, a tumultuous sound arose from Rama's rear. Some said, 'Alas, Rama!' Others said, 'Alas, Rama's mother!' All those in the prosperous inner quarters started to weep and lament. As he glanced back, Rama saw his father and mother, following along the path, distressed and not in control of their senses. He was bound in the noose of dharma and could not look at them directly. They deserved happiness and did not deserve this unhappiness. Though they deserved vehicles, they were on foot. On seeing this, he instructed the charioteer to drive swiftly. The tiger among men caught the miserable sight of his father and mother and could not bear it, like an elephant struck by a goad. The weeping Kousalya ran after the chariot, wailing, 'Alas, Rama! Rama! Alas, Sita! Alas, Lakshmana!' His mother seemed to be dancing and he could not stand the sight. The king said, 'Wait.' Raghava said, 'Go. Go.' Sumantra was caught between the two, as if in the midst of a whirlpool. Rama told him, 'It is wicked to witness their grief for a long period of time. When the king berates you later, you can say that you did not hear him.'[129] Hearing Rama's words, the charioteer acted in accordance with them. He took his leave of the people and urged the horses to proceed even faster.

Circumambulating Rama mentally,[130] the king's attendants returned. However, the men were incapable of controlling the flow of their tears. The advisers addressed the great king Dasharatha in these words. 'If one wishes for a person to return, one should

[129] Sumantra was caught in two minds about whom to obey. This is a rare instance of Rama asking someone to lie.

[130] Obviously, they couldn't do it physically.

not follow him for a long distance.' The king heard their words, which were full of all the qualities. His body was perspiring and his form was dejected. With his wives, the miserable king stood there, looking towards his son.

## Chapter 2(36)

Having joined his hands in salutation, the tiger among men departed. Great sounds of sorrow and lamentation arose from the inner quarters. 'Where is our protector going, like an ascetic, leaving the people weak and without a protector? He was our refuge and destination. Even when he was accused, he was never angry. He cast aside all kinds of rage. He pacified all those who were angry, sharing in their sorrow. Where is he going? The immensely energetic and great-souled one's mother is Kousalya and he respected us the way he respected her. Where is he going? Urged and afflicted by Kaikeyee, the king sent him to the forest. He is the saviour of the people and the world. Where is he going? Alas! The king is bereft of his senses. Rama's vow is dharma and truth. He is loved by all living beings on earth. Yet, he has been exiled for living in the forest.' All the queens were afflicted by grief. They wept and lamented loudly, like cows separated from their calves. On hearing those terrible sounds of sorrow that arose from the inner quarters, the great king was tormented by sorrow on account of his son and became extremely miserable. Despite the sun having set, no agnihotra oblations were offered. The cattle were neglected and not given their food. The cows and calves were not given water to drink. Trishanku, Brihaspati and Budha assumed a red tinge throughout.[131] All the planets assumed a terrible form and were in conjunction with the moon. The nakshatras lost their lustre. The planets lost their energy. Vishakha nakshatra was enveloped

[131] Brihaspati is Jupiter and Budha is Mercury. In this context, Trishanku means the Trishanku nakshatra, identified as the Southern Cross.

in smoke and no longer shone in the firmament. All the people in
the city were suddenly overcome by distress. Their minds turned
away from eating or finding pleasure. The faces of people along the
royal roads overflowed with tears. Everyone was full of sorrow.
Not a single happy person could be discerned. The wind that blew
was no longer cool. The moon was no longer pleasant to behold.
The sun did not heat the world any more. Everything on earth was
in disarray. Women no longer asked about their sons, husbands
and brothers. Thinking about Rama alone, they abandoned each
other. All of Rama's well-wishers were bereft of their senses. They
suffered from that great burden of sorrow and did not leave their
beds. Deprived of the great-souled one, Ayodhya was like the earth
with its mountains, abandoned by Purandara. Oppressed by that
terrible burden of fear, it seemed to quake. There was a road among
the large number of elephants, warriors and horses.

# Chapter 2(37)

When he departed, as long as the dust raised could be seen, the
best of the Ikshvaku lineage[132] could not withdraw his gaze.
His beloved son was extremely devoted to dharma and as long as
the king wished to see him, the dust arose from the earth so that he
could see his son. When the king could no longer see the dust raised
by Rama, he became distressed and miserable and fell down on the
ground. On the right, the lady Kousalya raised him in her arms. On
the left flank, the lady Kaikeyee, who loved Bharata, raised him. The
king was accomplished in policy, dharma and humility. However,
afflicted in his senses, the king glanced towards Kaikeyee and said,
'O Kaikeyee! You are wicked in conduct. Do not touch my limbs. I
do not wish to see you. You are not my wife, or my relative. I do not
depend on you. I do not belong to you and you do not belong to me.
For you, artha alone is supreme. Since you have discarded dharma,

---

[132] Dasharatha. The dust raised by Rama's chariot.

I discard you. I accepted your hand and circumambulated the fire. I am giving all of that up, in this world and in the next. If Bharata is delighted at having obtained this undecaying kingdom, if he gives anything to me in the form of funeral oblations, let those not reach me.'[133] The lord of men was covered in dust and Queen Kousalya, afflicted by grief, made him return.[134] The one with dharma in his soul thought about his ascetic son. He was tormented, as if he had wilfully slain a brahmana, or touched the fire with his hand. Distressed, he turned repeatedly towards the path followed by the chariot. The king was no longer radiant, like the one with rays[135] at the time of an eclipse. Remembering his beloved son, he lamented in grief and affliction. Discerning that his son had reached the boundaries of the city, he said, 'My son has been borne by the best of mounts. That is the reason marks of hooves can be seen along the road, but the great-souled one cannot be seen. It is certain that he will have to find a refuge at the foot of a tree today. He will have to lie down with its trunk, or a rock, as a pillow. The unfortunate one will wake on the ground, covered in dust. He will sigh like a bull elephant, surrounded by she elephants, does in a stream. It is certain that those who roam around in the forest will see a long-armed man, when Rama awakes and leaves. Though he is the protector of the world, he is like one without a protector. O Kaikeyee! May your wishes be fulfilled. May you reside in the kingdom like a widow. Without that tiger among men, I am not interested in remaining alive.' The king was surrounded by a crowd of people and lamented in this way. He entered that supreme city, like one who has bathed after an unfortunate event.[136]

The crossroads and houses were deserted. The shops and temples were covered. Exhausted, weak, miserable and afflicted, not too many people could be seen along the wide roads. Thinking of Rama, he looked at the entire city. Lamenting, the king entered

[133] That is, Dasharatha does not want Bharata to perform funeral oblations for him.
[134] To the city.
[135] The sun.
[136] Meaning death and the bath that one takes before entering the house after a funeral ceremony.

his residence, like the sun disappearing amidst clouds. It was like a large lake that was no longer agitated, since Suparna[137] had emptied it of all the serpents. Without Rama, Vaidehi and Lakshmana, that is what the residence looked like. 'Convey me quickly to the residence of Kousalya, Rama's mother.' This is what the king told the gatekeepers. Having entered Kousalya's residence, he lay himself down on a bed, but his mind was agitated. The great and valiant king looked around. He lamented in a loud voice, 'Alas, Raghava! You have left me. The best among men who survive this period and see Rama, and embrace him on his return, are happy. O Kousalya! O virtuous one! I am unable to see you. Touch me with your hand. My eyesight has followed Rama and has not returned.' The queen saw that though the Indra among men was lying down on the couch, he was thinking of Rama. She became even more distressed and sat down. Because of the hardship, she too sighed and lamented.

## Chapter 2(38)

The king was lying down, afflicted by grief. On seeing this, Kousalya, who was also grief-stricken because of her son, addressed the lord of the earth. 'Having released her poison on Raghava, tiger among men, Kaikeyee will roam around like a fork-tongued female serpent that has cast of its skin. The immensely fortunate one has satisfied her wish of banishing Rama. Self-controlled, she will now terrify me, like a wicked snake in a house. It would have been better had a boon been granted of my son dwelling in the house as a servant who roams around in the city, like a beggar looking for alms. As she desired, Kaikeyee has brought Rama down from his position. She is like a person who offers oblations into the fire on an auspicious occasion, but offers the indicated shares to rakshasas instead. The brave one possesses the

---

[137] Garuda.

stride of a king of elephants. He is a mighty-armed archer. He must certainly have entered the forest with his wife and with Lakshmana. Because of Kaikeyees's instruction and yours, in the forest, he will face hardships that he has not faced before. When he finishes his dwelling in the forest, what state will he be in? Devoid of riches, those young ones have been exiled and will be deprived of the fruits their ages warrant. Miserable, how will they live there, surviving on fruits and roots? When will that auspicious time, when I will see Raghava, with his wife and brother, and when my sorrows will be destroyed, arrive? When will Ayodhya hear that the brave ones have returned? When will the city be illustrious, with standards and garlands, full of happy people? When will we see those two tigers and men return from the forest? When will the city be happy and delighted, like the ocean at the time of the full moon? When will the brave and mighty-armed one enter the city of Ayodhya, placing Sita at the front of the chariot, like a bull behaving towards a cow? When will my sons, scorchers of enemies,[138] enter and proceed along the royal road, with thousands of people showering them with parched grain? When will they, with cheerful minds, happily circumambulate the city, offering fruits to maidens and brahmanas? When will the one who knows about dharma, as radiant as an immortal, return, with mature intelligence and age, and nourish me for three years?[139] O brave one! It is certain that I must have committed a cruel act earlier.[140] When calves wished to suck at milk, I must have sliced off the teats of mother cows. I am like a cow with a calf, rendered calf-less by a lion. O tiger among men! I am like a cow with a tender calf, forcibly rendered calf-less by Kaikeyee. He is ornamented with all the qualities and is accomplished in all the sacred texts. I only have one son. Without the son, I do not desire to remain alive. I cannot discern any capacity to remain alive. I am unable to see my beloved son, who is mighty-armed and immensely strong. My body is being scorched by grief, from the heat of a fire that has arisen. It

---

[138] In the dual, including Lakshmana.
[139] The imagery is of rains, specifically, three consecutive years of good rainfall.
[140] In an earlier life.

is as if the illustrious sun is scorching this earth with the radiance of its blazing rays during the summer.'

# Chapter 2(39)

Kousalya, supreme among women, lamented in this way. Established in dharma, Sumitra addressed her in words that were full of dharma. 'O noble one! Your son is supreme among men and possesses all the virtuous qualities. Why are you lamenting? Why are you weeping piteously? O noble one! Your immensely strong son has forsaken the kingdom and has left. The great-souled one has performed a virtuous act and has made his father's words come true. If one acts properly and virtuously, one obtains eternal fruits, even after death. Rama has been established in the best of dharma and one should never sorrow over him. The unblemished Lakshmana follows excellent conduct and is devoted to him. His compassion towards all creatures will bring benefit to the great-souled one.[141] Vaidehi is used to happiness and will know misery during her residence in the forest. However, she has followed your son, who has dharma in his soul. The radiance of the lord's deeds will flutter like a flag in the world. He possesses self-control and the vow of truth. After this, what can your son not obtain? Knowing about Rama's evident purity and supreme greatness, the sun will not be able to scorch his body with its rays. Auspicious breezes, appropriate for all seasons, will be released from the groves. Whether it is hot or cold, these cheerful winds will serve Raghava. When he lies down in the night to sleep, the cool beams of the moon will touch him and gladden him, like a father's embrace. On seeing that he had slain the Indra among danavas, Timidhvaja's son,[142] in a battle, the greatly energetic brahmana gave him divine weapons. The bull among men will obtain prosperity, together with

---

[141] Lakshmana's conduct will bring benefits to Rama.

[142] Timidhvaja is Shambara, whom Dasharatha fought against. Shambara's son is Subahu, killed by Rama. The brahmana who gave the weapons is Vishvamitra.

Vaidehi, who came out of the earth. With these three,[143] Rama will be consecrated as king. On seeing him leave this place, people shed tears of sorrow. You will soon see tears of joy emerge from their eyes. On seeing the well-wishers honour your son, you will soon release tears of joy, like an array of clouds during the monsoon. Your son, the granter of boons, will quickly return to Ayodhya. He will knead your feet with his thick, but gentle, hands.' Hearing these words of Lakshmana's mother, Rama's mother, the wife of the king, instantly made all sorrow disappear from her body, like an autumn cloud vanishes with only a little bit of water.[144]

## Chapter 2(40)

There were men who were devoted to the great-souled Rama, for whom, truth was his valour. When he left to live in the forest, they followed him. The king and his army returned. However, the groups of well-wishers did not return and followed Rama's chariot. He possessed all the qualities. Therefore, when he lived in Ayodhya, he was loved by those immensely illustrious men, as if he was the full moon. Despite being entreated to the contrary, Kakutstha rendered his father's pledge true and took to the forest. They glanced at him affectionately, as if they were drinking him in with their eyes. Affectionately, Rama addressed those subjects, as if they were his own offspring. 'O residents of Ayodhya! You have shown me affection and great respect. For the sake of bringing me pleasure, display this particularly towards Bharata. His character is fortunate and he extends Kaikeyee's delight. He will do whatever is appropriate, for benefit and pleasure. He may be young in age, but he is aged in wisdom. He is mild, but has the qualities of valour. He is worthy to be your lord and will dispel your fears. He possesses the qualities of being a king and has been identified as the heir apparent.

---

[143] The earth, Sita and prosperity.
[144] Probably meaning that an autumn cloud rains little.

In addition, we must abide by virtue and follow the commands of our master.[145] As I leave for the forest, ensure that the great king does not suffer. If you wish to bring me pleasure, this is what you should do.' The more Rama abided by the principles of dharma, the more the ordinary people desired him as their lord. They were distressed, overflowing with tears. The people who resided in the city were tied to Rama because of his qualities, and to Soumitri.

There were brahmanas who were aged in three ways—learning, age and energy. Their heads trembled because of their age.[146] From a distance, they cried out, 'O swift steeds that are bearing Rama! O fast horses born in noble lineages! If you desire the welfare of your lord, return and do not proceed to the destination. Your lord deserves to be brought back to the city. He does not deserve to be taken to the forest.' The aged brahmanas suffered and lamented in this way. On seeing that they were lamenting, Rama quickly descended from his chariot. With Sita and Lakshmana, Rama, headed for the forest, walking on foot and keeping pace with them.[147] Rama's character was affectionate and because of compassion, he was incapable of looking at the brahmanas who were on foot. Therefore, he abandoned the chariot. On seeing that Rama was still proceeding, the brahmanas were scared in their minds. Suffering greatly, they addressed Rama in these words. 'Just as you follow brahmanas, all the brahmanas are following you. These brahmanas are following you, carrying their sacred fires on their shoulders. Behold our white umbrellas from *vajapeya* sacrifices, held aloft.[148] They are following at the rear, like swans at the end of the monsoon. You do not have an umbrella and are tormented by the rays.[149] We will offer you shade from umbrellas obtained at vajapeya sacrifices. Our intelligence has always followed the mantras of the Vedas. O child! For your sake, we are now following you as you leave for

---

[145] Dasharatha.

[146] Because of their age, they couldn't follow.

[147] The brahmanas.

[148] Brahmanas who officiate at vajapeya sacrifices are given white umbrellas, normally the exclusive right of kings.

[149] Of the sun.

the forest. The Vedas are our supreme treasure and they are stored in our hearts. Our wives will be protected by their good characters and will reside in our homes. There is no need to think again about our course of action. We have taken the excellent decision of going with you. Since you are considering dharma, who is capable of not adhering to dharma? Our grey hair is like the white feathers on swans. We wish that you should return. Because our heads touched the ground, they are covered with dust from the earth.[150] O child! The brahmanas who have come here have commenced many sacrifices and their completion is conditional on your return. Both inanimate objects and animate creatures are devoted to you. They desire your affection. You should show them your affection. These trees seem to be weeping, raised by the force of the wind. Since they are unable to follow you, they are forcibly tugging at their roots. The birds are also beseeching you. They are perched in one spot on the trees, not trying to gather food. You are compassionate towards all creatures.' In this fashion, the brahmanas lamented, wanting his return. At this time, the river Tamasa was seen, as if it was also restraining Raghava.

# Chapter 2(41)

Raghava reached the beautiful banks of the Tamasa. He looked towards Sita and Soumitri and spoke these words. 'O Soumtri! Today is the first night of our residing in the forest. O fortunate one! You should not be anxious about dwelling in the forest. Behold. In every direction, the empty forest seems to be crying. Seeking shelter, the animals and birds are returning to their own abodes. The city of Ayodhya, my father's capital, and all the women and men there, will no doubt grieve about our departure. Bharata has dharma in his soul. He will no doubt comfort my father and mother with words that are full of dharma, artha and kama. O Lakshmana! Repeatedly

---

[150] When the brahmanas prostrated themselves and begged him to return.

thinking about the fact that Bharata does not cause injury, I am not sorrowing over my father and mother. O tiger among men! You have done your duty by following me. Otherwise, for Vaidehi's protection, I would have had to search for help. O Soumitri! Tonight, I will only subsist on water. Though there are many kinds of forest fare, this is what appeals to me.'

Having addressed Soumitri in this way, Raghava spoke to Sumantra. 'O amiable one! Tend attentively to the horses.' With the sun having set, Sumantra tethered the horses close by and gave them sufficient grass. On seeing that the evening was auspicious and that night had presented itself, with Soumitri, the suta prepared a bed for Rama to lie down on. On the banks of the Tamasa, a bed was prepared with the leaves of trees. With Soumitri's help, Rama and his wife entered that place. On seeing that his brother was asleep with his wife, Lakshmana told the suta about Rama's manifold qualities. Soumitri remained awake the entire night on the banks of the Tamasa, recounting Rama's qualities to the suta. The sun arose.

Not very far from the banks of the Tamasa, there were many herds of cows. With the ordinary people, Rama had spent the night there. Having awoken, the immensely energetic Rama saw those ordinary people and spoke to his brother Lakshmana, who possessed auspicious signs. 'O Soumitri! Look. Ignoring their homes, these people are looking towards us. O Lakshmana! See. They are sleeping near the roots of trees. These citizens are making efforts to make us return.[151] They will give up their lives, but will not give up their determination. In the limited time that we have while they are still asleep, let us ascend the chariot and leave, along a path that is devoid of fear. These residents from the capital city of the Ikshvakus, who are devoted to me, must not sleep near the roots of trees again. Because of two princes, these citizens have brought this suffering on themselves and must be freed from it. This misery is for us and the residents of the city must not be made to suffer.' Rama was stationed like Dharma[152] himself and Lakshmana told

[151] The citizens of Ayodhya who were still with them.
[152] The god of dharma.

him, 'O immensely wise one! This idea appeals to me. Ascend the chariot quickly.'

The charioteer swiftly yoked the excellent horses to the chariot. He joined his hands in salutation and told Rama that the yoking had been done. To confuse the citizens, Rama addressed the suta in these words. 'O charioteer! Mount the chariot and drive it towards the north. After swiftly driving for some time, bring the chariot back. Do this carefully, so that the citizens do not know where I am.' Hearing Rama's words, the charioteer drove the chariot around in a circle. Retracing the steps, he informed Rama that the chariot had returned. With all the accompanying objects, Raghava ascended the chariot. They quickly crossed the river Tamasa, which was full of whirlpools. The mighty-armed and prosperous one reached a large and auspicious road that was free from all obstructions and had no reason to scare even those who were afraid.

When night was over and it was morning, the citizens saw that Raghava wasn't there. Devoid of their senses and grief-stricken, they couldn't move. Their eyes overflowing with tears of grief, they cast their eyes here and there. However, they couldn't see Rama and were miserable. For some time, they followed the path. But unable to discern the tracks, they were filled with great sorrow. The chariot's tracks had vanished. Those spirited ones returned, exclaiming, 'What will we do? We have been struck by destiny.' Exhausted, senseless and full of distress, all of them returned to the city of Ayodhya along the path they had followed while coming there.

## Chapter 2(42)

The residents of the city gave up their attempt to follow Rama. They were dispirited and were ready to give up their lives. They reached their own respective houses and were surrounded by their sons and wives. All of them wept and their faces were covered with tears. No one was happy. No one was delighted. No trader displayed his wares. No merchandise glittered. No one who was responsible for a house cooked. No one was delighted at great riches, once lost, having been regained. No mother was joyous that the first son had been born. When the husbands returned home, there was weeping in every house. Afflicted by grief, like striking elephants with goads, they[153] struck them with words. 'What work do they have at home? What will they do with wives and riches? If they cannot see Raghava, what happiness will they obtain from sons? There is only one virtuous man in this world, Lakshmana. With Sita, he has followed Kakutstha Rama, so as to serve him. The rivers and lotus ponds must have earned good merits with their deeds, since Kakutstha will enter their auspicious waters and bathe there. The forests with charming groves, lands with great rivers and peaked mountains will beautify themselves for Kakutstha. Whenever Rama goes to a grove or a mountain, like a beloved guest who has arrived, it cannot but worship him. There are colourful blossoming trees that bear many kinds of flowers. The mountains will speak of Rama's arrival and the best of flowers and fruits will be shown to him, even if it is not the right season. Diverse colourful waterfalls will be displayed to him. On the summits of mountains, trees will cause delight to Raghava. Where Rama is, there is no fear. There is no defeat there. Dasharatha's son is brave and mighty-armed. Raghava is in front of us. He has not gone a long distance away. The shadow of the feet of such a great-souled lord constitutes happiness. He is the protector of the people. He is the supreme destination. We will tend to Sita, while you serve Raghava.' Thus, afflicted by grief, the women of the city told their husbands. 'In the forest, Raghava will ensure yoga and *kshema* for us.[154] Sita will ensure yoga and kshema for the womenfolk. Who will be happy in this place, populated by anxious people? Unless senseless, who will wish to dwell in such an unpleasant place? If this kingdom belongs to Kaikeyee, it will be full of adharma and

---

[153] The wives.

[154] Yoga has several meanings. In this context, it means getting objectives that one aspires for, but doesn't yet possess. In contrast, kshema means protecting and preserving what one already possesses.

we will be without a protector. There is no purpose to remaining alive. What is the point of sons? What is the point of riches? Who else will Kaikeyee, the defiler of the lineage, cast aside for the sake of riches? Her husband and son have abandoned her. We will not reside as servants in Kaikeyee's kingdom. We swear on our living sons that we will not do this as long as we are alive. Without any pity, she has banished the son of the king. She is wicked in conduct and has followed adharma. Having obtained it in this way, who can live happily? With Rama having been exiled, the lord of the earth will not remain alive. It is evident that after Dasharatha is dead, only lamentations will remain. Your[155] merits have been exhausted and you face a great catastrophe. Stir up some poison and drink it. Either follow Raghava, or follow the path of the ignorant. It is by resorting to deceit that Rama, his wife, and Lakshmana have been banished. We have been handed over to Bharata, like animals to an executioner.' In the city, the women who lived in the city lamented in this fashion. They wept, tormented by grief, as if they faced the fear of death. The women were afflicted on account of Rama, as if their sons or brothers had been exiled. Grief-stricken, they lamented, and senseless, wept. For them, he was superior to their own sons.

# Chapter 2(43)

Remembering his father's command, when night descended, Rama, tiger among men, travelled a great distance away. He travelled in this way throughout that auspicious night. He travelled beyond the boundaries of the kingdom and worshipped the morning sandhya. He proceeded swiftly on those excellent horses, which were like arrows, and passed by villages. He saw that their boundaries had flowering groves. He heard the words of the men who lived in those villages. 'Shame on King Dasharatha, who succumbed to

---

[155] Addressing the men.

desire. Alas! The wicked and cruel Kaikeyee has now been bound down by sin. Having fiercely transgressed norms, she has engaged in a fierce act. She has exiled such a son and prince, who is devoted to dharma. With her senses clouded by rage, she has dispatched the immensely wise one to residence in the forest.' He heard such words from the men who dwelt in those villages.

The brave lord of Kosala went beyond the boundaries of Kosala. There was a river named Vedashruti there, the bearer of auspicious waters. Having travelled towards the north, he next advanced towards the direction occupied by Agastya.[156] After travelling for a long period of time, he reached the river Gomatee, with cool waters. Its banks were ornamented with large numbers of cattle and it was headed towards the ocean. With those swift horses, Raghava crossed the Gomatee. He also crossed the river Syandika, resounding with the calls of peacocks and swans. In ancient times, this land had been given to the Ikshvakus by King Manu. Rama showed Vaidehi the boundaries of this prosperous kingdom. The handsome bull among men then glanced towards the charioteer and addressed him in a voice that was like that of a swan in love. 'When will I again return to the flowering forests on the banks of the Sarayu? When will I unite with my mother and my father and roam around on hunts? I do not excessively crave for hunting in the forests along the banks of the Sarayu. I love that place, unmatched in the world, and revered by rajarshis.' The descendant of the Ikshvaku lineage addressed the suta in these sweet words and spoke other desired words that were full of meaning. He continued to advance.

## Chapter 2(44)

Lakshmana's mighty-armed elder brother crossed the beautiful and extensive land of Kosala and reached Shringaverapura.

---

[156] Agastya's direction is the south. Rama crossed Tamasa and headed north. When he reached Vedashruti (which is difficult to identify), he turned south.

There Raghava saw the auspicious Ganga of the three flows, with divine and auspicious waters that were free of moss, populated by sacred rishis. There were the sounds of swans and cranes, the crying of *chakravaka* birds. Dolphins, crocodiles and serpents resided there. The maharatha saw waves and eddies and told the suta Sumantra, 'Let us reside here today. There is an extremely large *inguda* tree[157] not far from this river, with many flowers and branches. O charioteer! We will reside here.' Lakshmana and Sumantra said that they agreed with what Raghava had said and tied the horses to the inguda tree. Rama, the descendant of the Ikshvaku lineage, approached that beautiful tree. With his wife and with Lakshmana, he descended from the chariot. Sumantra also descended and released the supreme horses. He presented himself before Rama, at the foot of the tree, and joined his hands in salutation.

There was a king named Guha. He was Rama's friend and Rama loved him like his own self. He was born as a powerful nishada and was famous as an architect.[158] He heard that Rama, tiger among men, had arrived in his dominion. Therefore, surrounded by elders, advisers and kin, he arrived there. From a distance, Rama saw that the king of the nishadas was arriving. With Soumitri, he went forward to receive Guha. Guha was distressed.[159] He embraced Raghava and said, 'O Rama! For you, this place is just like Ayodhya. What can I do for you?' He brought the best quality of rice and other objects. He swiftly offered arghya and spoke these words. 'O mighty-armed one! Welcome. This entire earth is yours. All of us are your servants and you are our lord. Rule our kingdom. *Bhakshya, bhojya, peya* and *lehya* have been presented.[160] There are the best of beds and fodder for the horses.' When Guha spoke in this way, Raghava replied to him. 'We are delighted and you have honoured us in every

---

[157] *Balanites roxburghii.*

[158] Architect or builder is the natural translation, but this can also be translated as king.

[159] Because of Rama's exile.

[160] The four types of food are those that are chewed (charvya), sucked (choshya or chushya), licked (lehya) and drunk (peya). Bhakshya is the same as charvya and bhojya is the same as choshya.

possible way. To display your affection, you have arrived here on foot.' He engulfed him in his thick and auspicious arms and added these words. 'O Guha! It is good fortune that I see that you and your relatives are healthy. Is everything well with your kingdom, friends and riches? I know everything about your affection, which is why you have arranged all this. However, I should not accept them. Know that I am certain to abide by the dharma of an ascetic who lives in the forest. I will wear kusha grass, rags and bark. I will eat fruits and roots. I do not wish for anything other than fodder for the horses. If you do only this much, I will be greatly honoured. These horses are extremely well trained and are loved by my father, King Dasharatha. I will be honoured if this is done.' Guha instructed the men present, 'Let food and water be given to the horses. Give it quickly.'

He[161] only wore an upper garment made of bark. He worshipped the western sandhya. For food, he only had water that Lakshmana had brought himself. As he lay down on the ground with his wife, Lakshmana washed his feet and stood near a tree there. Guha conversed with the suta and Lakshmana. Without being distracted, the archer[162] remained awake and guarded Rama. The intelligent, illustrious and great-souled son of Dasharatha slept in this way. He had never faced unhappiness and deserved happiness. The long night passed in this way.

## Chapter 2(45)

Lakshmana was tormented. On account of his brother, he remained awake. Also grief-stricken, Guha humbly addressed Raghava[163] in these words. 'O father![164] This comfortable bed has

---

[161] Rama.

[162] This could mean Guha, but Lakshmana is more likely.

[163] Lakshmana.

[164] The word used is tata. While this does mean father or son, it is affectionately used for anyone who is senior or junior. While there are no indications as to whether Guha would address Lakshmana as a senior or a junior, senior seems more likely.

been constructed for you. O prince! Cheerfully, lie down and relax on it. All these people are used to hardships. You are used to ease. For the sake of protecting Kakutstha, we will remain awake during the night. There is nothing on earth that is as dear to me as Rama. I am telling you this truthfully. If this is not true, you can curse me. Through his favour, I hope to attain extremely great fame in this world. I will not only obtain artha, but will also obtain great dharma. My beloved friend, Rama, is lying down with Sita. With all my kin, I will protect him with the bow in my hand. Though I always roam around in the forest, there is nothing that is unknown to me. We are capable of repulsing a great army that consists of the four kinds of forces.'

At this, Lakshmana replied, 'O unblemished one! You look towards dharma and protected by you, all of us have nothing to fear here. When Dasharatha's son is lying down on the ground with Sita, as long as I am alive, how is it possible for me to lie down happily? All the gods and asuras are incapable of standing before him in a battle. Look at him, sleeping happily on the grass with Sita. Through mantras, austerities and many other kinds of efforts, Dasharatha obtained this son, with such qualities. With him exiled, the king will not live for a long time. It is certain that the earth will soon become a widow.[165] Having wept extremely loudly, the women must be exhausted. O son![166] I think the sounds must have ceased in the king's abode. I am not certain that Kousalya, the king and my mother will survive the night. However, looking towards Shatrughna, my mother may remain alive. But it will be misery if Kousalya, the mother of a brave son, dies. The king brought happiness to this world and that place is full of devoted people. With the catastrophe that results,[167] the city will perish. His extremely fond desire to see Rama instated as heir apparent in the kingdom has not been accomplished. With that not accomplished, my father will be destroyed. When that time presents itself, those who are around my father will be successful

---

[165] Figuratively, since the king is the lord of the earth.

[166] The word used is tata.

[167] Were the king to die.

in their objectives and will perform all the funeral rites for the
lord of the earth. The crossroads are beautiful and the large roads
have been laid out well. There are mansions and palaces, adorned
with the best of courtesans. Obstructions are created by chariots,
horses and elephants. There is the sound of trumpets blaring.
There are all the fortunate signs and the place is populated by
happy and well-nourished people. There are gardens for pleasure,
maintained by the communities. Everything in my father's capital
is full of happiness. After completing the pledge of truth and the
period of exile in the forest faithfully, will we return to Ayodhya
together?' Afflicted by grief, the great-souled one lamented in this
way. As the prince stood there, the night passed. For the sake of
the subjects, the son of the Indra among men spoke these true
words, out of affection for his senior.[168] Overcome by the calamity,
Guha released warm tears, like an elephant suffering from fever
and afflicted by pain.

## Chapter 2(46)

When night was over, the broad-chested and immensely
illustrious Rama spoke to Soumitri Lakshmana, who
possessed all the auspicious qualities. 'The illustrious night has
passed and it is time for the sun to rise. O son![169] This extremely
dark bird, the cuckoo, is calling. The sounds of peacocks crying in
the forest can be heard. O amiable one! We will cross the swift-
flowing Jahnavee, which heads towards the ocean.' Standing in
front of Rama, Soumitri, the extender of the delight of his friends,
heard his brother's words and summoned Guha and the suta. Those
two archers, the two Raghavas, girded swords with ornamented
handles around their loins and prepared to swiftly head towards the
Ganga, with Sita.

---

[168] Probably meaning Dasharatha, but could mean Rama too.
[169] The word used is tata.

The suta, conversant with dharma, humbly arrived before Rama. He joined his hands in salutation and asked, 'What will I do?' He was addressed in these words. 'Return. This is all that I required. Abandoning the vehicle, we will now proceed to the great forest on foot.' On seeing that he had been thus instructed, the charioteer was distressed. Sumantra addressed the descendant of the Ikshvaku lineage, the tiger among men, in these words. 'No man in the world has ever had to go through anything like this—like an ordinary person, you will have to live in the forest with your brother and your wife. I do not think that there are any fruits from brahmacharya or self-study, or from mildness or uprightness, since this kind of a hardship has befallen you. O Raghava! O brave one! By residing in the forest with Vaidehi and your brother, you will obtain ends obtained by one who has conquered the three worlds. O Rama! Since you have been deceived, we have also been destroyed. Having come under the subjugation of the wicked Kaikeyee, we will have our share of misery.' To the charioteer, Sumantra, Rama was like his own soul. He spoke in this way and wept for a long time. Afflicted by grief, from a distance, he looked on. When the weeping was over, the suta touched water and purified himself. Rama repeatedly spoke these sweet words to him. 'For the lineage of the Ikshvakus, a well-wisher like you cannot be discerned. Act so that King Dasharatha does not grieve over me. The lord of the earth is aged and his senses are afflicted by grief. He suffers from the burden of desire. That is the reason I am telling you this. Whatever the great-souled lord of the earth commands you to do, in an attempt to bring pleasure to Kaikeyee, do that without any hesitation. Lords of men rule their kingdoms with this objective in mind, that whatever tasks their minds desire should be carried out without impediments. O Sumantra! Act so that the great king does not suffer from sorrow that his commands are in vain. The king is noble and aged and has conquered his senses. He faces a sorrow that he has not confronted earlier. For my sake, bow down before him and address him in these words. "I, Lakshmana and Maithilee are not grieving that we have been dislodged from Ayodhya and have to reside in the forest. After fourteen years have passed, we will quickly return and you

will again see me, Lakshmana and Sita." O Sumantra! Speak to the
king and my mother in this way. Repeatedly tell Kaikeyee and the
other queens this. Bow down before Kousalya's feet and tell her I
am well. Say this about Sita, me and the noble Lakshmana. Tell
the great king that he should swiftly summon Bharata. As the king
wishes, once Bharata has arrived, let him be consecrated. Embrace
Bharata and get him consecrated as the heir apparent. Let the grief
and torment on our account not overcome you. Bharata should
be told that, without any distinction, he should behave towards
the mothers as he would towards the king. Sumitra is no different
from Kaikeyee. In particular, this is also true of my mother, Queen
Kousalya.' Sumantra was thus sent back by Rama and he was full
of sorrow.

Hearing all these words, he spoke affectionately to Kakutstha.
'If I speak fearlessly and without due courtesies, that is because of
my affection. I am devoted to you. Therefore, you should pardon
any misdemeanour in my words. How can I return to a city where
you are not present? O son![170] Without you, I will suffer the
separation from a son. The people lamented when they saw my
chariot with Rama astride it. On seeing a chariot without Rama, the
city will be shattered. On seeing the empty chariot, the city will be
submerged in grief. It will be as if the charioteer alone is left when a
hero and all his soldiers have been slain in a battle. Even when you
reside far away, you are always topmost in their minds. It is certain
that today, thinking of you, the subjects have starved. The citizens
uttered cries of distress when you were exiled. On seeing my chariot,
those cries will be multiplied a hundredfold. Can I tell the queen
the following? "I have conveyed your son to his maternal uncle's
house. Do not unnecessarily sorrow over him." I cannot speak such
words, since they are false. How can I speak truthful words, since
they are exceedingly unpleasant? I have engaged these mounts to
carry you and your relatives. How can I tell these excellent steeds
to bear a chariot that doesn't have you? If you ask me to leave you

---

[170] The word used is tata. Because of the affection, son seems more appropriate than
father.

here, as soon as I am abandoned by you, with the chariot, I will hurl myself into a fire. O Raghava! When you proceed to the forest, there are creatures that will cause obstructions in your austerities. Using this chariot, I will repulse them. It is on your account that I have obtained pleasure from driving this chariot. I hope that I will obtain happiness from residing in the forest with you. Show me your favours. In the forest, I desire to remain near you. I wish to hear your agreeable words that you want me to remain near you. Residing in the forest, I will bow down my head and serve you. In every way, I am ready to give up Ayodhya, and even the world of the gods. Without you, I am incapable of entering Ayodhya, just as a person who performs evil deeds is incapable of entering the great Indra's capital. O brave one! Residing in the forest, if these horses serve you, they will attain the supreme objective. My heart's desire is that once the period of residing in the forest is over, I will again convey you back to the city in this chariot. With you, the fourteen years in the forest will pass like an instant. Without you, it will seem like a hundred times longer. You are devoted to your servants and I am a servant who has been like a son to you. I am a servant who has remained within the bounds of devotion. Therefore, you should not abandon one who has been thus established.' Distressed, he repeatedly entreated in many kinds of ways. Compassionate towards servants, Rama addressed Sumantra in these words. 'I know of your supreme devotion and I know that you are devoted towards me, your master. Listen to the reason why I want you to leave this place and proceed to the city. On seeing you return to the city, my younger mother, Kaikeyee, will be reassured that Rama has indeed left for the forest. The queen will be content that I have left for dwelling in the forest. She will not suspect the king, who is devoted to dharma, of having uttered a falsehood. This is my first intention, that my younger mother should be prosperous and protected, on account of her son, Bharata, having obtained the kingdom. To bring pleasure to me and the king, go to the city with the chariot. As you have been instructed, respectively tell them about what has transpired.' Addressing the suta in these words, he repeatedly comforted him.

Without any lassitude, Rama then addressed Guha in words that were full of reason. 'Please bring me the sap of a *nyagrodha* tree.[171] Before proceeding further, I want to wear matted hair.' Guha quickly brought the sap for the prince and Rama used it to make his and Lakshmana's hair matted. They wore garments made of bark and their hair was matted. Those two brothers, Rama and Lakshmana, were as resplendent as rishis. With Lakshmana, Rama adopted the path followed by a hermit, ready for the vows. He addressed his aide Guha, 'O Guha! It has been held that a kingdom is extremely difficult to protect. Without any distraction, protect its army, treasury, forts and habitations.' The delight of the Ikshvaku lineage took his leave of Guha. Without any anxiety, he quickly left, with his wife and with Lakshmana.

The descendant of the Ikshvaku lineage saw the boat on the banks of the river.[172] Desiring to cross the swift-flowing Ganga, he told Lakshmana, 'O tiger among men! Hold the boat steady, so that the spirited Sita can climb on to it. You get into it later.' Hearing his brother's command, which he never ignored, he made Maithilee ascend first and climbed on to it later. After this, Lakshmana's energetic elder brother himself climbed in. Guha, the lord of the nishadas, urged his kin.[173] Taking his leave of Sumantra, his forces and Guha, Rama resorted to the boat and instructed the boatmen. The well-trained helmsmen of the boat were thus instructed and swiftly using oars, forcefully conveyed it across those auspicious waters. On reaching the middle of the Bhageerathee, the unblemished Vaidehi joined her hands in salutation and addressed the river. 'This is the son of the intelligent and great King Dasharatha. O Ganga! Protected by you, he is observing what he has been commanded to. Having spent a full fourteen years in the desolate forest, with his brother and me, he will return again. O goddess! O extremely fortunate one! O Ganga! Happy on returning safely and prosperous with all my desires fulfilled, I will worship you. O goddess with

---

[171] The Indian fig tree.

[172] The Critical Edition has excised some shlokas towards the beginning of this chapter, telling us that Guha had readied the boat.

[173] To ferry them across.

the three flows! You are seen in Brahma's world. You are also seen in this world as the wife of the lord of the waters.[174] O goddess! I bow down before you. O beautiful one! I praise you. When the tiger among men returns safely and gets the kingdom back, to give you pleasure, I will give away one hundred thousand cows, food and delicate garments to brahmanas.' The unblemished and accomplished Sita addressed Ganga in this way. They swiftly reached the southern bank.

On reaching the bank, the bull among men descended from the boat. With his brother and Vaidehi, the scorcher of enemies proceeded. The mighty-armed one spoke to the one who extended Sumitra's joy. 'O Soumitri! Advance in front and let Sita follow you. I will follow at the rear and protect you and Sita. From now on, Sita will experience the hardships of dwelling in the forest.' As Rama swiftly reached the other bank of the Ganga, Sumantra steadily continued to glance at him. But because of the great distance, grieving and distressed, he released tears.

They slew four large animals there—varaha, *rishya*, *prishata* and *maharuru*.[175] Hungry, they quickly ate the parts that could be eaten. They then went to a tree and took refuge there.

# Chapter 2(47)

Rama, best among those who cause delight, reached the tree and worshipped the western sandhya.[176] He spoke to Lakshmana. 'This is our first night, away from a habitation and without Sumantra. However, you should not be anxious. From tonight, we must attentively remain awake at night. O Lakshmana!

[174] The ocean.

[175] Rama and Lakshmana slew a varaha (this can mean boar or ram), rishya (antelope), prishata (spotted antelope) and maharuru (another kind of antelope). The word *mriga* means deer, but also means animal. They probably killed four kinds of deer. But it can also mean that they killed three kinds of deer and a boar.

[176] Evening.

Sita's comfort and security depend on us. O Soumitri! Let us spend
the night, in whatever way we can. Let us cover the ground with
whatever we collect ourselves and lie down there.' Though he was
used to expensive beds, Rama lay down on the ground and addressed
Soumitri in these auspicious words. 'O Lakshmana! It is certain
that the great king is sleeping in misery. With her desires satisfied,
Kaikeyee should be content. On seeing that Bharata has arrived,
Queen Kaikeyee, for the sake of the kingdom, will not take away
the great king's life. He is aged and without a protector and he has
been separated from me. Overcome by desire and under Kaikeyee's
subjugation, what will he do? On seeing the hardship the king has
suffered on account of the distraction in his senses, it is my view
that kama can be superior to artha and dharma. O Lakshmana!
Which man, however ignorant he is, will voluntarily, for the sake
of a woman, abandon a son like me? Kaikeyee's son, Bharata, is
happy with his wife. Like a supreme king, he will alone happily
enjoy Kosala. He will alone be foremost in the kingdom. My father
is aged and I have resorted to the forest. Like King Dasharatha, if a
person follows kama and abandons artha and dharma, he is swiftly
reduced to such a state. O amiable one! It seems to be that Kaikeyee
arrived to bring about Dasharatha's end, my exile and Bharata's
obtaining of the kingdom. Perhaps Kaikeyee is now intoxicated by
her good fortune and pride and on my account, is causing difficulties
for Kousalya and Sumitra. On my account, let not Queen Sumitra
live in misery. O Lakshmana! Tomorrow, leave this place and go
to Ayodhya. I will go to Dandaka with Sita alone. Kousalya has
no protector. Be her protector. Kaikeyee is inferior in conduct and
acts with enmity towards others. O one who knows about dharma!
Hand my mother over to Bharata. O Soumitri! In another life, my
mother must have separated women from their sons, and that is
the reason this has now happened. Kousalya has nourished me for
a long time and reared me with difficulty. Shame on me! When
it is time to reap the fruits, she has been separated from me. O
Soumitri! Let no woman give birth to a son like me, who brings
infinite sorrow to his mother. It is my view that the *sarika* bird
displays greater affection, since it listens to the words, "O *shuka*!

Bite the feet of my enemy."[177] O scorcher of enemies! She is grieving
and is unfortunate. Her son cannot help her. On my account, it is as
if she is without a son. Separated from me, my mother, Kousalya,
is limited in good fortune. Immersed in an ocean of grief, she is
lying down in misery and affliction. O Lakshmana! When I am
enraged, with my arrows, I can single-handedly save Ayodhya
and even the entire earth. However, one must certainly not exhibit
valour without reason. O unblemished one! O Lakshmana! I am
terrified of adharma and the world hereafter. Therefore, I do not
want myself to be consecrated now.' In that desolate spot, Rama
lamented piteously in many other ways. His face overflowing with
tears, he sat silently.

Rama lamented and was like a fire whose flames had gone
out, or an ocean without any force. Lakshmana comforted him.
'O Rama! O supreme among those who fight! With you having
left, it is certain that the city of Ayodhya is without any radiance
now, like the moon when the night has passed. O Rama! It is not
appropriate that you should be tormented in this way. O bull
among men! You are making Sita and me also grieve. O Raghava!
Without you, Sita and I will not be alive for even an instant, like fish
taken out of water. O scorcher of enemies! Without you, I do not
wish to see our father, Shatrughna or Sumitra, or even go to heaven
now.' Lakshmana's words were excellent and after listening to all of
them, Raghava, scorcher of enemies, accepted the idea of following
dharma and living in the forest for an extremely long period of time.

# Chapter 2(48)

Having spent the auspicious night under that large tree, when
the sparkling sun arose, they left that spot. They entered that
extremely large forest and headed for the region where Bhageerathee

---

[177] A sarika bird is a kind of thrush, *Turdus salica*, a talking bird kept as a pet.
Kousalya had a sarika bird as a pet. But a shuka is a parrot, though the two words are being
used synonymously. A female parrot is sometimes referred to as a sarika.

Ganga and Yamuna have a confluence. Those illustrious ones saw many beautiful countries and tracts of land that they had never seen before. Advancing comfortably, Rama saw many trees. When day had passed, he told Soumitri, 'O Soumitri! Behold. Smoke is rising from near Prayaga.[178] I think this illustrious fire is a sign that the sage[179] is close. We have certainly reached the confluence of the Ganga and the Yamuna. That is the reason the sound of water dashing against water can be heard. Many trees can be seen in Bharadvaja's hermitage. Those who make their living from the forest are splitting wood.' When the sun was long and it was evening, the two archers cheerfully reached the confluence of the Ganga and the Yamuna and the sage's abode. When Rama reached the hermitage, the animals and birds were frightened. After spending a short while along the path, they reached Bharadvaja. On reaching the hermitage, those two brave ones, with Sita following them, wished to see the sage, but halted some distance away.

The immensely illustrious one was offering agnihotra oblations into the fire. Rama, with Soumitri and Sita, joined his hands in salutation and worshipped him. Lakshmana's elder brother introduced himself. 'O illustrious one! We are Rama and Lakshmana, Dasharatha's sons. This is my fortunate wife Vaidehi, Janaka's daughter. The unblemished one has followed me to the desolate forest to perform austerities. When my father banished me, my beloved younger brother, Soumitri, was firm in his vows that he would follow me. O illustrious one! Commanded by our father, we have entered the forest to perform austerities. We will follow dharma there, living on roots and fruits.' Hearing the words of the intelligent prince, the one with dharma in his soul, offered him a cow, arghya and water.[180] The sage was seated, with animals and birds

---

[178] The confluence of Ganga and Yamuna, today's Allahabad.

[179] Bharadvaja.

[180] The text uses the word *ga*, Bharadvaja offered Rama ga. This is interpreted in translations as *madhuparka*, a mixture of milk and honey offered to a guest. However, a cow was also offered to a guest as a gift. Ga means cow and there is no reason why Bharadvaja shouldn't have symbolically offered a cow. The madhuparka interpretation is possible, but is unnecessary.

around him. When Rama arrived, the sage honoured and welcomed him. Having accepted these honours, Raghava seated himself and Bharadvaja addressed him in words that were full of dharma. 'O Kakutstha! It has indeed been a long time since you came here and I saw you. I have heard about your being exiled without reason. This region of the confluence of the two great rivers is secluded. It is sacred and beautiful. Dwell here happily.' Addressed by Bharadvaja in these words, Raghava, engaged in the welfare of everyone, replied in these auspicious words. 'O illustrious one! Inhabitants of the city and the countryside live near this spot. Wishing to see me and Vaidehi, those people will come here. That is the reason the idea of living here does not appeal to me. O illustrious one! Think of some lonely and excellent hermitage, so that Vaidehi, Janaka's daughter who deserves every kind of happiness, can find pleasure there.' On hearing these auspicious words, the great sage, Bharadvaja, addressed Raghava in words that were full of meaning. 'O son![181] You can reside in a mountain that is ten *krosha*s from this place.[182] That spot is sacred, pleasant to see everywhere and frequented by maharshis. It is populated by golangulas, apes and bears. The place is like Gandhamadana and is known by the name of Chitrakuta. As long as a man can see the summit of Chitrakuta, he performs auspicious deeds and the mind does not turn towards sin. Many rishis have spent hundreds of autumns there, performed austerities and ascended to heaven, to obtain the company of Kapalashiras.[183] I think that this lonely spot will be a happy place for you to reside in. O Rama! Otherwise, for the duration of your abode in the forest, live here with me.' Bharadvaja thus offered all the objects of desire for Rama, his beloved guest. With his wife and his brother, the one who knew about dharma accepted them.

When Rama approached the maharshi in Prayaga, the auspicious night arrived and they conversed about wonderful

---

[181] The word used is tata.

[182] This has a bearing on Chitrakuta and where it was, Madhya Pradesh or Uttar Pradesh. One krosha is two miles and ten kroshas make it twenty miles from Prayaga. However, the definition of krosha was not standardized.

[183] Shiva.

accounts. When night was over and it was morning, the tiger among men approached Bharadvaja.[184] He spoke to the sage, who blazed in his energy. 'O illustrious one! O one who is truthful in conduct! We have spent the night in your hermitage. Now grant us permission to find our abode.' With the night over, Bharadvaja said, 'Go to Chitrakuta, which possesses plenty of honey, roots and fruits. O Raghava! Around the extremities of the forest there, you will see herds of elephants and herds of deer roaming around. The auspicious ground there resounds with the cheerful notes of water hens and cuckoos. There are many kinds of crazy deer and elephants. Dwell there, in an extremely beautiful hermitage.'

## Chapter 2(49)

When the night was over, the two princes, scorchers of enemies, greeted the maharshi and left for that mountain. When they left, the great sage glanced towards them, like a father towards his sons, and addressed them in these words. 'From here, you will reach the Kalindi,[185] swift in its flow. Prepare a raft and cross the river Amshumati[186] there. After that, approach the giant nyagrodha tree, enveloped in green. This dark-green tree is surrounded by many trees and is frequented by siddhas. After having advanced hardly a krosha from that spot, you will see a blue grove. O Rama! It is full of beautiful palasha and badari trees, and bamboo leans over the Yamuna. That is the path towards Chitrakuta and there are many occasions when I have gone along it. It is beautiful and mild and is free from forest conflagrations.' After indicating the path, the maharshi returned.

---

[184] Inexplicably, the Critical Edition excises a shloka which mentions their sleeping happily during the night. Hence, there is a break in continuity.

[185] The Yamuna.

[186] Another name for the Yamuna. Yamuna was the daughter of the sun god and Amshumati means Amshumat's (the sun god's) daughter.

When the sage returned, Rama told Lakshmana, 'O Soumitri! Since the sage has shown us his compassion, we must have performed auspicious deeds.' The two spirited tigers among men consulted each other. Placing Sita ahead of them, they headed for the river Kalindi. Fastening timber together, they fashioned a large raft. Severing reeds,[187] Lakshmana created a comfortable seat for Sita. His beloved was as unthinkable as Shri and was a trifle ashamed. Rama, Dasharatha's son, helped her climb on to the raft. Using the raft, they crossed the swift-flowing Amshumati, garlanded by waves. They crossed the river Yamuna, with many trees standing along the banks. Once they crossed the Yamuna, they abandoned the raft. They reached the dark-blue nyagrodha, enveloped in a cool and green canopy. Sita approached the tree. She joined her hands in salutation and said, 'Let us again see Kousalya and the illustrious Sumitra.' After having proceeded hardly one krosha, the two brothers, Rama and Lakshmana, killed many deer that could be killed[188] and ate in the grove alongside the Yamuna. They roamed around in that auspicious forest, full of herds of elephants and apes and resounding with the cries of peacocks. They reached some flat terrain along the river and without showing any sorrow, readied an abode.[189]

## Chapter 2(50)

When the night was over, the descendant of the Raghu lineage gently awoke Lakshmana, who was sleeping without any interruptions. 'O Soumitri! Hear the beautiful sounds of the forest echo. O scorcher of enemies! The time for our departure has arrived.' His brother, Lakshmana, was asleep and was awakened at the right time. Because of the exhaustion along the path, he was

---

[187] Because the Critical Edition excises the relevant shloka, reeds is left implicit. Lakshmana severed reeds and branches.

[188] Some animals were not permitted to be killed.

[189] For the night.

prone to laziness, but abandoned the thought of sleep. Having awoken, all of them touched the sacred waters of the river. They followed the path towards Chitrakuta, as indicated by the rishi. At the right time, Rama, together with Soumitri, spoke these words to the lotus-eyed Sita. 'O Vaidehi! The *kimshuka* trees are blazing in every direction.[190] Behold. At the end of the winter, with their own blossoms, they have formed garlands. Behold the flowering *bhallatakas*,[191] plucked by men. They are bending down, because of the fruit and leaves. We are capable of surviving here. O Lakshmana! Behold. There are honeycombs in each tree, long and as large as a *drona*,[192] and bees collect honey from these. A *chataka* bird is crying and a peacock is crying back in response. This beautiful spot in the forest is strewn with flowers. Look at Mount Chitrakuta, with a tall and imposing summit. It echoes with the sound of birds and herds of elephants wander around.' On foot, with Sita, they advanced and reached the beautiful Mount Chitrakuta.

On reaching the mountain, frequented by hordes of many kinds of birds, 'We will dwell in this beautiful and peaceful spot.[193] O Lakshmana! Bring firm and beautiful wood. O amiable one! Construct a residence here. My mind finds delight at the prospect of living here.' Hearing his words, Soumitri collected many kinds of trees. The scorcher of enemies made a hut out of leaves. He[194] was attentive in serving him and he[195] addressed him in these words. 'O Soumitri! Bring the meat of an antelope and we will perform a sacrifice in this hut.' The powerful Lakshmana slew a black antelope, of the kind that could be killed. Soumitri flung this into the kindled fire. When he discerned that it was cooked and cleansed of all blood, Lakshmana addressed Raghava, tiger among men. 'This has been cooked and is dark in all its limbs, so that is truly a black antelope. O one who is like a god! You are accomplished. Worship

[190] Because of the red blossoms.
[191] Cashew nut.
[192] Drona has different meanings. Here, it is a measure of capacity.
[193] In English, the sentence is without a subject, but it is Rama speaking.
[194] Lakshmana.
[195] Rama.

the gods now.' Rama possessed the qualities of being conversant with techniques of chanting. He controlled himself and bathed. To pacify all kinds of sin, Rama offered that supreme sacrifice.

The abode was beautiful, covered with leaves from trees. It had been constructed well, in a place that was free from winds. Together, they entered it, like the congregation of gods entering the assembly hall Sudharma.[196] That supreme forest was full of many kinds of animals and birds. The trees had clumps of wonderful flowers. There were the sounds of predatory beasts. Extremely happy and in conquest of their senses, they wandered around there. They reached the extremely beautiful region of Chitrakuta and the river Malyavati,[197] which was a great place of pilgrimage. Cheerfully, collections of birds and animals called there. They forgot any misery that was due to their having been banished from the city.

# Chapter 2(51)

When Rama crossed over to the southern bank, extremely miserable and afflicted, Guha conversed with Sumantra for a very long time and finally returned to his own house. Having been permitted to leave,[198] Sumantra yoked the supreme steeds and grieving severely, proceeded towards the city of Ayodhya. He saw fragrant groves, rivers, lakes, villages and cities and extremely swiftly, passed through them. On the evening of the third day, the charioteer reached Ayodhya and saw that it was bereft of joy. Extremely distressed in his mind, he saw that it was silent, as if it was deserted. Immersed in waves of sorrow, Sumantra thought, 'Have the elephants, horses, people, kings and the city been consumed in a fire of grief, tormented and miserable on account of Rama?' Thinking in this way, the suta entered quickly. On seeing Sumantra arrive, hundreds and thousands of men rushed towards

---

[196] Sudharma is the assembly hall of the gods.
[197] This river is also known as Mandakinee.
[198] By Rama, not by Guha.

the suta and asked, 'Where is Rama?' He told them, 'I left him on the banks of the Ganga. The great-souled Raghava, devoted to dharma, then asked me to withdraw and return.' Hearing that they had crossed, the faces of the people filled with tears. They sighed and shrieked, 'Shame! Alas, Rama!' standing around in groups. He heard them say, 'We do not see Raghava here. It is certain that we will be destroyed. At the time of donations, sacrifices, weddings and grand assemblies, we will never again see Rama, who is devoted to dharma. Knowing what the people were capable of and what would bring them benefit and happiness, Rama protected the city, like a father.' As he drove along the roads between the shops, through the windows, he heard the lamentations of women, extremely tormented and miserable on account of Rama.

As he passed through the royal road, Sumantra covered his face. He reached the house where King Dasharatha was. He quickly descended from the chariot and entered the king's residence. He passed through seven chambers that were full of large crowds of people. Dasharatha's wives were scattered here and there in the palace. On account of Rama, they were tormented by grief and he could hear them converse softly. 'The suta departed with Rama and has returned here without Rama. How will he reply to the grieving Kousalya? I think it is extremely difficult to live in this way. It is certainly not easy. Despite her son having left, Kousalya remains alive.' The king's wives uttered words that were full of truth. Hearing these, he quickly entered the residence, which seemed to be blazing in its sorrow. He entered the eighth chamber and saw the distressed and grief-stricken king there, in that white house, pale because of sorrow on account of his son. The Indra among men was seated and Sumantra approached and greeted him, reporting exactly the words that Rama had uttered. With his senses in a whirl, the king heard silently. Overcome by grief on account of Rama, he lost his senses and fell down on the ground. When the lord of the earth lost his senses, it was as if the inner quarters were struck. When the king fell down on the ground, they[199] raised their arms up and shrieked.

---

[199] The residents.

With Sumitra, Kousalya raised her husband, who had fallen down. She then addressed him in these words. 'O immensely fortunate one! This messenger has accomplished an extremely difficult deed. He has arrived after living in the forest. Why are you not replying to him? O Raghava![200] Having acted inappropriately, today you are embarrassed. Do a good act and get up. There can be no help from sorrow. O king! Who do you fear that you are not asking the charioteer about Rama? Kaikeyee is not present here. You can reply without any fear.' Kousalya yielded to grief and addressed the great king in this way. She spoke in the midst of her tears and suddenly fell down on the ground. On seeing that Kousalya had fallen down on the ground, all the women glanced at their husband[201] and wailed. They wept loudly. An uproar arose from inside the inner quarters. All the women, in every direction, cried, and so did the aged and young men. Yet again, the city was disturbed.

## Chapter 2(52)

When the king regained his senses and his composure, he summoned the suta near him, so that he could hear about Rama's conduct. The aged one was extremely tormented, like an elephant that had just been caught.[202] As he reflected, he sighed, like an elephant that was ill. The suta's limbs were covered with dust. When he approached, the king, who was supremely afflicted, cheerless in his face and with eyes full of tears, spoke to him. 'How will the one with dharma in his soul reside at the foot of a tree? O suta! Raghava is used to great comfort. What will he eat? How will the son of a king lie down on the bare ground, as if he is without a protector? When he advanced, foot soldiers, chariots and elephants used to follow him. Having resorted to a desolate forest, how will Rama live there? Predatory beasts wander around there. The

---

[200] That is, Dasharatha.

[201] Dasharatha.

[202] Implying a wild elephant.

place is populated by black snakes. With Vaidehi, how have the princes entered the forest? O Sumantra! The ascetic Sita is delicate. With her, how have the princes descended from the chariot and proceeded on foot? O suta! Since you have seen my sons enter the extremities of the forest, like the two Ashvins entering Mandara, you have indeed been successful in your objective. What were the words that Rama uttered? What were the words that Lakshmana uttered? O Sumantra! On reaching the forest, what did Maithilee say? O suta! Recount where Rama seated himself. Where did he lie down? What did he eat?'

When the Indra among men urged him thus, the suta answered the king in a trembling voice and in words that choked with tears. 'O great king! Raghava continued to observe dharma. He joined his hands in salutation, lowered his head and bowed down and said,[203] "O suta! Convey my words to my father, who is one who knows about his own soul. The great-souled one is a person, before whom, one must lower one's head down at his feet. O suta! Convey my words to all those in the inner quarters and without any partiality, ask them about their welfare. Honour those who deserve it. Honour my mother, Kousalya, and ask about her welfare. Revere the feet of the king and the queen, as you would to a god. Ask about Bharata's welfare and also convey my words to him. Tell him to follow the conduct of being fair towards all the mothers. The mighty-armed descendant of the Ikshvaku lineage should be told that he must be instated as the heir apparent, so as to protect my father, who is still instated in the kingdom." O great king! This is what the immensely illustrious Rama, with coppery red eyes like a lotus, said, shedding tears profusely. However, Lakshmana was extremely angry. He sighed and addressed me in these words. "What is the crime that has led to the prince being exiled? Whether the act of banishing Rama was done on account of greed, or whether it was done because a boon had been granted, it was in every respect, something that should not have been done. I do not discern any reason behind

---

[203] This message is meant to be relayed by Sumantra to Dasharatha and the respect is also being shown to Dasharatha.

the abandonment of Rama. Whether this was undertaken without thinking about it, or whether it was done because of lack of intelligence, there will be resentment and rage at Raghava being exiled. I do not discern any traits of a father in the great king. For me, Raghava is the brother, lord, relative and father. He is engaged in the welfare of all beings. He is loved by all the worlds. Why will all the worlds be delighted at this act of abandoning him?" O great king! The ascetic Janakee sighed. Forgetting her own self, as if her intelligence had been overtaken by a demon, she stood there. The illustrious princess has not faced such a hardship ever earlier. She wept in misery and was incapable of saying anything to me. With her mouth parched, she glanced towards her husband. On seeing me leave, she suddenly started to cry. Tears also flowed down Rama's face and he joined his hands in salutation. He stood there, obtaining support from Lakshmana's arms. The ascetic Sita also wept, as she glanced at the royal chariot and at me.'

## Chapter 2(53)

'When Rama left for the forest, my horses shed warm tears and refused to return along the path. I controlled my misery and joined my hands in salutation before the two princes. I then ascended the chariot. In the hope that I might again hear Rama's words addressed to me, I remained with Guha for many days.[204] O great king! Your kingdom has also been affected by this hardship. Without yielding flowers, shoots or buds, the trees have withered away. Creatures are not moving and predatory beasts have stopped roaming around. Overcome by sorrow on account of Rama, no sounds emerge from the forest. O Indra among kings! Lotuses have drawn in their petals and the water is muddied. The lilies in the lakes have become warm. Fish and waterbirds have disappeared. Aquatic flowers and blossoms on the land are no longer radiant

---

[204] This contradicts what has been said earlier.

and have very little fragrance left. The fruits are no longer as they used to be. As I entered Ayodhya, no one greeted me. Having not seen Rama, the men sighed repeatedly. When the chariot returned, suffering because they couldn't see Rama, women lamented from mansions, buildings and palaces. Their large and sparkling eyes were filled with flows of tears. They glanced towards each other and it was evident that the women suffered more.[205] I do not discern any difference in the sorrow exhibited by those who are not friends, those who are friends and those who are neutral. Men are unhappy. Elephants and horses are distressed. They are jaded and screaming in affliction, or they are sighing silently. O great king! Miserable at Rama having been exiled, Ayodhya seems to me to be like Kousalya, separated from her son.'

On hearing the suta's words, the king became even more miserable. Shedding tears, he told the suta, 'I was persuaded by Kaikeyee, whose sentiments were driven by wickedness. I went along with her, without consulting the accomplished and the aged. I did not seek the views of well-wishers, advisers, ministers and those who know about the sacred texts. Urged by a woman, I was confused and did this suddenly. It is certain that this great catastrophe has come about because of destiny. O suta! As it desires, it will bring about the destruction of this lineage. O suta! If I have done any good deed towards you, quickly take me to Rama. The breath of life is about to leave me. If there is anyone who still listens to my command, let Raghava be brought back. Without Rama, I am incapable of remaining alive even for an instant. Or perhaps the mighty-armed one has gone a long distance away. In that event, make me ascend the chariot and quickly show me Rama. Where is the great archer with the rounded teeth? Where is Lakshmana's elder brother? If I can see him, with Sita, I will manage to remain alive. If I do not see the mighty-armed Rama, red-eyed and wearing bejewelled earrings, I will go to Yama's eternal abode. What can be a greater misery than attaining this state, where I cannot see Raghava, the descendant of the Ikshvaku lineage? Alas, Rama! Alas, Rama's younger brother!

[205] Than the men.

Alas, the ascetic Vaidehi! You do not know that I am without a protector and am about to die in misery. O queen![206] It is difficult for me to remain alive. It is unseemly that I cannot see Raghava now, nor can I see Lakshmana.' The immensely illustrious king lamented in this way. He became senseless and suddenly fell down on his couch. Lamenting in this way, the king became unconscious. The queen heard his words and her grief was doubled on account of Rama. Rama's mother was frightened yet again.

## Chapter 2(54)

Kousalya seemed to be possessed by a spirit and trembled repeatedly. As if lifeless on the ground, she spoke to the suta. 'Take me to the place where Kakutstha and Sita are, where Lakshmana is. Without them, I am not interested in remaining alive, not even for an instant. Retrace the chariot immediately and take me to Dandaka. If I do not follow them, I will go to Yama's eternal abode.' Her words choked with tears and she spoke softly. The suta joined his hands in salutation and addressed the queen. 'Abandon sorrow, delusion and any fright that gives rise to misery. Cast aside all torment, so that Raghava can reside in the forest. In the forest, Lakshmana will serve at Rama's feet. He knows about dharma and has conquered his senses. He is serving the cause of the world hereafter. Even though she is in a desolate forest, it is as if Sita is dwelling at home. She is not scared. Because her mind is devoted to Rama, she is at peace. Not even the most subtle kind of grief can be discerned in her. It seems to me that Vaidehi is used to living in exile. In earlier times, she used to visit groves in the city and find delight there. Despite it being a desolate forest, Sita finds a similar delight there. Her face is like the young moon and Sita finds pleasure like a child. Since her soul is immersed in Rama, even in

---

[206] This is addressed to Kousalya. Since the Critical Edition has excised some shlokas, there is a break in continuity.

that desolate forest, she finds delight. Her heart is in him. She lives
for his sake. Had she been in Ayodhya, without Rama, it would
have been like a forest to her. Along the path, on seeing villages and
towns, the courses of rivers and many kinds of trees, Vaidehi asked
about them. Vaidehi's radiance is like the beams of the moon and
has not suffered from travelling, from the force of the wind, from
fear, or from the heat. Her radiance is like the full moon, she is
like a lotus.[207] The generous Vaidehi's face has not trembled. She is
deprived of the red *alakta* juice and can no longer apply the alakta
juice.[208] Even then, her feet are as radiant as the buds of lotuses. The
beautiful one walks as if in sport, with her playful anklets tinkling.
Because of her affection for him, even now, Vaidehi adorns herself
in ornaments. Resorting to the forest, when she sees an elephant, a
lion or a tiger, she resorts to Rama's arms and is not terrified. They
do not grieve and you and the lord of men shouldn't grieve either.
Such conduct will eternally be established in this world. They have
cast aside grief and their minds are cheerful. They have properly
established themselves along the path followed by maharshis. They
reside in the forest and survive on wild fruit. They are following
the auspicious pledge given to their father.' In this way, the suta
spoke eloquently. However, though she was restrained, the queen
was grief-stricken over her son and her lamentation did not cease.
She exclaimed, 'O beloved son! O Raghava!'

# Chapter 2(55)

Rama was supreme among those who caused delight and
supremely devoted to dharma. Thus, he left for the forest.
However, Kousalya was herself afflicted. She wept and addressed
her husband in these words. 'Your great fame is renowned in the
three worlds. Raghava is compassionate, generous and pleasant

---

[207] The text uses the word *shatapatra*. This means something with one hundred
petals, that is, a lotus.

[208] Alakta is a red juice obtained from resin and is used to colour the soles of the feet.

in speech. O best among supreme men! Your two sons and Sita
have been reared in happiness. Miserable, how will they be able to
withstand the misery in the forest? She is young, *shyama*,[209] delicate
and used to happiness. How will Maithilee be able to withstand
the heat and the cold? With her beautiful teeth, the large-eyed Sita
has eaten auspicious broth. How will she be able to partake food
cooked from wild rice? The auspicious and unblemished one has
heard the sounds of singing and musical instruments. How will she
be able to hear the inauspicious sounds of predatory beasts and
lions? The mighty-armed one[210] is like the great Indra's standard.
How will the immensely strong one lie down, using his own arm
as a pillow? His complexion is like that of a lotus. The tips of
his hair are excellent. His excellent breath has the fragrance of
lotuses. When will I see the lotus-eyed Rama's face? There is no
doubt that my heart possesses the essence of a diamond. Despite
my being unable to see him, it has not shattered into a thousand
fragments. Even if Raghava returns in the fifteenth year, it is not
evident that Bharata will give up the kingdom and the treasury. O
lord of the earth! The kingdom will thus have been enjoyed by a
younger brother. Why will an elder and superior brother not refuse
to accept such a kingdom? A tiger does not wish to eat food that
has been brought and tasted by another. In that fashion, a tiger
among men will not accept something that has been enjoyed by
another. Once they have been used at a sacrifice, oblations, clarified
butter, cakes, kusha and altars made of khadira wood[211] are not
again used for another sacrifice. Enjoyed by another, this kingdom
will be like liquor that has lost its essence. It is like a soma plant
that has already been used in a sacrifice and indeed, Rama will not
accept it. Raghava will not commit such an act of dishonour, just
as a powerful tiger does not tolerate anyone touching the hair on
its tail. The bull among men possesses the strength of a lion. He has

---

[209] We have deliberately not translated shyama. Usually, this means dark. But
shyama also means a woman who has not had children and it is this second meaning that
is intended here.

[210] Rama.

[211] A kind of tree.

been destroyed by his own father, like a fish devouring its young. The dharma followed by *dvijas*[212] has always been instructed as the dharma of the sacred texts. Having banished your son, how have you been devoted to that dharma? A husband is a woman's first refuge, a son is the second refuge. O king! A kin is the third refuge and in this world, there isn't a fourth one. Among those, you do not exist for me and Rama has resorted to the forest. I do not wish to go to the forest. Therefore, I have been destroyed in every way. This kingdom and the country have been destroyed by you. You have destroyed yourself and your ministers. I and my son have been destroyed. The citizens have been destroyed. Only your son and wife[213] are happy.' She used such terrible words. Having heard them, the king was confounded and miserable. Remembering his misdeed yet again, the king was immersed in grief.

## Chapter 2(56)

In grief, Rama's mother angrily said this. Hearing these harsh words, the king was miserable and started to think. He thought about the terrible misdeed he had perpetrated earlier.[214] Ignorantly, he had struck, depending on sound alone. The lord's mind was distracted by this and by sorrow on account of Rama. Addressed by Kousalya, the king was afflicted by these two different kinds of sorrow. He said, 'O Kousalya! I have joined my hands in supplication. Show me your favours. You have always been affectionate and non-violent towards others. O queen! Whether he possesses qualities or does not possess qualities, one must remember the dharma that a husband is like a divinity himself. You have witnessed the superior and the inferior in this world, but have always been supremely devoted to

---

[212] Dvija means twice-born, a reference to the sacred thread ceremony, a kind of second birth. Though dvija often means brahmana, the three superior varnas were all entitled to sacred thread ceremonies and were therefore dvijas.

[213] Bharata and Kaikeyee respectively.

[214] This will be explained subsequently.

dharma. Whether you are miserable or extremely miserable, you should not have spoken these disagreeable words to me.'

Hearing the piteous words of the king, uttered in misery, Kousalya shed tears, like fresh water[215] flowing down a drain. She cupped her hands in the form a lotus and held the king's head, weeping as she did this. She was terrified and scared and she spoke so fast that the syllables were indistinct. 'I am bowing down my head and seeking your favours. I am lying down on the ground in front of you. O king! I am afflicted and am requesting you, though I do not deserve to be pardoned. O brave one! In both the worlds, there is no intelligent woman who has thus been lauded by her husband. O one who knows about dharma! I know about dharma. I know you to be truthful in speech. Afflicted on account of grief over my son, what have I said to you? Sorrow destroys patience. Sorrow destroys learning. Sorrow destroys everything. There is no enemy like sorrow. One is capable of withstanding a blow that is struck by the hands of an enemy. However, if it is sorrow, even if it is very subtle, that is impossible to tolerate. Five nights have passed since Rama left for residing in the forest. However, since my joy has been destroyed by grief, it seems like five years to me. Thinking of him, the sorrow of my heart is enhanced. It is like the great water of the ocean, enhanced by the force of rivers.' As Kousalya spoke these auspicious words, the sun's rays turned mild and night arrived. The king was cheered by Queen Kousalya's words. Though overcome by sorrow, he came under the subjugation of sleep.

## Chapter 2(57)

King Dasharatha was senseless with sorrow. However, he regained his senses in an instant and started to think. He was Vasava's equal. But because of Rama and Lakshmana's exile, he faced a calamity, like the sun darkened by the asura.[216]

---

[215] From a shower.
[216] Rahu, responsible for an eclipse.

On the sixth night after Rama had left for the forest, in the middle of the night, King Dasharatha remembered the wicked deed that he had done. Afflicted by grief on account of his son, he addressed Kousalya in these words. 'O fortunate one! According to whether he performs an auspicious act or an inauspicious act, the doer reaps the consequences of any deed that he has done. A person who commences a deed without considering whether it is grave or trivial, the fruits of the deed and its taints, is said to be a child. Some look at flowers and, desiring fruits, cut down mango trees and nurture palasha trees.[217] They sorrow when the fruits are obtained. I have also cut down a grove of mango trees and nurtured palasha. Being evil-minded, I have forsaken the fruit that is Rama and am grieving later. O Kousalya! When I was young, I became proficient with the bow and could strike at the sound.[218] As a young man, I was known as *shabdabhedi*.[219] That is when I perpetrated a wicked deed. O queen! Because of what I myself did, I am now faced with this misery. It is as if I consumed poison through childish confusion. In my ignorance, I have reaped this fruit of being a shabdabhedi. O queen! I was the heir apparent then and was not married to you. The monsoon season arrived and it increased my desire.[220] Having drunk all the juices from the earth, the sun, the one who pervades the earth with its rays, had entered the terrible southern direction, frequented by those others.[221] The heat suddenly disappeared and cool clouds could be seen. All the frogs, antelopes[222] and peacocks were filled with joy. Water continued to pour down on water that had already showered down. Inhabited by maddened antelopes, the mountains were submerged in torrents of water. This was an

---

[217] Palasha trees have lovely flowers and no fruit, it being the reverse for mangoes.

[218] Without visually seeing the target.

[219] One who can strike at the sound.

[220] To go on a hunt.

[221] Though not explicitly stated, this seems to imply that the sun had moved to *dakshinayana*, the southern solstice. In today's terms, this would mean the month of July. Dakshinayana is associated with the *pitris*, the ancestors. With this interpretation, 'others' would mean the ancestors. However, the south is also regarded as inauspicious, associated with death, ghosts and spirits. 'Others' might also mean that.

[222] *Saranga*, this can also mean a type of bird.

extremely pleasant period. I resolved to have some exercise. With
a bow and arrows and on a chariot, I followed the course of the
Sarayu river. I was in control of my senses and wished to kill a
buffalo, elephant or any other predatory beast that would come to
the river in the night.[223] In the darkness, I heard the sound of a pot
being filled with water. Since I wasn't able to see, I thought that
it was the sound of an elephant trumpeting. Therefore, I affixed
a blazing arrow that was like virulent poison. I released the sharp
arrow that was like virulent poison. I heard a human voice scream
"Alas! Alas!" as the person fell down. It was evident that these
sounds were uttered by a resident of the forest, who said, "How did
a weapon strike down an ascetic? In the night, I came to the river
to collect some water. Who has struck me with this arrow? What
have I done to anyone? I am a rishi who has cast aside the staff.[224]
I dwell in the forest on forest fare. Who has recommended the use
of a weapon to slay a person like me? I wear a mass of matted hair.
My garments are made of bark and deer skin. What purpose will be
served by killing me? What injury have I caused to anyone? This is
a pointless act that is full of ill intent. No one will say that this act
is virtuous. It is like transgressing the preceptor's bed.[225] I am not
grieving because my own life has come to an end. Since I will die, I
am sorrowing about my mother and my father. For a long time, this
aged couple has been nurtured by me. After my death, how will they
sustain themselves? It is as if I and my aged mother and father have
been slain by that single arrow. Who is the extremely foolish person
who has killed all of us?" Always desirous of dharma, I heard those
piteous words. Since I was distressed, the bow and arrows fell down
from my hands on the ground. Distressed in spirit and miserable in
my mind, I went to that spot. On the banks of the Sarayu, I saw the
ascetic who had been struck by the arrow. I stood there, terrified,
with my senses distracted. He glanced at me with his eyes, as if he
would burn me down through his energy. He then spoke these cruel
words. "O king! While I resided here, what injury have I caused to

[223] To drink water.
[224] The staff used for chastisement or punishment.
[225] Having intercourse with the preceptor's wife.

you? I wished to collect water for my seniors and you have struck me down. Indeed, a single arrow has been enough to strike at my vital organs. But it has also slain my aged and blind mother and father. They are weak, blind and thirsty and are waiting for me. Bearing their thirst and difficulties, they have been waiting for me for a long time. There may indeed be ascetics who have obtained the fruits of their yoga and learning. But my father does not know that I have fallen down and am lying down on the ground here.[226] He does not know. He is weak and incapacitated. What will he do? He is like a tree that is unable to save another tree that is being cut down. O Raghava! Go there quickly and tell my father, so that he does not angrily burn you down, like a forest by a fire. O king! This path will take you to my father's hermitage. If you go and seek his favours, he will not curse you in his anger. O king! Take out this stake of the sharp arrow from my body. It is tormenting me, just as even gentle flows of water can stir an unstable riverbank. O king! I am not a brahmana. Do not be distressed on that account.[227] O lord of habitations! My mother is a shudra and my father is a vaishya." Since the arrow had struck at his vital organs, he spoke these words with difficulty. As he was losing his senses, I drew out the arrow. His body was drenched with water and he lamented at this calamity. With his inner organs struck by the arrow, he sighed repeatedly. O fortunate one! Extremely miserable, I lay him down in the Sarayu and looked at him.'

# Chapter 2(58)

'I had committed a great crime in my ignorance and my senses were afflicted. I used my intelligence to think about what could best be done under the circumstances. I brought the pot and filled it with auspicious water. Following the indicated path, I reached the

---

[226] Since my father has not obtained fruits that lead to such insight.

[227] Killing a brahmana would have been a terrible crime.

hermitage. There I saw the two weak, blind and aged ones, without anyone to support them now. I saw the parents there, like birds whose wings had been severed. They were seated there, without anything to do, and were conversing among themselves. Since they had lost hope because of me,[228] they were miserable, immobile and without a protector. On hearing my footsteps, the hermit spoke these words. "O son! Why did you take such a long time? Quickly give me a drink. O son! That is the reason you had gone. Why did you tarry to play in the water? Your mother is anxious. Quickly enter the hermitage. O son! If your mother or I have done anything unreasonable towards you, you should not have secreted that in your mind. O son! You should have behaved like an ascetic. You are the refuge for those who have no refuge. You are the eyes for those who have no eyes. Our lives depend on you. Why are you not saying anything?" When the hermit spoke these words, I was terrified and glanced towards him. Like one who was scared, I spoke indistinctly, in words that were not properly formed.[229] Then I invoked my mental strength and imparted strength to my speech. I told him the fearful news of the catastrophe that had befallen his son. "I am a kshatriya named Dasharatha. I am not your great-souled son. Through my own deeds, I have caused this misery that is condemned by virtuous people. O illustrious one! With a bow in my hand, I arrived at the banks of the Sarayu. I wished to kill an elephant or a predatory beast that would come to drink water. I heard the sound of a pot being filled with water. Taking this to be an elephant, I struck with my arrow. Upon going to the banks of the river, I saw an ascetic lying down lifeless on the ground, the arrow having shattered his heart. O illustrious one! Wishing to kill an elephant, I aimed in the direction of the sound in the water. Thus released, the iron arrow slew your son. O illustrious one! I

---

[228] Of their son returning. A considerable amount of time has elapsed. Dasharatha struck the young ascetic in the middle of the night. In non-Critical versions, Dasharatha waits out the night before he discovers the young ascetic in the morning. The Critical text excises these shlokas, so that the discovery seems to be immediate. These incidents are actually happening next morning.

[229] Literally, in words that lacked the appropriate consonants.

approached him and he lamented and grieved about the two of you, since you are blind. When I took out the arrow, he went to heaven. In my ignorance, I violently killed your son. O hermit! Show me your favours and tell me what should be done about his remains."

'Hearing these cruel words, he was afflicted by grief and sighed. I stood before him, with my hands joined in salutation. The immensely energetic one said, "O king! If you had not yourself told me about this inauspicious act, as a consequence, your head would have shattered into a hundred thousand fragments. O king! If a kshatriya knowingly kills a person who has resorted to vanaprastha, he is dislodged from his state, even if the perpetrator happens to be the wielder of the vajra himself.[230] You are still alive because you did not do this knowingly. Had it been otherwise, not only would you have been destroyed today, but so would have been the lineage of the Raghavas.[231] O king! Take me to the spot that you have spoken about. We now wish to take a last look at our son, whose limbs are covered with blood and whose garment of deer skin has got dishevelled. He is lying down unconscious on the ground and has come under the subjugation of Dharmaraja."[232] I took those two extremely miserable ones to the spot and made the hermit and his wife touch their son. Those two ascetics approached and touched the fallen body of their son. The father said, "O son! O one devoted to dharma! I love you, but behold your mother. O delicate son! Why are you not embracing us? Why don't you say something? In the second half of the night,[233] whose words will I hear, so that they touch the heart? Who will recite sweet words from the sacred texts or from something else? Who will make us perform the sandhya worship? Who will bathe us and make us offer oblations into the fire? O son! When I am afflicted by sorrow and grief, who will sit beside me and assure me? As if I am a beloved guest, who will bring me roots and fruits? Who will feed me? I cannot do anything. I cannot act on my own. I am without my guide. Your ascetic mother

[230] Indra.
[231] A conscious act would have destroyed the entire lineage.
[232] The lord of dharma, Yama.
[233] This suggests that it is still night.

is blind and aged. O son! She desires her son and is in a pitiable
state. Who will sustain her? O son! Stay here. Do not leave for
Yama's abode. Depart tomorrow, with your mother and me. In
the forest, both of us are grieving and miserable. We are without
a protector. Without you, we will quickly leave for Yama's eternal
abode. On seeing Vaivasvata,[234] I will address him in these words.
'O Dharmaraja! Pardon him. Let him nurture his parents.' O son!
You did not commit a sin. This perpetrator of wicked deeds has
killed you. Because this is true, quickly go to the worlds reserved
for those who fight with weapons. That is where brave ones who
do not retreat from the field of battle and face the front go, when
they are slain. O son! Go to that supreme destination. O son! Attain
the destination obtained by Sagara, Shaibya, Dileepa, Janamejaya,
Nahusha and Dhundumara.[235] There are destinations obtained by
those who devote themselves to studying and austerities, those who
donate land, offer oblations into the fire and observe the vow of
having a single wife. Go there and to destinations obtained by those
who repay debts to their preceptors by gifting them thousands of
cows. O son! Go to the destinations obtained by those who cast
aside their bodies.[236] A person who has been born in this lineage
will not obtain an inauspicious end." In this fashion, he lamented
piteously. With his wife, he then performed the water rites. Because
of his own deeds, the hermit's son manifested himself in a divine
form. He assured his parents for a while and spoke these words.
"Because I served both of you, I have obtained this exalted state.
You will also quickly come to where I am." Having said this, in
control of his senses, the hermit's son quickly ascended to heaven in
a radiant and divine vimana.

'I stood there, with my hands joined in salutation. Having
performed the water rites with his wife, the immensely energetic
ascetic addressed me. "O king! Using a single arrow and killing my

[234] Yama.

[235] There could have been a different Janamejaya. But otherwise, Janamejaya does not
belong in this list. Nor for that matter does Shaibya.

[236] Such as through *prayopavesa*, voluntary fasting to death, adopted by someone who
has no worldly desires left.

son, you have rendered me without a son. Kill me now. I have no
sorrow in dying. In your ignorance, you have killed my virtuous son.
Therefore, I am cursing you that you will suffer from an extremely
terrible grief. On account of my son, you have presented me with this
calamity and misery. O king! Therefore, you will also die grieving over
your son."[237] O fortunate one! I face that generous person's words
now. They have come true. Though I am still alive, I am grieving on
account of my son. Can I immediately see Rama or touch him now?
O queen! Having done this to Raghava, there is no one like me. I
cannot see him with my eyes and my memory is fading. O Kousalya!
Vaivasvata's messengers are hurrying towards me. What can be more
miserable than my life ending in this way? I am unable to see Rama,
who knows about dharma and for whom truth is his valour. He is
handsome, with auspicious earrings. Those who will be able to see
Rama's face again in the fifteenth year are gods, not humans. His
eyes are like lotus petals. He possesses excellent brows and excellent
teeth. His nose is beautiful. Those who will be able to see Rama, with
a face like that of the lord of the stars,[238] are blessed. His face is like
the autumn moon and like a blooming lotus. Those who are able to
see my fragrant lord are blessed. After the period of exile in the forest
is over, he will return to Ayodhya again, like Shukra[239] returning to
its path. Those who see Rama then will be happy. I have brought this
sorrow on myself. I am without a protector and senseless. I am like
the bank of a river, being destroyed by the water. Alas, Raghava! O
mighty-armed one! Alas! O one who destroys my discomfort!'

As he sorrowed in this way, King Dasharatha's life ended. The
lord of men spoke in this miserable fashion. He was afflicted because
his beloved son had been exiled. At midnight, severely suffering from
grief, the one who was generous in appearance gave up his life.[240]

[237] The Critical text excises shlokas where the aged parents immolate themselves in
a fire.

[238] The moon.

[239] Venus.

[240] The Critical text excises part of a shloka, telling us that Kousalya and Sumitra
were present then. Because of what we are told in the next chapter, Dasharatha seems to
have died alone, in the sense that Kousalya and Sumitra were deep in slumber.

## Chapter 2(59)

Night passed and the next day arrived. The bards presented themselves at the king's residence. Those who were accomplished in the auspicious rites presented themselves. As used to be the practice, women and the best of eunuchs also arrived. They brought golden pots, filled with water mixed with yellow sandalwood paste. At the right time, as was the practice, those who were skilled in bathing brought these.[241] There were other women, most of whom were maidens. They brought auspicious objects, food and decorations. There were women who were authorized to approach the place where the Indra of Kosala slept.[242] They approached and sought to wake up their lord. They trembled when they thought that the king was no longer alive. They trembled like blades of grass facing a flood. Trembling in this way, those women looked at the king. They became certain that the calamity they had suspected was true. Those beautiful women began to wail in loud and miserable voices. They were like female elephants in a forest, when the leader of the herd has been dislodged. At the sound of this shrieking, Kousalya and Sumitra suddenly regained their senses and woke up from their sleep. Kousalya and Sumitra looked at the king and touched him. Lamenting 'Alas, lord!' they fell down on the ground. The daughter of the Indra of Kosala writhed around on the ground. Covered with dust, she was no longer radiant and was like a star that had been dislodged from the sky. The entire place was filled with a crowd of anxious and terrified people. As the miserable relatives lamented, there were sounds of wailing everywhere. All joy instantly vanished and despondency and misery were seen everywhere. This is what happened when the god among men met his end. Knowing that the illustrious bull among kings had passed away, his wives surrounded him. They were extremely miserable

---

[241] To bathe the king.

[242] This reference to Dasharatha as the Indra of Kosala is odd. Perhaps Kousalya's Indra is meant.

and wailed in piteous tones. As if without a protector, they clung
to each other's arms.

## Chapter 2(60)

He was like a fire that had been pacified, like an ocean without
water, like the sun robbed of its radiance. On seeing that
the lord of the earth had left for heaven, Kousalya's eyes filled
with tears and she was afflicted by many kinds of grief. Taking
the king's head on her lap, she spoke to Kaikeyee. 'O Kaikeyee!
You have accomplished your desire. Without any thorns, enjoy the
kingdom alone, abandoning the king. O cruel one! O one evil in
conduct! Abandoning me, Rama has departed and my husband has
left for heaven. Dislodged from the path, I am without any sense
of purpose. I have no interest in remaining alive. Abandoning a
husband who was himself like a divinity, which woman would wish
to remain alive, with the sole exception of Kaikeyee, who has cast
aside dharma? Like a person who eats what should not be eaten,
a greedy individual does not understand a sin. Because of Kubja,
Kaikeyee has destroyed the lineage of the Raghavas. She forced the
king to do what should not be done and exiled Rama and his wife.
Hearing this, Janaka will lament, just as I am. Though he is alive, the
lotus-eyed Rama has been destroyed and so has the ascetic Sita, the
daughter of the king of Videha. She does not deserve unhappiness
and will be miserable at the difficulties in the forest. In the night,
animals and birds will shriek in terrible tones. On hearing these, it
is certain that she will be frightened and seek refuge with Raghava.
He is aged and has no sons. Thinking of Vaidehi, it is certain that
he will be immersed in grief and will give up his life.'

The ascetic Kousalya embraced him and lamented in this way,
extremely miserable. The attendants removed her from the spot.
The advisers immersed the king in a vessel of oil and thereafter
did everything else that needed to be done for the king. Without a
son being present, the ministers did not wish to perform the king's

last rites. Knowing everything about what needed to be done, they therefore preserved the king's body in this way. The advisers laid down the king in a vessel of oil. Knowing that he was dead, the women lamented. They threw up their arms and were in a pitiable state, their eyes and faces overflowing with tears. Tormented by grief, they wept and wailed piteously. The city of Ayodhya was deprived of the great-souled king and was like a night without stars, or like a woman abandoned by her husband. The eyes of people were full of tears and women from noble lineages lamented. The crossroads and houses were empty and were no longer resplendent, as they used to be earlier. It was as if the firmament, bereft of the sun, had lost its lustre and the night was bereft of its large number of nakshatras. Without the great-souled one, the city lost its radiance. The roads and crossroads were crowded with people whose voices choked with tears.[243] Crowds of men and women gathered and condemned Bharata's mother. When the god among men died, the city was afflicted and could not find any peace.

## Chapter 2(61)

When night was over and the sun arose, there was an assembly of the king's officers and brahmanas. There were Markandeya, Moudgalya, Vamadeva, Kashyapa, Katyayana, Goutama and the immensely famous Jabali. One by one, these brahmanas and the advisers faced Vasishtha, best among royal priests, and spoke to him. 'The night of misery has passed and it has been like one hundred years. Overcome by sorrow on account of his son, the king has died. The great king has gone to heaven and Rama has resorted to the forest. The energetic Lakshmana has also departed with Rama. Bharata and Shatrughna, scorchers of enemies, are in Kekaya. They are in the beautiful city and royal palace, in their maternal uncle's abode. Someone from the lineage of the Ikshvakus should now

---

[243] However, it has just been said that the crossroads were empty.

be made the king. In the absence of a king, the kingdom will be destroyed. If there is no king in a habitation, clouds garlanded with lightning will not loudly thunder in the sky and Parjanya will not shower down water from the sky on earth. If there is no king in a habitation, even a fistful of seeds does not sprout. If there is no king, a son does not remain under a father's control, nor a wife under her husband's. In the absence of a king, there is no wealth. In the absence of a king, there is no wife either. There is yet another misfortune too. If there is no king, how can there be truth? If there is no king in a habitation, men do not construct assemblies, beautiful groves and cheerful and auspicious houses. In the absence of a king, brahmanas do not engage in sacrifices and generous rites. Nor are brahmanas devoted to their vows. If there is no king in a habitation, large numbers of actors and dancers do not gather at assemblies and festivals and thereby enhance the prosperity of the kingdom. If there is no king in a habitation, disputes do not come to a satisfactory resolution. Those who love tales and are accomplished in reciting the accounts do not delight hearers with their stories. If there is no king in a habitation, men do not leave for the forest in swift-moving vehicles, desiring to find pleasure there with women. If there is no king in a habitation, prosperous people are not protected properly and cannot sleep with their doors open, nor can those who earn a living from agriculture and animal husbandry. If there is no king in a habitation, merchants cannot safely travel long distances, carrying with them large quantities of merchandise. There are controlled sages who roam around alone at will, thinking only of the *atman*, and making a home for the night wherever evening falls. If there is no king in a habitation, they cannot do this. If there is no king in a habitation, yoga and kshema are not ensured. Without a king, soldiers cannot defeat the enemy in a battle. A kingdom without a king is like a river without water, a forest without grass and cows without a cowherd. If there is no king in a habitation, there is nothing like one's own property. Then, like fish, men devour each other. Without any fear, non-believers violate the ordinances, thinking that their inclinations will no longer be chastised by the king's rod. Alas! Without a king,

it will be impossible to differentiate between anything in this world
and separate the virtuous from the wicked. When the great king
was alive, we never transgressed your words, like the ocean does
not cross the shoreline. O noble brahmana! Look at us around you.
Without a king, the kingdom will become a forest. You can yourself
consecrate a young and generous descendant of the Ikshvaku lineage
as the king.'

## Chapter 2(62)

Hearing their words, Vasishtha replied to the large number
of friends, advisers and all the brahmanas in these words.
'Bharata, together with his brother Shatrughna, is happily residing
in the city of his maternal uncle, in the royal palace. Using swift
steeds, let messengers quickly go there and bring the two brave
brothers here. What else do we need to think about?' All of them
told Vasishtha, 'Let them go.' Hearing what they said, Vasishtha
spoke these words. 'Siddhartha, Vijaya, Jayanta, Ashoka and
Nandana—come here. Listen to me. I will tell all of you about
everything that needs to be done. Using horses that can travel fast,
go to the city and the royal palace. Abandon all sorrow and convey
my instructions to Bharata. "The priest and all the ministers have
asked about your welfare. Depart quickly. There is an extremely
urgent work that you have to undertake here." Do not tell him
about Rama's exile and do not tell him that his father is dead.
Do not tell him about the catastrophe that confronts the Raghava
lineage. Quickly collect the best of garments and ornaments from
the treasury, so that they can be given to the king and to Bharata.
Then leave.'

Taking Vasishtha's permission, the messengers left quickly.
They crossed the river at Hastinapura and headed in a western
direction. In the midst of Kurujangala,[244] they reached the Panchala

---

[244] The area around Kurukshetra.

kingdom. They quickly crossed the divine Sharadanda river,[245] filled with sparkling water and populated by many birds, and proceeded through a region populated by people. They approached the divine *nikula* tree, also known as *satyopayachana*.[246] Passing beyond it, they entered the city of Kulinga. From there they reached Abhikala and the extensive region of Tejobhibhavana. Through the midst of the Bahlika region, they reached Mount Sudama. They saw Vishnupada, Vipasha and Shalmali. Because of the difficult journey that had been undertaken, the mounts and the messengers were exhausted. However, swiftly and safely, they reached the supreme city of Girivraja.[247] To do what would bring pleasure to their lord,[248] to protect the lineage and to bring welfare to the lineage of their lord,[249] the messengers obeyed their instructions quickly and respectfully. They reached the city in the night.

## Chapter 2(63)

On the same night that the messengers entered the city, Bharata had an unpleasant dream during the night. He had that unpleasant dream when night was about to turn into dawn.[250] Because of this, the son of the king of kings was extremely tormented. His friends, pleasant in speech, got to know that he was tormented. To dispel this and to comfort him, they arranged for stories to be told in an assembly. Some played on peaceful musical instruments, others arranged for the production of plays. There were many kinds of jokes that were cracked. The friends,

---

[245] Literally, a river that had many clumps of reeds. Identification of these geographical places is difficult and a lot has been speculatively written on these. We are deliberately avoiding any such references, because they are inherently speculative.

[246] Because prayers made before the tree came true.

[247] The capital of Kekaya.

[248] Vasishtha.

[249] Now meaning Dasharatha.

[250] It is believed that dreams seen at dawn turn out to be true.

pleasant in speech, sought to bring pleasure to the great-souled Bharata through these joyous gatherings. However, Raghava did not rejoice.

When he was surrounded by his friends, his most beloved friend asked Bharata, 'O friend! Why are you not happy, even when you are served by your well-wishers?' Thus addressed by the well-wisher, Bharata replied, 'Listen to the reason why I am overcome by this despondency. I saw my father in my sleep. He was faded and his hair was dishevelled. From the summit of a mountain, he fell down in a lake that was filled with filth and cow dung. I saw him float away in that lake filled with cow dung. He seemed to drink oil from his cupped hands and laughed repeatedly. With his head facing downwards, he repeatedly fed on sesamum seeds. With his limbs covered in oil, he then immersed himself in oil. In the dream, I saw the ocean turn dry and the moon fall down on the ground. Suddenly, the blazing fire seemed to be extinguished. The earth was shattered and many kinds of trees dried up. I saw mountains being whirled around, enveloped in smoke. I saw the king seated on an iron seat, attired in black garments. Women dressed in black and brown seemed to be laughing at him. The one with dharma in his soul was decorated in red garlands and paste. In a chariot drawn by asses, he seemed to be hurrying towards the southern direction.[251] This is the terrible sight I saw in the night, as if I, Rama, the king or Lakshmana will die. In a dream, if a man sees a vehicle that is drawn by asses, in a short period of time, the smoke from a funeral pyre will be seen above him. That is the reason for my distress, the reason why I am unable to honour you properly. My throat is parched and my mind is not at peace. Since I cannot comprehend the reason, I am hating myself. Having had this bad dream in different forms, the like of which I have not seen earlier, my mind is disturbed. A great fear has arisen in my heart. I have been thinking about the unthinkable sight of the king.'

[251] The direction of death.

# Chapter 2(64)

As Bharata was speaking about his dream, the messengers, with their exhausted mounts, crossed over the impenetrable moats and entered the beautiful royal palace in the city. They met the king and was honoured by the prince.[252] Having touched the king's feet, they addressed Bharata in these words. 'The priest and all the ministers have asked about your welfare. You should leave quickly. There is an extremely urgent task that you have to undertake. O son of a king! This complete collection of thirty crores is to be given to the king, your maternal uncle.' Bharata was devoted to his well-wishers and accepted all this. Having honoured them with all the objects of desire, he told the messengers, 'I hope that my father, King Dasharatha, is well. I also hope that the great-souled Rama and Lakshmana are healthy. Is Rama's intelligent mother, Kousalya, healthy? The noble one knows about dharma and is devoted to dharma. She possesses the insight of dharma. Is the mother in the middle, Sumitra who knows about dharma and is the mother of the brave Lakshmana and Shatrughna, healthy? My mother, Kaikeyee, always pursues her own desires. She is wrathful and prone to anger, though she prides herself on her wisdom. What has she said?' The messengers were thus addressed by the great-souled Bharata. They respectfully replied to Bharata in the following words. 'O tiger among men! Everyone that you have asked about is well.' Thus addressed, Bharata told the messengers, 'I will take the great king's permission and tell him that the messengers are urging me to hurry.'

Bharata, the son of a king, told the messengers this. Having urged the messengers in these words, he told his maternal uncle, 'O king! The messengers have urged me to go to my father's residence. Whenever you remember me, I will come here again.' Having been thus addressed by Bharata, the king, his maternal uncle, inhaled the fragrance of Raghava's head and addressed him in these auspicious

---

[252] Yudhajit, the son of Ashvapati, the king of Kekaya. However, the way the sentence is structured, 'prince' could also mean Bharata.

words. 'O son![253] Go, you have my permission. Kaikeyee has a
good son like you. O scorcher of enemies! Tell your mother and
father that I have asked about their welfare. O son! Ask about the
welfare of the priest, the other excellent brahmanas and your two
brothers who are great archers, Rama and Lakshmana.' The king
of Kekaya generously offered Bharata gifts of excellent elephants,
colourful blankets and deer skin, riches, two thousand gold
coins and sixteen hundred horses. The king of Kekaya honoured
Kaikeyee's son by offering all these riches. Ashvapati also provided
beloved and trusted advisers who possessed all the qualities, so
that they could follow Bharata on the fast return journey. There
were handsome Airavata elephants from the Indrashira region.[254]
There were well-trained and swift mules. His maternal uncle gave
him all these riches. As a gift, he also gave him extremely large
dogs that had been bred in the inner quarters of the palace. These
were powerful, with the valour of tigers, and could use their teeth
in fighting. Having taken the leave of his maternal grandfather,
his maternal uncle, Yudhajit, Bharata, with Shatrughna, ascended
the chariot and got ready to leave. There was a circle of more than
one hundred chariots, yoked to camels, cattle, horses and mules.
There were also servants who would follow Bharata. The great-
souled Bharata was protected by this large force. He was also
accompanied by advisers who were as noble as him. Possessing no
enemies, he also took Shatrughna with him. They left the residence,
like the Siddhas leaving Indra's world.

## Chapter 2(65)

From the royal palace, the valiant one headed in an eastern
direction. He crossed the wide Hladini river, which flowed in

[253] The word used is tata.

[254] While Airavata is the name of Indra's elephant, there were different species
of elephants and Airavata was also one of these. Indrashira was a mountainous area in
Kekaya. Kekaya was famous for its animals, elephants and horses included.

an eastern direction.[255] The handsome descendant of the Ikshvaku lineage crossed the Shatadru river. Having crossed the Eladhana river, he reached the region of Aparaparpata. At the places known as Agneya and Shalyakartana, he used rocks to cross over. Truthful in his objective and pure, the handsome one looked at the rocks that were being borne along in the flow. He crossed over a giant mountain and headed for the grove of Chaitraratha. There was the forceful flow of the river named Kulinga. This was surrounded by mountains and gladdened the heart. He reached the banks of the Yamuna and made his forces rest there. Their limbs were cooled and the exhausted horses were comforted. They bathed and drank and collected water for use. The prince traversed a gigantic forest that was rarely visited and rarely inhabited. The fortunate one crossed it on well-trained mounts, like the wind coursing through the sky. He reached Jambuprastha, located on the southern parts of the Torana region. Dasharatha's son reached the beautiful village of Varutha. Having set up camp in the beautiful forest and dwelt there, they headed eastwards. They reached a grove in Ujjihana, full of *priyaka* trees. Having reached there, the horses were tethered to the sala and priyaka trees. Having given the forces permission to rest there, Bharata left swiftly. He spent some time in Sarvatirtha and crossed the Uttanaka river. Using the horses, he crossed many other mountainous rivers. Astride an elephant, he crossed Kutika. The tiger among men crossed the Kapeevati at Louhitya. He crossed the Sthanumatee at Ekasala and the Gomatee river at Vinata. He reached a grove of sala trees in the city of Kalinga. Though the mounts were extremely exhausted, Bharata proceeded swiftly. Through the night, he swiftly traversed through the forest. When the sun was about to rise, he saw the city of Ayodhya, built by King Manu. Having spent seven nights on the road, the tiger among men saw that city.

From the chariot, he saw Ayodhya in front of him and told the charioteer, 'O charioteer! Ayodhya can be seen at a distance, like

[255] As will become apparent, this route from Rajagriha to Ayodhya doesn't seem to be quite the same as the route from Ayodhya to Rajagriha followed by the messengers. In addition, it is difficult to understand what some of the expressions mean.

a mass of white clay. It is illustrious and filled with sacred groves, though it cannot be seen clearly from here. Because of sacrifices performed, it possesses all the qualities and it is full of brahmanas who are accomplished in the Vedas. It also has a large number of aged people, protected by the best of royal sages.[256] Earlier, a large and tumultuous sound used to be heard from Ayodhya in every direction, spoken by the men and women. However, I do not hear that today. In the evening, in every direction, the gardens would be full of sporting men who would run around. However, it seems to me to be otherwise today.[257] Abandoned by those who seek pleasures, the gardens seem desolate now. O charioteer! To me, the city seems to be like a forest. Vehicles cannot be seen there, nor can the neighing of horses be heard. Earlier, the best among men used to constantly enter and leave. I see many kinds of evil signs and inauspicious portents. That is the reason my mind is distressed.'

With the exhausted mounts, he entered through the Vaijayanta gate.[258] With pronouncements of victory uttered by gatekeepers who stood up, he entered with his followers. With an anxious heart, he greeted the many people at the gate. Raghava told Ashvapati's exhausted charioteer, 'Earlier, we have heard about what happens when kings are destroyed. O charioteer! I see all those signs here. I see anxious people, men and women, in the city—distressed, eyes full of tears, miserable, deep in thought and extremely afflicted.' Distressed in his mind, Bharata spoke these words to the charioteer. Witnessing all these inauspicious signs, he proceeded towards the royal palace. He saw the city, which used to be like Indra's city. The tops of the gates and houses and the roads were deserted. The red gates and the machines on the gates were covered with dust. He saw many such things that were disagreeable to the mind, those that had never been seen in the city earlier. He was unhappy and distressed in his mind, with his head lowered down. He thus entered his great-souled father's residence.

---

[256] Dasharatha.

[257] Though it was morning when Bharata reached.

[258] Gate that signifies victory.

# Chapter 2(66)

He did not see his father there, in his father's residence. To see his mother, Bharata went to his mother's residence. Kaikeyee saw that her son, who had been away, had arrived. Delighted in her mind, she leapt up from her golden seat. The one with dharma in his soul entered his own house, which was devoid of all signs of prosperity. On seeing his mother, Bharata touched her auspicious feet. She embraced the illustrious one and inhaled the fragrance of his head. Placing Bharata on her lap, she started to question him. 'How many nights have passed since you left the Aryaka's residence?[259] Having swiftly come on a chariot, are you not exhausted? Is Aryaka well? How is Yudhajit, your maternal uncle? O son! Was your residence there happy? Tell me everything.' Kaikeyee asked these questions to her beloved son of the king. The lotus-eyed Bharata told his mother everything that he had been asked. 'This is the seventh night since I left Aryaka's residence. My mother's father is well and so is Yudhajit, my maternal uncle. The king, the scorcher of enemies, gave me riches and jewels as gifts. However, my companions became exhausted along the way and I arrived ahead of them. I came quickly because the messengers conveyed the king's message. O mother! You should answer what I wish to ask you. This gold-decorated bed, used for lying down, is empty. The people of the Ikshvaku lineage do not seem to be happy to me. The king is usually here, in my mother's residence. I do not see him here now. I came here to meet him. I wish to touch my father's feet. Tell me what I am asking you. I see. Perhaps he is there in my eldest mother, Kousalya's, residence.'

At this, Kaikeyee told him the terrible and disagreeable news, as if she was recounting something pleasant. She told him what she knew, but he did not, about how she was confounded by her greed for the kingdom. 'Your father has confronted the end that is attained by all living creatures.' Bharata followed dharma and was born in a noble and auspicious lineage. Hearing these words, afflicted by great grief on account of his father, he suddenly fell down on the ground.

[259] Ashvapati's father.

He was extremely miserable on account of his father's death and was senseless with grief. His senses awhirl and distracted, the immensely energetic one lamented. 'In earlier times, this extremely beautiful bed of my father's used to be radiant. Deprived of the intelligent one, that is the reason it does not shine any longer.' She saw that the one who was like a god was afflicted and had fallen down on the ground. She raised the afflicted one and addressed him in these words. 'Arise! O immensely illustrious prince! Why are you lying down? Arise! Those like you, revered in the assemblies of men, do not grieve in this way.' Writhing around on the ground, he wept for a long time. Afflicted by many kinds of grief, he replied to his mother. 'I thought that the king was going to consecrate Rama, or that he had decided to perform a sacrifice. Having thought in this way, I cheerfully undertook this journey. Everything has turned out to be the opposite and my mind is shattered. I do not see my father, who was always engaged in my welfare. O mother! Before I returned, what disease did my father die of? Tell me that quickly. My elder, Rama, whose deeds are unblemished, is like a father now. A noble one who follows dharma knows this. I will grasp his feet. He is my refuge now. O noble lady! For my father, truth was his valour. What did he say? I want to myself hear his last and virtuous words.'

Thus asked, Kaikeyee told him words that were in conformity with the truth. 'The king lamented, uttering the names of Rama, Sita and Lakshmana. Thus did the great-souled one, supreme among all refuges, go to the world hereafter. These were the last words spoken by your father. He was like a giant elephant in a noose, entangled in the dharma of time. "Men who see Rama, Sita and the mighty-armed Lakshmana return again will accomplish their objective."' Hearing this second piece of unpleasant news, he was distressed again. With a miserable face, he again asked his mother, 'Where is the extender of Kousalya's delight, the one with dharma in his soul, now? Where have my brother, Lakshmana, and Sita gone with him?' Thus asked, his mother started to tell him everything that had happened. This was unpleasant news, though she thought it was pleasant. 'O son! The prince has attired himself in bark and has gone to the great forest. With Vaidehi and Lakshmana following him, he has gone to Dandaka.' Hearing this, Bharata was terrified, because he suspected this might have had something to do with his brother's character and would therefore reflect on his lineage's greatness. He asked, 'Has Rama seized the riches of a brahmana? Has he caused injury to a rich or poor person, or to an innocent one? Has the prince sought after another person's wife? Has he been exiled to Dandakaranya because of foeticide?' At this, the fickle mother narrated the truth about what she had exactly done, because of her feminine sentiments. 'Rama has not seized any brahmana's riches. He has not caused injury to a rich or poor person, or to one who is innocent. Nor has Rama cast a glance at another person's wife. O son! I heard about Rama being consecrated as the heir apparent. I immediately asked your father for the kingdom and for Rama's exile. Following standards of conduct he set for himself, your father acted accordingly. He sent Rama, Soumitri and Sita away. The king could no longer see his beloved and immensely illustrious son. He died on account of sorrow over his son. O one who knows about dharma! You can rightfully claim the kingship now. All that I did was done for your sake. O son! Following the ordinances, quickly meet the ones who know about the rites—the Indras among brahmanas, led by Vasishtha. At the right time, without any distress in your heart, consecrate yourself as the king over this earth.'

## Chapter 2(67)

He heard the account about his father and about his brothers being banished. Bharata was tormented by grief and spoke these words. 'As I am grieving, what use is this devastated kingdom to me now? I am deprived of my father and of my brother, who is like a father. Like applying salt on a wound, you have imposed a sorrow on another sorrow. You have made my father die and have turned Rama into an ascetic. You have brought about the destruction of the lineage, as if a night of destruction has arrived. My father did not know that he had embraced a burning piece of coal. You are my mother. But overcome by sorrow on account of their sons, Kousalya and Sumitra will find it extremely difficult to reside with you. The noble one[260] had dharma in his soul and displayed supreme conduct towards you, treating you like his own mother. He knew about how one should behave with seniors. In that way, my eldest mother, Kousalya, possesses foresight. Resorting to dharma, she behaved with you as if with one's own sister. You have made her son don garments of rags and bark and leave for residing in the forest. Despite this wickedness, you are not sorrowing. You do not realize the evil you have caused to that illustrious one. You have exiled him, with bark as attire. Do you see any reason for this? I do not think you know how much I desire Raghava. Otherwise, for the sake of the kingdom, you would not have brought about this great and unnecessary calamity. In the absence of the strength brought about by those tigers among men, Rama and Lakshmana, why will I be interested in protecting the kingdom? He[261] is powerful and extremely strong and the great king always found succour in him. The one with dharma in his soul was like the forest around Meru, sustaining Meru. This great burden has been thrust upon me. How can I bear this load? It requires energy. I do not possess the insolence to attempt this burden. On account of your son, you are greedy. Even if I were to possess the capacity brought about through yoga, intelligence and strength, I will not allow you to accomplish your objective. I will bring back my brother, who is loved by his relatives, from the forest.' The great-souled Bharata spoke in this way and added a multitude of other pleasant words. Though he was afflicted by grief, like a lion in a mountainous cavern, he roared.

# Chapter 2(68)

Bharata censured his mother in this way. Overcome by great rage, he again spoke these words. 'O Kaikeyee! O cruel one!

[260] Rama.
[261] Rama.

O one who is wicked in conduct! Go away from this kingdom.
You have abandoned dharma. When I am dead, weep over me.
What harm has the king, or Rama, who is extremely devoted to
dharma, done to you? Because of what you have done, his death
and the exile have occurred simultaneously. Because you have
brought about the destruction of this lineage, it is as if you have
committed foeticide. O Kaikeyee! Go to hell. You will not obtain
the world obtained by your husband. You have perpetrated an
extremely terrible deed like this. Having abandoned someone
who is loved by all the worlds, you have created a great fear in
me too. My father is dead and Rama has resorted to the forest
because of you. For me, you have brought about ill fame in the
world of the living. O cruel one! O one who is greedy for the
kingdom! In the form of a mother, you are my enemy. I will not
speak to you. O evil in conduct! You have killed your husband.
O defiler of the lineage! Because of you, Kousalya, Sumitra and
my other mothers are immersed in great misery. The intelligent
king, Ashvapati, is devoted to dharma. You are not his daughter.
You have been born as a rakshasa lady, to destroy your father's
lineage. Rama was always devoted to the truth and abided by
dharma. Because of you, he has left for the forest and, grieving,
my father has gone to heaven. Your grievous sin has been to
deprive me of my father. O one hated by all the worlds! You
have also made my brothers abandon me. Kousalya is devoted
to dharma. Having turned your mind towards wickedness, you
have deprived her. Having done this, you will now obtain worlds
destined for those who go to hell. O cruel one! Did you not
comprehend that Rama, my elder brother and Kousalya's son, is
like a father to me? He is a refuge for all his relatives. The son
is born from the limbs and the heart. That is the reason a son is
most loved by a mother. All the other relatives come after that.
Surabhee[262] is revered by the gods and knows about dharma.
There was an occasion when she lost her senses on seeing her
two sons bear heavy burdens on earth. She saw that her two

---

[262] The mother of cows and the cow of the gods.

sons were exhausted on earth, having borne the burden for half a day. Afflicted on account of her sons, she wept, her eyes overflowing with tears. The great-souled king of the gods was travelling below her and those fine and fragrant drops fell on his body. Indra, the wielder of the vajra, saw that the illustrious one was tormented by grief. Anxious, the king of the gods joined his hands in salutation and spoke these words. "I hope no great fear has been caused to you by us. O one who wishes everyone's welfare! What has given rise to this sorrow? Tell me." Thus addressed by the intelligent king of the gods, Surabhee, eloquent in the use of words, replied in these patient words, "O lord of the immortals! May anything that causes you evil be pacified. I am immersed in grief because my two sons are facing a hardship. They are distressed and weak, because they have been scorched by the rays of the sun. O lord of the gods! Dragging the plough, the two bulls are being killed. They have been born from my body. They are suffering and are afflicted by the burden. I am tormented on seeing them. There is nothing as beloved as a son." The cow which provides all the objects of desire sorrowed, even though she possessed a thousand sons. Without Rama, how will Kousalya sustain herself? The virtuous one has a single son and because of what you have done, she has been separated from her son. Therefore, you will always suffer from grief, in this world and in the world hereafter. I will do everything that needs to be done for my father and compensate my brother by enhancing his fame. There is no doubt about this. I will bring back Kousalya's immensely radiant son. I will myself go to the forest that is frequented by the hermits.' Like an elephant in the forest, which has been prodded by a javelin or a goad, he fell down angrily on the ground and sighed like a serpent. His eyes were red and his clothing was dishevelled. All his ornaments were thrown around. The king's son, scorcher of enemies, fell down on the ground, like the standard of Shachi's consort, once the festival is over.[263]

---

[263] Shachi's consort is Indra. As long as the festival is observed, Indra's standard is raised. Thereafter, it is flung away.

# Chapter 2(69)

Hearing the words spoken by the great-souled Bharata and recognizing the voice, Kousalya spoke to Sumitra. 'Bharata, the son of Kaikeyee, the perpetrator of cruel deeds, has arrived. I wish to see the far-sighted Bharata.' She was trembling and she wasn't in control of her senses. Pale and dressed in faded garments, she told Sumitra this and left for where Bharata was. Meanwhile, together with Shatrughna, Bharata, Rama's younger brother, also left for Kousalya's residence. Bharata and Shatrughna saw the miserable Kousalya. Afflicted with grief, she had lost her senses and fallen down along the way. They embraced her. Kousalya, extremely miserable, addressed Bharata. 'You desired this kingdom and you have obtained the kingdom, bereft of thorns. Thanks to Kaikeyee, the performer of cruel deeds, you have quickly obtained it. My son, dressed in rags, has left, to reside in the forest. What merit did the evil-sighted Kaikeyee see in this? Kaikeyee should quickly grant me permission to leave for the place where my extremely illustrious son, Hiranyanabha,[264] is. Or perhaps I can cheerfully leave on my own, with Sumitra following me. With the agnihotra fire in front, I will go to wherever Raghava is. But perhaps that is what you yourself desire now. You should convey me there, where my ascetic son, tiger among men, is tormenting himself through austerities. This extensive kingdom, with its store of grain, riches, elephants, horses and chariots, has been handed over to you.'

When she lamented in this way, Bharata joined his hands in salutation. Kousalya was suffering from many kinds of grief and he spoke to her. 'O noble lady! Why are you reprimanding me? I am ignorant and innocent of any sin. You know that my affection for Raghava is great. The noble one is devoted to the truth and is best among virtuous ones. May the intelligence of anyone who ensured his departure never turn to the sacred texts. May the servants of any such wicked person release urine in the direction of the sun. May the

---

[264] The one with the golden navel, Vishnu's name. It is odd that Kousalya should use this expression.

person who ensured his departure kill a sleeping cow with his foot. A servant who causes great injury and performs a great misdeed is imposed a punishment by his master. May the person who ensured the adharma of his departure endure that punishment. May the person who ensured his departure suffer from the sin committed by an individual who causes injury to a king who protects his subjects like his own sons. A king who extracts more than one-sixth of taxes makes his subjects suffer and commits adharma. May the person who ensured his departure suffer from that sin. An individual who promises ascetics dakshina at sacrifices and deviates from the pledge commits a sin. May the person who ensured his departure suffer from that sin. In a tumultuous battle where weapons are used, there are rules for fighting with elephants, horses and chariots and any deviation is not dharma. May the person who ensured his departure suffer from that sin. An evil-souled person destroys the extremely subtle meaning of the sacred texts, taught by intelligent instructors. May the person who ensured his departure suffer from that sin. Without offering it first to seniors, there are those who pointlessly eat the shunned food of payasam, *krisara* and goat meat.[265] May the person who ensured his departure suffer from that sin. It is a sin to eat alone in one's house, when one is surrounded by sons, wives and servants. May the person who ensured his departure suffer from that sin. It is a sin to kill a king, a woman, a child or an aged person, just as it is a sin to abandon a servant. May that kind of sin visit the person. Sleeping during both the sandhyas has been thought of as a sin. May the person who ensured his departure suffer from that sin. It is a sin to indulge in arson. It is a sin to transgress a preceptor's bed. It is a sin to cause injury to a friend. May the person suffer from that sin. It is a sin not to serve the gods, the ancestors, the mother and the father. May the person suffer from that sin. It has been recounted that there are worlds for the virtuous and for those who perform virtuous deeds. May the person who ensured his departure be swiftly dislodged from those.' Kousalya had been deprived of her

---

[265] Krisara is a dish made out of sesamum and grain. The point is that shares must first be offered to gods and other seniors. Otherwise, it is abhorred food and any sacrificial food, not offered first to the gods, is a pointless sacrifice.

husband and her son. While comforting her in this way, the king's son was also overcome by grief and fell down.

Bharata had just taken extremely difficult pledges. Having taken those pledges, he had become unconscious. Kousalya spoke these words to the one who was tormented by grief. 'O son! My sorrow has become greater. Through the pledges that you have taken, you are making me suffer even more. It is good fortune that, like Lakshmana, your soul is devoted to dharma. O son! You have sworn on the truth and you will obtain worlds meant for the virtuous.' Afflicted by grief, the great-souled one[266] lamented in this way. His mind was agitated. He was confused and racked by tides of grief. He lamented and lost his senses. With his intelligence devastated, he fell down on the ground. He repeatedly emitted long sighs. The night passed in the midst of such misery.

## Chapter 2(70)

In this way, Bharata, Kaikeyee's son, was tormented by grief. Vasishtha, foremost among rishis and best among eloquent ones, spoke to him. 'O fortunate one! O immensely illustrious prince! Enough of this sorrow. The time has come to perform the last rites for the lord of men.' Hearing Vasishtha's words, Bharata prostrated himself. The one who knew about dharma performed all the funeral rites. The body of the king was raised from the vessel of oil. The face was yellow in complexion, as if he was asleep. The body was first laid down on the best of beds, decorated with many kinds of jewels. At this, Dasharatha's son lamented in great misery. 'O king! When I was away and had not returned from my trip, why did you send off Rama, who knows about dharma, and the immensely strong Lakshmana on exile? O great king! Abandoning these grieving people, where will you go? They have also been deprived of Rama, the performer of unblemished deeds and lion among men. O king!

[266] Bharata.

Who will now think of yoga and kshema for this city? O father! You have gone and Rama has left for the forest. O king! Without you, the earth is a widow and does not shine any more. The city seems to me to be like the night without the moon.' Distressed in his mind, Bharata lamented in this way.

The great rishi, Vasishtha, again addressed him in these words. 'Funeral and other rites need to be performed for the king. O mighty-armed one! Without any distraction or reflection, perform those rites.' Bharata worshipped Vasishtha and agreed to his words. He quickly welcomed all the officiating priests, priests and preceptors. Following the indicated ordinances, the officiating priests and assistants initially kindled the fire for the king outside the fire chamber. The king's senseless body was then placed on a palanquin and borne by distracted attendants whose voices choked with tears. Ahead of the king, people advanced along the road, scattering silver, gold and many kinds of garments. The funeral pyre was prepared with wood from *sarala*, *padmaka* and devadaru trees and sprinkled with the essence of sandalwood and aloe. Many other kinds of fragrances were flung there and the officiating priests placed the king in the midst of all these. The officiating priests poured oblations into the fire and chanted. Following the sacred texts, those accomplished in the Sama Veda chanted Sama hymns.

As each one deserved, the women mounted palanquins and vehicles. Surrounded by the elders, they left the city and reached the place. The king was on the funeral pyre and the officiating priests circumambulated him anticlockwise. With Kousalya at the forefront, the women were tormented by grief. Like the sound of female curlews, the wails of the women could be heard. At the time, thousands of them lamented in piteous tones. On the banks of the Sarayu, those beautiful women descended from their vehicles and distressed, repeatedly wept and lamented. With the royal women, the ministers and the priests, Bharata performed the water rites. Eyes full of tears, they entered the city. In misery, they spent ten days on the ground.[267]

---

[267] That is, they slept on the floor for ten days.

# Chapter 2(71)

After ten days had passed, the son of the king purified himself. On the twelfth day, he performed the *shraddha* ceremony. He gave brahmanas large quantities of jewels, riches, food, many white goats, hundreds of cows, female servants, male servants and extremely expensive houses. As part of the funeral rites, the king's son gave these to brahmanas.

On the morning of the thirteenth day, the mighty-armed Bharata went for cleansing.[268] He became senseless with sorrow and lamented. The words choked in his throat. Extremely miserable, at the foot of the funeral pyre, he addressed his father in these words. 'O father! I entrusted your care to my brother, Raghava. But you exiled him to the forest. Abandoned by you, I am alone now. O father! Mother Kousalya's refuge was her son. But you exiled him to the forest. O king! Forsaking her, where have you gone now?' He saw the red ashes and the burnt circle of skin and bones. He grieved that his father had given up his body. He was miserable on seeing the remnants and fell down on the ground. It was as if Shakra's standard had been raised, but fell down because the machines to work the standard failed. All the advisers, pure in their vows, approached. It was like the rishis rushing to Yayati when the time for his death arrived.

Shatrughna also saw that Bharata was overcome with sorrow. Remembering the king, he also lost his senses and fell down on the ground. It was as if he[269] went mad. He lamented in great misery. He remembered all the many qualities that his father had possessed. 'We are being agitated and have been immersed in this ocean of grief. This is because of Manthara's terrible influence and Kaikeyee is like a crocodile swimming in the two boons. O father! As a child, you have always tended to the delicate Bharata. He is lamenting. Abandoning him, where have you gone? You have always given us

---

[268] This doesn't convey the sense. He went to clean the cremation ground and collect the remaining bones.

[269] Shatrughna.

everything that we desired—food, drink, garments and ornaments. Why don't you do that now? As a king, you knew about dharma and were great-souled. Without you, the earth should be shattered. Why is it not being shattered? Our father has gone to heaven and Rama has resorted to the forest. What is the point of remaining alive? I should enter the fire. I am without a brother. I am without a father. Ayodhya, ruled by the Ikshvakus, is empty. Why should I return there? I should enter a hermitage.'

Hearing their lamentations and witnessing their distress, all their followers were again immersed in great grief. Both Shatrughna and Bharata were exhausted and distressed. They writhed around on the ground, like insensate bulls whose horns had been broken. Vasishtha was the priest of their father. Like a physician who restores to normalcy, he raised Bharata and addressed him in these words. 'Without exception, there are three kinds of opposite sentiments all living creatures have to face.[270] Since this is inevitable, you should not behave like this.' Sumantra knew about the truth. He raised Shatrughna and comforted him, telling him about the origin and destruction of all creatures. Those two illustrious tigers among men were raised. They were as radiant as Indra's standard, having suffered through rains and the heat. Their eyes were still red and their speech was miserable. But they wiped away their tears. The advisers urged them to hurry with the remaining rites.

## Chapter 2(72)

Bharata was tormented by grief and wished to undertake the journey.[271] Shatrughna, Lakshmana's younger brother, addressed him in these words. 'The spirited Rama is the refuge of all creatures. What can be a greater grief to us than that he has been exiled to the forest by a woman? Lakshmana is so named

---

[270] Birth and death, joy and misery and heat and cold.
[271] To meet Rama.

because he possesses strength and valour.[272] Why did he not free
Rama and restrain our father? Even before the act had happened,
on considering good and bad policy and on seeing that the king
had resorted to a wrong path, having come under the subjugation
of a woman, he should have restrained him.' While Shatrughna,
Lakshmana's younger brother, was speaking in this way, Kubja
appeared at the eastern gate, adorned in every kind of ornament.
She was radiant in royal garments and was smeared with the essence
of sandalwood. Attired in colourful girdles, she looked like a female
monkey, bound with ropes. She was the perpetrator of an extremely
wicked deed. On seeing her, the doorkeepers seized the cruel Kubja.
Delivering her to Shatrughna, they said, 'It is because of what she
did that Rama has left for the forest and your father has given up his
life. This is the wicked and cruel one. Do what you want with her.'

Shatrughna, firm in his vows, was extremely miserable. He
instructed all those in the inner quarters in these words. 'This
perpetrator of cruel deeds has led to this great calamity and owes
a debt to my brothers and my father. Let her reap the fruits of her
action.' Kubja was surrounded by her friends. Having said this, he
powerfully seized her, so that the residence echoed with her cries.
Hearing Shatrughna's angry words, all her friends became extremely
miserable and fled in different directions. All those friends came to
the following conclusion. 'The way he is advancing, he will destroy
all of us. The illustrious Koushalya knows about dharma and is
generous and compassionate. Let us seek refuge with her. It is certain
that she is our only refuge.' The eyes of Shatrughna, tormentor of
enemies, were coppery red with rage. He dragged the shrieking
Kubja along the ground. As Manthara was dragged along the
ground, her many colourful ornaments were strewn around on the
floor. When those ornaments were strewn around, the radiant royal
palace was as resplendent as the autumn sky.[273] The powerful one,
bull among men, seized her in his rage. He reprimanded Kaikeyee
in harsh words. Kaikeyee was extremely miserable and pained at

[272] The word *lakshmana* means mark or sign.
[273] The ornaments looked like stars.

these harsh words. Terrified of Shatrughna, she sought refuge with her own son. On seeing her and the angry Shatrughna, Bharata said, 'Among all living beings, women should never be killed. She should be pardoned. Kaikeyee is wicked and evil in conduct. However, Rama is devoted to dharma and will be angry if I were to kill my mother. But for this, I would have killed her. Raghava has dharma in his soul. If he gets to know that this Kubja has been killed, it is certain that he will not speak to you or to me.' Hearing Bharata's words, Shatrughna, Lakshmana's younger brother, controlled his rage and released Manthara. Manthara fell down at Kaikeyee's feet. Suffering greatly, she lamented piteously and sighed. Flung away by Shatrughna, Kubja was senseless and grief-stricken, like a female curlew that had been captured. On seeing her, Bharata's mother gently comforted her.

# Chapter 2(73)

It was the morning of the fourteenth day. Those entrusted with the task of anointing a king assembled and addressed Bharata in these words. 'Dasharatha, senior to all our seniors, has gone to heaven. Rama, the eldest, has been exiled and so has the immensely strong Lakshmana. O greatly illustrious king! You should be our king now. Without a leader, it is fortunate that the kingdom has not suffered from a calamity so far. O Raghava! O son of a king! With everything required for a consecration, your own relatives and the citizens are awaiting you. O Bharata! Accept this great kingdom of your father and grandfathers. O bull among men! Consecrate yourself and save us.'

Bharata circumambulated all the vessels kept for the consecration. Firm in his vows, he replied to all those people. 'In our lineage, it has always been proper that the kingdom should be vested with the eldest. O those who are accomplished! You should not speak to me in this way. My brother, Rama, is elder to me and he will be the lord of the earth. I will reside in the forest for fourteen years. Let a large and extremely strong army, with the four kinds of forces, be yoked. I will bring my elder brother, Raghava, back from the forest. Placing all these objects required for the coronation in front of me, for Rama's sake, I will go to the forest. With these objects, I will consecrate that tiger among men there. I will bring Rama back, like bringing back the sacrificial fire.[274] I will not allow the one who pretends to be by mother to be successful. I will reside in the impenetrable forest and Rama will be the king. Let artisans create a path through flat and uneven terrain. Let those who know about impenetrable paths protect us along the way.' For Rama's sake, the son of the king spoke in this way. All the people replied in these supreme and excellent words. 'Since you have spoken in this way, let Padma always be with you, in the form of Shri.[275] You have desired to give away the earth to your elder, the son of the king.' They heard those supreme words spoken by the son of the king. Because of their delight, tears of joy fell down from their noble eyes. Hearing those words, the advisers and the counsellors were delighted and abandoned their misery. They said, 'O supreme among men! Following your instructions, devoted men and large numbers of artisans will be engaged to construct the road.'

## Chapter 2(74)

Those who knew about land and the regions, those accomplished with strings,[276] brave ones engaged in their own tasks, diggers, those who worked with machines, labourers, architects, men accomplished about machines, carpenters, road builders, those who would cut down trees, those who would dig wells, those who would do plaster work, those who would work with bamboo and those

[274] The image is of a sacrifice performed outside a city, the sacrificial fire then brought back to the city.

[275] Lakshmi, also known as Shri, the goddess of wealth and prosperity. Since Lakshmi is seated on a lotus, she is also known as Padma.

[276] For levelling the ground.

who were capable, departed, placing the supervisors at the front.
That large crowd of men departed joyously and was as radiant as
the great force of the ocean at the time of the full moon. They were
accomplished in building roads and each engaged himself in his
own appointed task, with his own respective implement. They thus
advanced. Those people cleared away creepers, lantanas, shrubs,
trees and rocks. Cutting down many kinds of trees, they created a
path. Some planted trees in spots where there were no trees. Others
used axes, hatchets and sickles to cut down thickets. Other strong
ones, stronger than the others, removed clumps of *veerana* grass.
Here and there, they levelled the impenetrable parts. Some filled
up wells and pits with earth. Some levelled the spots that sloped
downwards. Bridges were built where they could be constructed.
Throughout the region, the men crushed and shattered obstructions
that stood along the way. In a short while, many canals and wells
were built. There were many such and some of them looked like
oceans. In spots where there was no water, many excellent wells
were dug and decorated with platforms around them. The surface
of the road was plastered and lined with blossoming trees, on which,
intoxicated birds chirped. The road was decorated with flags. The
road was decorated with many kinds of flowers and sprinkled with
water mixed with the fragrance of sandalwood. Constructed for
those many soldiers, the road was as radiant as a road to heaven.
The supervisors were men who had been instructed for the purpose.
In a beautiful spot that had many kinds of succulent fruit, they
constructed a residence for the great-souled Bharata. Adorned with
many kinds of ornaments, this itself looked like an ornament. Those
who knew about such things determined an auspicious nakshatra
and at that time, camps were set up for the great-souled Bharata.
Each of these was surrounded by moats and walls of earth. Each
of these possessed excellent roads and looked like sapphires. There
were garlands of mansions and walls and fortifications were erected
around them. Each had excellent and large roads, decorated with
flags. The tops of the mansions were like vimanas and extended up
into the sky. As they rose up, they were as resplendent as Shakra's
city. With many trees and groves, the road approached the Jahnavee,

which was full of cool and sparkling water and populated by giant fish. The clear and sparkling night is radiant with the moon and a large number of stars. Constructed progressively and auspiciously by the artisans, the beautiful royal road was as resplendent as that.

## Chapter 2(75)

There were bards and minstrels, eloquent in the use of words. On that *nandimukha* night,[277] they praised Bharata with auspicious words of praise. There was a drum that was used to sound the progress of the yamas. This was struck with a golden drumstick. Hundreds of conch shells, with loud and soft notes, were blown. The sky was filled with the extremely large sound of trumpets. Bharata was already tormented by sorrow and this increased his grief. Awoken by the sound, Bharata instructed that it should cease. He said 'I am not the king.' He next told Shatrughna, 'O Shatrughna! Look at the great injury Kaikeyee has caused to the world. King Dasharatha has left, releasing this grief on me. This royal prosperity, with dharma as its foundation, belongs to the great-souled king who followed dharma. It is now being tossed around, like a boat without a steersman in the water.' On seeing Bharata senseless, lamenting in this way, all the women wept piteously, in loud tones.

When they were lamenting in this way, the immensely illustrious Vasishtha, who knew about the dharma of kings, entered the assembly hall of the lord of the Ikshvakus. It was beautiful, decorated with molten gold, gems and jewels and was like Sudharma.[278] The one with dharma in his soul entered with his followers. The one who knew all the Vedas seated himself on a golden seat that was strewn with spreads. He then instructed the messengers, 'Without being distracted, quickly summon the brahmanas, kshatriyas,

---

[277] Nandimukha has different meanings. Here, it simply means joyous night. The word is also used for a special shraddha ceremony.

[278] The assembly hall of the gods.

warriors, advisers and leaders of the armies. We have to perform an extremely urgent task.' A large and tumultuous sound was generated, as chariots, horses, elephants and people started to assemble. Bharata arrived, like Shatakratu of the immortals, and all the subjects greeted him, as if he was Dasharatha. Adorned by Dashratha's son, the assembly hall was like a lake with tranquil waters, filled with water, gems, conch shells, gravel, whales and serpents, just as, in earlier times, it used to be with Dasharatha.

## Chapter 2(76)

The well-designed assembly hall was full of noble people and was like the night, adorned by the full moon. Bharata, full of understanding, saw it. The noble ones were seated on their own respective seats and he saw it, dazzling like a night of the full moon after the end of the monsoon. The priest, knowledgeable about dharma, looked at all the royal and ordinary people and addressed Bharata in these gentle words. 'O son!279 Having followed dharma, King Dasharatha has gone to heaven. He has given you this prosperous earth, full of riches and grain. Rama is virtuous and upholds the truth. Remembering dharma, he did not cast aside his father's command, just as a rising moon does not cast aside the moonlight. Bereft of thorns, your father and your brother have given you this kingdom. Enjoy it. With the delighted advisers, quickly arrange for the coronation. Let those from the north, from the west, from the south, those without kingdoms280 and those from the boundaries of the ocean bring you crores of jewels.'

Hearing these words, Bharata, knowledgeable about dharma, was filled with sorrow. He mentally thought of Rama and desired to ensure dharma. In a voice overcome with tears and in a tone like that of a swan, in the midst of the assembly, the youth reprimanded

---

279 The word used is tata.
280 The word used is *kevala*. It is not obvious that this refers to those from the east. Literally, the word would mean isolated countries.

the priest. 'I have followed brahmacharya and having acquired learning, have bathed.[281] I am intelligent and endeavour to pursue dharma. How can someone like me steal someone else's kingdom? How can someone born from Dasharatha steal a kingdom? Both I and the kingdom belong to Rama. You should speak in accordance with dharma. He is elder and superior, possessing dharma in his soul. He is the equal of Dileepa and Nahusha.[282] As did Dasharatha, Kakutstha should receive the kingdom. If I commit this crime, I will act like an ignoble person and will not go to heaven. In this world, I will become the defiler of the lineage of the Ikshvakus. I do not take delight in the wicked act perpetrated by my mother. From here, I am joining my hands in salutation and bowing down before the one who is in the impenetrable forest. He is supreme among bipeds and I will follow King Rama. Raghava deserves the kingdom of the three worlds.' Hearing those words, in conformity with dharma, all the courtiers shed tears of joy, their minds immersed in Rama. 'If I am incapable of bringing back the noble one from the forest, I will reside in the forest, as the noble Lakshmana is doing. I will use every means, even force, to bring him back. I will present the noble one before this assembly of virtuous people who possess all the qualities.' With dharma in his soul and affectionate towards his brother, Bharata spoke in this fashion. Sumantra, skilled in counsels, was nearby and he addressed him in these words. 'O Sumantra! Arise. Follow my command and go quickly. Summon the forces and ask them to leave swiftly.' Thus addressed by the great-souled Bharata, Sumantra cheerfully instructed that everything should be done as he[283] had desired. The ordinary soldiers and the commanders of the forces were delighted on learning about the journey to bring back Raghava. Knowing this, in every house, the wives of all the warriors were also filled with joy and urged their husbands to hurry. The commanders of the forces urged all the forces—horses, bullock carts, chariots that were as fleet as thought and warriors. Bharata saw that the army was ready. In the

---

[281] The ritual bath at the end of a period of studies.
[282] While Dileepa is from the solar dynasty, Nahusha is from the lunar dynasty.
[283] Bharata.

presence of his preceptor,[284] he spoke to Sumantra, who was by his side. 'Swiftly prepare my chariot.' Happy, he accepted Bharata's instructions. He yoked the chariot to excellent steeds and brought it, ready to leave. Raghava[285] was powerful and firm in adherence to the truth. He spoke what was appropriate. He was firm and truth was his valour. The illustrious one wanted to go to the great forest to seek the favours of his elder. Bharata said, 'O Sumantra! Arise quickly and go. Tell the leaders of the forces to yoke the army. For the welfare of the world, I desire to seek Rama's favours and bring him back from the forest.' The son of the suta was thus directly instructed by Bharata to accomplish his desire. He instructed all the leaders of the ordinary soldiers, the commanders of the armies and the well-wishers. Every family arose and started yoking chariots to camels, mules, elephants and well-bred horses—royalty, vaishyas, *vrishalas* and brahmanas.[286]

## Chapter 2(77)

When it was morning, Bharata arose and wishing to see Rama, ascended an excellent chariot and swiftly departed. All the ministers and priests ascended chariots that were like the sun's chariot, yoked to horses, and proceeded ahead of him. There were nine thousand elephants that had been prepared in the proper way. They followed Bharata, the delight of the Ikshvaku lineage, on his journey. There were six thousand chariots with archers armed with many kinds of weapons. They followed illustrious Prince Bharata on his journey. There were one hundred thousand horses and riders. They followed illustrious Prince Bharata Raghava on his journey. Kaikeyee, Sumitra and the illustrious Kousalya left on a radiant

---

[284] Vasishtha.
[285] Bharata.
[286] Vrishala means shudra, but also outcast in general. Royalty obviously represents kshatriyas.

vehicle, delighted at the prospect of bringing Rama back.[287] Cheerful in their minds at the prospect of seeing Rama and Lakshmana, that noble assembly left, conversing about his[288] wonderful exploits. 'He is mighty-armed and as dark as a cloud. He is firm in his spirit and firm in his vows. When will we see Rama, the dispeller of the world's misery? As soon as we see him, Raghava will dispel our grief, just as the rising sun dispels darkness from all the worlds.' Delighted, they addressed each other in these auspicious words. The citizens embraced each other and proceeded. There were others there who were respected, merchants and ordinary people. All of them also left, delighted at the prospect of seeing Rama. There were some who worked with gems, those who fashioned beautiful pots, those who were carpenters, those who made weapons, those who worked with peacock feathers, those who used saws, those who fashioned ornaments, those who pierced gems, those who worked with tusks, those who worked with plaster, those who made their living through fragrances, famous goldsmiths, those who wove woollen blankets, those who bathed and attired people, physicians, incense makers, those who distilled liquor, washermen, tailors, leaders of villages and habitations, dancers, fishermen and their women. All of them proceeded. There were self-controlled brahmanas, learned in the Vedas and respected for their conduct. Astride thousands of bullock carts, they followed Bharata. They were attired in pure and excellent garments, anointing themselves with red sandalwood paste. All of them swiftly followed Bharata, on many kinds of vehicles. Delighted and comforted, the soldiers followed Bharata, Kaikeyee's son.

The army was thus stationed there. On seeing the army following him and Ganga, full of auspicious waters, ahead of him, Bharata, accomplished in the use of words, spoke to all his advisers.[289] 'It is my desire that the entire army should set up camp. They are exhausted. We will cross this great river tomorrow. I desire to descend into the waters of the river and offer the funeral water

---

[287] Kaikeyee seems to have repented.
[288] Rama's.
[289] Some time had been spent on the journey.

rites to the king who has left for heaven.' Hearing his words, the
self-controlled advisers agreed. They arranged for separate camps
for everyone, in accordance with each one's wishes. They carefully
set up camp on the banks of the great river, Ganga. With all the
equipment, the army looked beautiful. The great-souled Bharata
resided there, thinking about how he would bring Rama back.

## Chapter 2(78)

The banks of the river Ganga were full of flags. On seeing these,
the king of the nishadas[290] spoke urgently to his kin. 'From
here, this giant army is seen to have the appearance of an ocean.
Though I have been thinking about this in my mind, I cannot see
an end to this. There is a giant *kovidara* standard on a chariot.[291]
Perhaps he will bind our fishermen or slay us. Dasharatha's son,
Rama, has been banished from the kingdom by his father. Perhaps
Bharata, Kaikeyee's son, has advanced so as to kill him. Rama,
Dasharatha's son, is my lord and my friend too. To accomplish his
desires, armour yourselves and remain on this bank of the Ganga.
Let all our servants station themselves along the river Ganga. Let the
army subsist on meat, roots and fruit and protect the river. Let there
be five hundred boats, each with one thousand fishermen. Let them
remain ready.' These were his instructions. 'If Bharata is kindly
disposed towards Rama, only then will he be allowed to safely cross
the Ganga now.' Having said this, Guha, the lord of the nishadas,
took fish, meat and honey as offerings and approached Bharata.
The powerful son of the suta[292] saw him approach and the humble
one spoke to Bharata with humility. 'This lord is surrounded by
one thousand of his kin. He is knowledgeable about the Dandaka
forest and has also been your brother's friend for a long time. O
Kakutstha! Therefore, let Guha, lord of the nishadas, see you. There

[290] Guha.
[291] Bharata's standard was made out of kovidara (a kind of orchid tree).
[292] Sumantra.

is no doubt that he will know where Rama and Lakshmana are.'
Hearing the auspicious words spoken by Sumantra, Bharata replied,
'Let Guha see me quickly.' Having obtained permission, Guha was
delighted. Surrounded by his kin, he humbly approached Bharata
and spoke these words. 'This region is like a pleasure garden and we
are your subjects. We are presenting ourselves before you. Reside
in this family of your servants. These roots and fruit have been
collected by the nishadas. There is fresh and dried meat and large
amounts of inferior and superior forest fare. I hope your army will
eat and spend the night here. After accepting these diverse objects of
desire, you can leave tomorrow with your soldiers.'

## Chapter 2(79)

Thus addressed by Guha, the lord of the nishadas, the immensely
wise Bharata replied in words that were full of purport and
meaning. 'O friend of my senior! An army like this is extremely
large. Your desire to extend hospitality to them is indeed great.'
Having spoken these excellent words to Guha, the immensely
energetic and prosperous Bharata again addressed the lord of the
nishadas in these words. 'O Guha! Which route should I follow to
reach Bharadvaja's hermitage? This difficult region is impenetrable
and the waters of the Ganga are difficult to cross.' Hearing the
words of the intelligent prince, Guha, who was used to travelling
in impenetrable regions, joined his hands in salutation and spoke
these words. 'O immensely illustrious prince! These self-controlled
servants, who are archers, will follow you. I will also follow you. I
hope you are not going because you harbour ill intentions towards
Rama, unblemished in deeds. This large army leads me to suspect
that.' Bharata was as clear as the sky.[293] Thus addressed, he spoke to
Guha in gentle words. 'Let there never be such a time. You should
not have suspected me. Raghava is my elder brother and is like a

---

[293] His mind was as clear as the sky.

father to me. Kakutstha is residing in the forest and I am going to make him return. O Guha! You should not think otherwise. I tell you this truthfully.' Hearing the words spoken by Bharata, his face became joyful and delighted, he again addressed Bharata in these words. 'You are blessed. On the surface of the earth, I do not see anyone like you. Though you did not strive for it, you obtained this kingdom and you wish to cast it aside. Your deeds will indeed be recounted in this world for an eternity, since you wish to bring Rama back from the calamity he is in.' While Guha was addressing Bharata in this way, the sun lost its radiance and night arrived.

Tended to by Guha, the handsome one[294] made the army set up camp and with Shatrughna, lay down on a bed. As he thought about Rama, who did not deserve this kind of misery, the great-souled Bharata grieved. He only looked towards dharma. At the time of a forest conflagration, a fire can be hidden inside a hollow tree. Like that, an inner fire burnt and tormented Raghava.[295] Generated by this fire of grief, perspiration exuded from all over his body, just as the rays of the sun scorch snow on the Himalayas and make them flow. His thoughts were like mountainous caverns. His sighs were like dark minerals. His misery was like clumps of trees. His sorrow and exhaustion were like summits. His swooning was like that of beasts. His torment was like herbs and bamboo. Kaikeyee's son was assailed by great grief that was like a mountain. Thereafter, the noble Bharata composed himself and with his relative,[296] went and met Guha. Bharata was low in spirits, but Guha again assured Bharata about his elder brother.

## Chapter 2(80)

Then Guha, who was familiar with impenetrable regions, told the immeasurable Bharata about the good conduct of the

[294] Bharata.
[295] Bharata.
[296] Shatrughna.

great-souled Lakshmana. 'I spoke to Lakshmana, the possessor of qualities. Extremely attentive to protecting his brother, he remained awake, wielding an excellent bow and arrows. "O father![297] This comfortable bed has been prepared for you. O descendant of the Raghava lineage! Lie down here, comfortably and happily. You are used to comfort and all of us are used to hardships. O one with dharma in your soul! It is appropriate for us to remain awake and protect him. There is no one on earth whom I love more than Rama. Do not be anxious. In your presence, I am telling you that this is not a falsehood. Through his favours, I desire to obtain great fame in this world. I wish to obtain great dharma, not only mere artha. Rama, my beloved friend, is lying down with Sita. With my kin, and with bows and arrows in our hands, we will protect him. There is no one who wanders around in this forest who is unknown to me. In a battle, we are capable of withstanding an army with the four kinds of forces." Thus did I speak to the great-souled Lakshmana. However, he only looked towards dharma and entreated all of us. "With Sita, Dasharatha's son is lying down on bare ground. How is it possible for me to get sleep, life or happiness? All the gods and asuras are incapable of withstanding him in a battle. O Guha! Behold. With Sita, he is lying down on a bed of grass. He alone, among Dasharatha's sons, possesses his[298] qualities and he was obtained after great austerities and many kinds of exertions. Having banished him, the king will not live for a long time. It is certain that the earth will soon become a widow. It is certain that the women in the royal palace will utter great shrieks now and exhausted thereafter, there will be silence there. I am not hopeful that Kousalya, the king and my mother will survive through this night. Perhaps my mother will look towards Shatrughna and remain alive. However, Kousalya, the mother of a brave son, will be destroyed. My father will not be able to accomplish his heart's desire of getting Rama consecrated in the kingdom and, countered and unsuccessful, will be destroyed. When the time of my father's

---

[297] The word used is tata. Guha would presumably address Lakshmana as a senior.
[298] Dasharatha's.

death presents itself tomorrow, all those who have been successful in their objective will perform the funeral rites for the king. The crossroads are beautiful, the wide roads are laid out well.[299] There are mansions and palaces, decorated with all the jewels. There are hordes of elephants, horses and chariots. There are the sounds of trumpets blaring. It is full of all the signs of welfare and populated by happy and healthy people. It is full of gardens for pleasure and there are assemblies and festivals. They roam around happily in the capital that was my father's. When he[300] has accomplished his pledge of truth and the period is over, together with him, will we, happy and well, enter that place?" Thus did the extremely great-souled prince lament, standing there. The night passed. When the sparkling sun rose in the morning, they matted their hair. On these banks of the Bhageerathee, I happily conveyed them across. Both of them sported matted hair and were attired in garments made out of the barks of trees. They were extremely strong, like two leaders of herds of elephants. Those two scorchers of enemies wielded supreme arrows, bows and swords. They glanced back at me and left with Sita.'

## Chapter 2(81)

Hearing those extremely unpleasant words from Guha, Bharata started to think about the unpleasant words that he had heard. He was delicate and great in spirit. He was mighty-armed and possessed the shoulders of a lion. He was young and handsome, with large eyes like lotus petals. He sighed for a while and after some time, became extremely distressed. He suddenly fell down, like an elephant that has been struck in the heart with a goad. Shatrughna was standing nearby. On seeing the state the unconscious Bharata was in, he was afflicted by grief, and embracing him in his arms,

[299] This is a description of Ayodhya.
[300] Rama.

began to lament loudly. All Bharata's mothers were lean from fasting. They were distressed and miserable on account of their husband. They rushed towards him, when he fell down on the ground. They surrounded him and wept. Distressed in her mind, Kousalya bent down and embraced him. Distressed by grief, she was affectionate towards him, as if towards her own child. Weeping, she asked Bharata, 'O son! Are you suffering from any disease in your body? This royal lineage is now dependent on your remaining alive. O son! Now that Rama has left with his brother, my survival is contingent on seeing that you are alive. King Dasharatha has died and you alone are our protector now. O son! I hope you have not heard anything unpleasant about Lakshmana, or about my only son, who left for the forest with his wife.'

The immensely illustrious one[301] regained his composure in an instant. Though he still seemed to be weeping, he comforted Kousalya and addressed Guha in these words. 'Where did my brother, Sita and Lakshmana spend the night? O Guha! Where did they make their beds for lying down? What did they eat? Tell me.' Asked by Bharata, Guha, the lord of the nishadas engaged in ensuring the welfare of his guests, reported the arrangements he had made for Rama. 'There were superior and inferior kinds of food and many kinds of fruit. For Rama's consumption, I brought many such. Rama, for whom truth is his valour, refused all these. Remembering the dharma of kshatriyas, he did not accept any of these.[302] O king! The great-souled one entreated us in this way. "O friend! We must not accept. We must always give." With Sita, the immensely illustrious Raghava fasted and drank the water that had been brought by Lakshmana. Lakshmana drank the water that was left. After that, the three of them observed silence and controlling themselves, observed the sandhya rites. After this, for Raghava's sake, Soumitri quickly brought kusha grass himself and prepared an auspicious bed. With Sita, Rama lay down on that bed. Washing their feet with water, Lakshmana withdrew. On this grass at the

---

[301] Bharata.
[302] A kshatriya should kill or collect his own food, not accept it from others as a gift.

foot of this inguda tree,[303] Rama and Sita lay down and spent the night. Lakshmana, scorcher of enemies, wore armour made of lizard skin on his palms and fingers. He tied a quiver full of arrows on his back. He strung a giant bow. Throughout the night, he stood there, circling them. With an excellent bow and arrows, I also stood there with Lakshmana. So were my kin, without distraction and with bows in their hands. Like the great Indra, he[304] protected him.'

## Chapter 2(82)

With his advisers, Bharata heard this entire accurate account. He arrived at the foot of the inguda tree and saw the spot where Rama had lain down. The great-souled one told all his mothers, 'This is where he lay down in the night, with his body pressing down on the ground. He was born in an immensely fortunate lineage from the intelligent and immensely fortunate Dasharatha. Rama does not deserve to sleep on the ground. The tiger among men used to lie down on a bed spread with the best collection of covers. How could he lie down on the bare ground, covered with hairy antelope skin? There was a palace, with tops like vimanas, with constant fortifications. The floor was decorated with gold and silver and there were the best of carpets. There were wonderful collections of flowers and fragrances of sandalwood and aloe. It[305] was like a white cloud in complexion, resounding with the sounds of a large number of parrots. There were the sounds of singing and musical instruments, the tinkling of the best of ornaments. He always woke to the sound of drums. At that right time, the scorcher of enemies awoke to the sounds of praise and ballads sung by many bards, minstrels and raconteurs. I no longer have faith in truth being manifested in this world. My mind is indeed confounded. It is my view that all this is nothing but a

[303] Inguda is a medicinal tree.
[304] Lakshmana.
[305] The palace.

dream. It is certain that there is no divinity who is greater than
destiny, since a person like Rama, Dasharatha's son, had to lie
down on the bare ground. The beautiful Sita is the daughter of the
king of Videha and Dasharatha's beloved daughter-in-law. She too
had to lie down on the ground. My brother made his bed on this
hard ground and as he tossed around in his sleep, the grass bears
the marks of being crushed by his limbs. Since, here and there,
specks of gold can be seen, I think that Sita must have slept on this
bed without taking her ornaments off. Since strands of silk have got
attached to the grass, it is clearly evident that Sita's upper garment
must have got entangled. I think that the young and ascetic lady
must have been happy lying down with her husband. Though she
is delicate, Maithilee cannot have experienced any sorrow. He was
born in a lineage of emperors. He is the one who brings happiness
to all the worlds. He is loved by all the worlds. He has cast aside
his beloved and supreme kingdom. Raghava is handsome, with red
eyes and the complexion of a blue lotus. He deserves happiness,
not unhappiness. How could he lie down on the ground? Since she
has followed her husband to the forest, Vaidehi has indeed been
successful in her objective. Without that great-souled one, there
is no doubt that all of us have suffered. The earth seems empty
to me, without anyone to steer it. Dasharatha has gone to heaven
and Rama has resorted to the forest. Even though he resides in the
forest, this earth is protected by the strength of his arms and no one
can covet it. The capital is unprotected. The ramparts are empty
of guards and there is no one to control the horses and elephants.
The gates of the city have been thrown open. It is evident that
the soldiers are distressed. Everything is exposed, as if during a
catastrophe. However, regarding it as poisoned food, even the
enemies do not wish to taste it. From today, I will lie down on
the ground, or on grass. I will subsist on fruits and roots. I will
always don matted hair and bark. For his sake, I will happily
reside for the rest of the time in the forest.[306] Thus, the pledge will

---

[306] Instead of Rama, Bharata will dwell in the forest.

not be rendered false, though he will be freed from it. Instead of his brother,[307] Shatrughna will dwell in the forest with me. With Lakshmana, let the noble one rule over Ayodhya. The brahmanas will crown Kakutstha in Ayodhya. May the gods make this wish of mine come true. Bowing down my head, I will seek his favours and entreat him in many ways. He should not disregard me. However, if he does not accept it, for a long time, I will live in the forest with Raghava.'

## Chapter 2(83)

Having reached the banks of the Ganga, Raghava Bharata spent the night there. Waking at the right time, he told Shatrughna, 'O Shatrughna! Awake. Why are you still asleep? Quickly bring the fortunate Guha, lord of the nishadas, here, so that the army can cross.' Urged by his brother, Shatrughna replied in these words. 'I am awake. I am not asleep. I have been thinking about the noble one.'[308] While those two lions among men were conversing with each other, Guha arrived. Joining his hands in salutation, he spoke to Bharata. 'O Kakutstha! Did you happily spend the night on the banks of the river? Are you well, with all your soldiers?' Hearing Guha's words, which were uttered with affection, Bharata, devoted to Rama, addressed him in these words. 'O king! Honoured by you, we have happily spent the night. Let servants with many boats ferry us across the river.'

Hearing Bharata's instructions, Guha hurried. He entered the city and spoke to his relatives. 'Arise. Awake. May you always be fortunate. Fetch boats, so that the army can be ferried across.' Thus addressed and obeying the commands of their king, they quickly arose. From every direction, they collected five hundred boats. Some were marked with the *svastika* sign. Some were excellent, with large

[307] Lakshmana.
[308] Rama.

bells. They were adorned with flags and sails were unfurled. To the sounds of praises, Guha brought an excellent boat that was marked with the svastika sign and was spread with a white blanket. Bharata, the immensely strong Shatrughna, Kousalya, Sumitra and the other royal women climbed on to this. However, even before this, the priests, the preceptors and the brahmanas climbed on. The royal women followed and so did the carts with provisions. The sky was filled with the sounds of camps being burnt,[309] people descending to the boats and of vessels being carried. The boats with flags were steered by the servants. Bearing the people who had ascended, they travelled swiftly. Some were filled with women. Others carried horses. Some carried wagons filled with great wealth, yoked to mounts. When they reached the other bank, the people descended. The servants and kin brought those boats back, as if they were colourful toy boats.[310] The elephants bore flags with signs of victory and were urged by drivers of elephants. As they swam across with their flags, they looked like mountains. While some climbed on to boats, others crossed over to the other bank on rafts. Some swam across with the use of pots and pitchers, others used their arms. The fishermen helped the sacred army cross the Ganga. At the time of *maitra* muhurta, they reached the excellent forest of Prayaga.[311] The great-souled Bharata comforted the army and as each one willed, made them set up camp. Surrounded by the officiating priests, he left to meet rishi Bharadvaja.

# Chapter 2(84)

From a distance that was one krosha away, the bull among men saw Bharadvaja's hermitage. Asking the entire army to remain

---

[309] Camps of soldiers were burnt so that there were no signs for the enemy to follow.

[310] Empty of loads, they moved as quickly as toy boats.

[311] A muhurta is a measure of time, equal to forty-eight minutes. Some muhurtas are good, others bad, maitra being a good one. The precise timing of maitra muhurta varies from day to day, but is roughly one-and-a-half hours after sunrise.

there, he proceeded with his ministers. He knew about dharma. Therefore, he cast aside his weapons and garments and proceeded on foot. He attired himself in silken garments and placed the priest[312] ahead of him. When he could see Bharadvaja, Raghava asked the ministers to remain and went alone, following the priest. On seeing Vasishtha, Bharadvaja, the great ascetic, quickly got up from his set and asked his disciples to offer arghya. Having met Vasishtha, he recognized Bharata to be Dasharatha's immensely energetic son and greeted him. The one who knew about dharma offered him arghya and padya. He then gave him fruits and one by one, asked him about the welfare of everyone in the family. He asked about the army, treasury, friends and ministers of Ayodhya. However, knowing that Dasharatha was dead, he did not ask about the king. Vasishtha and Bharata also asked about his physical welfare, the sacrificial fires, trees, disciples, animals and birds.

Bharadvaja, the great ascetic, said that everything was well. Because he was tied to Raghava[313] with bonds of affection, he then addressed Bharata in the following words. 'You are the ruler of the kingdom. Why have you come here? Tell me everything about this. Otherwise, my mind harbours a doubt. He is the slayer of enemies and being born from Kousalya, is the extender of her joy. With his brother and his wife, he has been exiled to the forest for a long period of time. He is immensely illustrious in this world. However, because he was commanded by a woman, his father instructed him to reside in the forest for fourteen years. He committed no crime. Do you wish to cause harm to him, so that you can enjoy the kingdom, bereft of thorns, with your younger brother?' Thus addressed by Bharadvaja, tears of sorrow began to flow from Bharata's eyes. He replied in an indistinct voice, 'If an illustrious one like you thinks in this fashion, I am devastated. I cannot even think of such wickedness. Do not accuse me in this way. I do not approve of what my mother did while I was away. I am not happy with her, nor do I accept her instructions. I have come to seek the

[312] Vasishtha.
[313] Rama.

favours of that tiger among men, worship his feet and take him back to Ayodhya. Knowing my intentions, you should show me your favours. O illustrious one! Tell me where Rama, the lord of the earth, is now.' Satisfied, Bharadvaja addressed Bharata in these words. 'O tiger among men! You have been born in the Raghava lineage. It is appropriate that you should possess good conduct towards your seniors, self-control and an inclination to follow virtuous people. I knew what was in your mind, but I wanted to be absolutely certain. I asked you so that your fame might increase even more. I know where Rama, knowledgeable about dharma, dwells, with Sita and with Lakshmana. Your brother is on the great mountain of Chitrakuta. With your ministers, reside here today. You can go to that region tomorrow. O one who is extremely wise! O one who knows about kama and artha. Act in accordance with what I want.' With his intentions clear, Bharata, generous in his outlook, agreed to this. The son of a king made up his mind to reside in that great hermitage during the night.

## Chapter 2(85)

When Bharata, Kaikeyee's son, made up his mind to reside there, the sage made all the arrangements to offer hospitality to the guest. Bharata said, 'You have already offered me padya and arghya and provided the guest with whatever forest fare is available.' Bharadvaja smiled and replied to Bharata, 'I know that you are kindly disposed and are content with whatever little is available. O bull among men! But I wish to feed your soldiers. Affectionate towards me, you should allow me to do this. Why did you leave your army at a distance and then come here? O bull among men! Why did you not come here with your army?' Bharata joined his hands in salutation and replied to the store of austerities. 'O illustrious one! I did not come with my soldiers because I was scared of you. O illustrious one! The best of horses, men and excellent and crazy elephants are following me, covering an extensive area. They might cause damage to the trees, water, ground and cottages in the hermitage. That is the reason I came alone.' When the supreme rishi commanded that the army should be brought there, Bharata instructed that the soldiers should be brought.

He[314] entered the place where the sacrificial fire was kept. He drank water and touched it. After this, he invited Vishvakarma[315] to arrange for hospitality towards the guests. 'I invite Vishvakarma. I invite Tvashtra too. I wish to extend hospitality. Let arrangements be made for this purpose. Let all the rivers that flow towards the east, those that flow towards the west, those that flow on earth and those that flow in the firmament come here now, from every direction. Let some have flows of maireya, let others have flows of other kinds of sura.[316] Let others flow with cool water that is like sugar cane juice. From every direction, I invoke the gods, the gandharvas, Vishvavasu, Haha, Huhu,[317] the apsaras, goddesses and female gandharvas. I invoke Ghritachee, Vishvachee, Mishrakeshee and Alambusa, those who tend to Shakra and those beautiful ones who tend to Brahma. Let all of them arrive with Tumburu and all the equipment.[318] Kubera has a divine and eternal garden in a forest in the Kuru region.[319] Let it manifest itself here, with the leaves taking the form of garments and ornaments and the fruits taking the form of celestial women. Let the illustrious Soma arrange for excellent food and many and diverse kinds of bhakshya, bhojya, choshya and lehya. Let the trees give rise to wonderful garlands. Let there be sura and other things to drink. Let there be many kinds of

---

[314] Bharadvaja.

[315] The architect of the gods. Tvashtra/Tvashtri is sometimes equated with Vishvakarma and is the carpenter of the gods. Tvashtra is also one of the sun's manifestations.

[316] Maireya is made from molasses or grain, while sura is a general term for liquor.

[317] Vishvavasu is the king of the gandharvas, Haha and Huhu are the names of specific gandharvas. Gandharvas are semi-divine species and celestial musicians, often described as Kubera's companions. Apsaras are also semi-divine and celestial dancers. Ghritachee, Vishvachee, Mishrakeshee and Alambusa are the names of specific apsaras.

[318] Tumburu is the name of a gandharva, sometimes described as a teacher of singing and dancing. But since equipment is mentioned, one should mention *tambura/tanpura*, the stringed musical instrument, though neither tambura nor tanpura is a Sanskrit word.

[319] This means northern Kuru.

meat.' The sage, with infinite energy acquired through meditation and austerities, pronounced these invocations in a trained voice. As he joined his hands in salutation, faced the east and meditated in his mind, one by one, all those divinities arrived. A pleasant and auspicious breeze that delighted the soul and removed the sweat began to blow from the Malaya and Dardura mountains. From the firmament, clouds started to shower down flowers. In every direction, the sounds of the drums of the gods could be heard. As that excellent breeze blew, large numbers of apsaras started to dance. The tones of the veenas of the gods and the gandharvas could be heard. The gentle, harmonious and rhythmic sound penetrated the earth, the firmament and the ears of living beings. Those divine sounds brought happiness to the eyes of men and Bharata's soldiers saw what Vishvakarma had arranged. There was a flat region that was five yojanas in every direction. It was covered by many layers of grass and assumed the complexion of blue lapis lazuli. There were trees there—bilva, *kapittha, panasa, beejapuraka, amalaka* and *chuta* laden with fruit.[320] The divine forest arrived from the northern Kuru region. A divine river, with many trees along its banks, also arrived. There were square and dazzling residences, with stables and lodgings for elephants. There were mansions and palaces with radiant turrets. With excellent gates, the royal residence was like a white cloud. This was festooned with white garlands and divine fragrances wafted through it. There was a square and extensive courtyard, with couches, seats and vehicles. It was filled with all kinds of divine drinks and divine food and garments. Every kind of food was prepared and placed in clean and sparkling vessels. All the seats were properly arranged and excellent beds were spread with handsome covers.

With the maharshi's permission, mighty-armed Bharata, Kaikeyee's son, entered the residence that was filled with jewels. All the ministers and priests followed him. On seeing that excellent residence, they were filled with joy. There was a divine

---

[320] Bilva is wood apple and a tree sacred to Shiva, kapittha is also a variety of wood apple, panasa is jackfruit, beejapuraka is a citrus tree, amalaka is myrobalan and chuta is mango.

royal throne there, with a whisk and an umbrella. Like a king, Bharata circumambulated it with his ministers. However, he only worshipped and honoured the seat as if Rama was seated there.[321] With the whisk made of hair in his hand, he sat down on a seat meant for an adviser. In due order, all the ministers and priests seated themselves. After this, the commander and the platoon leaders seated themselves. In a short while, on Bharadvaja's instructions, a river began to flow towards Bharata, with payasam as its mud. Through Brahma's favours, divine and beautiful residences appeared on both banks of this, plastered with white clay. In an instant, on Brahma's instructions, twenty thousand women arrived, adorned in celestial ornaments. On Kubera's instructions, another twenty thousand women arrived, beautifully adorned in gold, jewels, pearls and coral. Twenty thousand apsaras arrived from Nandana.[322] If a man was embraced by any of these, he would be seen to turn mad. Narada, Tumburu, Gopa, Prarvata and Suryavarchasa—these kings of gandharvas started to sing in front of Bharata. On Bharadvaja's command, Alambusa, Mishrakeshee, Pundareeka and Vamana started to dance before Bharata. On Bharadvaja's command, divine garlands from the grove of Chaitraratha were seen at Prayaga. Through the energetic Bharadvaja's command, bilva trees assumed the form of drummers, *bibheetaka* trees[323] assumed the form of those who played on cymbals and *ashvattha* trees assumed the form of dancers. Sarala, *tala*, *tilaka* and *naktamalaka* trees were delighted and arrived there in the form of kubjas and vamanas.[324] On Bharadvaja's command, *shimshapa*, amalaka, jambu and other creepers from groves assumed the form of women[325] and said, 'O those who drink! Drink this liquor. O those who are hungry! Eat the payasam. The meat is fresh. Eat as you will.' Seven or eight women

---

[321] He did not occupy the royal throne.

[322] Indra's pleasure garden.

[323] A type of myrobalan.

[324] Sarala is a species of pine, tala is a palm tree, tilaka is a tree with beautiful flowers and naktamalaka is a tree that flowers in the night. Kubja means hunchbacked and vamana means dwarf. However, these two words are probably being respectively used in the sense of female and male servants.

[325] Shimshapa is the ashoka tree and jambu is the rose apple tree.

massaged each man with oil and bathed him on the beautiful banks of the river. The women with beautiful eyes cleansed them and one after another, wiped them. Those beautiful women made them drink. Horses, elephants, mules, camels, Surabhee's offspring[326] and other mounts were fed sugar cane and roasted grain mixed with honey, urged on by the extremely strong warriors of the Ikshvaku lineage. A horse keeper no longer recognized his horse. An elephant keeper no longer recognized his elephant. The entire army was crazy, intoxicated and delighted. All the objects of desire were satisfied. The bodies were smeared with red sandalwood paste. Surrounded by large numbers of apsaras, the soldiers said, 'We will certainly not go to Ayodhya. We will not go to Dandaka. Let Bharata be well. Let Rama also be happy.' Having been tended to in this way, the foot soldiers and the riders and keepers of elephants and horses no longer recognized their leaders and told them that. Happy, the thousands of men who had followed Bharata said, 'This is heaven.' They had eaten the food that was like amrita. However, when they looked at this divine food, they felt like eating again. In every direction, servants, slaves, young women and soldiers were all greatly content, attired in new garments. Elephants, donkeys, camels, bullocks, horses, animals and birds were fed exceedingly well and one's share did not eat into another one's share. There was no one there who was in soiled garments, hungry or jaded. No man could be seen with his hair covered in dust. There was the meat of goats and wild boar, in delicious sauces. There was fragrant and tasty soup, cooked well in the juice of fruits. In every direction, there were heaps of white rice, decorated with flowers that were like flags. Amazed, the men saw thousands of vessels made out of rare metals. There were wells along the flanks of the forest and their mud was turned into payasam. The trees exuded honey and turned into cows that yielded all the objects of desire. The ponds were filled with maireya, while some were filled with venison and the meat of wild cocks and peacocks, cooked in hot vessels. There were thousands of vessels made out of molten gold and well-cleaned

[326] Bulls, Surabhee is the mother of cattle.

plates, pots and shallow dishes filled with curds, shining, fragrant and with the complexion of kapittha fruit. There were lakes filled with curds mixed with spices, others being filled with white curds. Still others were filled with payasam and heaps of sugar. As they went down to the river, the men saw ointments, powders, unguents and other objects used for bathing. There were twigs for cleaning the teeth, as white as the moon. White sandalwood paste was kept in caskets. There were polished mirrors and piles of clothing. There were thousands of pairs of footwear and sandals. There were collyrium, combs, brushes, umbrellas and bows. There were colourful beds and couches to comfort the inner organs. The ponds for drinking were full of donkeys, camels, elephants and horses. There were lakes that these could descend and bathe in, filled with lotuses and lilies. For feeding the animals, stores of gentle grass were seen in every direction, blue in complexion, like lapis lazuli. The men were astounded to see the hospitality the maharshi had arranged for Bharata. It was extraordinary and like a dream. They sported themselves there, like the gods in Nandana.

As they found pleasure in Bharadvaja's hermitage, the night passed. Having taken Bharadvaja's permission, the rivers, the gandharvas and all the beautiful women went away to wherever they had come from. The men were crazy and intoxicated with liquor, smeared with divine sandalwood paste and aloe. Many kinds of excellent and celestial garlands were strewn around, crushed by the men.

## Chapter 2(86)

Bharata was extended hospitality by Bharadvaja. Having spent the night there, with his retinue, he desired to leave. The rishi saw that the tiger among men had arrived, hands joined in salutation. Having offered oblations into the agnihotra fire, Bharadvaja addressed Bharata. 'O unblemished one! Have you spent the night happily, having arrived in our region? Have your people received hospitality? Tell me.' The rishi, excellent in his energy, had emerged from his hermitage. Thus addressed, Bharata joined his hands in salutation and bowed down before him. 'O illustrious one! I, and all the soldiers and mounts, have spent the time happily. Thanks to you, the advisers and the soldiers have been satisfied with every object of desire. We have eaten well. We obtained an excellent abode. All our exhaustion and hardship has been dispelled. Having obtained everything, all our servants have also spent the time happily. O illustrious one! O supreme rishi! I seek your permission to leave and approach my brother now. Please cast a friendly eye towards me. O one who knows about dharma! Where is the hermitage of the great-souled one who is devoted to dharma? Tell me which path I should follow and how far it is from this spot.' Bharata, desirous of seeing his brother, asked this and the immensely energetic Bharadvaja, great in austerities, replied. 'O Bharata! Three-and-a-half yojanas from here, there is a desolate forest.[327] Mount Chitrakuta is there, with beautiful caverns and groves. If you approach the northern flank, there is the river Mandakinee, shrouded by blossoming trees and beautiful and flowering groves. Mount Chitrakuta is beyond that river. O son![328] It is certain that they are dwelling there, in a cottage made of leaves and twigs. O lord of the army! Make the army full of elephants, horses and chariots follow the southern path, or go left and then south. O immensely fortunate one! You will then be able to directly see Raghava.'

The women of the king of kings[329] deserved to be in carriages. However, hearing about the path, they got down from their carriages and surrounded the brahmana. Kousalya was wan, distressed and trembling. With Queen Sumitra, she seized the sage's feet with her hands. Kaikeyee's objectives had not been accomplished and she had been censured by all the worlds. Ashamed, she too seized his feet. She then circumambulated the illustrious and great sage and distressed in her mind, stood near Bharata. Bharadvaja, firm in

[327] This makes it twenty-eight to thirty-two miles.
[328] The word used is tata.
[329] Dasharatha.

his vows, told Bharata, 'O Raghava! I wish to know the special characteristics of your mothers.' Thus addressed by Bharadvaja, Bharata, who was devoted to dharma and accomplished in the use of words, joined his hands in salutation and replied, 'O illustrious one! This one is distressed and miserable, afflicted through fasting. She is my father's chief queen. You can see that she is like a goddess. Rama is a tiger among men, with a valorous stride like that of a lion. Kousalya gave birth to him, just as Aditi did to Dhata.[330] There is the one who is distressed in her mind and clings to her[331] left arm. She is like the branch of a *karnikara* tree,[332] with dried flowers, standing at the end of a forest. This queen's sons are the two brave princes Lakshmana and Shatrughna, for whom truth is their valour and whose complexion is like that of the gods.[333] This is the one because of whom the lives of the two tigers among men have been destroyed and, deprived of his sons, King Dasharatha has gone to heaven. This is Kaikeyee, who desired prosperity and is ignoble, though noble in appearance. Know her to be my cruel mother, wicked in her determination. I discern that she is the root cause behind my great hardship.'

The tiger among men said this, in a voice choking with tears. With his eyes coppery red, he sighed like an irate serpent. The immensely intelligent maharshi Bharadvaja replied to Bharata in words that were full of meaning. 'O Bharata! Understand that you should not ascribe any wickedness to Kaikeyee. Rama's exile will lead to the generation of happiness.'[334] Content, Bharata honoured him and circumambulated him. He instructed that the soldiers should be yoked. Divine chariots decorated with gold were yoked to steeds. Desiring to leave, many kinds of people ascended these.

[330] The words Dhata (Dhatri) and Vidhata (Vidhatri) are used synonymously, but have slightly different nuances. Vidhata is more like creator, while Dhata is more like presever. Hence, Dhata can be interpreted as Vishnu.

[331] Kousalya's.

[332] The Indian laburnum.

[333] Referring to Sumitra.

[334] The Critical Edition excises a shloka that expands on this, mentioning the purification of gods, danavas and rishis. With or without that shloka, Bharadvaja's statement can only mean the rishi had some inkling about the future course of events.

There were female and male elephants with golden harnesses and flags. They left, trumpeting like clouds at the end of the summer. Many other vehicles, large, small and expensive, departed. The foot soldiers walked on foot. Desiring to see Rama, the women, with Kousalya at the forefront, happily left on their excellent vehicles. The handsome Bharata and his companions left on an auspicious palanquin that had been kept ready and was as radiant as the young moon. Full of elephants, horses and chariots, that great army left in this way, enveloping the southern direction like a gigantic cloud that had arisen. They passed through the forest that was full of animals and birds. The elephants, horses and warriors were delighted, but they terrified the large number of animals and birds. As it penetrated that great forest, Bharata's army was resplendent.

## Chapter 2(87)

As that large army with its flags marched, the residents of the forest, the maddened leaders of the herds[335] were frightened and fled, with their herds. In every direction, along forest paths, mountains and rivers, large numbers of bear, spotted dear and *ruru* antelopes could be seen. Dasharatha's son, with dharma in his soul, happily marched. He was surrounded by a roaring army with the four kinds of forces. The great-souled Bharata's army was like the waves of the ocean and covered the earth, like clouds cover the sky before showers. Because of the waves of speedy horses and extremely swift elephants, for a long period of time, the earth could not be seen. Having travelled a great distance, the mounts were extremely exhausted.

The handsome Bharata spoke to Vasishtha, supreme among ministers. 'Matching the appearance of this place with what I had heard, it is evident that we have reached the region Bharadvaja spoke

[335] Of animals.

about. This is Mount Chitrakuta and that river is Mandakinee.
From a distance, the forest has the complexion of a blue cloud.
This beautiful spot at the foot of Mount Chitrakuta is now being
trampled by my elephants, which are themselves like elephants.
These trees on the summit of the mountain are showering down
flowers, just as at the end of the summer, dark and dense clouds
shower down water on the earth. O Shatrughna! Behold the spot
on the mountain, frequented by kinnaras. In every direction, it is
now covered by horses, like makaras in the ocean. These herds of
deer are swift in food. They are being driven away, like a mass of
clouds driven away by the wind in the autumn sky. These trees
are crested with fragrant flowers and have clumps of fruit that
have the complexion of clouds, like men from the south.[336] This
forest, terrible in form, used to be silent. Filled with people, it now
seems like Ayodhya to me. The dust raised by the hooves covers
the sky, but is swiftly carried away by the wind, thus causing me
pleasure. O Shatrughna! Behold. The chariots are yoked to horses
and controlled by the best among charioteers. They are swiftly
entering the forest. Look at these beautiful peacocks and birds.
Terrified, they are entering their nests in the mountain. To me, this
region appears to be extremely pleasant. It is evident that this is the
residence of ascetics and the path to heaven. In the forest, there are
many male spotted deer, with female deer. Their beautiful forms
can be seen, as if they are decorated with flowers. Let the virtuous
soldiers explore the forest to see where the two tigers among men,
Rama and Lakshmana, can be seen.'

Hearing Bharata's words, the brave men, with weapons in their
hands, entered the forest and saw some smoke. On seeing the smoke
in front of them, they came and told Bharata, 'There cannot be a
fire without men. It is evident that the two Raghavas are there.
If the two princes, tigers among men and scorchers of enemies,
are not there, it is evident that other ascetics who are like Rama
must be there.' Hearing their words, which were in conformity
with what the virtuous would say, Bharata, the destroyer of the
forces of the enemy, spoke to all the soldiers. 'Remain here. You

[336] Implying darkness in complexion.

should not proceed further ahead. I will go alone, with Sumantra and the preceptor.'[337] Thus addressed, in every direction, they spread themselves out there. Bharata looked towards the smoke and proceeded ahead. Bharata's army could see the smoke in front, but remained there. Knowing that they would soon meet their beloved Rama, they were delighted.

## Chapter 2(88)

Dasharatha's son, who loved mountains and forests and was like an immortal, had lived near that mountain for a long period of time. He wished to please his own mind and bring pleasure to Vaidehi. He showed his wife the beauty of Chitrakuta, like Purandara to Shachi. 'O fortunate one! On seeing this beautiful forest, my mind is no longer distressed at being dislodged from the kingdom or from the absence of the well-wishers. O fortunate one! Behold this mountain, populated by many kinds of birds. Decorated with minerals, the summits rise up into the sky. Some places are like silver, others have the complexion of wounds.[338] Some places are yellow in hue, others possess the complexion of excellent jewels. Some have the complexion of topaz, crystal and ketaka.[339] Others possess the radiance of jyotirasa.[340] Decorated by minerals, this spot in this Indra among mountains is dazzling. The place is surrounded by large numbers of many kinds of deer, elephants, hyenas and bears. This spot in the mountain is radiant with many kinds of birds that aren't injurious. There are mangoes, jamuns, lodhras,[341] priyalas,[342] jackfruit, dhavas,[343] ankola trees,

[337] Vasishtha.
[338] They are red.
[339] Flowering plant.
[340] A kind of gem.
[341] The lotus bark tree.
[342] The chironji tree, also known as piyala.
[343] The axle-wood tree.

bhavyas,[344] tinishas,[345] bilvas, tindukas, bamboos, kashmiras,[346] arishtas,[347] varanas,[348] madhukas,[349] tilakas,[350] badaris, amalakas, neepas,[351] cane, dhanvana trees and pomegranates. They are laden with flowers. They are laden with fruit. They provide shade and the spot is beautiful. This place on the mountain is covered with such beautiful flowers. O fortunate one! Behold these spirited kinnara couples, roaming around on the slopes of the mountain, delighted and in the throes of desire. They have slung their swords and their excellent garments from the branches. Behold the beautiful spots where the vidyadharas are sporting with their women. Here and there on the mountain, shining waterfalls are emerging, like musth exuding from crazy elephants. A breeze bearing the fragrances of many flowers wafts through the caverns, pleasing to the nose. Which man will not be delighted? O unblemished one! If I have to reside here, with you and Lakshmana, for many autumns, I will not suffer from any sorrow. It is beautiful with many kinds of flower and fruit. Large numbers of birds populate it. O beautiful one! I am indeed enraptured by this wonderful summit. I have obtained two kinds of fruit through residing in this forest—I have followed dharma in repaying my father's debt and I have brought Bharata pleasure. O Vaidehi! Are you happy that you are in Chitrakuta with me? Look at these many kinds of things that bring pleasure to the mind, words and the body. The kings and rajarshis, my great grandfathers, have said that for objectives after death, one must reside in the forest, since it is like amrita. In every direction, hundreds of large boulders of this mountain are shining. There are many with many colours—blue, yellow, white and red. In the night, on this Indra among mountains, the radiance of thousands of herbs can be seen, shining with their own resplendence, like the tips of flames from a

---

[344] The starfruit tree.
[345] The Indian rosewood.
[346] The Indian rubber plant.
[347] Medicinal plant.
[348] The sacred garlic pear tree.
[349] The honey tree.
[350] The bleeding heart plant.
[351] The kadamba tree.

fire. Some parts have the complexion of mansions. Others possess
the complexion of groves. O beautiful one! In other parts of this
mountain, a single boulder shines. Chitrakuta seems to have arisen
after shattering the earth. In every direction, Chitrakuta's summit is
seen to be auspicious. Behold. Coloured and fragrant white lotuses
and leaves of birch provide excellent covers, while mats of kusha
grass act as beds for those who wish to indulge in desire. O lady!
Behold. Garlands of lotuses can be seen, crushed and cast aside by
those who have indulged in desire. There are many kinds of fruits
too. With many kinds of roots, fruit and water, Mount Chitrakuta
is superior to Vasvoukasara, Nalini and Uttara Kuru.[352] O lady! O
Sita! With you and Lakshmana, I will roam around here for some
time. I will obtain delight from extending the dharma of the lineage.
I will engage in supreme rituals and follow the path of the virtuous.'

## Chapter 2(89)

Maithilee and the lord of Kosala emerged from the mountain
and saw the auspicious and beautiful waters of the river
Mandakinee. The lotus-eyed Rama spoke to the daughter of the
king of Videha, who possessed a face that was as beautiful as the
moon and lovely thighs. 'Behold the wonderful and beautiful banks
of the river Mandakinee, frequented by swans and cranes and with
flowers leaning down over it. There are many kinds of trees, with
flowers and fruit, which grow along the banks. In every direction, it
is resplendent, like Rajaraja's Nalini.[353] Herds of deer are drinking
now and dirtying the water. The beautiful descents into the water are
creating great pleasure in me. O beloved one! At the right time, rishis
who wear matted hair and have upper garments made up of bark and
antelope skin immerse themselves in the river Mandakinee. O large-
eyed one! There are other sages, rigid in their vows. They follow the

---

[352] Vasvoukasara is another name for Alaka, Kubera's capital. Nalini is the name of
Kubera's lake. The Uttara Kuru region is beautiful.

[353] Rajaraja is one of Kubera's names.

rituals, raise up their arms and worship the sun god. On both sides of the river, the crests of trees are stirred by the wind and make leaves and flowers shower down, creating the impression that the mountain is dancing. In some places, the water sparkles like a jewel. In others, there are sand banks. Behold the river Mandakinee. In some places, it is full of siddhas. Behold the heaps of flowers that are shaken down by the wind. Behold the others that are floating away in the water. There are birds, the red ducks,[354] with extremely melodious voices. O fortunate one! They are ascending,[355] uttering auspicious tones. O beautiful one! I think that this sight of Chitrakuta and Mandakinee and the sight of you are better than residing in a city. The siddhas have cleansed themselves of sin and possess austerities, self-control and restraint. They always stir the waters. You should also have a bath with me. O Sita! Immerse yourself in this Mandakinee, it is like a friend to you. O beautiful one! Immerse yourself amidst the red and white lotuses. O lady! Think of the predatory beasts as citizens, this mountain as Ayodhya and this river as Sarayu. Lakshmana has dharma in his soul and his mind is devoted to commands. O Vaidehi! You are also kindly disposed towards me and this causes me delight. I bathe thrice a day. I subsist on honey, roots and fruit. With you, I don't desire Ayodhya or the kingdom now. These beautiful waters are agitated by herds of elephants. Elephants, lions and apes drink it. Blossoming flowers adorn the ground. Who is there who will not overcome his exhaustion and be happy here?' Rama spoke many other appropriate words about the river. Chitrakuta possessed the complexion of collyrium used on the eyes. With his beloved, the extender of the Raghu lineage roamed around in that beautiful spot.

# Chapter 2(90)

While they were there, Bharata's soldiers approached. The noise and dust created by them rose up and touched the sky.

---

[354] The ruddy shelduck.
[355] The banks.

At that moment, terrified by the great noise that was created, the crazy leaders of herds were afflicted and, with their herds, fled in different directions. Raghava heard the clamour that was created by the soldiers. He saw that all the herds were running away. Having seen them run away and having heard the noise, Rama spoke to Soumitri Lakshmana, who blazed in his energy. 'O Lakshmana! Alas! Sumitra has given birth to a good son like you. A tumultuous sound can be heard, like the terrible and deep thunder of a cloud. Is a king or a prince roaming around in the forest in search of a hunt, or is it some predatory beast? O Soumitri! You should find out. You should quickly find out everything about this.'

Lakshmana swiftly ascended a flowering sala tree. He glanced towards all the directions and looked at the eastern direction. He saw a giant army in the northern direction. It had a large number of chariots, horses and elephants and well-trained infantry. There were many horses and elephants. The chariots were adorned with flags. He told Rama about the army and spoke these words. 'O noble one! Extinguish the fire and let Sita find refuge in a cave. Ready your bow, arrows and armour.' At this, Rama, tiger among men, replied to Lakshmana. 'O Soumitri! Look at the signs. Whose army do you think this is?' Lakshmana was like an enraged fire, wishing to burn down the soldiers. Thus addressed, he replied to Rama in these words. 'It is evident that having accomplished the objective of obtaining the kingdom and having been crowned, Bharata, Kaikeyee's son, is coming here to kill us. An extremely large and dazzling tree can be seen. On a chariot, a standard with a kovidara, raising up its shining trunk, can be seen.[356] As they will, horse riders are prancing around astride their horses. There are resplendent and delighted riders astride the elephants. O brave one! Let us seize our bows and ascend the mountain. Or let us remain here, armoured and with weapons upraised. In a battle, perhaps the kovidara standard will come under our control. O Raghava! Perhaps we will see Bharata, because of whom we—you, Sita and I—have faced this great hardship. O Raghava! You have been dislodged from the eternal kingdom because of him. O brave one! That enemy Bharata is approaching. He should be slain

[356] Bharata's standard.

by me. O Raghava! I do not see any sin attached to slaying Bharata. If
one abandons a person who has caused an injury earlier, no adharma
has been said to be attached to that. When he has been killed, you
will rule over the entire earth. Kaikeyee desires the kingdom. In the
encounter today, she will see her son slain by me, like a tree by an
elephant, and will be extremely miserable. I will also slay Kaikeyee,
with all her followers and relatives. Today, I will free the earth from
this great taint. O one who grants honours! Because of the slight, my
rage has been ignited and I will destroy the soldiers of the enemy,
like a fire amidst dry wood. Today, I will mangle the bodies of the
enemy with sharp arrows and make the forest of Chitrakuta overflow
with the consequent blood. The hearts of elephants and horses will
be shattered with arrows. Predatory beasts will drag them away and
the bodies of the men who are killed by me. In this great forest, I will
repay my debt to my bow and arrows. There is no doubt that I will
slay Bharata, with his soldiers.'

## Chapter 2(91)

Soumitri Lakshmana was enraged and senseless with anger. Rama
pacified him and spoke these words. 'In this case, where is the
need for a bow, sword or shield? The great archer and immensely
wise Bharata is coming himself. Bharata wishes to see us and this
is the right time for him to come here. Even in his thoughts, he
has never acted injuriously towards us. Earlier, has Bharata ever
acted disagreeably towards you? Why are you scared in this way
and why are you suspecting Bharata today? Indeed, Bharata should
not hear these cruel and disagreeable words from you. If you speak
disagreeably about Bharata, it is as if you have spoken disagreeably
about me. O Soumitri! Even if there is a hardship, how can sons
slay their father? How can a brother slay a brother whom one loves
like his own life? If you have spoken these words for the sake of the
kingdom, when I see Bharata, I will ask him to give the kingdom
to you. O Lakshmana! In truth, if I tell Bharata to give you the

kingdom, he will reply in words of assent.' He was thus addressed
by his brother, who was engaged in his welfare and followed dharma
and good conduct. In shame, Lakshmana seemed to shrink into his
own body. On seeing that Lakshmana was ashamed, Raghava said,
'I think that the mighty-armed one[357] has come here to see us. This
Vaidehi has been used to great happiness. Perhaps he has thought
of taking her home from residence in the forest. O brave one! Two
excellent horses, beautiful and born of noble lineages, can be seen.
They are swift and like the wind in their speed. Ahead of the army,
an extremely large elephant is walking. His name is Shatrunjaya
and he belongs to our intelligent and aged father.' Lakshmana, who
was victorious in assemblies, got down from the top of the sala tree.
He joined his hands in salutation and stood by Rama's side.

Bharata had instructed that the soldiers should not cause any
destruction. Therefore, they set up their camps all around the
mountain. The army of the Ikshvakus, full of elephants, horses and
chariots, covered the area around the mountain, to the extent of one-
and-a-half yojanas. Bharata placed dharma at the forefront and gave
up any sense of pride. His army was properly instructed to remain in
Chitrakuta in this way. The one who knew about good policy found
pleasure in seeking the favours of the descendant of the Raghu lineage.

## Chapter 2(92)

The lord[358] made arrangements for the army to be camped.
Supreme among those who walked on foot, he then sought
to approach Kakutstha, who was following his senior,[359] on foot.
Once the soldiers had been camped, as they had been instructed,
Bharata humbly addressed his brother, Shatrughna, in these words.
'O amiable one! With groups of men and trackers to aid them, you
should quickly search the forest on all sides of this forest. I will not

---

[357] Meaning Dasharatha.
[358] Bharata.
[359] Rama was following the instructions of Dasharatha.

obtain peace until I see Rama, the immensely strong Lakshmana and the immensely fortunate Vaidehi. I will not obtain peace until I see the auspicious face of my brother, which is like the moon and which has eyes like lotuses. I will not obtain peace until I place the feet, marked with all the signs, of my brother, the king, on my head. I will not obtain peace until his head is sprinkled with water for crowning him in this kingdom of our father and grandfather. He is the one who deserves the kingdom. The immensely fortunate Vaidehi, Janaka's daughter, has been successful in her objective. She is the one who follows her husband on this earth, right up to the frontiers of the ocean. Mount Chitrakuta is like the king of the mountains.[360] Since Kakutstha is residing here, like Kubera in Nandana,[361] it is extremely fortunate. This impenetrable forest is populated by predatory beasts. Since the immensely energetic Rama, supreme among those who wield weapons, resides here, it has been successful in its objective.'

Having said this, the immensely energetic Bharata, bull among men, energetically entered that great forest on foot. The summit of the mountain was dense with many different species of trees, with flowers blossoming at the top. The supreme among eloquent ones proceeded through them. On Mount Chitrakuta, he climbed up a flowering sala tree and saw the smoke from Rama's hermitage, curling up like an upraised standard. On seeing this, the handsome Bharata and his relatives were delighted, like those who have been able to cross a body of water. Having instructed the army to again set up camp, the great-souled one quickly proceeded, with Guha, towards Rama's hermitage on Mount Chitrakuta.

# Chapter 2(93)

Bharata instructed the soldiers to be camped. Having shown Shatrughna,[362] he left, eager to see his brother. He asked rishi

---

[360] The Himalayas.

[361] Kubera's pleasure garden.

[362] The signs of Rama's hermitage.

Vasishtha to quickly bring the mothers. Devoted to his seniors, he then quickly went on ahead. Sumantra was as anxious to see Rama as Bharata was. Therefore, he also followed Shatrughna at a distance. The place was full of the abodes of ascetics. As Bharata proceeded, he saw a handsome cottage. This was his brother's, constructed with leaves. In front of the cottage, Bharata saw that wood had been splintered and flowers had been gathered. Because of the cold, he also saw in the forest huge heaps of the dung of deer and buffaloes.[363] As he proceeded, the mighty-armed and radiant Bharata cheerfully spoke to Shatrughna and all the advisers. 'I think that we have reached the spot Bharadvaja spoke about. I think that the river Mandakinee cannot be far from here. These barks must have been tied by Lakshmana. These are signs to mark the path, in case one wishes to return at odd times.[364] The slopes of the mountain are marked with the tusks of spirited elephants, as they roamed around and trumpeted at each other. In the forest, ascetics always desire to light fires.[365] The smoke can be seen, trailing black plumes. I am delighted that I will see the noble tiger among men here, devoted to attending to his seniors. Raghava is like a maharshi.' After having proceeded for some time along Chitrakuta, Raghava[366] reached Mandakinee and spoke these words to those people. 'The Indra of men, the tiger among men, seated himself on the ground in *virasana* in this desolate spot.[367] Shame on my birth and life. It is on account of me that the immensely radiant lord of the world has faced this hardship. Having given up all the objects of desire, Raghava is residing in the forest.'

On seeing that large, sacred and beautiful hut made out of leaves in that forest, Dasharatha's son lamented in this way. It was large and covered with many delicate leaves from sala, tala and *ashvakarna*[368] trees. It looked like a sacrificial altar covered with kusha grass. There

---

[363] Gathered so that these could be burnt to ward off the cold.

[364] Such as at night. The barks were tied to trees.

[365] To keep away wild animals.

[366] Bharata.

[367] Literally, posture of a hero. A seated position used by ascetics.

[368] Similar to sala.

were many heavy bows that were like Shakra's weapons. These
were immensely heavy, capable of obstructing the enemy. They
were ornamented and overlaid with gold. There were arrows in
the quivers. These were terrible, like the rays of the sun. They were
adorned with blazing tips, like serpents in Bhogavati.[369] The place
was adorned with two swords that were in sheaths of silver. It was
also adorned with two colourful shields that were dotted with gold.
Colourful finger guards made of lizard skin hung there, decorated
with gold. A large number of enemies were incapable of assailing the
spot, like deer attacking the cave of a lion. A large sacrificial altar
sloped down towards the north-east and it blazed like the fire. In
Rama's sacred residence, Bharata saw this. After looking at this for
an instant, Bharata saw his senior, Rama, seated there in the cottage,
wearing a circle of matted hair. He was attired in black antelope skin
and garments made out of bark. He saw the fearless Rama seated
there, like a fire. His shoulders were like those of a lion. He was
mighty-armed and lotus-eyed. He followed dharma and was the lord
of the earth, right up to the frontiers of the ocean. On the ground
covered with darbha grass, the mighty-armed one was seated there,
like the eternal Brahma, and with Sita and Lakshmana.

On seeing him, the handsome Bharata was overcome with grief
and confusion. Bharata, Kaikeyee's son, with dharma in his soul,
rushed forward. On seeing him, he started to lament in an afflicted
tone, his voice choking with tears. He was incapable of remaining
patient and spoke these words. 'The ordinary people worshipped
my brother in an assembly. Wild animals now attend to him in
the forest. Earlier, the one who follows dharma possessed many
thousands of garments. He has now covered himself in deer skin.
Earlier, he decorated himself with many colourful flowers. How can
that Raghava now bear this mass of matted hair? He observed the
prescribed sacrifices and accumulated a store of dharma. He is now
following a path of dharma that involves oppression of the body.
His limbs used to be smeared with expensive sandalwood paste.
How can this noble one's limbs now be smeared with filth? Rama

---

[369] The capital of the nagas in the nether regions.

was used to happiness and it is because of me that he is facing this hardship. Shame on my life. Because of my cruelty, I am condemned by the world.' Distressed, he lamented in this way. His face was like a lotus and it began to perspire. Bharata wept and fell down at Rama's feet. Bharata, the immensely strong prince, was tormented by grief. Having said, 'O noble one,' he was so miserable that he was unable to say anything further. His voice choked with tears and he glanced towards the illustrious Rama. He could only loudly say 'O noble one' and was incapable of saying anything more. Weeping, Shatrughna also worshipped at Rama's feet. Rama also shed tears and embraced both of them. In the forest, Sumantra and Guha saw those sons of the king, like the sun and the moon in the sky, together with Venus and Jupiter. Those princes met in that great forest, like the leaders of herds of elephants. All the residents of the forest saw them and forgetting all their happiness, started to shed tears.

# Chapter 2(94)

Rama Raghava controlled himself. He embraced Bharata and inhaled the fragrance of his head. Placing him on his lap, he asked about him. 'O son![370] Where is our father, since you have come to the forest? As long as he is alive, you should not come to the forest. O Bharata! From a distance, for a long time, I saw you come to this forest, with a mournful face. O son! Why have you come to the forest? Is King Dasharatha, devoted to the truth, well?[371] Having turned his mind towards dharma, he is the performer of royal and horse sacrifices. O son! Are you properly honouring the immensely radiant and learned brahmana, who is always devoted to dharma and is the preceptor of the lineage of the Ikshvakus?[372] O

[370] The word used is tata.

[371] There is an inconsistency in this section. Having asked about Dasharatha, Rama doesn't wait for the answer. But the succeeding questions seem to suggest that Rama knows that Bharata is the ruler now. In any event, this section doesn't seem to belong.

[372] This is a reference to Vasishtha.

son! Are Kousalya and Sumitra, the mother of offspring, happy? Does the noble Queen Kaikeyee rejoice? Is the priest who possesses humility and is extremely learned revered by you?[373] He has been born in a noble lineage, possesses insight and is without envy. I hope intelligent and upright ones who know about the rituals light the sacrificial fire at the right time and always inform you that oblations have been offered into the fire at the right time. O son! I hope you show respect to the preceptor Sudhanva. He is supreme among those who know about arrows and weapons and is accomplished in *arthashastra*.[374] O son! I hope you have appointed as ministers noble ones who know about the signs, those who are brave, learned and have conquered the senses, those who are like your own self. O Raghava! The foundation of a king's victory lies in good counsel, from well-trained advisers who are accomplished in the sacred texts and can maintain secrets. I hope you have not come under the subjugation of sleep. I hope you wake up at the right time. During the second half of the night, I hope you think about the appropriateness of policies. I hope you do not seek counsel from a single person, nor do you seek counsel from too many. I hope your secret counsels with ministers do not spread throughout the kingdom. O Raghava! I hope you determine whether an objective has minimum cost and maximum gain and having decided, act swiftly, without delays. I hope other kings get to know about all the acts you have successfully completed and also those you have commenced, but not those that are yet to begin. O son! I hope your debates and discussions, within your own self, or secretly with your advisers, are not divulged to others. I hope you prefer a single learned person over one thousand foolish ones. To accomplish an objective, a learned person can bring about great gain. Even if a king engages one thousand foolish people, their help will not bring about any benefit. A single intelligent, brave, accomplished and skilled adviser can bring about great prosperity to a king, or to one

---

[373] The name isn't mentioned. This could be a reference to Vasishtha, but is more likely to be a reference to Vasishtha's son, since Vasishtha has already been mentioned. Vasishtha's son was named Suyajna.

[374] Loosely, political economy, or the science of creating wealth.

who aspires to be a king. I hope the best servants are engaged in superior tasks, medium ones in medium tasks and the inferior ones in inferior tasks. For your tasks, I hope you engage advisers who have learned lineages, with unsullied fathers and grandfathers, those who are the best among the best. I hope those who perform sacrifices do not regard you as an outcast, one who accepts terrible gifts and one whose desires are like those of a woman. If a person does not kill a physician who is unskilled, a servant who is engaged in reviling and a brave person who desires prosperity, he is himself destroyed.[375] I hope the commander-in-chief appointed is someone who is happy, brave, wise, intelligent, pure, noble in birth, devoted and accomplished. I hope powerful and foremost warriors skilled in fighting, whose bravery has been witnessed earlier, are honoured and respected by you. I hope you give the appropriate food and wages to the soldiers when the time arrives, without any delays. It has been said that if the right time passes, salaried servants, even if they are devoted, are angry at their master and censure him, thus leading to an extremely great calamity. I hope all those who are foremost in their lineages are devoted to you. Are they self-controlled? For your sake, are they ready to lay down their lives? O Bharata! As ambassador in any specific habitation, I hope you have appointed a person who is learned, accomplished and talented, speaking what should be spoken. In every tirtha, do you employ three spies, who do not know about each other's existence, to find out the eighteen functionaries of the enemy and the fifteen on your own side?[376] O slayer of enemies! There are those who are exiled, but always return to cause injury. Taking them to be weak, I hope

[375] The king destroys himself in the process. A brave person who desires prosperity might seek to become the king himself.

[376] The eighteen officers of the enemy are the prime minister, the royal priest, the crown prince, the commander in chief, the chief warder, the treasurer of the palace, the superintendent of jails, the treasurer of the kingdom, the herald, the public prosecutor, the judge, the assessor of taxes, the one who disburses salaries to soldiers, the one who disburses salaries to workers, the superintendent of public works, the protector of the borders, the magistrate and the supervisor of forests and waterbodies. On one's own side, the prime minister, the royal priest and the crown prince are exempted from scrutiny, thus yielding fifteen.

you do not ignore them. O son! I hope you do not serve brahmanas
who are excessively addicted to worldly pursuits. Those who are
foolish, but pride themselves to be learned, are skilled at causing
harm. Though the foremost among sacred texts exist and though
intelligent ones look on, those who are evil in intelligence continue
to prattle about futile things. O son! Earlier, Ayodhya was inhabited
by our brave ancestors. With its firm gates and full of elephants,
horses and chariots, it is true to its name.[377] Brahmanas, kshatriyas
and vaishyas are always engaged in their own tasks. There are
thousands of advisers who have conquered their senses and are
great in enterprise. Surrounded by many kinds of palaces, it is full
of learned people. I hope it is happy and prosperous and that you
protect it. In the habitations of people, I hope hundreds of altars are
properly laid out. I hope the temples are adorned with stores of
drinking water and lakes. I hope assemblies and festivals are
decorated with happy men and women. I hope pens for the animals
are laid out well and they are not subjected to violence. I hope the
agricultural land is excellent and free of predatory beasts. O
Raghava! I hope the habitations are prosperous and happy places of
residence. O son! I hope that people who earn a living from
agriculture and animal husbandry are cherished by you and are
indeed happy. I hope that everything is being done for protecting
them, maintaining them and tending to their needs. Following
dharma, the king must protect all those who reside inside his
kingdom. I hope you comfort the women and protect them well. I
hope you do not trust them and tell them secrets. I hope the places
frequented by elephants are protected and elephants are not
tormented. O prince! Do you wake in the forenoon and having
woken, always ornament and show yourself to the people along the
great highways? I hope all the forts are stocked with riches, grain,
weapons and water and full of machines, artisans and archers. I
hope the revenue is a lot and that the expenditure is limited. O
Raghava! I hope the treasury does not reach those who are
undeserving. I hope your expenditure is meant for the gods, for

[377] Ayodhya means something that cannot be attacked or fought against.

ancestors, for brahmanas, for guests, for warriors and for those who
are in the nature of friends. I hope a noble and virtuous person, pure
in soul, when accused of an act of theft, is not killed out of avarice,
without having been questioned by those who are accomplished in
the sacred texts. O bull among men! I hope that a thief when seen,
caught and sufficiently questioned at the time of the act, is not freed
because of a desire for riches. O Raghava! I hope that when there is a
dispute between a rich and a poor person, your extremely learned
advisers resolve it impartially, without differentiating because of the
relative prosperity. O Raghava! If a person rules wilfully, out of
pleasure alone, the tears that fall from the eyes of one who is falsely
accused, kill that person's sons and animals. O Raghava! I hope that
through gifts, thoughts and words, you please three categories of
people—the aged, the children and the foremost among those who
are learned. I hope you bow down before seniors, the aged, ascetics,
gods, guests, *chaityas*[378] and all the brahmanas who have become
successful in their objectives. I hope you do not obstruct the
observance of dharma through the pursuit of artha, or the observance
of artha through the pursuit of dharma, or the pursuit of either
through excessive attachment to kama. O supreme among victorious
ones! O Bharata! O one who knows about the apportioning of time!
I hope you devote your time equally to artha, dharma and kama. O
immensely wise one! I hope that brahmanas who are accomplished
about the purport of all the sacred texts and inhabitants of the city
and the countryside hope for your happiness. I hope you abandon the
fourteen kinds of sins for kings—non-belief, falsehood, anger,
distraction, procrastination, disregard for the learned, laziness,
pursuit of the five senses, single-minded devotion to artha, seeking
counsel of those who don't know the objectives, failure to start
projects that have been decided, failure to protect secrets, failure to
observe auspicious signs and a readiness to rise from one's seat for
everyone. O Raghava! I hope you do not eat tastily prepared food
alone. I hope you also give shares to friends who so desire.'

[378] The word chaitya has several meanings—sacrificial shed, temple, altar, sanctuary
and a tree that grows along the road.

# Chapter 2(95)

Hearing Rama's words, Bharata replied, 'How can someone like me violate the canons of dharma and perform the dharma of kings? O bull among men! The eternal dharma has always been followed by us. O king! As long as an elder son is present, the younger can never be a king. O Raghava! Therefore, with me, go to prosperous Ayodhya. For the lineage and for our sake, crown yourself. A king is said to be a man. However, if his conduct is in conformity with dharma and artha, he is said to be superhuman. For me, such a person is revered like a divinity. While I was in Kekaya and while you resorted to the forest, the king who performed sacrifices[379] and was revered by the virtuous has gone to heaven. O tiger among men! Arise and perform the water rites for our father. I and Shatrughna have already performed the water rites earlier. O Raghava! In the world of the ancestors, it has been said that what is given by the beloved becomes inexhaustible and you are our father's beloved.'

Hearing those piteous words uttered by Bharata, conveying news about the death of his father, Raghava lost his senses. The disagreeable words spoken by Bharata were like words with a vajra in them. Rama, scorcher of enemies, stretched out his arms and fell down on the ground, like a tree with blossoms at the top, when it is severed by an axe in the forest. Rama, the lord of the universe, fell down in this way, like an exhausted elephant sleeping on a bank that has now been washed away. His brothers, great archers, were afflicted by grief and surrounded him from all sides, weeping. So did Vaidehi and they sprinkled him with water. When he regained consciousness, tears began to flow from Kakutstha's eyes and he spoke many piteous words of lamentation. 'My birth is in vain. What task can I perform for the great-souled one? He has died on account of sorrow over me and I have been unable to perform the last rites for him. Alas! O Bharata! O unblemished one! Since you and Shatrughna have been able to perform all the funeral rites, you

---

[379] Dasharatha.

are indeed successful. Without its leader and without that Indra among men, Ayodhya is in a deranged state. When the period of exile in the forest is over, I am not interested in returning there. O scorcher of enemies! Since our father has gone to the other world, when the period of exile in the forest is over, who will instruct me in Ayodhya? In earlier times, on witnessing my good conduct, my father used to comfort me and address me in words that were pleasant to hear. Where will I hear such words now?' Having addressed Bharata in this way, Raghava sought out his wife, whose face was like the full moon. Tormented with grief, he spoke to her. 'O Sita! Your father-in-law is dead. O Lakshmana! You are without a father. Bharata has brought the sorrowful tiding that the lord of the earth has gone to heaven.' Rama comforted Janaka's daughter, who was weeping.

Lakshmana was miserable and he addressed him in these words of grief. 'Bring the pulp of an inguda tree. Bring bark for an upper garment. I will go and perform the water rites for our great-souled father. Let Sita walk in front. Follow her at the rear. I will follow thereafter in this extremely terrible procession.' The immensely intelligent Sumantra was always devoted to them and knew about the soul. He was firm in his devotion to the mild, self-controlled and composed Rama. He comforted Raghava and holding him by the hand, made him descend into the auspicious river Mandakinee. With blossoming trees, river Mandakinee was always beautiful. Faced with the catastrophe, the illustrious one reached this excellent tirtha.[380] This auspicious tirtha was free of mud and the waters flowed fast. He[381] said, 'O king! Accept this water that is being offered to you.' The lord of the earth cupped his hands and filled them with water. He faced the southern direction and weeping, spoke these words. 'O tiger among kings! This sparkling water is eternal. As soon as I offer it to you, may it reach you in the world of the ancestors.' Ascending the banks of the Mandakinee again, the energetic Raghava, with his brothers, offered funeral cakes to

---

[380] Tirtha is a ford, a sacred place of pilgrimage.
[381] Rama.

their father. The pulp of inguda and badari were mixed and laid out on darbha grass by Rama. Grieving and weeping, he spoke these words. 'O great king! Be pleased and eat this. This is what we also eat. What is food for a man is also food for the gods.'[382] Following the same path, the tiger among men then ascended from the banks of the river and reached the beautiful summit of the mountain.

The lord of the universe reached the cottage made out of leaves. He embraced Bharata and Lakshmana in his arms. The sounds of the brothers and Vaidehi weeping could be heard and echoed in the mountain, like the roaring of lions. Hearing this tumultuous sound, Bharata's soldiers were alarmed. They said, 'It is certain that Bharata has met Rama and this great sound is because they are sorrowing over their dead father.' All of them abandoned their camps and headed in the direction of the sound. Their single intention was to rush towards the spot. Some men went on horses. Some went on elephants. Some went on ornamented chariots. Those who were young proceeded on foot. All the people suddenly rushed towards the hermitage, desiring to see Rama. Though he had been away only for a short period, it was as if he had been away for a long period of time. They rushed, eager to witness the meeting of the brothers. They resorted to different kinds of mounts and vehicles, with hooves and with wheels. As the earth was struck by many different kinds of vehicles, with hooves and axles, a tumultuous sound arose, like clouds dashing against each other in the sky. There were male elephants surrounded by female elephants[383] and they were terrified at this. Releasing the scent of their musth, they left for another forest. Large numbers of boars, wolves, lions, buffaloes, bears, apes, tigers, *gokarna*s, *gavaya*s and spotted deer were frightened.[384] Red ducks, waterfowl, swans, *karanda*s,[385] herons, male cuckoos and curlews lost their senses and fled in different directions. The sky

---

[382] This explains why forest fare is being offered, instead of properly prepared funeral cakes.

[383] Wild ones.

[384] Gokarna means cow-eared and is a kind of antelope. Gavaya is the *gayal*, it is the wild variety of domesticated cattle.

[385] Kind of duck.

was filled with birds frightened by the sound. The earth was filled with men and both looked beautiful at the time.

The men had tears in their eyes and were extremely miserable. On seeing them, the one who knew about dharma[386] embraced them, like their own father and mother. He embraced some of the men. Some other men worshipped him. The son of the king met them all, including his friends and relatives and treated each one according to what was deserved. The sounds of the great-souled ones weeping filled the earth and the sky and the sound echoed in the mountain caverns and all the directions, as if the beating of drums could be heard.

## Chapter 2(96)

Vasishtha placed Dasharatha's wives at the forefront and desiring to see Rama, approached the spot. The king's wives gently approached Mandakinee and saw the tirtha frequented by Rama and Lakshmana. Kousalya's eyes were full of tears and her mouth was dry. Distressed, she spoke to Sumitra and the other royal women. 'The performers of unblemished deeds have been banished from the kingdom and this is the tirtha towards the east of the forest that those unfortunate ones, deprived of protectors, frequent. O Sumitra! This is the spot from where, without any distraction, Soumitri, your son, himself draws water for my son.' On the ground, laid out on darbha grass, the large-eyed one saw the pulp of inguda offered to his father, with the tip pointing to the south. She saw what the unfortunate Rama had laid out on the ground for his father. On seeing this, Queen Kousalya spoke to all of Dasharatha's women. 'Look at this. Following the prescribed rites, Raghava[387] has offered this to his great-souled father, Raghava,[388] the protector of the lineage of the Ikshvakus. The great-souled king was the equal

[386] Rama.
[387] Rama.
[388] Dasharatha.

of a god. Given the objects of pleasure that he enjoyed, I do not think that this is appropriate food. On earth, he was the equal of the great Indra and was the lord of the earth, ruling over the four quarters of the earth. How can he eat this pulp of inguda? I cannot see a greater misery in this world than that the prosperous Rama has to offer a pulp of inguda to his father. I have seen the pulp of inguda that Rama has offered to his father. At the misery of this, why does my heart not shatter into one thousand fragments?'

She was afflicted and her co-wives comforted her. They went and saw Rama in his hermitage, like an immortal who has been dislodged from heaven. On seeing that Rama had given up all the objects of pleasure, his mothers were afflicted. Afflicted by grief, they shed tears and lamented loudly. Rama, tiger among men and devoted to the truth, arose and seized the auspicious feet of all his mothers. Those large-eyed ones used their hands, pleasant to the touch, and their gentle and auspicious fingers and palms to wipe the dust off Rama's back. On seeing that all the mothers were miserable, immediately after Rama, Soumitri gently worshipped all the mothers. Lakshmana was born from Dasharatha and bore the auspicious signs. All the women acted towards him just as they had acted towards Rama. Miserable and with tears in her eyes, Sita also seized the feet of her mothers-in-law and stood before them. She was afflicted by grief and lean from residing in the forest. Kousalya embraced the miserable one, like a mother does to a daughter, and spoke these words. 'This is the daughter of the king of Videha. This is Dasharatha's daughter-in-law. This is Rama's wife. What misery has led to her being in this desolate forest? O Vaidehi! I can see your face. It is like a lotus scorched by the heat. It is like a water lily that has faded. It is like gold defiled by dust. It is like the moon shrouded in clouds. The grief is tormenting my mind like a fire and it is as if the hardship has acted like kindling that generates the fire.'

While the miserable mothers were speaking in this way, Raghava, Bharata's elder brother, approached Vasishtha and seized his feet. Extremely great in his energy, the priest was Agni's equal. Raghava, the lord of men, seized his feet, like Indra does to Brihaspati, and sat down beside him. After they were seated, Bharata, who knew about dharma and followed dharma, approached and sat down below his elder brother, with the advisers, the foremost citizens, the soldiers and other people. The valiant Raghava was seated in the garb of an ascetic and blazed in his prosperity. On seeing him, Bharata joined his hands in salutation, like the great Indra bowing down before Prajapati.[389] After having worshipped and honoured him, what virtuous words would Bharata speak to Raghava? All the noble people were supremely curious to know the truth about this. Raghava was devoted to the truth, Lakshmana was extremely generous and Bharata was devoted to dharma. Surrounded by their well-wishers, these three were like the three fires surrounded by assistant priests.[390]

# Chapter 2(97)

Rama comforted his brother, who was devoted to his seniors. With Lakshmana, he questioned his brother. 'I wish to hear the reason behind your coming to this place, with matted hair and attired in bark and antelope skin. Why have you come to this region, with black antelope skin and matted hair? Why have you abandoned the kingdom? You should tell me everything.'

When the great-souled Kakutstha addressed him in this way, Kaikeyi's son forcibly controlled his sorrow. He joined his hands in salutation and said, 'O noble one! Father abandoned you and performed an extremely difficult deed. Overcome by sorrow on account of his son, the mighty-armed one went to heaven. O scorcher of enemies! He was urged by a woman, my mother, Kaikeyee. She performed an extremely wicked act that brought her ill fame. Desiring the fruit of the kingdom, she has become a

---

[389] Brahma.

[390] The three sacrificial fires are *ahavaniya, garhapatya* and *dakshinatya* (the fire that burns in a southern direction). Garhapatya is the fire that burns in households. Ahavaniya has various meanings, the simplest being the monthly sacrificial rites offered to the ancestors on the day of the new moon.

widow and is afflicted by grief. My mother will descend into an
extremely terrible hell. Though I am her son, I am your servant and
you should show me your favours. Like Maghavan,[391] consecrate
yourself in the kingdom today. These ordinary people and all the
widowed mothers have come before you. You should show them
your favours. O one who grants honours! Following the norm of
progression[392] and dharma, you yourself are the one who should be
united with the kingdom. Satisfy the desires of your well-wishers.
Like the autumn sky when there is a sparkling moon, this entire
widowed earth will obtain you as a husband. With these advisers, I
am bowing my head down and beseeching you. I am your brother,
disciple and servant and you should show me your favours. O tiger
among men! This entire circle of advisers was always revered by our
father and you should not contradict what they want.' Kaikeyee's
mighty-armed son said this, his voice choking with tears. Bharata
repeatedly touched Rama's feet with his head. He was like a
maddened elephant and sighed repeatedly.

Rama embraced his brother, Bharata, and said, 'You have been
born in a noble lineage. You possess spirit and energy and are good
in conduct. For the sake of the kingdom, how can you commit a
wicked act, like an ordinary person? O slayer of enemies! I do not
see the slightest bit of taint in you. Like a child, you should not
censure your mother. O one who knows about dharma! O supreme
among those who uphold dharma! The honour and respect a father
receives in this world is exactly the same as the honour that a
mother receives. O Raghava! These two, mother and father, who
are devoted to dharma in conduct, asked me to leave for the forest.
How could one have acted contrary to this? You should receive
the kingdom of Ayodhya and be revered by the people. With bark
as a garment, I need to reside in Dandakaranya. In the presence
of people, this is the division that the great king had ordained and
instructed. The immensely energetic Dasharatha has now gone to
heaven. The king, with dharma in his soul, is the preceptor of the

[391] Indra.
[392] Primogeniture.

worlds and of ours too and this is the norm he set. You should
enjoy the share that our father has given. O amiable one! I will
remain in Dandakaranya for fourteen years. Enjoy the share that
our great-souled father has given to you. Our great-souled father is
like the lord of the gods. He is respected in the world of men. I think
what he told me is supremely beneficial for me, not an undecaying
lordship over all the worlds.'

## Chapter 2(98)

While the lions among men were still grieving, surrounded
by a large number of their well-wishers, the night of misery
passed. When night turned into a wonderful morning, surrounded
by their well-wishers, the brothers meditated and offered oblations
in Mandakinee, then approaching Rama. They sat in silence and no
one uttered a word. In the midst of the well-wishers, Bharata then
spoke these words to Rama. 'Having given this kingdom to me, my
mother has now been pacified. I am giving the kingdom back to
you, bereft of thorns. Enjoy it. When a dam has been breached by
the great force of water that the advent of the monsoon brings, it is
difficult to mend it. Like that, this giant dominion of the kingdom
cannot be ruled by anyone other than you. O lord of the earth!
The speed of a horse cannot be replicated by a donkey, nor that
of Tarkshya[393] by an ordinary bird. I do not have the capacity to
mimic your speed. A person on whom others depend for a living
always lives well. O Rama! A person who depends on others for
a living lives badly. A tree planted and tended to by a man may
become a gigantic tree with a firm trunk, which always has flowers,
but does not show any fruit. However, a dwarf finds it difficult to
climb it. No pleasure is obtained by the person who planted it for a
reason.[394] O mighty-armed one! You should understand the reason

---

[393] Garuda.
[394] Because it does not yield any fruit.

behind this simile. You are the bull and lord among us. Instruct us, your servants. O great king! O scorcher of enemies! May all the classes look upon you established in front of them in the kingdom, scorching like the sun. O Kakutstha! Let crazy elephants follow you and trumpet. When you reach the inner quarters, let all the self-controlled women rejoice.' When they heard Bharata's words, beseeching Rama, the many people from the city thought that he spoke virtuous words.

Seeing that the illustrious Bharata was extremely miserable and was lamenting in this way, Rama, self-restrained and in control of his soul, comforted him. 'A man is not the master and cannot act according to his own desires. From here to there, he is dragged around by the one who brings an end to all action.[395] Everything that is stored up is destroyed. Anything that goes up, ends in a fall. Union ends in separation. Life ends in death. A ripened fruit has no other fear other than that of falling down. In that way, a man who is born, has no other fear other than that of death. A house built on a firm foundation is eventually dilapidated and destroyed. Like that, a man comes under the subjugation of old age and death and is destroyed. In this world, as day and night pass, the lifespan of every living being is diminished, just as during summer, the sun's rays quickly do the same to water. You should sorrow over your own self. Why are you sorrowing over another?[396] Whether you are in one place or whether you roam around, your lifespan will be diminished. Death roams around with us. Death is seated with us. Even if one travels a long distance away, death returns with us. Wrinkles appear on the body. The hair on the head turns grey. A man decays because of old age. How can he regain his old powers? Men are delighted when the sun arises and are delighted when the sun sets. They do not comprehend that their own lifespans decrease. They are delighted when they see the onset of a season, as if something new and newer has arrived. However, the change of the seasons heralds the destruction of the lifespans of

---

[395] The text uses the word *kritanta*, meaning fate, destiny, death.
[396] Dasharatha.

living creatures. In the great ocean, a piece of wood rubs against another piece of wood. Having come together for a time, they drift apart again. Wives, sons, relatives and riches are like that. They come together, but their separation is also certain. No living being can transgress its destiny. Therefore, there should be no capacity to grieve over death. When a caravan passes, someone who is standing along the road says, "I will also follow you at the rear." In that way, we must certainly follow the path taken by our fathers and grandfathers earlier. That being the case, since there is no violation to this, why should one sorrow? Age rushes on and like a flow, does not return. The atman should be engaged in something that brings happiness. It has been said that subjects deserve happiness. The lord of the earth, our father, had dharma in his soul. He performed all the sacrifices and gave away copious quantities of dakshina. Having cleansed his sins, he has gone to heaven. He maintained the servants and protected the subjects properly. Having followed dharma in accumulating artha, our father has gone to heaven. He performed many kinds of rites and sacrifices. He enjoyed all the objects of pleasure. Having spent an excellent life, the lord of the earth has gone to heaven. Our father has cast aside a decayed human body. He has obtained divine prosperity and roams around in Brahma's world. Someone who is as wise as you should not grieve in this fashion. Someone like you and someone like me are learned and possess superior intelligence. All those who are patient and intelligent in all situations should abandon these many kinds of sorrow, lamentations and weeping. Therefore, be steady. Do not grieve. Go and reside in that city. O supreme among eloquent ones! That is what our self-controlled father engaged you to do. I have also been thus engaged by that performer of auspicious deeds. I will act in accordance with our noble father's instructions. O scorcher of enemies! It is not proper for me to cast aside his instructions. He was our relative and our father and you must always also respect his wishes.' Rama, devoted to dharma, spoke these words that were full of meaning and stopped.

Bharata replied in wonderful words that were full of dharma. 'O scorcher of enemies! Where in this world is there a person like you? You are not distressed at misery, nor are you delighted at joy. You are revered by the aged and you ask them when there is a doubt. If a person has obtained the intelligence to look upon death and life equally, and existence and non-existence equally, why should he be tormented? He does not deserve to grieve even when he confronts an adversity. Your spirit is like that of the immortals. You are great in soul and devoted to the truth. O Raghava! You know everything. You see everything. You are intelligent. You possess such qualities and know about existence and non-existence. You do not deserve to suffer from the most terrible of miseries. While I was away, for my sake, my mother performed a wicked deed. It was inferior and injurious, but you should show me your favours. I am tied by the bond of dharma.[397] That apart, she is my mother. I should kill her and chastise her with this terrible punishment. She is the perpetrator of a wicked deed and deserves to be punished. But I have been born from Dasharatha, whose deeds were noble and pure. Knowing about dharma, how can I perform an act of adharma, even though I might desire to commit that act? He was my senior. He performed rites and was aged. He was the king. He was my father. He is now dead and one should not condemn a father. In an assembly, he was like a divinity. How could a person who knew about dharma and artha have performed such a sinful act? He knew about dharma and followed dharma, but acted in this way to bring pleasure to a woman. There is an ancient saying that at the time of destruction, creatures are confounded. Having done what he did, in the eyes of the world, the king has made that saying come true. Our father knew the meaning of virtue. Yet, he transgressed it because of anger,[398] confusion or rashness. Therefore, correct that transgression. It is the view of the world that if a son thinks it virtuous to counter a father's transgression, such a son is regarded as a true son, not one who acts in a contrary way. You should be a son like that, do not be one who assents to a wicked act committed by our father. The act that he perpetrated is condemned by the patient people of this world. Save

---

[397] Of not killing a woman.
[398] Kaikeyee's anger.

all of us—Kaikeyee, me, our father, the well-wishers, our relatives
and all the inhabitants of the city and the countryside. What is this
forest? Where is the duty of a kshatriya? What is this matted hair?
What about ruling? You should not act in this contrary way. If
you wish to follow dharma by accepting a hardship, then accept
the hardship of ruling the four varnas in accordance with dharma.
Among the four ashramas, garhasthya is the best ashrama.[399] This
has been said by those who know about dharma. O one who knows
about dharma! How can you give that up? Compared to you, I am
a child in learning, status and birth. When you are there, how can
I rule over the earth? I am inferior to you in intelligence. I am like
a child in qualities. I am inferior in status. Without you, I have no
interest in remaining alive. O one who knows about dharma! With
your relatives and without any distraction and thorns, follow your
own dharma and rule over this entire kingdom of our father. With
all the ordinary subjects, let the officiating priests with Vasishtha
and those who know about the mantras crown you here with the
appropriate mantras. After having been crowned, you can leave
with us and go and rule Ayodhya. You will quickly conquer the
worlds, like Vasava with the Maruts.[400] You will repay the three
debts[401] and properly punish all those who commit wicked deeds.
You will satisfy the well-wishers with all the objects of desire. And
you will also instruct me. O noble one! The well-wishers will rejoice
today at your coronation. Today, the evildoers will be terrified
and will flee in the ten directions. O bull among men! Wipe away
the outrage that my mother has caused. Today, protect our father
from the sin he has committed. With my head bowed down, I am
beseeching you. Show compassion towards me. To relatives and all
creatures, you are like Maheshvara.[402] Or, if you turn your back

[399] The four ashramas are brahmacharya, garhasthya, vanaprastha and sannyasa.
Stated simply, brahmacharya is the state of being a celibate student, garhasthya is the state
of being a householder, vanaprastha is when one resorts to the forest and sannyasa is the
state of being an ascetic.

[400] The Maruts are wind gods who are companions of Indra (Vasava).

[401] The three debts are owed to gods, ancestors and sages.

[402] The great lord, also a name for Shiva.

towards me and leave this place for the forest, I will also follow you wherever you may go.'

Bharata bowed his head down and sought the favours of Rama, the lord of the earth. However, the spirited one had no intention of returning. He was established in the word given by his father. On witnessing that extraordinary perseverance in Raghava, the people were delighted and miserable at the same time. They were miserable because he was not going to Ayodhya. However, on seeing that he would stick to his pledge, they were also delighted. Bharata prostrated himself before Rama. The officiating priests, the aged leaders of the people and the weeping and senseless mothers praised Bharata's words and also added their entreaties to his.

## Chapter 2(99)

Lakshmana's elder brother, handsome and extremely revered amidst his kin, again responded to Bharata, who had spoken. 'The words that you have spoken are deserving of a son from Kaikeyee and Dasharatha, excellent among kings. O brother! In ancient times, when our father married your mother, he promised your maternal grandfather this excellent kingdom as a bride price. In a battle between the gods and the asuras, the lord, the king, was extremely delighted with your mother. The king offered her two boons. With that pledge having been made, your illustrious and beautiful mother sought those two boons from that best of men. O tiger among men! Thus urged by her, the king gave her those boons—the kingdom for you and my exile. O bull among men! Because that boon was given, I have been instructed by our father to reside in the forest for fourteen years. Without any violation of the truthful pledge that our father had given, I have thus come to this desolate forest, followed by Lakshmana and Sita. You should also ensure that our father, Indra among kings, was truthful in his speech. You should swiftly crown yourself. O Bharata! For my sake, release the lord, the king, from his debt. O one who knows about dharma! Save our father and delight your mother. O son![403] The sacred texts recount a chant by the illustrious Gaya. This is when he performed a sacrifice to repay the debt to his ancestors in Gaya.[404] 'A son is said to be putra because he saves his ancestors from the hell known as *pum*.[405] One who repays debts to his ancestors is a true son. It is desired that there should be many sons who possess all the qualities and are extremely learned. Among all those, there will be at least one who will go to Gaya.' O delight of the king! This is what all the rajarshis felt. O best among men! O lord! Therefore, save your father from the hell. O Bharata! Go to Ayodhya and delight the ordinary subjects. O brave one! Go with Shatrughna and all the brahmanas. O king! With Vaidehi and Lakshmana, without any delay, I will enter Dandakaranya. O Bharata! Become the king of men yourself. In the forest, I will be the king of the animals. Now cheerfully go to the most excellent of cities. I will also cheerfully enter Dandaka. O Bharata! Let the umbrella cast a cool shadow over your head and protect you from the rays of the sun. For me, there are the plentiful trees in the forest to cast a shadow. I will happily seek refuge under them. Shatrughna is accomplished and intelligent and will be your aide. Soumitri is known to be my foremost friend. We four are excellent sons for that Indra among men. O Bharata! We will resort to the path of the truth. Do not grieve.'

## Chapter 2(100)

Rama knew about dharma and addressed Bharata in these excellent words. However, a brahmana named Jabali spoke these words that were against dharma.[406] 'O Raghava! Excellent,

---

[403] The word used is tata.

[404] The place known as Gaya.

[405] The hell is known as pum. *Pumnama* means 'known as pum'. One who saves (*trayate*) from pum is *putra*.

[406] Jabali is an exponent of the *lokayata* school. While there are nuances as to what this school believed in, the emphasis is on the material world and not on the metaphysical and the world hereafter.

but do not turn your intelligence towards a futile end. O noble one! Your intelligence should be like that of an ascetic, but you are behaving like an ordinary man. Who is related to what man? What can ever be obtained by anyone? A creature is born alone and is also destroyed alone. O Rama! If a man clings to anyone as a mother or a father, he should be known as a person who is mad. No one ever belongs to another person. Having entered a village, a man resides for a while in a certain place. However, on the very next day, he abandons that residence and moves on elsewhere. For men, a father, a mother, a house and riches are like that. O Kakutstha! They are just like a residence. Virtuous people do not find delight in these. O supreme among men! You should not forsake your father's kingdom and dwell in this desolate place that is full of great misery and full of many thorns. Crown yourself in prosperous Ayodhya. The city is waiting for you, with a single braid of hair.[407] O son of a king! Enjoy the extremely expensive royal objects of pleasure. Pleasure yourself in Ayodhya, like Shakra in heaven. Dasharatha is nothing to you and you are nothing to him. He was a different king and you are another. Therefore, do what I am telling you. That king has gone wherever he was supposed to go. That is the nature of everyone who is mortal. You are concerned with this in vain. I sorrow over all those who are excessively devoted to artha and dharma. They suffer in this world and are destroyed after death. There are people who say that the eighth day is for the divinity who was a father.[408] Look at the wastage of food. What will a dead person eat? If in the course of a shraddha, food is meant to reach another body and be enjoyed by it, then let it be given to those who are setting out on a journey. At least they will have food for the road. Perform sacrifices, give donations, consecrate yourself for a sacrifice, torment yourself through austerities, renounce— intelligent people wrote these injunctions down in texts so as to persuade people to give. O immensely intelligent one! Therefore,

---

[407] There is the image of a woman, *ekavenidhara*, wearing a single braid of hair. This is done by a mourning woman, when the husband is away or dead.

[408] The word used is *ashtaka* (eighth). This is a special kind of funeral ceremony (shraddha) performed on the eighth day of the bright lunar fortnight (*shukla paksha*), where food is offered to the deceased ancestors.

arrive at the conclusion that nothing exists beyond this world. Resort to whatever is directly in front of you. Turn your back on whatever is not manifest. Place at the forefront the intelligence of the virtuous, that which has been demonstrated by all the worlds. Placated by Bharata, accept the kingdom.'

# Chapter 2(101)

Rama, supreme among those who have truth in their souls, heard Jabali's words. Without any disturbance to his own intelligence, he spoke these excellent words. 'You have spoken these words with a view to ensuring my pleasure. Though it seems to be a possible course of action, it is actually impossible. Though it seems to be sanctioned food, it is actually food that should not be eaten. If a man is full of evil conduct and violates pledges, he does not receive respect from the virtuous and destroys perceptions about his character. Conduct makes it evident whether a person is noble or ignoble, brave or vain, pure or impure. If I am ignoble but appear noble, devoid of purity but appear pure, bereft of signs but seem to possess signs, practise bad conduct in the garb of good conduct, practise adharma dressed up as dharma, create confusion in this world, abandon everything auspicious and forsake rites and rituals, will any man who can distinguish between what should be done and what should not be done show me great respect in this world? I will be censured by the world as someone who is wicked in conduct. If I follow bad policies, how can I expect good conduct from anyone? If I deviate from pledges, how will I obtain heaven? The entire world will then conduct itself as it wills. Whatever is the conduct followed by kings, that is indeed the conduct followed by the subjects. Truth and non-violence are the eternal conduct of kings. Therefore, there must be truth in the soul of the kingdom. The world is established in truth. The rishis and the gods also revere truth. A person who speaks truth in this world obtains what is supreme after death. A man who practises falsehood is feared like a snake. In this world, truth is supreme dharma. It is said to be the foundation for heaven. Truth is the lord of this world. Padma[409] is established in truth. Truth is the foundation of everything. There is no objective that is superior to truth. Donations, sacrifices, oblations, tormenting through austerities and the Vedas—all these are established in truth. Therefore, there is nothing superior to truth. A single person can rule over the world.[410] A single person can protect the lineage. A single person can immerse it in hell. A single person can obtain greatness in heaven. For what purpose should I not follow the instructions of my father? I am true to pledges. He was truthful and he made a pledge in accordance with the truth. My senior has taken a pledge of truth. Because of greed, confusion, or ignorance of darkness, I will not shatter that bridge of truth. The gods and the ancestors will not accept the offerings of those who are fickle and unstable in their intelligence and deviate from the truth. This is what we have heard. I can myself see that the dharma of truth pervades the atman. This burden of the truth has been accepted by virtuous people and has been respected as an objective. I forsake the dharma of kshatriyas. It is adharma in the name of dharma. It is practised by the greedy, the violent, the inferior and the performers of evil deeds. After having been thought of by the mind, the body performs wicked deeds and the tongue utters a falsehood. All three are forms of sin. The earth, deeds, fame, prosperity and heaven desire and seek a man who serves the truth. You have used words of reason to persuade me to do seemingly beneficial things. However, what you have presented as superior is actually ignoble. I gave a pledge to my senior to reside in the forest. How can I abandon the pledge given to my senior and act in accordance with Bharata's words? The pledge and promise I made in the presence of my senior is inviolate. That is when Queen Kaikeyee was delighted in her mind. I will reside in the forest. I will control myself and eat pure food. With auspicious roots, flowers and fruits, I will render offerings to the gods and ancestors. In this world, I will satisfy my five senses and embark on this journey. Able to discriminate between what should be done and what should not be done, I will do this faithfully and without deceit. Having obtained this earth, an arena for action, I will undertake auspicious deeds.

[409] Lakshmi, the goddess of wealth, who is seated on a lotus (*padma*).
[410] All of these are a function of adherence to the truth.

Agni, Vayu and Soma will receive their shares in the fruits of these acts. Having performed one hundred sacrifices, the lord of the gods went to heaven. Having practised fierce austerities, the maharshis obtained heaven. The virtuous have said that truth, dharma, valour, compassion towards beings, agreeable speech and worship to brahmanas, gods and guests are the paths to heaven. Those who are devoted to dharma, associating with virtuous men, those who are spirited and possess the foremost quality of generosity, those who are non-violent and those who are devoid of taints in this world are worshipped as the foremost among sages.'

## Chapter 2(102)

Discerning that Rama was angry, Vasishtha replied, 'Even Jabali knows about the comings and goings of this world. He spoke these words with a view to making you return. O lord of the world! Hear from me about the creation of this world. Everything was submerged in water and the earth was created from this. Svayambhu Brahma was created, together with all the gods. Assuming the form of a boar, he raised up the earth.[411] With sons who were created from his own self, he created this universe and everything in it. The eternal, everlasting and undecaying Brahma was created from space. Marichi was born from him[412] and Marichi's son was Kashyapa. Vivasvat was born from Kashyapa. Manu is known as Vivasvat's son. He was the first Prajapati and Ikshvaku was Manu's son. This prosperous earth was first given by Manu to him. Know that Ikshvaku was the first king of Ayodhya.[413] Ikshvaku's son was the handsome Kukshi, who was famous. Kukshi gave birth to a brave son named Vikukshi. Vikukshi had an immensely energetic and powerful son named Bana. Bana's son was the mighty-armed and immensely illustrious Anaranya. When

---

[411] From the water. The implied identification is with Brahma, though Vishnu assumed the varaha (boar) incarnation.

[412] Marichi was one of the sons born through Brahma's mental powers.

[413] There are some inconsistencies with the genealogy given in 'Bala Kanda'.

the supremely virtuous and great king Anaranya ruled, there was
no lack of rain and no famine. There were no thieves. Anaranya
gave birth to the mighty-armed King Prithu. From Prithu was
born the great king, Trishanku. The brave one spoke the truth and
went to heaven in his own physical body. Trishanku's son was the
immensely illustrious Dhundumara. Dhundumara gave birth to the
immensely energetic Yuvanashva. Yuvanashva had a handsome
son named Mandhata. The immensely energetic Susandhi was
born from Mandhata. Susandhi had two sons—Dhruvasandhi
and Prasenjit. The illustrious Bharata, the slayer of enemies,
was born from Dhruvasandhi. Asita was born from the mighty-
armed Bharata. Kings who were his enemies were also born—the
Haihayas, the Talajanghas and the brave Shashabindus. Having set
up counter-battle formations in an encounter, the king was exiled.
He[414] became a devoted sage on a beautiful and excellent mountain.
It has been heard that his two wives became pregnant. Bhargava
Chyavana had resorted to the Himalayas. Kalindee[415] approached
and worshipped that rishi. She desired a boon from the brahmana
that a son might be born to her. The queen returned home and
gave birth to a son. However, desiring to destroy the foetus, her
co-wife gave her poison. Because he was born with poison, he came
to be known as Sagara. On the day of the full moon and in the
course of a sacrifice, it was King Sagara who dug up the ocean, thus
terrifying the subjects through this force. We have heard that a son
named Asamanja was born to Sagara. Because he was engaged in
wicked deeds, his father spared his life, but exiled him. Asamanja
had a valiant son named Amshuman. Dileepa was Amshuman's
son and Dileepa's son was Bhageeratha. Bhageeratha's son was
Kakutstha and the Kakutsthas are named after him. Kakutstha had
a son named Raghu and the Raghavas are descended from him.
Raghu's energetic son was Pravriddha. However, he is famous on
earth as Purushadaka, Kalmashapada and Soudasa. Kalmashapada
had a son who was famous as Shankhana. However, though he was

---

[414] Asita.
[415] One of Asita's wives.

valiant, he and his soldiers were destroyed. Shankhana's son was the brave and handsome Sudarshana. Sudarshana's son was Agnivarna and Agnivarna's son was Sheeghraga. Sheeghraga's son was Maru and Maru's son was Prashushruka. Prashushruka's son was the immensely radiant Ambareesha. Ambareesha's son was Nahusha, for whom, truth was his valour. Nahusha had a son named Nabhaga and he was supremely devoted to dharma. Nabhaga had two sons named Aja and Suvrata. Aja's son was King Dasharatha, who possessed dharma in his soul. O Rama! You are his eldest and famous heir. O king of the universe! Considering this, accept your own kingdom. In the entire lineage of the Ikshvakus, it is only the eldest who becomes the king, not a younger one when the elder is alive. The eldest is consecrated as the king. O one with dharma in your soul! This is the eternal practice in the lineage of the Raghavas. You should not forsake this now. Rule the earth with its great store of jewels and this extensive kingdom, as your immensely illustrious father did.'

## Chapter 2(103)

Vasishtha, the royal priest, told Rama this. Then, he again spoke words that were full of dharma. 'O Raghava! O Kakutstha! When a man is born, he has three teachers—the preceptor, the father and the mother. O bull among men! The parents only give birth to the being. Since the preceptor gives wisdom, he is known as a true teacher. O scorcher of enemies! I was your father's preceptor and am yours too. Act in accordance with my words and do not violate the path of the virtuous. O son![416] The courtiers and classes have assembled. For their sake, follow dharma. Do not violate the path of the virtuous. Do not cross your mothers. They are aged and devoted to dharma. Act in accordance with their words. Do not violate the path of the virtuous. O Raghava! Bharata's words have entreated you. O one who possesses valour and the dharma

---

[416] The word used is tata.

of truth! Do not cross yourself.' The preceptor, who was seated, himself addressed him in these sweet words.

Raghava, bull among men, replied to Vasishtha. 'It is not very easy to perform good deeds towards the mother and the father so as to compensate for the good deeds that they always undertake towards a son. To the best of their capacities, they bathe him and give him clothing, they always speak to him in pleasant words and rear him. My father, King Dasharatha, gave birth to me. His instructions to me cannot be rendered false.' The extremely generous Bharata was seated near him. When Rama spoke in this way, he became extremely distressed and addressed the suta.[417] 'O charioteer! Quickly spread out some kusha grass on this ground. Until the noble one shows his favours, I will commit *praya*.[418] Until he returns, I will be like a brahmana who lies down before a cottage, without food, without light and without riches.'[419] Distressed in his mind, he then looked towards Rama and looked towards Sumantra. He himself began to spread out kusha grass on the ground there. At this, the immensely energetic Rama, supreme among rajarshis, said, 'O Bharata! O son![420] Why are you engaged in this act of praya? This is the single-minded objective for a brahmana. The rite of praya is not recommended for someone who has sprinkled his hair[421] with the objective of saving men. O tiger among men! Arise. Give up this terrible vow. O Raghava! Quickly go to Ayodhya, supreme among cities.' Bharata remained seated. He looked all around, at the inhabitants of the city and the countryside, and asked, 'Why aren't you saying anything?' The great-souled soldiers and the inhabitants of the city and the countryside said, 'O Kakutstha![422] We know that Raghava[423] has

---

[417] Sumantra.

[418] The practice in question is prayopavesa. While this does mean voluntary fasting to death, it is adopted by someone who has no worldly desires left.

[419] This doesn't mean the brahmana is poor. He has simply given everything away, including his wealth.

[420] The word used is tata.

[421] That is, has crowned himself as a king.

[422] Bharata.

[423] Rama.

said the right thing. This immensely fortunate one firmly adheres to the words given by his father. Therefore, we are incapable of asking him to return quickly.'[424] Hearing their words, Rama spoke these words. 'Listen to the words of the well-wishers who possess the insight of dharma. O Raghava! Listen to their words about what is proper and what is not proper. O mighty-armed one! Arise and do not touch the water.'[425] Arising, Bharata touched water and spoke these words. 'O courtiers, ministers and classes! Listen. I do not desire my father's kingdom or the words of my mother. Nor do I know Raghava, who is noble and supremely devoted to dharma. If it is mandatory that one must follow one's father's instructions and dwell in the forest for fourteen years, then I will reside there.' Rama, with dharma in his soul, was astounded at these true words spoken by his brother. He looked at the people from the city and the countryside and said, 'While he was alive, if my father undertook an act of sale or purchase,[426] then I or Bharata are incapable of transgressing it. As my representative, I do not wish to send someone to reside in the forest. A good deed is to adhere to what Kaikeyee urged my father to do. I know that Bharata is self-controlled and devoted to performing tasks for his seniors. He always looks at what is beneficial. The great-souled one is devoted to the truth. When I return again from the forest, with my brother, who possesses dharma in his conduct, I will become an excellent king on earth. Let me act in accordance with the words spoken by the king and Kaikeyee. Let us free our father, the king, from any act of falsehood.'

# Chapter 2(104)

All the assembled maharshis were astounded on witnessing this meeting, which made the body hair stand up, between

---

[424] That is, before the period of exile is over.

[425] Water is touched before taking a vow.

[426] A reference to a contract of sale.

these two brothers who were unmatched in energy. Large numbers of invisible rishis, siddhas and supreme rishis praised the two brothers, the great-souled Kakutsthas. 'We love the conversation that we have heard between these two. They know about dharma and have dharma as their valour. A person who has two sons like these is blessed.' The large number of rishis desired to ensure that Dashagriva was quickly killed. They approached Bharata, tiger among kings, and addressed him in these words. 'O immensely wise one! You have been born in a noble lineage. You are great in conduct and immensely illustrious. If you have respect towards your father, accept Rama's words. Now that Dasharatha has gone to heaven, we always desire to see Rama freed from the debt he owes to his father and the debt to Kaikeyee.' Having said this, all the gandharvas, the maharshis and the rajarshis returned to their own respective destinations. Delighted at these auspicious words, Rama, auspicious in form, worshipped the rishis with a gladdened face.

Bharata's body was trembling. He joined his hands in salutation and in a choking voice, again addressed Raghava in these words. 'O Kakutstha! Look towards the dharma of kings and the dharma revered by our lineage. You should do what I and your mother desire. I am not interested in protecting and ruling this large kingdom alone. In that way, I will not be able to delight the inhabitants of the city and the countryside and others who are devoted. Our kin, warriors, friends and well-wishers are waiting for you, like farmers for rain. O immensely wise one! When you return, establish this kingdom. O Kakutstha! You are capable of ruling over the world.' Having said this, Bharata, who was pleasant in speech, fell down at his brother Rama's feet and earnestly beseeched him. Rama's eyes were like those of a lotus. He was dark. He raised his brother up on his lap and in a voice like that of a maddened swan, himself addressed him in these words. 'You have obtained the intelligence, that which was innate and that which has been taught. O son! You are extremely competent to protect the earth. In all acts, consult and use the intelligence of advisers, well-wishers and ministers. Perform great deeds. Radiance may desert the moon, snow may desert the Himalayas and the ocean may breach the shoreline, but I am incapable of crossing my father's pledge. O son! Your mother acted in this way because of greed and avarice and on your account. You should not harbour this in your mind. Behave towards her as a mother.'

Thus addressed by Kousalya's son, who was like the sun in his energy and as handsome as the moon during *pratipada*,[427] Bharata replied, 'O noble one! These sandals are decorated with gold. Wear them on your feet. It is from these that the entire world will obtain yoga and kshema.' Thus addressed, the tiger among men wore the sandals on his foot. The immensely energetic one then handed them over to the great-souled Bharata. The powerful Bharata, who knew about dharma, worshipped those ornamented sandals. He circumambulated Raghava and placed them on the head of an excellent elephant. The extender of the lineage of Raghava[428] was as firm in his own dharma as the Himalaya mountains. In due order, he honoured the people, the seniors, the ordinary subjects and his younger brothers, and took their leave. The voices of the mothers choked with tears and because of their grief, they were incapable of saying anything. Rama worshipped all his mothers and weeping, entered his own cottage.

# Chapter 2(105)

Bharata placed those sandals on his head and with Shatrughna, cheerfully ascended the chariot. Vasishtha, Vamadeva, Jabali, firm in his vows and all the ministers who were revered because of their intelligence proceeded ahead. After circumambulating the great mountain of Chitrakuta, they advanced eastwards, along the beautiful river Mandakinee. Seeing thousands of many beautiful kinds of minerals, with his soldiers, Bharata proceeded along its

---

[427] Pratipada means the first quarter from the start, so this is the first quarter of shukla paksha.

[428] Rama.

flank.[429] Not very far from Chitrakuta, Bharata saw the hermitage where the sage Bharadvaja had made his abode. On reaching the hermitage, the extender of the lineage descended from his chariot and worshipped at the feet of the intelligent Bharadvaja. Delighted, Bharadvaja addressed Bharata in these words. 'O son![430] Have you been successful in your intention of meeting Rama?' Bharata was thus addressed by the intelligent Bharadvaja. Bharata, devoted to dharma, replied to Bharadvaja. The seniors and I beseeched him. However, firm in his valour and extremely happy, Raghava spoke the following words to Vasishtha. 'I will truthfully abide by my father's pledge. I have given word to my father about fourteen years.' When the immensely wise one, Raghava, who is eloquent in the use of words, addressed him in this way, Vasishtha, who is also eloquent in the use of words, replied in these great words. 'Cheerfully give these sandals that are ornamented with gold.[431] O immensely wise one! They will ensure yoga and kshema in Ayodhya.' Thus addressed by Vasishtha, Raghava stood up and faced the east. For the sake of the kingdom, he gave me the sandals embellished with gold. Having accepted the auspicious sandals, I took the permission of the extremely great-souled Rama and am leaving for Ayodhya.' Hearing the words of the great-souled Bharata, the sage Bharadvaja addressed him in words that were even more beneficial. 'O tiger among men! It is not surprising that you should be supreme among those who are good in conduct. Nobility is natural in you, just as water naturally proceeds downwards. With a son like you, who possesses dharma in his soul and is devoted to dharma, your mighty-armed father, Dasharatha, has become immortal.' Hearing the words of the great-souled rishi, he[432] joined his hands in salutation and touching his feet, took leave of him. Having repeatedly circumambulated Bharadvaja, with his ministers, the prosperous Bharata departed for Ayodhya.

[429] The flank of the mountain.

[430] The word used is tata.

[431] This makes it unclear whether the idea was originally Vasishtha's or Bharata's. Perhaps the idea was Bharata's, but Bharata gave the credit to Vasishtha.

[432] Bharata.

The extensive army of vehicles, carriages, horses and elephants followed Bharata on his return journey. They crossed the divine river Yamuna, garlanded with waves. All of them again saw the river Ganga, with auspicious waters. With his relatives, he crossed the river that was full of beautiful water. With his soldiers, he saw the beautiful region of Shringaverapura. From Shringaverapura, he saw Ayodhya. Tormented by grief, Bharata told the charioteer in a sorrowful voice, 'O charioteer! Behold. Ayodhya seems devastated and is not radiant. It seems to have no form and is miserable. It is distressed.'

## Chapter 2(106)

The immensely illustrious Lord Bharata quickly entered Ayodhya astride a chariot that made a gentle and deep sound. Cats and owls roamed around. The men and elephants crouched down. The place seemed to be covered in darkness. It was indistinct, as if during the night. Rohini alone is the beloved wife, blazing in her radiance and prosperity.[433] It was as if the planet Rahu had arisen and was oppressing her. It was like a thin mountain stream with limited and agitated waters, the birds scorched by the summer and small and large fish and crocodiles destroyed. It was like a golden fire that rises up when oblations are offered into it, bereft of smoke, but with the flames extinguished after the oblations have been devoured. It was like an army devastated in a great battle, armour, chariots and standards shattered, elephants and horses suffering and the best of warriors dead. It was like an ocean that had risen up with foam and sound, but the water and the waves now rendered quiet and silent by a wave that has arisen. It was like a silent sacrificial altar when the time for offering oblations is over and the place has been cleared of all the sacrificial objects

---

[433] The nakshatras are the wives of the moon, but the moon loves Rohini more than the others.

and officiating priests. It was like the anxious wife of a bull, which is standing miserable in the middle of a pen and does not graze on new grass, because it has been abandoned by the bull. It was like a resplendent, blazing and excellent necklace made of coral and fresh pearls, now devoid of lustre because the collection of good gems had been taken away. It was like a star dislodged from the firmament because its store of merit had got exhausted, thus violently descending on the earth and losing its radiance. It was like a creeper from the forest, laden with flowers during the spring and with maddened bees hovering around it, now withered and consumed in a forest blaze. All the movement stopped on the roads. The shops and stores were closed. It was like the sky, completely covered with clouds and with the moon and the stars shrouded. It was like a dirty drinking house in the open ground, when the excellent liquor was exhausted, the best of vessels strewn around and all the drinkers having left. It was like a place with drinking water that was now devastated, the flat ground below strewn with empty and shattered vessels for drinking, the store of water having been exhausted. It was like bow that was once large and stretched, strung with a spirited bowstring, now lying down on the ground because it had been severed with arrows. It was like a horse that was violently urged by a rider in a battle, but turned out to be a weak and young female horse and thus had its decorations and harness flung away.[434] It was like the radiance of the sun, enveloped by dark monsoon clouds when the sun enters a dense cluster of clouds.

The handsome Bharata, Dasharatha's son, was astride his chariot. Borne by the best of chariots, he addressed the charioteer in these words. 'Earlier, the sounds of singing and the noise of musical instruments could be heard from Ayodhya. Why can't that deep music be heard today? The maddening fragrance of *varuni*,[435] the scent of garlands and the fragrance of incense and aloe are no longer wafting around everywhere. There used to be the excellent sound

---

[434] Killed by the enemy in the battle.
[435] Liquor.

of carriages, the gentle sound of horses neighing, the trumpeting of crazy elephants and the loud roar of chariots. Earlier, before Rama was exiled, such sounds were heard. The large roads in Ayodhya are no longer radiant with the young attired in beautiful garments and men straight in their strides.' Conversing thus in many ways, he entered his father's residence. Without that Indra among men, it was like a cave without a lion.

## Chapter 2(107)

Firm in his vows, Bharata took his mothers to Ayodhya. Tormented by grief, he then addressed his seniors. 'I am now taking my leave of all of you. I will go to Nandigrama. Without Raghava, I will bear all the hardships there. The king has gone to heaven and my senior has resorted to the forest. For the sake of the kingdom, I will await Rama. The immensely illustrious one is the king.' Hearing the auspicious words of the great-souled Bharata, all the ministers and the priest Vasishtha said, 'O Bharata! The words that you have spoken are praiseworthy. These words show your affection for your brother and are deserving of you. You are always affectionate towards your relative and are established in love for your brother. O noble one! Which man will not approve of the path that you have resorted to?' He heard the agreeable and desired words of his ministers. He addressed the charioteer in these words. 'Yoke my chariot.' With a cheerful face, taking leave of all the mothers, the handsome one ascended the chariot with Shatrughna. Extremely happy, Shatrughna and Bharata quickly ascended the chariot and left, surrounded by the ministers and priests. The brahmanas, with the priest Vasishtha at the forefront, led the way. All of them headed east, in the direction where Nandigrama was. Though not asked, the army, full of elephants, horses and chariots, followed Bharata and so did all the residents of the city. Bharata, devoted to his brother and with dharma in his soul, was astride the chariot. With the sandals atop his head, he quickly went to Nandigrama.

Bharata quickly entered Nandigrama. Swiftly descending from his chariot, he addressed his seniors. 'My brother has himself given me this kingdom as a trust. These sandals, ornamented with gold, will bring yoga and kshema. I will rule it until Raghava returns. I will myself quickly put them back on Raghava's feet. I will see Rama's feet, with the sandals on them. When Raghava returns, I will thus give the burden back to him. Having given the kingdom back to my senior, I will serve him the way one should serve a senior. These excellent sandals are marks of trust and I will give them back to Raghava, with the kingdom of Ayodhya. I will thus be cleansed of my sins. Kakutstha will be crowned and the people will be delighted. My joy and the kingdom's fame will multiply fourfold.' The immensely illustrious Bharata lamented in this way. Though distressed, with his ministers, he ruled the kingdom from Nandigrama. The lord donned bark and had matted hair. He was in the garb of a hermit. With his soldiers, the brave Bharata resided in Nandigrama. Bharata, devoted to his brother, desired Rama's return. Devoted to his pledge, he carried out his brother's words. He crowned those sandals in Nandigrama. Bharata ruled the kingdom in the name of the sandals.

# Chapter 2(108)

When Bharata left, Rama continued to reside in the hermitage. He noticed that the ascetics were anxious and disturbed. However, earlier, the ascetics who dwelt in hermitages in Chitrakuta, under Rama's protection, were not seen to display any signs of anxiety. Rama could discern their fear from their eyes and frowns. They conversed with each other, secretly and softly. Noticing their anxiety, Rama was himself worried. He joined his hands in salutation and spoke to the rishi who was the leader of the group. 'O illustrious one! I had not noticed this kind of behaviour earlier. I see an agitation, as if something is disturbing the ascetics. Has my younger brother committed an act causing offence? Has Lakshmana

looked at the rishis in a way that is not deserving of his own self?
Has Sita not followed the conduct that is deserving of women? She
serves me well. Has she not served you?' The aged rishi was aged in
austerities and he also suffered from old age. Trembling, he replied
to Rama, who was compassionate towards all beings. 'O son![436]
Vaidehi is benevolent in her spirit and in her conduct, always does
what is beneficial, especially for ascetics. It is because of you that this
hardship has come upon the ascetics. They anxiously and secretly
converse about the depredations of the rakshasas. Ravana has a
younger brother and he is a rakshasa named Khara. He oppresses
all the ascetics who have made their residences in Janasthana.[437] He
is insolent and desires victory. He is cruel and devours human flesh.
O son! He is proud and wicked and cannot tolerate you. O son! Ever
since you came to this hermitage, the rakhsasas have acted against
the ascetics. They exhibit many terrible, gruesome and cruel forms.
Some forms are so ugly that those forms are unpleasant to see. They
fling filth and impure objects on the ascetics. There are ignoble ones
who remain in front and quickly kill others.[438] Unseen, they hide
themselves in those hermitages. They are evil in intelligence and find
delight in destroying the ascetics there. When the time for rendering
oblations presents itself, they throw away the sacrificial vessels
and ladles, sprinkle water on the fire and break the pots. Since the
hermitage has been infiltrated by those evil-souled ones, the rishis
have decided to leave and have urged me to go to some other region
today. O Rama! Before the wicked ones cause some physical harm
to the ascetics and display such inclinations, they wish to abandon
this hermitage. Not far from this forest, there is an ancient and
colourful hermitage with an abundance of roots and fruits. With
my companions, I will again find a refuge there. O son! Before
Khara does something against you too, if your intelligence is so
inclined, go with us to that place. O Raghava! You are with your
wife and you will always be anxious. Though you are capable, a

---

[436] The word used is tata.

[437] Janasthana is another name for the Dandakaranya region. Sometimes, Janasthana
is also described as the capital of Dandakaranya.

[438] That is, kill other ascetics.

residence here now is fraught with hardship.' When he had spoken in this way, since the ascetics were so very anxious, Prince Rama was unable to restrain them with his reply. Having explained his reasons, the leader of the group greeted Raghava and sought his leave. With his group, he then left the hermitage. Rama understood why the large number of rishis wanted to leave the region and he greeted the rishi who was the leader of the group and accompanied them for a while. They were happy that their reasons had been understood. He then took their leave and returned to his own sacred residence.

## Chapter 2(109)

Raghava thought about the departure of the ascetics and could think of many reasons why it was no longer desirable to live in that place. 'This is where Bharata met me, with the mothers and the citizens. That memory remains with me and I always sorrow over it. The great-souled one's army set up camp here and the dung from the horses and the elephants has caused a great deal of devastation here. Therefore, we should go somewhere else.' This is what Raghava thought and left, with Vaidehi and Lakshmana.

He reached the hermitage of the immensely illustrious Atri and worshipped him. The illustrious one welcomed him like a son. He personally instructed that all the arrangements should be made for treating the guests well. He honoured Soumitri and the immensely fortunate Sita. He summoned his aged wife and welcomed her too. The one who knew about dharma and was engaged in the welfare of all beings spoke to her. Anasuya was an immensely fortunate ascetic lady who followed dharma. The excellent rishi told her, 'Welcome Vaidehi.' He told Rama about the ascetic lady who was devoted to dharma. 'The world incessantly suffered from ten years of drought and she is the one who created roots and fruits and made the Jahnavee flow then. She performed fierce austerities and was ornamented with all the rituals. She performed great austerities for ten thousand years. O son![439] Through her vows, Anasuya removed all the impediments. O unblemished one! To accomplish the task of the gods, she converted ten nights into one night.[440] She is like a mother to you. This aged and illustrious one is never angry and all creatures bow down before her. Let Vaidehi approach her. When the rishi said this, Raghava agreed. He spoke these excellent words to Sita, who knew about dharma. 'O princess! You have heard what the sage has said. For the sake of your own welfare, quickly approach the ascetic lady. Because of her deeds, Anasuya has obtained fame in the world. You should swiftly approach the ascetic lady.'

Raghava always sought Sita's welfare. On hearing this, Maithilee circumambulated Atri's wife, who knew about dharma. She was aged and weak and her body was marked with wrinkles. Because of old age, her hair had turned grey. Her limbs always trembled, like a plantain tree in the wind. Sita attentively worshipped the immensely fortunate Anasuya, who was devoted to her husband, and told her her own name. Vaidehi worshipped the unblemished ascetic lady. Cupping her hands in salutation, she cheerfully asked about her welfare. The one who followed dharma saw the immensely fortunate Sita. Comforting her, she happily said, 'It is good fortune that you look towards dharma. O Sita! O beautiful one! It is good fortune that you have given up your relatives, honours and prosperity and have followed Rama in his exile to the forest. For a woman who loves her husband, regardless of whether he resides in a city or a forest and irrespective of whether he is wicked and vile, the great worlds result. For a noble woman, the husband is the supreme divinity, even if he is evil in conduct, addicted to desire and bereft of riches. O Vaidehi! When I think about it, I do not see a relative who is superior to an appropriate husband. He is like the undecaying result of austerities. Wicked

---

[439] The word used is tata.

[440] The story is that the sage Mandavya cursed Shandeeli, a lady sage and a friend of Anasuya's that she would become a widow within ten nights. Anasuya responded with her own curse that there would be no dawn. To remedy the situation, and thus accomplish the task of the gods, Anasuya subsequently transformed ten nights into one night and Shandeeli did not become a widow.

women who make their hearts drive their desire and those who lord it over their husbands do not understand what is a good quality and what is a sin. O Maithilee! Indeed, women who act in this undesirable way of controlling[441] obtain ill fame and are dislodged from dharma. However, women like you, who possess the quality, regardless of prosperity or adversity in this world, roam around in heaven, like the performers of auspicious deeds.'

## Chapter 2(110)

Vaidehi was thus addressed by Anasuya, who was without jealousy.[442] She worshipped her in gentle words and said, 'It is not extraordinary that a noble one like you should address me in this way. I also know that the husband is the preceptor for a woman. O noble one! Even if my husband is without a means of subsistence, I should show no hesitation in obeying him. What more can one say for someone who is praised for his qualities, compassion, conquest of the senses, firmness in devotion and for one who has dharma in his soul, following his mother and loved by his father? Whatever conduct the immensely strong Rama exhibits towards Kousalya is identical to the conduct he exhibits towards all the other women of the king. He knows about dharma and is devoid of false pride. Even if the affectionate king has looked towards a woman with a favourable glance, the brave one treats her like a mother. When I left for the desolate forest that conveys fear, my mother-in-law told me something great and it is firmly lodged in my heart. I also bear the words my mother used to instruct me in earlier times, when my hand was given in marriage, with the fire as a witness. "O one who follows dharma! Your words will render everything new. Serving a husband represents austerities for a woman. Nothing else has been recommended. Having

---

[441] Their husbands.
[442] The name Anasuya means someone without jealousy (*asuya*).

served her husband, Savitree obtained greatness in heaven.[443] If you follow that kind of conduct of serving your husband, you will obtain heaven. The goddess Rohini is supreme among all the women in the sky and the moon is not seen without her, not even for an instant. Such supreme women are firm in their devotion to their husbands. Through their own auspicious deeds, they have obtained greatness in the world of the gods."' Hearing Sita's words, Anasuya was delighted. She happily inhaled the fragrance of Maithilee's head and said, 'O Sita! O one who is pure in vows! Because I have tormented myself through many rituals, great austerities exist in me. Using that strength, I wish to confer a boon on you. O Maithilee! Your words are appropriate and right and I am pleased. Tell me. What can I do for you?' Sita told the one who possessed the store of austerities, 'I have already obtained success.'[444]

Thus addressed, the one who knew about dharma became happier still. She said, 'O Sita! I will do something that will make you successful and happy. O Vaidehi! Here are some divine and excellent garlands, garments, ornaments, unguents for the limbs and extremely expensive pastes. O Sita! I am giving these to you so that your body can be ornamented. You deserve them. Even when they have been used, they will remain fresh. O Janaka's daughter! With these pastes and unguents smeared on your limbs, you will be beautiful with your husband, like Shri with the undecaying Vishnu.' Maithilee accepted the garments, pastes, unguents, ornaments and garlands that had been given as a supreme gift of love. Having accepted those gifts of love, the illustrious Sita joined her hands in salutation and patiently sat down near the store of austerities.

When Sita was seated, Anasuya, firm in her vows, started to question her, conversing about the pleasant things that had once happened. 'O Sita! I have heard the story that you were obtained by the illustrious Raghava in an act of svayamvara. O Maithilee! I wish to hear that account in detail. You should tell me everything, exactly as you felt it.' Thus addressed, Sita said, 'Listen to the

[443] Savitree's husband, Satyavan, died. Savitree followed the dead body to Yama's abode and obtained the boon of bringing her husband back to life.

[444] She didn't want a boon.

account.' She told the one who followed dharma the story. 'The brave lord of Mithila was Janaka and he followed dharma. Devoted to the dharma of kshatriyas, he ruled over the earth properly. With a plough in his hand, he was tilling a plot of land. It is said that I split the earth and arose as the king's daughter. King Janaka was engaged in scattering seeds from his fist and was astounded to see me, all my limbs covered in dust. Affectionately, he placed me on his own lap. Since then, lovingly, he has referred to me as his daughter. It is said that an invisible human voice was heard from heaven. "O king! Following dharma, she will be your daughter." My father, the lord of Mithila with dharma in his soul, was delighted at this. After having obtained me, the lord of men obtained great prosperity. The performer of auspicious deeds gave me to the eldest queen, like something obtained from a sacrifice. She gently reared me, with maternal affection. My father saw that I had attained the age when I should be united with a husband. He was overcome by thoughts, like one without riches when his wealth has been destroyed. Even if a daughter's father is Shakra's equal on earth, in this world, he is reviled by those who are his equal and inferior.[445] The king saw that such condemnation was not far away. He was immersed in an ocean of thoughts, like a person without a boat who is unable to cross over to the other shore. He knew that I was not born from a womb and was unable to find an answer to his thoughts. Where was an equal or similar king who would be my husband? After thinking incessantly about this, he arrived at a determination. The intelligent one decided that he would marry his daughter off through a svayamvara. In a great sacrifice, the great-souled Varuna was delighted with him and had given him a supreme bow and two quivers with an inexhaustible supply of arrows.[446] It was so heavy that even if men made efforts, they were unable to move it. Even in their dreams, the lords of men were unable to bend it. My father, truthful in speech, invited the kings first. When they assembled, he told the Indras among men that the bow would have to be raised.

---

[445] If the daughter is not married.
[446] In some versions, this bow and the quivers were received from Shiva.

"If a man raises this bow and strings it, I will bestow my daughter on him as a wife. There is no doubt about this." That excellent bow was as heavy as a mountain. The kings were incapable of raising it. They worshipped it and went away. After a long period of time, the immensely radiant Raghava came to witness a sacrifice, together with Vishvamitra. Rama, for whom truth is his valour, was with his brother Lakshmana. Vishvamitra, with dharma in his soul, was honoured exceedingly well by my father and told my father, "These two Raghavas, Rama and Lakshmana, are the sons of Dasharatha and they wish to see the bow." When the brahmana said this, the bow was brought there. In a mere instant, the valiant one bent the bow. The valiant one then quickly strung the bow and stretched it. Because of the force of the stretching, the bow snapped in the middle into two parts. The resultant sound was terrible, as if a bolt of thunder had descended. My father, fixed to the truth, fetched an excellent vessel of water and immediately bestowed me on Rama, with that vessel. Though bestowed, Raghava did not accept me then, not until the views of his father, the lord who was the king of Ayodhya, had been ascertained. My father, the aged King Dasharatha was invited and my father bestowed me on Rama, who knows about his atman. My younger sister is the virtuous Urmila, lovely to behold. My father himself bestowed her on Lakshmana as a wife. In this way, I was bestowed on Rama in that svayamvara. Following dharma, I am devoted to my husband. He is supreme among valiant ones.'

# Chapter 2(111)

Anasuya, who knew about dharma, heard this great account. She inhaled the fragrance of Maithilee's head and embraced her in her arms. 'You have recounted it in distinct, colourful and sweet syllables and sentences. I have heard everything about the story of the svayamvara. O one who is pleasant in speech! I am delighted and happy to hear about this account. The sun has set and the auspicious and beautiful night has arrived. The chirping of birds can be heard. During the day, they travelled long distances in search of food. Now that it is evening, they are back in their nests, desiring to sleep. The sages are wet from their ablutions, having eaten fruits. They are returning together, their garments of bark wet with water. Following the prescribed ordinances, the rishis are offering oblations into the agnihotra fire. Raised by the wind, the smoke can be seen, red like a pigeon's neck. In every direction, though they possess limited leaves, the trees seem dense. In this region, where the senses are restrained, the directions are never visible. The animals that roam around in the night are travelling everywhere. The deer of the hermitage are sleeping around the sacrificial altar. O Sita! The night has arrived, adorned with nakshatras. The moon can be seen to have arisen in the sky, surrounded by moonlight. I grant you permission. Go and follow Rama now. I am satisfied with the pleasant conversation with you. O Maithilee! In front of me, adorn yourself with these ornaments. O child! I will be delighted when you become beautiful with these divine ornaments.' Sita adorned herself with those ornaments and was like a daughter of the gods. She bowed her head down and prostrated herself and left to meet Rama.

The supreme among eloquent ones saw the ornamented Sita. Raghava rejoiced at what the lady ascetic had given as a gift of affection. Sita Maithilee showed Rama everything that was given as a gift of affection by the lady ascetic—the garments, the ornaments and the garlands. Rama and maharatha Lakshmana were delighted on seeing that Maithilee had been honoured in this excellent way, extremely difficult for a human to obtain. The descendant of the Raghu lineage, with a face like the moon, was delighted and spent the auspicious night there, worshipped by the ascetics and the siddhas.

When the night was over, the two tigers among men asked the ascetics, who had offered oblations into the fire and dwelt in the forest. The ascetics who resided in the forest and followed dharma told them about parts of the forest that teemed with rakshasas. 'This is the path that the maharshis follow to fetch fruits from the forest. O Raghava! It is proper that you should follow this. There

is this other one through this impenetrable forest.'[447] The scorcher
of enemies joined his hands in salutation before the ascetics, and
the brahmanas pronounced words of benediction over them. With
Lakshmana and his wife, Raghava entered the forest, like the sun
entering a mass of clouds.

*This ends Ayodhya Kanda.*

[447] Though not stated very clearly, there seems to have been a choice of two paths
through Dandakaranya.